Moloka'i and Lāna'i

Maui

0 kilometers   50
0 miles   25

MOLOKA'I

Kaunakakai •

LĀNA'I

Lāna'i City •

Kahului •

MAUI

KAHO'OLAWE

Hawai'i Island

• Kailua-Kona

Hilo •

HAWAI'I
ISLAND

HAWAII

EYEWITNESS TRAVEL

HAWAII

DK

DK

LONDON, NEW YORK,
MELBOURNE, MUNICH AND DELHI
www.dk.com

Project Editor Helen Townsend

Art Editor Anthony Limerick

Editor Freddy Hamilton

Designers Tessa Bindloss, Tim Mann

Map Co-Ordinators Emily Green, David Pugh

Production David Proffit

Picture Research Ellen Root

DTP Designer Ingrid Vienings

Senior Revisions Editor Esther Labi

Contributors
Gerald Carr, Bonnie Friedman, Rita Goldman, Clemence Mclaren, Melissa Miller, Alex Salkever,
Stephen Self, Greg Ward, Paul Wood

Photographers
Rob Reichenfeld, Mike Severns

Illustrators
Robert Ashby, Richard Bonson, Gary Cross, Chris Forsey, Stephen Gyapay, Claire Littlejohn,
Chris Orr & Associates, Robbie Polley, Mike Taylor, John Woodcock

Printed in China

First published in Great Britain in 1998 by
Dorling Kindersley Limited 80 Strand, London WC2R ORL

14 15 16 17 10 9 8 7 6 5 4 3 2 1

**Reprinted with revisions 1999, 2000, 2001, 2002, 2003, 2004, 2005, 2006,
2007, 2009, 2011, 2013, 2015**

Copyright © 1998, 2015 Dorling Kindersley Limited, London
A Penguin Random House Company

The secluded Secret Beach near Kilauea Point *(see*

Contents

How to Use
This Guide **6**

Introducing
Hawai'i

Visitors in an underwater tunnel at the
Maui Ocean Center *(see p123)*

◀ The beautiful Kalalau Valley on the Nā Pali Coast, Kaua'i

near Kīlauea Point *(see p168)*

Honolulu and Waikīkī

Summit depression of the Haleakalá volcano *(see p132)*

Hawai'i Island by Island

Travelers' Needs

Dancer at the Polynesian Cultural Center at Lā'ie, O'ahu

The twin Wailua Falls, north of Lihu'e, cascading into the Wailua river *(see p165)*

Survival Guide

Decorative scrimshaw made from whale bones *(see p117)*

Geological diagram of the Hawaiian Islands *(see pp22–3)*

HOW TO USE THIS GUIDE

This guide helps you to get the most from your visit to Hawai'i. It provides both detailed practical information and expert recommendations. *Introducing Hawai'i* maps the island chain and sets it in its historical and cultural context. The five island chapters, plus *Honolulu and Waikīkī*, describe important

sights, using maps, photographs, and illustrations. Tips for hotels, restaurants, shops, entertainment, and sports are found in *Travelers' Needs*. The final section, *Survival Guide*, contains practical advice on everything from personal security to using public transportation.

Honolulu and Waikīkī

This chapter is divided into three areas: Downtown Honolulu, Waikīkī, and Greater Honolulu. Each area has its own section that opens with a list of the sights described. All sights are numbered and plotted on the chapter's Area Map. Information on each sight is easy to locate as it follows the numerical order on the map.

Sights at a Glance lists the chapter's sights by category: Cathedrals and Churches, Museums and Galleries, Historic Streets and Buildings, Parks and Gardens, Cemeteries and Memorials.

Each area has colour-coded thumb tabs.

A locator map shows where you are in relation to other areas on the island of O'ahu.

1 **Area Map** For easy reference, the sights in each area are numbered and plotted on a map. The sights are also shown on the Honolulu and Waikīkī Street Finder (see pp80–83).

2 **Street-by-Street Map** This gives a bird's-eye view of the key areas in each chapter.

A suggested route for a walk is shown in red.

3 **Detailed information** The sights in the three main areas are described individually. Addresses, telephone numbers, opening hours, admission charges, tours, photography, and wheelchair access are also provided, as well as public transportation links.

1 Introduction
The landscape, history, and character of each island is outlined here, showing how the area has developed over the centuries and what it has to offer to the visitor today.

Hawai'i Area by Area

Apart from an initial section on Honolulu and Waikīkī, the state has been divided into five island groups, each of which has a separate chapter. The most interesting towns and places to visit are numbered on a Regional Map at the beginning of each chapter.

2 Regional Map
This shows the main road network and gives an illustrated overview of the whole island group. All interesting places to visit are numbered and there are also useful tips on getting around the region.

Each area of Hawaii can be quickly identified by its colour coding, shown on the inside front cover.

A Recreational Areas Chart shows where to head for the top activities on each island.

3 Detailed information
All the important towns and other places to visit are described individually. They are listed in order, following the numbering on the Regional Map. Within each town or city, there is detailed information on important buildings and other sights.

A Visitors' Checklist provides the practical information you will need to plan your visit.

4 Hawai'i's top sights
These are given two or more full pages. Museums and galleries have color-coded floor plans to help locate the most interesting exhibits; national parks have maps showing facilities and trails.

INTRODUCING HAWAI'I

DISCOVERING HAWAI'I

The following tours have been designed to cover as many of the state's highlights as possible, while keeping long-distance travel at a minimum. First come the 2-day tours of Hawai'i's largest city (Honolulu) and smallest islands (Lāna'i and Moloka'i). With abundant attractions, a thriving cultural scene, and one of the world's most famous beaches, Honolulu offers much for every traveler. At the opposite end of the spectrum are the tiny, untouched islands of Lāna'i and Moloka'i, each of which

can be explored in a single day. Next come multi-day tours for the state's most visited islands: Maui, Hawai'i Island, Kaua'i, and O'ahu. These islands are filled with countless activities and attractions, including some of America's most stunning beaches and natural vistas. The routes can be combined to make a superb multi-week trip through the entire state. Follow your favorite tours, or simply dip in and out and be inspired.

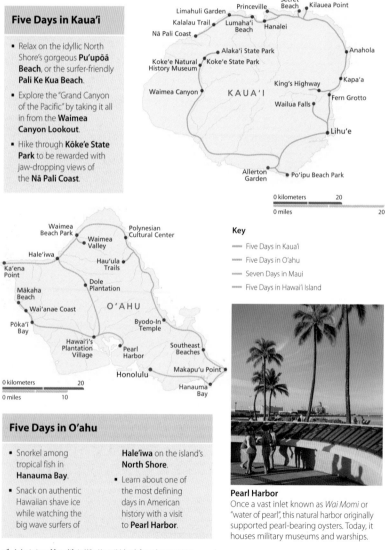

Five Days in Kaua'i

- Relax on the idyllic North Shore's gorgeous **Pu'upōā Beach**, or the surfer-friendly **Pali Ke Kua Beach**.

- Explore the "Grand Canyon of the Pacific" by taking it all in from the **Waimea Canyon Lookout**.

- Hike through **Kōke'e State Park** to be rewarded with jaw-dropping views of the **Nā Pali Coast**.

(Map labels: Limahuli Garden, Princeville, Secret Beach, Kilauea Point, Kalalau Trail, Lumaha'i Beach, Hanalei, Nā Pali Coast, Alaka'i State Park, Anahola, Koke'e Natural History Museum, Koke'e State Park, King's Highway, Kapa'a, Waimea Canyon, KAUA'I, Wailua Falls, Fern Grotto, Lihu'e, Allerton Garden, Po'ipu Beach Park)

0 kilometers 20
0 miles 20

Key

— Five Days in Kaua'i
— Five Days in O'ahu
— Seven Days in Maui
— Five Days in Hawai'i Island

(Map labels: Waimea Beach Park, Polynesian Cultural Center, Waimea Valley, Hale'iwa, Hau'ula Trails, Ka'ena Point, Dole Plantation, Mākaha Beach, Wai'anae Coast, O'AHU, Pōka'i Bay, Byodo-In Temple, Hawai'i's Plantation Village, Pearl Harbor, Southeast Beaches, Honolulu, Makapu'u Point, Hanauma Bay)

0 kilometers 20
0 miles 10

Five Days in O'ahu

- Snorkel among tropical fish in **Hanauma Bay**.

- Snack on authentic Hawaiian shave ice while watching the big wave surfers of

Hale'iwa on the island's **North Shore**.

- Learn about one of the most defining days in American history with a visit to **Pearl Harbor**.

Pearl Harbor
Once a vast inlet known as *Wai Momi* or "water of pearl", this natural harbor originally supported pearl-bearing oysters. Today, it houses military museums and warships.

◀ A depiction of farm life in Hilo, Hawai'i Island, from the year 1855

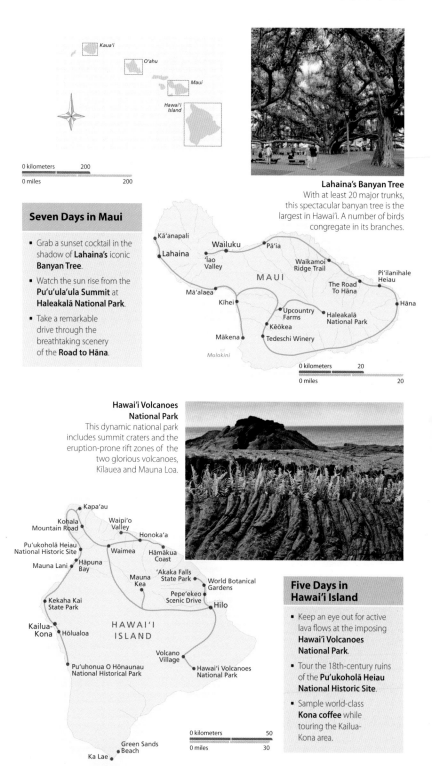

Lahaina's Banyan Tree
With at least 20 major trunks, this spectacular banyan tree is the largest in Hawai'i. A number of birds congregate in its branches.

Seven Days in Maui

- Grab a sunset cocktail in the shadow of **Lahaina's** iconic **Banyan Tree**.
- Watch the sun rise from the **Pu'u'ula'ula Summit** at **Haleakalā National Park**.
- Take a remarkable drive through the breathtaking scenery of the **Road to Hāna**.

Hawai'i Volcanoes National Park
This dynamic national park includes summit craters and the eruption-prone rift zones of the two glorious volcanoes, Kilauea and Mauna Loa.

Five Days in Hawai'i Island

- Keep an eye out for active lava flows at the imposing **Hawai'i Volcanoes National Park**.
- Tour the 18th-century ruins of the **Pu'ukoholā Heiau National Historic Site**.
- Sample world-class **Kona coffee** while touring the Kailua-Kona area.

View of the magnificent Diamond Head, as it towers over Waikīkī

Two Days in Honolulu

Apart from Waikiki's crowds and traffic, the vibrant capital offers famous sites and experiences for all.

- **Arriving** Honolulu International Airport, located a few miles to the west of Waikīkī, is serviced by hotel shuttles, buses, and rental cars.

Day 1

Morning Begin your day with a self-guided tour of **Waikīkī** *(pp64–9)*, the epicenter of Hawai'i's tourism industry. Stroll along the **Waikīkī Beach Front** *(pp66–7)*, an area full of surfers and beaches, until you reach the gorgeous **Kūhiō Beach** *(p69)*. View the flower-adorned statue of **Duke Kahanamoku** *(p69)*, widely considered the father of modern surfing. Afterwards, take a walk down the bustling Kalakaua Avenue, lined with inviting boutiques and restaurants. Here, you

Statue of Duke Kahanamoku, the father of modern-day surfing, on Kūhiō Beach

can visit the neighborhood's most impressive retail facility, the **Royal Hawaiian Shopping Center** *(p67)*.

Afternoon After lunch, head east until you reach the verdant **Kapi'olani Park** *(pp76–7)*. Towering over the park is the imposing **Diamond Head** *(p77)*, an extinct volcano with breathtaking views of the island from its summit. Wind the day off with a well-deserved *pupu* (appetizer) and a tropical cocktail at the city's iconic **Royal Hawaiian Hotel** *(pp66–7)*.

Day 2

Morning A must-see for any visitor of the **Capitol District** *(pp56–7)*, is the **'Iolani Palace** *(p59)*, the only royal palace in the United States. Across the street from here is the **State Capitol** *(p59)*, which features interesting architectural features and impressive banyan trees. Before leaving the district, take a picture with the **King Kamehameha Statue** *(p58)*, a statue of one of the state's most revered monarchs.

Afternoon Hop on a public bus to **Chinatown** *(pp62–3)*, where you can have lunch at one of the many restaurants and takeaway eateries. Be sure to stop by the **Izumo Taisha Shrine** *(p62)* and the statue of **Dr. Sun Yat-sen** *(p62)*. Round off the day with a visit to the tranquil **Foster Botanical Gardens** *(p63)*.

> **To extend your trip…**
> Catch the current exhibits at the **Bishop Museum** *(pp72–3)*, and the **Honolulu Museum of Art** *(p75)*.

Two Days in Moloka'i and Lāna'i

With only a fraction of the businesses of Hawai'i, Moloka'i and Lāna'i offer a peaceful getaway.

- **Arriving** The airports of Moloka'i and Lāna'i offer services to the primary airports. There is no public transportation, so visitors rent vehicles.

Day 1

Morning Start the day with a visit to the town of **Kaunakakai** *(p102)* in Moloka'i, where you can grab a treat at the popular Kanemitsu Bakery *(p102)*. From here, head to **East Moloka'i** *(pp102–3)*, with a stop at the **'Ualapu'e Fish Pond** *(p103)*. Thereafter, enjoy a picnic lunch along the **Twenty-Mile Beach** *(p103)*.

Afternoon Head north until you reach the island's most scenic spot, the **Hālawa Valley** *(p103)*. The more adventurous can take a two-hour hike to the breathtaking **Moa'ula Falls** *(p103)*.

Day 2

Morning Arrive in **Lāna'i City** *(p108)*, the only pineapple plantation town in Hawai'i. Check out the historic **Hotel Lāna'i** *(p108)*, and visit the stunning **Luahiwa Petroglyphs** *(p108)*, once believed to possess sacred powers. Next, head south until **Mānele Bay** *(p108)* and **Hulopo'e Bay** *(p108)*, home to countless Hawaiian spinner dolphins. Unwind on the breezy patio at the **Four Seasons Lāna'i and Mānele Bay** *(p108)*, where you can eat a hearty gourmet lunch.

Afternoon Head north of Lānai City, to the incredible **Garden of the Gods** *(p109)*. Affected by wind erosion over thousands of years, the garden is home to a variety of unusual, lunar-like rock formations. Afterwards, spend the evening at the nearby **Shipwreck Beach** *(p109)*, with its view of the World War II supply ship.

Seven Days in Maui

From lively lu'aus and world-class resorts to a dormant volcano, the "Valley Isle" is Hawai'i's second-largest island, with something for everyone.

- **Arriving** Kahului Airport is Maui's only major airport. Direct flights bring visitors from cities as well as neighboring Hawaiian islands. There are limited public bus services, and visitors tend to rent vehicles.

Day 1

Morning Stroll through the historic town of **Lahaina** (*pp114–17*), which is the island's primary commercial hub. The **Baldwin Home** (*p116*) is well worth a visit, as is the **Lahaina Courthouse** (*p117*). Stop to admire the town's majestic **Banyan Tree** (*p116*), a National Historic Landmark. Grab lunch at one of the town's many award-winning restaurants.

Afternoon Visit the **Wo Hing Temple** (*p117*) for an insight into the life of the local Chinese community. Next, visit the **Hale Pa'i** (*p117*) museum. Wrap up the day with happy-hour cocktails at an outdoor bar.

Day 2

Morning Spend your morning aboard one of the frequent whale-watching cruises that

The altar of the Wo Hing Temple, built by the Chinese in 1912

depart from Lahaina Harbor. If you're lucky, you'll spot several humpback whales (*p119*).

Afternoon Head north via the **Lahaina Kā'anapali & Pacific Railroad** (*p118*), a steam locomotive also referred to as the "Sugar Cane Train." Enjoy lunch in the island's largest resort area, **Kā'anapali** (*p118*). Pop into the **Whalers Village Museum** (*p118*) to learn about the area's maritime history.

Day 3

Morning Travel south along the coast, until you reach **Mā'alaea** (*p123*). Charter a boat, and dabble in sport fishing or snorkeling. Alternatively, visit the area's major attraction, the **Maui Ocean Center** (*p123*), which is home to an array of exotic Hawaiian creatures.

Afternoon Grab lunch at **Kīhei** (*p124*), where there are plenty of cafés, shops and beaches. Visit the nearby Big Beach and Little Beach in **Mākena** (*p124*). For the nature-loving soul, the observation deck at the **Hawaiian Islands Humpback Whale National Marine Sanctuary** (*p124*) is a must-see.

Day 4

Morning Greet the day with a tour of **Upcountry Maui** (*pp126–7*). As you wind through the region, visit the charming country town of **Kēōkea** (*p126*), and the **Tedeschi Winery** (*p126*).

Afternoon Travel north to the **Upcountry Farms** (*p125*), where a fantastic range of vegetation flourishes. Discover everything about goats at **Surfing Goat Dairy** (*p125*), and visit the lavender farm at **Ali'i Kula Lavender** (*p125*).

Day 5

Morning Start your day early by making a trek to **Haleakalā National Park** (*pp132–3*). Catch the sunrise at the **Pu'u'ula'ula Summit** (*132*), the highest point on the island. The more adventurous can hit the **Sliding Sands Trail** (*p133*), or the **Halemau'u Trail** (*p133*).

The 'Īao Needle, a popular landmark in the beautiful 'Īao Valley

Afternoon Muster all remaining energy to make a trip to **Hāna** (*p129*). Stop by the **Hāna Cultural Center** (*p129*) to learn more about the history of this authentic Hawaiian town.

Day 6

Morning Drive down the breathtaking **Road to Hāna** (*pp128–9*), and check out sights, such as the **Waikamoi Ridge Trail** (*p128*) and the **Pi'ilanihale Heiau** (*p129*) along the way.

Afternoon Head west until you reach the royal center of **Wailuku** (*p122*). Spend the afternoon discovering local artifacts at the **Bailey House Museum** (*p122*).

Day 7

Morning Begin by exploring the impressive **'Īao Valley** (*p123*), with its relaxing **Kepaniwai Heritage Gardens** (*p123*) and its educational **Hawai'i Nature Center** (*p123*).

Afternoon Head to the island's most quirky destination, the bohemian beachtown of **Pā'ia** (*p128*). This is one of Maui's top spots for food lovers. Spend your remaining time exploring the town's hippie-friendly shops.

> **To extend your trip…**
> Spend a day on the little island of **Molokini** (*p125*), a submerged volcano that peeks out 50-m above the snorkelers and scuba divers.

Tourists explore the prehistoric interiors of the Thurston Lava Tube

Five Days in Hawai'i Island

The "Big Island" offers visitors unique sights such as the Hawai'i Volcanoes National Park, the Mauna Loa, and the Mauna Kea.

- **Arriving** Two airports serve the island: Kona International Airport and Hilo International Airport. For the purpose of this itinerary, arrive at either airport, rent a car, and depart from the other airport.

Day 1
Morning Begin your day by exploring the rainy city of **Hilo** *(pp152–3)*. If it's a Wednesday or a Saturday, head to the acclaimed **Farmers' Market** *(p152)*. Afterwards, pop into the **Pacific Tsunami Museum** *(p152)*.

Afternoon After lunch, take the **Pepe'ekeo Scenic Drive** *(p151)*, and head north until you reach the **World Botanical Gardens** *(p147)*. Continue north to see the **'Akaka Falls State Park** *(p151)*.

Day 2
Morning Explore the intimidating **Hawai'i Volcanoes National Park** *(pp156–9)*, which includes fantastic hiking trails. Make a stop at the **Volcano Art Center** *(p158)* on your way in.

Afternoon Bike to the **Kilauea Iki Overlook** *(p157)*, where you can take the trail to the **Thurston Lava Tube** *(p157)*.

For breathtaking views, head to the **Halema'uma'u Overlook** *(p156)*, or hike down the easy **Earthquake Trail** *(p158)*.

Day 3
Morning Start off by heading to the dormant volcano, **Mauna Kea** *(p150)*. Continue north until **Waimea** *(p141)*, where you can visit the **Keck Observatory Center** *(p141)*. To learn about the area's *paniolo* (cowboy) culture, head to the **Historic Parker Ranch Homes** *(p141)*. Grab an all-natural beef burger at one of their eateries.

Afternoon Drive to the rural town of **Honoka'a** *(p147)*, stopping by the **Hāmākua Coast** *(p147)*. Explore the **Waipi'o Valley** *(p146)*, or the "Valley of the Kings".

Day 4
Morning Begin with a drive along the spectacular **Kohala Mountain Road** *(p146)*. Take a detour to the historic town of **Kapa'au** *(p145)*. Afterwards, visit the ruins of the **Pu'ukoholā Heiau National Historic Site** *(p144)*.

Afternoon Head back along the beautiful **Hāpuna Bay** *(p144)*. Take a dip in the stunning Hāpuna Beach, and round the day off at the popular **Mauna Lani** *(p141)* resort area.

Day 5
Morning Start with a swim at the pretty **Kekaha Kai State Park** *(pp140–41)*, before arriving at the island's western hub, **Kailua-Kona** *(p138)*. Coffee lovers should continue to the town of **Hōlualoa** *(p138)*, to discover world-class **Kona coffee** *(p139)*.

Afternoon Devote the rest of the day to the incredible **Pu'uhonua O Hōnaunau National Historical Park** *(pp142–3)*. Wrap up the day with a *pupu* and cocktail in Kailua-Kona at sunset.

To extend your trip...
Drive along **Green Sands Beach** *(p155)* to **Ka Lae** *(p155)*, that sits at the southern tip of the island.

Five Days in Kaua'i

The oldest of the Hawaiian Islands, the "Garden Island", is also considered the most beautiful. However, the imposing geographical barriers make renting a car a necessity.

- **Arriving** Lihue Airport offers a small terminal that services both inter-island flights and non-stop jumbo jets for a steady stream of passengers.

Day 1
Morning Head to **Līhu'e** *(pp164–5)*, where you can visit the lovely **Grove Farm Homestead** *(p164)* for a pre-booked guided tour of the private orchard. Then, drive north through the old sugarcane fields until **Wailua Falls** *(p165)*. Enjoy a picnic lunch at the falls.

Afternoon Drive north to the beautiful cave, **Fern Grotto** *(p166)*. Then, visit the historic sites of **Hikinaakalā Heiau** *(p166)* and the **Birthing Stones** *(p166)* on the **King's Highway** *(p166)*. Devote the evening to **Kapa'a** *(p167)*, the eastern shore's largest commercial area.

Day 2
Morning Start early with a drive to the village of **Anahola** *(p167)*, and admire the pretty **Anahola Baptist Church** *(p167)*. Carry on to rocky **Kilauea Point** *(p168)*, home to the **National Wildlife**

The breathtaking twin Wailua Falls, dropping from a height of 80 ft (24 m)

Refuge (*p168*), a sanctuary for rare Pacific seabirds. Next, unwind on the glorious sands of **Secret Beach** (*p168*).

Afternoon A short distance to the west is **Princeville** (*p169*), one of the most famous resort and golf destinations. End the day at the gorgeous **Pu'upōā Beach** (*p169*), or at the surfer-friendly **Pali Ke Kua Beach** (*p169*).

Day 3
Morning Start the day at **Hanalei** (*p170*), or "Crescent Bay". For a sense of the area's history, check out the **Wai'oli Hui'ia Church** (*p170*) and the **Wai'oli Mission House** (*p170*). Nearby, **Lumaha'i Beach** (*p170*) is worth a stop. Nature lovers must visit the **Limahuli Garden** (*p171*).

Afternoon Spend the rest of the day hiking on the **Kalalau Trail** (*pp172–3*). Don't forget to visit **Hanakāpī'ai Falls** (*p173*) and the **Hanging Valleys** (*p173*), before returning to Līhu'e. Alternatively, take a charter cruise for views of the famous **Nā Pali Coast**.

Day 4
Morning Start off with a trip to the idyllic **Allerton Garden** (*p176*), and enjoy a peaceful moment at the Diana Fountain.

Afternoon Head east to **Po'ipū** (*p177*), a popular beach resort area. See the **Spouting Horn** (*p177*), and take a stroll at **Po'ipū Beach Park** (*p177*).

Day 5
Morning Spend a few hours exploring the **Waimea Canyon** (*pp174–5*). Learn the history of the region at the **Kōke'e Natural History Museum** (*p174*).

Afternoon Head to **Kōke'e State Park** (*pp174–5*) for additional hiking trails, including one that reaches into the imposing **Alaka'i Swamp** (*p175*).

> **To extend your trip…**
> Visit the historic village of **Hanapēpē** (*p176*). Discover a surprising collection of galleries, shops, and eateries.

Panoramic view of the spectacular Waimea Canyon, Kaua'i

Five Days in O'ahu

O'ahu offers many quiet pockets and world-class beaches, perfect for escaping a 21st-century life.

- **Arriving** Honolulu International Airport, just west of downtown, provides easy access to the city. To explore the rest of the island, renting a car is a necessity.

Day 1
Morning Pick a day from the Two Days in Honolulu itinerary on p12.

Day 2
Morning Head east from Honolulu to **Hanauma Bay** (*p92*). Spend the morning snorkeling among tropical fish.

Afternoon Travel to **Makapu'u Point** (*p92*), stopping to admire the views below the Makapu'u lighthouse. Head up along the coast to the exclusive beaches of **Southeast O'ahu** (*p93*). Those interested in history should venture inland to the **Byodo-In Temple** (*p92*), a replica of a 900-year-old Japanese temple.

Day 3
Morning Nature lovers should carve out time to explore the **Hau'ula Trails** (*p92*). Alternatively, head up the coast to the **Polynesian Cultural Center** (*p96*), an educational theme park that allows you to learn and interact with various Polynesian tribes.

Afternoon Enjoy lunch at one of the no-frills food trucks on the North Shore. Afterwards, visit the **Waimea Valley** (*p96*) and the pretty **Waimea Beach Park** (*p96*). Devote the evening to **Hale'iwa** (*p96*), where you can explore charming boutiques. Catch the sunset at **Ali'i Beach Park** (*p96*).

Day 4
Morning Families should visit the **Dole Plantation** (*p97*), home to the daunting **Pineapple Garden Maze** (*p97*). For a quieter experience, the remote **Ka'ena Point** (*p97*) offers a tranquil hiking trail with impressive mountain views.

Afternoon On the way back towards Honolulu, visit **Hawai'i's Plantation Village** (*p97*) for a glimpse of the sugar plantation culture.

Day 5
Morning Head along the water to the quiet **Wai'anae Coast** (*p97*). Visit the handsome **Pōka'ī Bay** (*p97*) and **Mākaha Beach** (*p97*).

Afternoon Travel south to **Pearl Harbor** (*p77*), where you can visit sights such as the **USS Arizona Memorial** (*p77*) and the **USS Bowfin Submarine Museum and Park** (*p77*).

> **To extend your trip…**
> Visit the **National Memorial Cemetery of the Pacific** (*p75*), located above Honolulu in the extinct volcanic crater, Punchbowl.

Putting Hawai'i on the Map

Hawai'i is an isolated archipelago in the middle of the Pacific Ocean. Part of the United States, it consists of eight main islands covering 6,425 sq miles (16,650 sq km). Most visitors arrive in Honolulu, the state capital, and travel to the other islands by inter-island flights or cruises.

Princeville
Kaua'i
Anahola
Kapa'a
Lihu'e
Kekaha
Ele'ele
Kōloa
Ni'ihau
Lihu'e
Mainland USA

Kaua'i Channel

O'ahu
Hale'iwa
Wahiawa
Ka'a'awa
Mākaha
Kāne'ohe
Honolulu
Honolulu

Pacific
Ocean

Asia,
Australasia

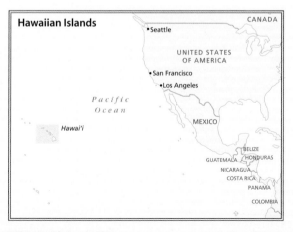

Hawaiian Islands

CANADA
• Seattle
UNITED STATES
OF AMERICA
• San Francisco
• Los Angeles
Pacific
Ocean
MEXICO
Hawai'i
BELIZE
HONDURAS
GUATEMALA
NICARAGUA
COSTA RICA
PANAMA
COLOMBIA

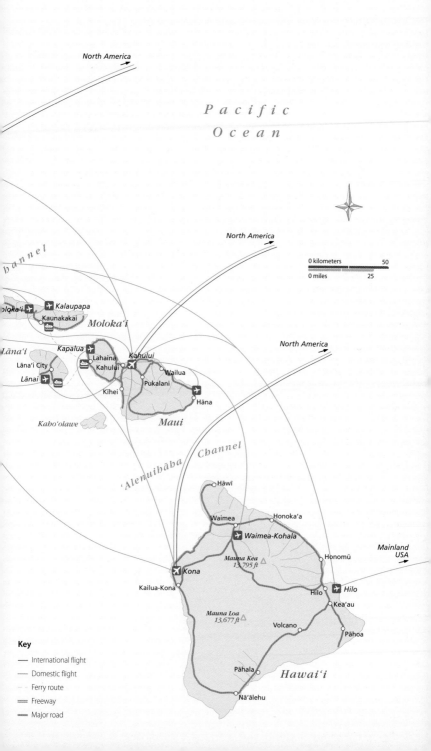

North America

P a c i f i c

O c e a n

North America

| 0 kilometers | | 50 |
| 0 miles | 25 | |

hannel

✈ Kalaupapa

oloka'i ✈

Kaunakakai

Moloka'i

North America

Lāna'i

Kapalua ✈

Lahaina

Kahului ✈

Lāna'i City

Kahului

Wailua

✈ *Lānai*

Pukalani

Kīhei

✈ Hāna

Mainland
USA

Kaho'olawe

Maui

'Alenuihāha Channel

Hāwī

Waimea

Honoka'a

✈ *Waimea-Kohala*

Mauna Kea
13,795 ft △

Honomū

✈ *Kona*

Kailua-Kona

Hilo

✈ *Hilo*

Kea'au

Mauna Loa
13,677 ft △

Volcano

Pāhoa

Key

Pāhala

Hawai'i

—— International flight

—— Domestic flight

Nā'ālehu

- - - Ferry route

══ Freeway

▬▬ Major road

A PORTRAIT OF HAWAI'I

Hawai'i is, quite simply, America's paradise. Its long stretches of white sand, crystal blue waters, swaying palms, and lush tropical rainforests dotted with pristine waterfalls attract millions of visitors each year. Hawai'i represents an ever-growing population encompassing a myriad of ethnic groups, development and tourism, agricultural diversity, and it is home to a rich cultural heritage.

The most isolated land masses and the longest island chain on earth, the Hawaiian Islands were all formed by volcanic eruptions deep beneath the sea and are, technically, the summits of submerged volcanoes. Of the archipelago's numerous islands and atolls, the six main islands are O'ahu, Moloka'i, Lāna'i, Maui, Hawai'i Island, and Kaua'i. The state's unique topography is most vividly apparent on Hawai'i Island where the world's most active volcano, Kīlauea, has been erupting constantly since 1983. As Kīlauea's lava empties into the sea, the island continues to grow and change shape. The isolation of the Hawaiian islands and their diverse habitats have resulted in spectacular native flora and fauna. These impressive and fragile ecosystems are home to more endangered species than anywhere else in the world. Climates vary considerably, with 12 of the earth's 13 climactic zones represented. Windward coasts to the north and west receive more rainfall and are characterized by jagged cliffs, lush valleys, and dense foliage. The sunnier leeward sides to the south and west are drier and make ideal locations for popular tourist resorts.

A pristine stretch of beach on Maui's north shore, with the West Maui mountains in the background

◀ The twin cascade of Wailua Falls, surrounded by sugarcane fields, Kaua'i

Tourists flock to the clear blue waters of O'ahu's North Shore

Tourism and Economics

Tourism is, by far, the islands' biggest industry and it continues to grow annually. More than seven million people from around the globe visit the Hawaiian islands each year. Resort hotels, restaurants, retail outlets, and operators that organize sports activities dominate the industry. Military installations, including Pearl Harbor, are the second leading source of outside income.

A tourist learns how to surf at one of Hawai'i's surf schools

The agricultural industry remains an important facet of Hawai'i's economy. Major agricultural products include coffee, macadamia nuts, tropical flowers, cane sugar, pineapples, bananas, and papayas. In addition to these larger agricultural ventures, small farmers are making a resurgence and are today driving a diversified agriculture movement thanks, in large measure, to their partnerships with island chefs. A myriad variety of vegetables, herbs, beef cattle, and locally grown and produced foodstuffs now appear on restaurant menus throughout the islands.

Hawai'i's strategic location in the Pacific Rim also fuels the state's modern economy. Hi-tech companies and financial institutions establish themselves here, the closest place in the United States to the markets of Asia.

People and Society

To call Hawai'i an ethnic melting pot is an understatement. Immigration to these islands started more than six centuries

Pineapple plantation, West Maui

ago, with the arrival of the first Polynesian settlers, and continued during the plantation era with waves of Chinese, Portuguese, Japanese, Filipino, Korean, German, and Puerto Rican laborers. Today, more ethnic and cultural groups are represented in Hawai'i than in any other state. Each group has brought traditions that have been tightly woven into the fabric of modern Hawaiian life.

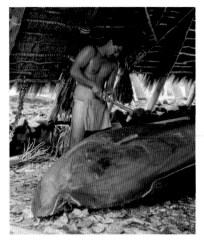

Crafting of a canoe using traditional methods

The tradition of removing one's shoes before entering a home, the annual Obon and Floating Lantern Festival which honors ancestors, the proliferation of sushi restaurants, and the extreme reverence for elders are all Japanese customs that today know few ethnic boundaries. The roots of the cattle industry, ranches, rodeos, 'ukulele music, and sweet bread lie in the influx of Portuguese immigrants in the 19th century.

Culture and the Arts

Traditional Hawaiian chanter

Hawai'i's cultural renaissance began in the late 1970s and continues to grow strongly and steadily to this day. There are many organizations and workshops dedicated to the preservation and perpetuation of the Hawaiian culture. Most important is the revival of the Hawaiian language in recent years. A lively contemporary music scene also flourishes throughout the islands, which blends mainstream reggae, rock 'n' roll, and jazz with more traditional sounds, including Hawaiian slack key guitar. It is still possible to see traditional *hula* performances, and the arts of Polynesian navigation and *lua*, a Hawaiian martial art, are also thriving. Hawaiian crafts – such as the making of hula implements, feather *lei* (garlands), and weaving – are also experiencing a welcome revival. And, of course, the ancient sports of surfing and canoe paddling are more popular than ever.

Artists from all over the world have been inspired by the people and beauty of Hawai'i, and Western and Asian visual and performing arts are very well represented. Honolulu boasts two world-class art institutions – the Honolulu Academy of Arts and The Contemporary Museum – and all of the islands are home to a number of galleries and artists' studios.

Floating lanterns at the annual Obon festival, Honolulu

Formation of the Hawaiian Islands

The Hawaiian Islands are the tips of a large chain of volcanoes stretching almost 3,100 miles (5,000 km) from Hawai'i Island to the Aleutian Trench in the north Pacific. Most are now underwater stumps, fringed by coral reefs, but many were once great shield (dome-shaped) volcanoes. The oldest, northernmost volcano is slowly disappearing into the Aleutian Trench. The youngest volcano – Kīlauea – today spews out basaltic lava, creating new land on Hawai'i Island. This cycle of destruction and creation, driven by the conveyor-belt movement of the Pacific plate over a stationary hot spot of magma, has been occurring for 70 million years.

Moloka'i's sea cliffs *(see pp104–105)* constitute the back wall of giant landslide scars formed when half of the Wailau shield volcano slumped into the sea. Marine erosion keeps the cliffs steep by undercutting the bases.

The areas of undulating ocean floor are deposits of giant landslides. Little is known about them because they sit in deep water, and their precise age of formation is unknown.

Kaua'i

Ni'ihau

O'ahu

Kaua'i's amazing Waimea Canyon *(see pp174–5)* is carved into the Wai'ale'ale shield volcano. The layers of lava flows that created the volcano are visible. Large canyons of this nature are typical of Hawaiian volcanoes in their late erosional stage.

Stretching almost halfway along O'ahu, the spectacular Nu'uanu Pali (cliffs) formed when a large section of the Ko'olau shield volcano slumped into the sea.

Ocean floor

The Pacific plate moves northwesterly at a rate of 2–3.5 in (5–9 cm) a year.

Conveyor Belt

As it moves, the Pacific plate – the huge slab of earth's crust underlying the Pacific Ocean – rides over a stationary hot spot (mantle plume) that feeds heat and basaltic magma toward the surface. Mauna Loa, Kīlauea, and the "new" underwater volcano Lō'ihi, are presently over the hot spot. As the plate moves to the northwest, volcanoes are gradually pulled off the hot spot while new volcanoes grow in their place.

O'ahu's Hanauma Bay *(see p92)* is a late-stage volcanic crater, one of several forming a line of cones, craters, and vents caused by an eruption at least 10,000 years ago. The ash cones are the result of explosive interaction of rising magma with sea water. Either the bay's present shape is due to breaching of the crater wall or, more likely, the wall was never complete.

Maui's Haleakalā *(see pp132–3)*, in its erosional, middle to late stage, is Hawai'i's only active shield volcano outside Hawai'i Island. Its last lava eruption was in 1790. Young cones and lava flows occur in and around the misnamed crater – actually an erosional depression formed where two large valleys coalesced.

Volcano Life Cycle

Shield volcanoes form while over a hot spot. As they move off it, volcanic activity decreases and erosion begins. Late stage volcanoes occur from a magma source deeper than the hot spot. Eventually, volcanoes disappear under the ocean surface.

1. Formation below sea level

2. Shield-building stage

3. Caldera stage

4. Erosional stage

5. Post-erosional late stage volcano

6. Atoll stage

Moloka'i
Lāna'i
Kaho'olawe
Maui
Hawai'i Island
Mauna Kea
Rift zone

Hot spot
Main conduit
Vent
Lithosphere
Underplating

Magma Reservoir

Mauna Loa *(see p151)* makes up over one-half the volume of Hawai'i Island.

Kilauea, a growing volcano perhaps calved off Mauna Loa some 200,000 years ago, has been erupting since 1983 and shows no sign of stopping *(see pp156–9)*. During this period lava has extended the coastline and formed about 2 sq miles (5 sq km) of new land.

Volcanic material

Lō'ihi, Hawai'i's newest shield volcano, lurks nearly 1 mile (1.5 km) below the ocean surface and is not expected to emerge for 100,000 to 200,000 years. It has all the features of a Hawaiian shield volcano, but none of its eruptions has broken the surface.

Hawai'i Island's Mauna Kea *(shown here)* and Mauna Loa, a pair of giant shield volcanoes, are hard to distinguish at their base beneath the sea. Mauna Kea *(see p150)* is older, in its post-shield stage with many smaller cones, giving it a rough appearance. Bulkier Mauna Loa's mass is so heavy that it has depressed the ocean floor. Together, they make up the earth's largest single volcanic structure.

Flora of the Hawaiian Islands

Prior to human settlement, the location of the Hawaiian islands in the middle of the Pacific Ocean was a natural barrier to the colonization of plants from other parts of the world. In prehistoric times, fewer than 300 immigrant flowering plant species – seeds borne by wind, carried by birds, or drifting on the ocean – colonized the islands. Extreme isolation produced a limited flora in comparison with continental floras; for example, Hawai'i has only three native orchids out of a worldwide family of 20,000 species. Some species evolved into new forms able to exploit a wide variety of habitats. Thorns and other defensive adaptations have largely been lost in Hawaiian plants as they con-ferred no advantage in a flora isolated from natural predators. As a result, native flora is unique, with 89 per cent of its flowering species found only in Hawai'i.

Koa is one of the most important forest trees in the Hawaiian islands. The largest specimens can attain heights of over 115 ft (35 m), and their huge trunks were used by Hawaiians to make voyaging canoes.

Grasses are found in virtually all vegetation zones, occasionally as the dominant species. In dry, lowland areas, *pili* grasslands provided thatching material for early Hawaiians *(see p73)*. About 150 native and naturalized species of this important and large family occur in Hawai'i.

'Ōhi'a lehua, probably the most common tree in the Hawaiian flora, occurs from near sea level to eleva-tions of 7,200 ft (2,200 m). It is also one of the most variable, with mature forms ranging from a few inches in bog habitats to 80 ft (24 m) or more in forest habitats. Epiphytes and a tree fern understory also characterize wet 'ōhi'a lehua forests.

Iliau, a relative of the silversword

Hibiscus, a favorite flower, is represented here by koki'o, one of seven native species and hundreds of orna-mental varieties and hybrids in Hawai'i.

Palm trees imported from Polynesia

Bougainvillea imported from Brazil

Pōhuehue, a typical beachfront plant

Naupaka is a dune-binding shrub with distinctive "half" flowers. Ocean currents have dispersed its buoyant fruits throughout the Pacific Basin. Scientists believe that two separate colonizations account for eight endemic species growing in a variety of upland habitats.

'Ākala, or native Hawaiian raspberries, appear to have lost an unnecessary defense mechanism (thorns in this case) that was present in their continental ancestors.

The silversword, or 'āhinahina *(see p133)*, occurs on Maui and Hawai'i Island in alpine desert habitats to elevations of over 12,000 ft (3,650 m). This species, together with the bog greensword and 25 other shrubs, trees, and a liana, actually evolved in the Hawaiian islands from one single ancestral immigrant.

Vegetation Zones

Alpine vegetation, a sparse array of shrubs dominated by silverswords and kūpaoa, occurs at 9,850–11,150 ft (3,000–3,400 m). A harsh, dry zone, it may freeze at night.

Subalpine communities occur in a relatively cool, dry zone from about 5,575–9,850 ft (1,700–3,000 m). Vegetation varies from grassland or shrubland to stunted trees.

Māmane tree, found in subalpine areas

Typical Island

The diversity of Hawaiian flora can be seen on this hypothetical island. At coast level, native shrubs and imported palm trees exist, gradually giving way to lowland shrubs and trees of increasing stature as rainfall increases. Bog vegetation may develop on flat, poorly drained areas. Above 6,000 ft (1,850 m), and at lower elevations in leeward areas, a dramatic reduction in rainfall usually results in sparse, low vegetation.

Montane dry areas are characteristic of leeward slopes at an elevation of 1,650–8,850 ft (500–2,700 m). Vegetation varies from dry grasslands to dry forests with a canopy 10–65 ft (3–20 m) high.

Montane wetlands, in areas of high rainfall at elevations of 3,950–7,200 ft (1,200–2,200 m), include wet herblands, sedgelands, shrublands, bogs, and forests with canopies up to 130 ft (40 m) high.

Raised hummocks of oreobolus

The greensword, a close relative of the silversword, is found in summit bogs of West Maui and at mid-elevations mostly in windward East Maui.

Lowland and coastal communities include a diverse array of dry, medium, and wet herb, grass, shrub, and forest vegetation occurring below 5,000 ft (1,500 m) elevation.

Tropical plants from around the world thrive in Hawai'i. This lush planting on O'ahu includes giant aroids and bananas. Alien plants pose a real threat to native species by displacing them and preventing their regeneration.

Marine Life of Hawai'i

Hawai'i's remote location in the middle of the Pacific Ocean supports a rich population of marine life and a relatively undisturbed coral reef habitat. This dynamic reef ecosystem is home to more than 7,000 marine species, of which approximately one third are unique to the Hawaiian Islands. It is also home to many endangered species which are protected under the 1973 Endangered Species Act, including Hawaiian monk seals and green sea turtles. In 2006, the Northwestern Hawaiian Islands National Monument was created in order to protect 140,000 sq miles (360,000 sq km) of this precious marine habitat, including ten islands and atolls, making this the largest area dedicated to marine conservation in the world.

Humuhumunukunukuapua'a (reef triggerfish) is the designated state fish of Hawai'i. Its name means "triggerfish with a snout like a pig". With sharp teeth and powerful jaws, it feeds off molluscs and crustaceans.

Cauliflower coral has heavy, leaf-like branches.

Corals are living animals that eat, grow, and reproduce.

Urchins inhabit crevices in the coral reef.

Antler coral, common in Hawai'i, is usually found in depths of 35 ft (11 m) to 150 ft (46 m). Its branches resemble moose antlers.

The seven eleven crab has seven prominent spots on the top of its shell and four more along the bottom for a total of eleven. It is most commonly seen at night.

The pencil-slate sea urchin is bright red and has large, blunt, pencil-thick spines.

The green sea turtle measures more than 3 ft (1 m) across and weighs up to 220 lbs (100 kg). Once a food source for islanders, it is now a protected species.

Sharks of the Coastline

There are about 40 species of sharks found in Hawaiian waters, ranging in size from the deep-water pygmy shark, about 0.7 ft (0.2 m) long, to the whale shark, up to 50 ft (15 m) long. The most frequently encountered near Hawaiian reefs are the whitetip reef, hammerhead, and, occasionally, tiger sharks. Sharks are essential in maintaining the balance of the ecosystem.

Whitetip reef shark

Hammerhead shark

Whale shark

Coral Reefs

Hawai'i's coral reefs are home to thousands of fish and other sea animals and plants that come in every size, shape, and color imaginable. The reefs house the majority of coral found in U.S. waters. They grow only 0.25 inches (0.6 cm) each year.

Moorish Idols are brightly-colored and move gracefully through the water feeding off the coral.

Butterfly fish live in depths of less than 20 ft (6 m). There are 25 species in Hawaiian waters.

The octopus is a master of camouflage. It escapes detection by changing its color to match its environment.

The Hawaiian stilt is a rare and threatened species. This slender wading bird with long pink "stilt" legs is endemic to the Hawaiian island chain. It can grow up to 1.3 ft (0.4 m) tall.

Spinner dolphins are the most common dolphin species in Hawai'i. They can be observed daily off the coast of O'ahu.

Hawaiian monk seals, so named because their folds of skin resemble a monk's hood, are the most endangered marine mammals in the U.S. Adults can grow to 600 lbs (272 kg).

Voices of Hawai'i

Ancient Hawai'i produced a wealth of oral literature and myth, which was passed down from generation to generation. A 12-letter alphabet, the smallest in the world, was developed by the missionaries in the early 19th century. Notable literary visitors wrote accounts of the islands and completed other works during their stays. Today, a new generation of Hawaiians is creating modern native literature, while maintaining a profound respect for the myths and chants that perpetuate the old ways of Hawai'i.

The demigod Maui fishing the Hawaiian islands out of the sea

Oral Tradition

The oral traditions of precontact Hawai'i played a vital role in island life. The literature, committed to memory, was often chanted to the accompaniment of music and dance. There were *oli* (chants), *mo'olelo* (stories and narratives), *mele* (songs), and *'ōlelo no'eau* (proverbs). The *kāhuna* (priests) composed and recited poetry to preserve history, genealogies, and the knowledge of traditional crafts. *Haku mele* (composers) often composed verses for special occasions, such as the birth of an *ali'i* (royal) child; such songs were considered sacred.

19th-century image of Kū

The *haku mele* took advantage of the fact that many words sound alike, building on repetitions and word play. The similarity of words was not considered accidental; if a sea creature's name matched that of a geographical feature, these phenomena were considered *kino*, manifestations of the same spiritual force.

The most famous creation chant, the *Kumulipo*, tells of life and the islands growing up gradually, on their own initiative. The progenitors of humans were the male *Wākea* (the Heavens) and the female *Papa* (the Earth). Hawaiians venerated four main gods: Kāne (light, life, water), Lono (productivity of the land), Kū (war, courage), and Kanaloa (sea). Each had numerous manifestations, all with names, and their deeds were visible in everyday nature.

Stories tell of Pele, the fiery-tempered volcano goddess who migrated from *Kahiki* (Tahiti, or simply the distant homeland) seeking a dry place for her eternal fires. Tracing the geological evolution of the islands, she resided first on Kaua'i and then O'ahu before settling for a time in Maui's Haleakalā Crater. She now lives in Hawai'i Island's Kīlauea Caldera *(see pp156–7)*.

Myths are told of Pele's entire clan, especially of her jealous relationship with her beautiful youngest sister, Hi'iaka, the first dancer of the *hula*. Pele's opponent in many stories is the shapeshifting pig-man Kamapua'a, a carnal, violent manifestation of Lono. Representing the productivity of the mountains and fields, his unending quest is to tame and fertilize the destructive goddess of lava. A cinder cone near Hāna on Maui is called Ka Iwi o Pele, or Pele's bones *(see p129)*, because the two titans met there for a cataclysmic battle.

Other stories tell of Maui, the Prometheus of Hawaiian mythology, who brought fire to the human race, lifted the roof of the heavens, slowed the speed of the sun, and fished the islands out of the sea with a magic hook.

Early Records

The first written words about Hawai'i are found in the logbooks and journals of the early visitors. Thomas Manby, on an expedition in 1791, wrote candidly of the seamen's amorous relations with Hawaiian women and gave a humorous portrait of Kamehameha I's first sight of a cow – startled, the great warrior knocked over half his retinue fleeing for his life.

The first missionaries kept more restrained records. The Reverend Hiram Bingham, leader of the first mission in 1820, set the pattern with his

An 1834 edition of *Ka Lama Hawaii* (The Hawaiian Luminary)

Missionaries versus Man-of-Warsmen. Within 14 years of their arrival, the missionaries had created a Hawaiian alphabet, translated the Bible, established a printing press, and put out the first Hawaiian language news-paper, *Ka Lama Hawaii*.

Native oral tradition was suppressed but never lost during this time. Traditional songs *(mele)* passed through the filter of hymns *(hīmeni)* and the introduction of the guitar and 'ukulele to emerge as "Hawaiian music." King Kalākaua (1874–91) started a renaissance of Hawaiian culture by calling for a revival of the *mele*, chants, and *hula*. In the same era, scholarly converts such as Samuel M. Kamakau and David Malo wrote invaluable records of life in precontact Hawai'i.

Jack and Charmian London on Waikīkī Beach in 1915

Portrait of Robert Louis Stevenson by Girolamo Piero Nerli (1892)

Literary Visitors

In the opening chapter of Herman Melville's *Moby Dick*, Ishmael says, "I love to sail forbidden seas and land on barbarous coasts." This urge to explore exotic realms was an echo of that felt by Ishmael's creator and many other writers, and in the 1800s, the lure of the South Seas was particularly strong. In 1843, Melville himself spent four months in Hawai'i, working in a Honolulu bowling alley and beach-combing in Lahaina.

Following in Melville's footsteps, the 31-year-old Mark Twain explored the islands in 1866 as a correspondent for the *Sacramento Union*. While touring, he wrote a series of *Letters from the Sandwich Islands* and later put several chapters about Hawai'i in his book *Roughing It*. Though he never visited again, he wrote that "no other land could so lovingly and so beseechingly haunt me, sleeping and waking, through half a lifetime, as that one has done."

In 1889, the Scottish writer Robert Louis Stevenson dined with King David Kalākaua. Suffering from tuberculosis, the author of *Treasure Island* traveled the South Seas from 1888 until his death in 1894. In Hawai'i, he befriended the royal family, studied the language, and visited Kalaupapa leprosy colony *(see pp104–105)*. Stevenson worked at fever pitch during his five-month visit, finishing *The Master of Ballantrae*, conceiving his novel *The Wrecker*, roughing out a collection of sketches about Hawai'i called *The Eight Islands*, and writing numerous poems and letters. Two of his best stories, "The Bottle Imp" and "The Isle of Voices," were also penned here.

Jack London arrived in Honolulu aboard his yacht *Snark* in 1907. The islands became his second home and where he wrote some of his famous works, such as *The Call of the Wild* and *White Fang*. He was the first literary figure to call himself a *kama'āina* (child of the land). His volumes of island-set stories, *On The Makaloa Mat* and *The House of Pride*, angered the authorities by depicting racial snobbery and the cruelty of official responses to leprosy.

Hawai'i Calls

Twentieth-century tourism produced a new mythology, casting the islands as a "paradise" filled with relaxed, 'ukulele-strumming natives. A surge of interest in 1916 stimulated songs such as "Oh, How She Could Yacki Hacki Wicki Wacki Woo (That's Love In Honolu)." A second wave in the 1930s prompted a string of Hollywood Waikīkī fantasies, including the 1936 film *Honolulu*, which turned *hula* into a form of tap dance.

Today, the Hawai'i Visitors and Convention Bureau continues to romanticize Hawai'i. However, island-born writers such as Oswald A. Bushnell and Milton Murayama are creating a wealth of native literature. With support from local intellectuals, many now write in pidgin, the hybrid language that evolved on the plantations so that different ethnic groups could communicate. The stories of Lois-Ann Yamanaka, for example, have received international acclaim.

Wild Meat and the Bully Burgers, a novel by Lois-Ann Yamanaka

Hula and Hawaiian Music

Hula began, it is believed, as a form of religious ritual to honor the ancient gods and chiefs while providing entertainment for the ruling classes. The traditional *hula kāhiko* was accompanied only by the human voice through chants *(oli)* or song *(mele)*, and by percussion instruments. In the early 19th century, the missionaries tried to abolish *hula* but succeeded only in driving it underground. King Kalākaua, the Merrie Monarch, encouraged the revival of *hula* in the late 19th century, giving rise to the modern *hula 'auwana*. This style was influenced by Western music and clothing – women wore, and still do, long-sleeved, floor-length dresses *(holokū)*. The 1930s ushered in the "Sweet Leilani" era when dancers in cellophane skirts and flower *lei* greeted the ocean liners bringing tourists to Honolulu. Today, *hula* enjoys great respect.

This 19th-century engraving is a European interpretation of a native woman with traditional tattoos dancing *hula noho* (sitting *hula*) in a *kapa* skirt.

The earliest hula was, some say, the domain of men, although there is no documented evidence. However, there has been a great resurgence of male *hula* in recent years.

Knee-length *ti*-leaf skirts are worn in *hula kāhiko*. The flat leaves rustle with the dancers' movements.

Dog-tooth leg ornaments, or *kūpe'e niho 'īlio*, were traditionally worn exclusively by male dancers. Only four teeth from each dog were used, and it took nearly 3,000 dogs to make some ornaments.

The *'uli'uli* is a small gourd containing seeds and fitted with a handle. It is often decorated with feathers.

The ipu heke is a percussion instrument made of two gourds. It is the most common accompaniment for *hula kāhiko*. The *kumu* (teacher) here is wearing a dried *ti*-leaf cape, which originally would have functioned as a raincoat.

The standing pahu drum is traditionally made from a section of coconut tree covered with shark skin, played with the hands. *Pahu* are often used in conjunction with the smaller *pūniu* – a drum made of coconut, lashed to the chanter's right thigh and played with a thong of braided fiber.

Where to Enjoy Hula and Music

Merrie Monarch Festival (p41)
Polynesian Cultural Center (p96)
Moloka'i Ka Hula Piko (p38)
Prince Lot Hula Festival (p38)
Nā Mele O Maui (p40)

Pū'ili are made of bamboo; one end is a handle and the other is split into a narrow "fringe" that makes a rattling sound.

This group of kūpuna (respected elders) dressed in *mu'umu'u* are singing and playing instruments that typically accompany *hula 'auwana* – *'ukulele*, guitar, and standing bass. The *ipu heke* and *'ulī'ulī* lying in the foreground are used for *hula kāhiko*.

The 'ukulele is one of many instruments brought to Hawai'i by immigrants, in this case the Portuguese. It is integral to contemporary Hawaiian music.

Flower *lei* are not authentic to *hula kāhiko*; dancers traditionally wear fern anklets and bracelets.

Maui's Keali'i Reichel is a well-known chanter, *hula* dancer, singer, composer, and teacher dedicated to the preservation of the culture.

Hula Kāhiko

This old form of hula is shown here with contemporary twists. The ti-leaf skirts, pū'ili, and 'ulī'uli are traditional, while the plumeria flower lei and colorful fabric tops are modern. Visitors can see this combined style of old and new elements on all the Hawaiian islands.

The Revival of Hula and Hawaiian Music

Today *hula kāhiko* is pursued by hundreds of students performing the same chants and using the same instruments as their ancestors, and *hula 'auwana* is more popular than in King Kalākaua's time. *Hula's* connection to Hawaiian music is inextricable. The "music" accompanying traditional dancers took the form of musical poetry – chants and song. When Western musical influence became widespread, *hula* embraced it in the *'auwana* style. In the early 19th century, missionaries brought sober hymns to Hawai'i, and increased sea traffic brought musicians from Europe and Asia with their varied secular music. The era from 1900 to the Hawaiian Renaissance of the 1970s saw an explosion of *hapa haole* – Hawaiian music influenced by ragtime, Tin Pan Alley, and even orchestrations from films and television shows. The instruments brought by immigrants – *'ukulele*, Hawaiian guitar, standing bass, piano – were stirred into the musical pot. The ongoing Hawaiian Renaissance has brought an enthusiastic revival of early Hawaiian music.

Child dancing *hula kāhiko*

Traditional Hawaiian Crafts

What we consider crafts today – woven baskets, feather *lei* (garlands), *poi* (taro paste) pounders, wooden bowls – were integral to the lives of ancient Hawaiians. They were made with care from readily available sources, such as coconut fronds, feathers of the *mamo* bird, local stone, and native *koa* wood. Many crafts are still made in the old, precontact ways. Even the ancient, almost lost art of beating and printing *kapa* (bark cloth) is undergoing a revival. Traditional implements are often favored over the modern, but certain tools have been updated. For instance, metal needles for stringing *lei* have replaced those made from coconut palm frond midribs. Not all crafts are indigenous. The missionaries introduced quilting, an art that is still passed from generation to generation *(see p72)*. Both the ancient and modern crafts are time-consuming pursuits requiring patience and skill – not unusual attributes among Hawaiians.

Netting was the most efficient method of fishing in old Hawai'i. The best nets were made with a netting needle and mesh gauge, using cord from the *olonā* shrub.

These two wooden bowls, connected by a human figure crowned with feathers, were probably used by an ali'i (chief) for Poi (taro paste) or 'awa (a ceremonial drink).

The Starbuck Cape

This superb 19th-century 'ahu'ula (cape) with a unique geometric pattern was made with the feathers of thousands of birds, which were released after giving up just a few feathers each. It was probably given to Captain Starbuck by Kamehameha II, who with his wife sailed to London on the captain's ship in 1824.

Feathers were arranged by size, tied together at the quills, and attached to the net with *olonā* thread.

Kapa Cloth

Common garments (*'a'ahu*) in ancient Hawai'i were made of *kapa* (bark cloth). The *wauke* (paper mulberry tree) produced the best cloth, which was pounded with wooden *kapa* beaters. Using dyes from native plants in every imaginable hue, bamboo implements were used to stamp patterns on the cloth. Today *kapa* is still made for certain ceremonies and is highly regarded for its variety of textures and beautiful, intricate designs.

Decorating *kapa* cloth

This late 18th-century pe'ahi (fan) is made out of coconut leaves, human hair, cordage, and dyes. Fans with this distinctive shape were probably used exclusively by the ali'i (chiefs).

Gourds with tubular necks were used in ancient Hawai'i to hold drinking water. It is believed that dyes created with infusions of bruised leaves, bark, or black mud were used to make the dark patterns on gourd bowls and water containers. Gourds of different shapes and sizes were also used as percussion instruments *(see pp30–31)*.

Two-ply cord made from the bark of the *olonā* shrub was used in the net foundation and the fasteners.

The irregular black shapes are made from the feathers of the 'ō'ō bird. Black feathers were rarely used.

The red background was made from the feathers of the 'i'iwi bird.

The 'ō'ō bird also provided the bright yellow feathers.

Hawaiian Lei

Lei are wreaths or garlands, made of flowers, leaves, shells, nuts, or feathers, which are worn around the neck. They range from simple strings of blossoms to complex woven garlands of native leaves and plants. *Lei* have always been important symbols of affection in Hawai'i and are bestowed frequently with a kiss. They are worn by everyone with pride on Lei Day *(see p38)*.

Woman with colorful flower *lei*

Stone poi *pounders* were used to grind taro *(see p129)*, a vital food source, into *poi* (a thick paste eaten with the fingers). It was heavy work, done by men who sat at a wooden pounding board, which was moistened with water, and mashed the cooked taro.

Traditional Braiding

In ancient Hawai'i, braiding or weaving was an important method of creating everyday objects, such as floor coverings, sleeping mats, pillows, baskets, and fans. *Lauhala* – the large leaves *(lau)* of the pandanus tree *(hala)* – were one of the most common materials. Sedge grass, including the coveted fine sedge *makaloa*, and certain palms were also used. The most extraordinary sleeping mats were made of *makaloa* on the island of Ni'ihau. In preparing the leaves for braiding, the weaver had to be careful because their edges and spines were sharp. Today, coconut palm fronds are commonly woven into hats and baskets. Generally speaking, the tighter the weave, the more valuable the item.

Coconut frond hat

Stiff, sharp leaves used as braiding material

Surfing in Hawai'i

Past and present, surfing has occupied an honored place in Hawaiian culture. Though its exact origins are unclear, *he'e nalu* (wave sliding) has been practiced here for centuries. The sport was dominated by the *ali'i* (chiefs), who had their own surf breaks that commoners were not permitted to enjoy; Kamehameha the Great himself was an avid wave rider. In the 19th century, the sport went into decline after the missionaries discouraged it. A revival started in the early 20th century when Waikīkī became an international playground. Today the islands remain the ultimate place to surf.

Hawaiian surfers ride the waves in this 19th-century engraving. In ancient times, entire villages flocked to the beach when the surf was up.

Duke Kahanamoku, shown here with fellow surfers in front of the Moana Hotel c.1915, was the father of modern surfing *(see p69)*. The Duke was a gifted surfer and the epitome of the carefree Waikīkī Beach life in the early 20th century.

The face of the wave, just before it breaks, is where the energy is most concentrated.

The surfer keeps knees bent and arms out for balance and to control speed and movement.

Banzai Pipeline

This spectacular wave on O'ahu's North Shore shows an expe[rt?] surfer engulfed in a tube of water. He must maintain an exac[t] position inside the "barrel" or risk being thrown over the "falls[."]

Most modern surfboards are made of lightweight fiberglass and range in length from 6–12 ft (2–4 m). They usually have three fins attached to the underside of their tails, though longer boards may only have one.

Short boards, the most maneuverable boards, are used for steep small- to medium-size waves. They are more difficult to stand on than long boards.

Long boards may be wide for riding gently sloped waves, like those of Waikīkī, or narrow for riding steep, very large waves, like those of Waimea Bay.

Fins add stability and maneuverability. They come in different shapes and sizes. In big waves, the fin would be backward and in small waves, it would be forward.

Boogie boards are small foam boards coated with fiberglass used to surf steep waves, often in shallow water. Riders lie flat on the boards and kick with fins to gain enough speed to catch the waves.

O'ahu's North Shore sees towering waves from October to April, when storms sweep across the North Pacific producing powerful swell lines. Waimea Bay *(above)* has always been known for the largest waves that can be surfed.

In the 1960s, daredevil surfers like American Mike Doyle, seen here with Duke Kahanamoku, came to Hawai'i in search of challenging surf. They found it on Oahu's North Shore, which soon became the surfing capital of the world.

The wave breaks just behind the surfer, creating a cascade of spray and foam.

Special techniques in surfing can involve the use of foot straps for aerial tricks, exotic board shapes, and towing by jet skis to surf giant waves.

Triple Crown of Surfing

Every year for three weeks in late November to mid-December, O'ahu's North Shore is transformed into a surf carnival. During this time, the Triple Crown of Surfing, the world's most prestigious series of surfing contests, takes place at Banzai Pipeline and Sunset Beach near Waimea, and at Ali'i Beach Park in Hale'iwa *(see p96)*. Giant waves and spectacular rides create a level of excitement and performance found almost nowhere else in surfing. The contests attract surfers from around the globe for competitions that often decide the world championship. The highlight is the PipeMasters at the Banzai Pipeline – the most coveted title in surfing. Live commentary makes the events accessible even to spectators watching surfing for the first time. Food is not generally available at the beach parks so spectators take a picnic.

Winners of O'ahu's famous Triple Crown, which is contested on waves bigger than 20 ft (6 m)

Scuba Diving and Snorkeling

Diving and snorkeling in Hawai'i is an experience like no other. The warm, crystalline waters teem with an incredible array of fish, coral, and other marine life. Visibility often exceeds 100 ft (33 m). Below the ocean's surface, the spectacular scenery includes reefs, lava formations, caves, and sandy plains. Beginners quickly get the hang of snorkeling. You can rent or buy a mask, snorkel, and fins on every island; if you go on a snorkeling boat excursion, instruction and gear are provided. Scuba diving usually takes place on the calmer, leeward sides of the islands. Instruction and gear are provided by dive shops and charter boats. Most offer introductory dives and internationally recognized certification courses. A wet suit is always recommended for scuba diving.

Snorkeling is a popular pastime on each of the islands and there are many sites to choose from. It offers the chance to see schools of tropical fish and colorful marine life at close range.

Kaua'i *(see pp160–77)* has some of the best protected reef lagoons. Po'ipū Beach Park offers a sheltered, shallow cove ideal for novice snorkelers. Kaua'i is known for its rugged and pristine diving. Popular sites include General Store, a reef 65–80 ft (20–24 m) deep with a 19th-century sunken steamship.

KAUA'I ② ③ ①

O'AHU ⑤ ⑥

Brennecke's Ledge is best viewed from below, to spot long nose hawk fish and Hawaiian lionfish.

Mahi Shipwreck is a former mine-sweeper where lemon butterfly-fish and other tropical species practically pose for photographs.

Dive Site Ratings

There is a good variety of dive sites around the Hawaiian island chain. Divers should find out the level of experience required at any dive site before braving the waters.

	Snorkeling	Novice Diving	Advanced Diving	Expert Diving
Po'ipū Beach Park ①	●	▣		
General Store ②			●	
Brennecke's Ledge ③			●	
Hanauma Bay ④	●	▣	●	▣
Hale'iwa Beach Park ⑤	●	▣	●	
Mahi Shipwreck ⑥			●	
Murphy's Beach ⑦	●	▣		
Fish Bowl ⑧			●	▣
Hulopo'e Beach ⑨	●	▣		
Cathedrals ⑩			●	
Molokini ⑪	●	▣	●	▣
Carthaginian ⑫			●	
Richardson's Beach Park ⑬	●	▣		

0 kilometers   100

0 miles   100

O'ahu *(see pp88–97)* has dive sites that range from lava formations to shipwrecks. Hanauma Bay, the most popular snorkeling destination, is a natural "fish bowl". Originally the cone of a volcano, depths range from 15 ft (5 m) to 70 ft (21 m). Hale'iwa Beach Park is also good.

Moloka'i *(see pp98–109)* boasts the longest barrier reef in Hawai'i. The best snorkeling spots are between mile markers 18 and 20, heading east from Kaunakakai along Kamehameha V Highway, such as Murphy's Beach. Sites like Fish Bowl offer superb scuba diving, but are seldom visited due to weather and sea conditions.

Getting to the Dive Sites

Organized diving excursions include equipment and transportation by boat or motor van. If you are certified and wish to dive on your own, you can get directions and maps at any dive shop when you pick up your equipment.

Getting there: Each island has at least one major airport, and there are limited ferry services between Maui and the islands of Lāna'i and Moloka'i. See pages 238–41 for the location of airports, ferry ports, and major roads.

Hulopo'e Beach on Lāna'i *(see pp108–9) is renowned* for its snorkeling; it is edged by tide pools full of tiny fish and anemones. The most popular scuba site is Cathedrals, named for the size of its lava tubes and the stained-glass effect created by the sun's rays coming through holes in the lava ceiling.

Most dive sites in Maui *(see pp110–33)* are located off the west coast, including Molokini. Maui's newest scuba diving attraction is the Carthaginian, a replica of a double-masted brigantine, which was sunk in 2005 off Lahaina to create an artificial reef.

Molokini *(see p125)* is perfect for snorkelers and learner divers. Charter boats drop anchor here so both can view the abundant trumpet-fish, octopus, and other marine life.

On Hawai'i Island *(see pp134–59), Richardson's Beach* Park, east of Hilo, is a good place for beginner snorkelers. The more adventurous can swim around the lava rock outcroppings to a reef with fish and sea turtles.

HAWAI'I THROUGH THE YEAR

Contrary to popular belief, Hawai'i does have distinct seasons but only two: summer and winter. To residents, the distinctions are clear. It is summer if the mango tree in the garden is weighed down with fruit, or the intoxicating aroma of white ginger wafts in the air. Sudden rains or storms mean the onset of winter, as do the big waves that surfers eagerly await.

Residents in the cooler upcountry areas of Kaua'i, Maui, and Hawai'i Island spend Christmas Eve gathered around the fireplace. A fair generalization for visitors is that May to October is hot and dry; November through April is slightly cooler and wetter. Happily for visitors, though, there are very few days during the year when Hawai'i's fine beaches do not beckon.

Summer

By May, the winter rains have ceased and summer bursts into life all over the Hawaiian islands with blooming flowers and myriad festivals. **Lei Day** takes advantage of the abundance of scented flowers, with everyone donning a flowered garland. Hawai'i's oldest state holiday, **King Kamehameha Day**, dates back to 1872; there are many celebrations on all the islands to honor the great chief who united Hawai'i (see p45). All summer long there are cultural, music, and food festivals, as well as great sports competitions, from big rodeos to outrigger canoe races and the grueling **Ironman Triathlon**. The summer draws to a close with the grandest of all annual parties, the **Aloha Week Festivals**.

May

Lei Day (May 1), all islands. Everyone is adorned with at least one of these traditional Hawaiian garlands; lei-making contests are held on the islands of O'ahu and Kaua'i.
Moloka'i Ka Hula Piko (3rd Sat), Pāpōhaku Beach County Park (see p107), Moloka'i. This celebration of the birth of hula features music, dancing, food, and traditional crafts.
Hawaiian Steel Guitar Festival (early May), Kā'anapali, Maui. Concerts and workshops featuring the Island's only indigenous stringed instrument.
Memorial Day (last Mon), all islands. This national holiday commemorates soldiers who lost their lives in battle.

June

King Kamehameha Day (Jun 11 and surrounding days), all islands. This state holiday is celebrated with parades, hula and chant performances, crafts festivals, and much more. The biggest celebration is held at the Neal Blaisdell Center in Honolulu (see p215).
Hawaiian Slack Key Guitar Festival (Jun to Jul), Maui, O'ahu, and Hawai'i. This uniquely Hawaiian guitar tuning is used in performances by the state's best guitarists.
Obon Festivals (late Jun to end Aug), all islands. At every Buddhist temple in Hawai'i, Japanese Bon dancers honor their ancestors. There are spectacular floating lantern ceremonies in Lahaina, Maui, (Jul) and at Honolulu's Ala Wai Canal (Aug).

July

Pu'uhonua O Hōnaunau Cultural Festival (late Jun or early Jul), Pu'uhonua O Hōnaunau National Historical Park (see pp142–3), Hawai'i Island. A royal

Dancers at the traditional Buddhist Obon Festival in Honolulu

court and demonstrations of traditional Hawaiian crafts.
Makawao Rodeo (weekend closest to Jul 4), Makawao (see p127), Maui. Hawai'i's biggest rodeo, where paniolo, Hawaiian cowboys (see p147), demonstrate their skill.
Parker Ranch Rodeo (weekend closest to Jul 4), Waimea (see p141), Hawai'i Island. Set in the ranching heartland.
Prince Lot Hula Festival (3rd Sat), Moanalua Gardens, O'ahu. Local hālau hula (hula schools)

Crowd-pleasing bull-riding at the annual Makawao Rodeo

Average Number of Sunny Days Per Month

Sunshine Chart
Hawai'i has few days without at least some sunshine, with leeward (southwest) coasts being sunnier than windward (northeast) ones. Blue skies and warm days are thus a fairly consistent feature, except at higher altitudes, which are often misty. The chart gives the number of days per month with little or no cloud cover, averaged across the islands.

honor Prince Lot (Kamehameha V) with both the ancient and modern styles.

Kōloa Plantation Days *(late Jul)*, Kōloa, Kaua'i. A parade and other celebrations which commemorate one of the first sugar plantations to be established in Hawai'i.

August

Hawaiian International Billfish Tournament *(late Jul to early Aug, or 1st half of Aug)*, Kailua-Kona *(see p138)*, Hawai'i Island. The world's leading international marlin fishing tournament. Fishermen and avid fans are drawn to this renowned event from all over the world.

Hawai'i Food and Wine Festival *(late Aug to early Sep)*, O'ahu, Maui, and Hawai'i Island. One of Hawai'i's largest annual culinary events, with an array of dinners, tastings, seminars, and parties. Some of America's top chefs appear at this festival.

September

Aloha Week *(mid-Sep to late Oct)*, all islands. Dozens of music and dance events, craft fairs and demonstrations, floral parades, delicious food, and even a royal ball make up this grandest of Hawai'i's annual celebrations. The festival begins on O'ahu and continues on each of the other main islands, lasting a week on each island.

Kaua'i Mokihana Festival *(Sep or Oct)*, Lihu'e *(see pp164–5)* and island-wide, Kaua'i. This weeklong celebration showcases contemporary Hawaiian music and *hula*, with concerts and competitions.

Nā Wahine O Ke Kai *(late Sep)*, Hale O Lono, Moloka'i. The most

Traditional costumes and flower-decked float at an Aloha Week parade

important women's outrigger canoe race of the year; finishes on O'ahu.

October

Princess Ka'iulani Keiki Festival *(date varies)*, Hanapēpē *(see p176)*, Kaua'i. A parade of stage peformances, children's activities, and tributes to Princess Ka'iulani, through the historic town.

Ironman Triathlon *(Sat closest to full moon)*, Kailua-Kona *(see p138)*, Hawai'i Island. The ultimate physical challenge for the 1,250 participants, this race combines a 2.4-mile (3.8-km) swim with a 112-mile (180-km) bike ride before finishing with a grueling 26-mile (42-km) marathon.

Coconut Festival *(early Oct)*, Kapa'a Beach Park *(see p167)*, Kaua'i. The cultural, social, and historical importance of

the versatile fruit is celebrated with coconut food items, crafts, games, contests, and entertainment.

Nā Moloka'i Hoe *(mid-Oct)*, Hale O Lono, Moloka'i. More than 50 men's teams from around the world compete in this outrigger canoe race to O'ahu. It has become the most important annual event in the sport in the world.

Halloween Mardi Gras of the Pacific *(Oct 31)*, Lahaina *(see pp114–17)*, Maui. The streets are closed to all traffic for this rollicking Halloween party.

Start of the Ironman Triathlon in Kailua-Kona

Average Monthly Rainfall

Rainfall Chart
This two-tiered chart gives average figures for all of Hawai'i. The dark green indicates rainfall on the sheltered, leeward coasts, while the light green indicates the higher rainfall on the exposed windward coasts. The winter months, from Nov–Apr, receive the most rainfall, while the summer, May–Oct, receives the least.

Winter

In ancient Hawai'i, winter was the time of Lono, the god of agriculture and peace (see p28). Lono made himself known with extreme weather that could change from minute to minute. Traditionally, wars were concluded by the onset of winter, and it was time for the people and the land to rest from the year's labors.

November, December, and January are the most unpredictable months, but Hawaiian winters are generally mild, and there are many sports and cultural events. The remarkable **Triple Crown of Surfing** displays feats of great skill and courage, while major Pro-Am golf tournaments are held statewide. Winter ends with the famous **Merrie Monarch Festival** of *hula*.

November

Kona Coffee Cultural Festival, Kona district (see p139), Hawai'i Island. With parades, arts and crafts, gourmet tasting, and a coffee-picking contest, the Kona district pays homage to the bean that made it famous.
Hawai'i International Film

Float at the Kona Coffee Cultural Festival

Festival (late Oct to mid-Nov), all islands. Dozens of screenings, workshops, and symposia starting on O'ahu, and then running concurrently on the other islands. Except for some films on O'ahu, screenings are free.
Triple Crown of Surfing (late Nov to mid-Dec), North Shore (see p35), O'ahu. The world's most prestigious surfing competition, which spans three weeks (see p35), waves and weather permitting.
Thanksgiving Day (4th Thu), all islands. National holiday celebrated with family feasts.
Mission Houses Museum Annual Christmas Fair (last weekend in Nov), O'ahu. An open-air market features artists and crafts-people showing and selling Christmas-related handicrafts.

December

Honolulu City Lights and Festival of Trees (early Dec to early Jan), Honolulu. A must-see display of lights and one-of-a-kind trees, all created by employees of different county and city departments.
Nā Mele O Maui (1st weekend), Kā'anapali (see p118), Maui. Cultural celebration of music featuring a student song contest to help preserve the knowledge and love of Hawaiian traditions.
Honolulu Marathon (2nd Sun), Honolulu. One of the most popular and scenic marathons in the US, it stretches 26 miles

(42 km) from the Aloha Tower to Kapi'olani Park, drawing 15,000 runners. **Christmas** (Dec 25), all islands. National holiday.
Hawai'i Bowl (Dec 25), Aloha Stadium, O'ahu. Annual event contended by college football teams.

Lion dancer at the Narcissus Festival in Honolulu's Chinatown

January

Narcissus Festival (Jan–Mar, lasting 12 weeks), all islands. This celebration of the Chinese New Year features lion dances, fireworks, a coronation ball, and traditional food. Honolulu's Chinatown (see pp62–3) hosts the best parties.
Ka Moloka'i Makahiki (late Jan), Kaunakakai (see p102), Moloka'i. Week-long cultural festival beginning with a fishing contest in outrigger canoes. There are traditional Hawaiian games, sports, *hula*, and music.
Pacific Island Arts Festival (Jan), Kapiolani Park, Waikīkī. Annual exhibit of works by native artists.

Average Monthly Temperature

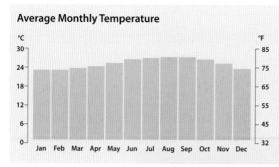

Temperature Chart
Hawai'i has consistently warm temperatures year round, with little variation between summer and winter. The coastal areas are warmest, particularly the leeward coasts, which are more sheltered from wind and rain. The upcountry and mountainous areas can be much cooler, with a marked difference in the mornings and evenings.

Sony Open in Hawai'i (mid-Jan), Wai'alae Golf and Country Club, O'ahu. Major tournament on the PGA tour.

February
Cherry Blossom Festival (late Jan or early Feb to Mar or early Apr), all over O'ahu. Japanese festival with tea ceremonies, cooking and flower arranging demonstrations, *mochi*-pounding, and traditional Taiko drumming.

Panaewa Rodeo Stampede (mid-Feb), Equestrian Center next to zoo outside Hilo (see p152), Hawai'i. Professional and amateur cowboys and cowgirls compete for prizes.

NFL Pro Bowl (late Jan or early Feb), Aloha Stadium, O'ahu. NFL stars play a post-season, all-star game. Reserve tickets early.

The annual NFL Pro Bowl game at O'ahu's Aloha Stadium

March
World Championship of Women's Bodyboarding (mid-Mar–mid-Apr), Banzai Pipeline, north shore O'ahu. Pro women bodyboarders compete for prize money.

Hula dancers with their flower *leis* at the Merrie Monarch Festival

Whale and Ocean Arts Fest (mid-Feb to early Mar), Banyan Tree Lahaina (see pp114–17), Maui. Celebration of marine life and the humpback whales that spend winters in Maui's coastal waters (see p119).

Prince Kūhiō Day (Mar 26), all islands. Holiday in celebration of Hawai'i's first delegate to the US Congress and a well-liked "people's prince." There are ceremonies at the Federal Building in Honolulu.

Windward Orchid Society Annual Spring Show (late Mar), O'ahu. Beautiful orchids on display in every imaginable hue. Demonstrations on plant care and plant sale.

April
Easter Sunrise Service (Easter Sun), National Memorial Cemetery of the Pacific (see p75), Honolulu. An inspiring ceremony held at "Punchbowl" crater with views of the city.

Merrie Monarch Festival (week starting Easter Sun), Hilo (see pp152–3), Hawai'i Island.

This week-long Hilo festival honoring King David Kalākaua culminates with the "Olympics" of *hula*. Plan well in advance for this extremely popular event, as tickets sell out almost immediately.

Public Holidays
New Year's Day (Jan 1)
Martin Luther King Day (3rd Mon in Jan)
Presidents' Day (3rd Mon in Feb)
Prince Kūhiō Day (Mar 26)
Memorial Day (last Mon in May)
King Kamehameha Day (Jun 11)
Independence Day (Jul 4)
Admission Day (3rd Fri in Aug)
Labor Day (1st Mon in Sep)
Columbus Day (2nd Mon in Oct)
Election Day (1st Tue in Nov)
Veterans' Day (Nov 11)
Thanksgiving Day (4th Thu in Nov)
Christmas Day (Dec 25)

THE HISTORY OF HAWAI'I

Spanning less than 2,000 years, Hawaiian history is one of the briefest in the world, with much of it shrouded in legend. And yet it equals the world's best for bloodshed, irony, and heroism. Hawai'i has had to adapt to waves of invasion and immigration, and now supports one of the world's most ethnically diverse cultures.

The islands were formed by volcanic eruptions in the Pacific Ocean, more than 2,500 miles (4,000 km) from the nearest landmass. Life on the isolated Hawaiian archipelago evolved from wind-borne spores and seeds, corky fruits that drifted in the sea, and the occasional hardy bird blown off course by a storm. Sea creatures had difficulty reaching the islands, as the North Pacific currents push life-rich plankton away from Hawai'i. As a result, the unspoiled island ecosystem consisted of thousands of unique species that evolved by adapting to the new environment.

The Polynesians, whose culture was established in the island clusters of Samoa and Tonga between 2,000 and 1,500 BC, possessed a remarkable seafaring technology. They traveled in twin-hulled voyaging canoes that carried up to 100 passengers plus planting stocks of crops (taro, coconut, sweet potato, banana) and pairs of domesticated animals (pigs, dogs, and chickens). These explorers colonized the Society Islands (Tahiti) and the Marquesas Islands in the first century AD. Around AD 300, the Marquesans dared the 3,000-mile (5,000-km) ocean crossing to discover the Hawaiian islands. Archaeologists have based this date on excavations of habitation sites at Waimānalo (O'ahu), Hālawa Valley (Moloka'i), and Ka Lae (Hawai'i Island). Hawaiian ancestral chants, which were rigorously preserved in oral tradition, carried family lines back further, to the first century.

Map from 1862 showing the Hawaiian archipelago and its location in the middle of the Pacific

◀ Early Hawaiians gathered around a thatched *hale* (house)

Hawaiian men dancing in front of a crowd

Kānaka Maoli ("Real People")

The early Hawaiians established an advanced, spiritual culture. Dedicated farmers and stone-builders, they were the first to alter a landscape that had evolved in isolation for millions of years. They divided the land into *ahupua'a*, pie-shaped wedges running from the mountaintop to the sea, providing each district with access to the full range of island resources. They also built monumental *heiau* (temples) and some of the largest irrigation systems in Polynesia.

Life centered on the *'ohana* (extended family) of 250 to 300 people, in which everyone from *keiki* (child) to *kupuna* (grandparent) was vital to the whole. Cultural values included *aloha 'āina* (love of land), *laulima* (cooperation), and *pa'ahana* (hard work).

Invasion of the Ali'i

During the 12th and 13th centuries, new waves of Polynesian settlers came from the Society Islands (Tahiti). According to oral tradition, the invasions were cruel and bloody. Casting themselves as reformers of a weakened Polynesian race, they established a rigid class system with themselves as *ali'i* (chiefs) who

regulated the lives of the *maka'āinana* (commoners) through the harshly enforced *kapu* system. Derived from the Tahitian term "taboo," *kapu* designated any activity that was forbidden because it interfered with the apportionment of *mana* (supernatural power). Women, for example, were forbidden to eat with men. Commoners could not touch the clothes or shadows of the nobility, or lift their heads higher than the chiefs'. Punishment for infractions was quick and fatal, and the *ali'i* rededicated temples as *luakini heiau*, for human sacrifice.

The chief figure in this reform was the Tahitian priest Pā'ao, who probably made several journeys between the two archipelagos. He established a line of *kuhina nui* (high priests) and brought a chief named Pili, probably from Samoa, to consolidate political power. For unknown reasons, these voyages ceased after the 13th century.

Contact

Although British sea captain and explorer James Cook is credited with the "discovery" of Hawai'i in 1778, convincing evidence suggests that Spanish ships preceded him by more than 200 years. In the mid-16th century, Spanish galleons made annual voyages across the Pacific between their colonies in Mexico and recently established bases in the Philippines. In 1542, a fleet commanded by Ruy Lopes de Villalobos and led by Portuguese navigator Joao Gaetano stumbled onto islands they named the Isla de Mesa

Traditional *ali'i* attire, as worn in the 13th century

AD 300 Marquesans discover and settle Hawaiian islands

Hawaiian stone idol

1250 Arrival of Tahitian priest Pā'ao, who rededicates *heiau* (temples) for human sacrifice

Early hale (house)

AD 300 **600** **900** **1200** **1500**

Early voyaging canoe (c.300)

AD 1100–1300 Tahitians invade Hawai'i

1542 Spanish expedition, led by Joao Gaetano, finds Hawai'i and suppresses the information group. Navigators were ordered not to mention the islands in their logs for fear that knowledge of them would fall into British hands. In 1742, the British burst into the Pacific with their man-of-war *Centurion*, commanded by Lord Anson, and captured

Confrontation at Kealakekua Bay, Hawai'i Island, in 1779

a Spanish galleon in its annual crossing. They seized its treasure and a chart showing the Isla de Mesa group; Cook must have had a copy of that chart.

The timing of Cook's arrival at Hawai'i Island's Kealakekua Bay constitutes one of history's oddest ironies. His ships, the *Resolution* and *Discovery*, appeared at the height of the annual *makahiki* festival honoring the Hawaiian god of agriculture, Lono. The British ships bore a startling resemblance to Hawaiian prophecies that said that one day Lono would return on a floating island. Much to Cook's surprise, the Hawaiians greeted him with reverence beyond anything he had experienced in the Pacific.

All went well until his departure in February 1779, when a storm snapped a mast, forcing Cook back to Kealakekua Bay. By now, the Hawaiians surmised that the *haole* (Westerners) were less than divine, and a series of squabbles, including the killing of a chief, escalated into violent confrontation over a stolen

Kamehameha the Great, ruler from 1795 to 1819

boat. Cook was knifed to death in the fray.

Other explorers followed, including Frenchman La Pérouse in 1786, the first Westerner on Maui. Four years later,

American Simon Metcalf ordered the slaughter of dozens of Maui natives in the Olowalu Massacre. In 1792, British captain George Vancouver introduced cattle, goats, and sheep to Hawai'i. Within a generation of "discovery," domestic animals had begun to denude the forests, and imported diseases were killing large numbers of Hawaiians.

Kamehameha the Great

An ambitious chief from Kohala (Hawai'i Island), Kamehameha could claim a direct kinship to the powerful chief Pili, who lived 500 years earlier. A skilled warrior and shrewd opportunist, he managed to quell centuries of internecine warfare by systematically conquering each of the islands. In 1790, he demoralized the Hawai'i Island chiefs by constructing Pu'ukoholā Heiau (*see p144*) and sacrificing his key rival on its altar. In 1795, he stormed Maui, terrifying the enemy with cannon plundered from an American ship. O'ahu fell the same year after bloody fighting along the Nu'uanu *pali* (cliffs). Twice he tried to invade Kaua'i, but storms turned back his fleet. Kamehameha then invited chief Kaumuali'i to visit him on O'ahu.

1758 Kamehameha I born

1779 Cook killed at Kealakekua Bay

1795 Kamehameha conquers Maui, Moloka'i, Lāna'i, and O'ahu

1778 British captain James Cook first sights Ni'ihau and Kaua'i

1790 Hundreds killed in Olowalu Massacre

1750   1760   1770   1780   1790

1786 La Pérouse explores Hawaiian islands

1791 Kamehameha begins conquest of islands

Captain Cook (1728–79)

Through threats and rewards, he forced the chief to cede Kaua'i, and Hawai'i became a united kingdom in 1809.

Mid-19th-century painting of an enormous whale effortlessly destroying a whaling boat

When the old conqueror died in 1819, he left a leadership void that his son Kamehameha II was unable to fill. The drunken youth was coerced that same year to abandon the strict *kapu* system. The crucial moment came when he shared a meal with women – his mother Keōpūolani and his father's favorite wife, Ka'ahumanu. This act of *'ai noa* (free eating) was taken as a symbolic deed that invalidated all traditional rules. Thus the kingdom was reduced to a class of leaders with no precise set of laws.

Missionary Years

The American Board of Foreign Missions provided relief just six months later. On April 19, 1820, the brig *Thaddeus* landed in Kailua Bay (*see p138*) carrying 23 Congregationalists, the first of 12 such groups to come to Hawai'i over the next three decades. In 1823, the second group established a church in Lahaina, Maui, which was by now the whaling capital. The missionaries had running battles with rowdy whalers. They also baptized Keōpūolani, the

Missionary preaching to Hawaiians on Kaua'i, 1840

dying queen mother, who commanded her people to embrace Christianity.

Kamehameha II had bankrupted the kingdom by now, despite stripping the native forests to sell Hawaiian sandalwood to China. To distract himself from his problems, he and his wife sailed to England where they arrived unannounced and unrecognized. Instead of meeting King George IV as they had hoped, they both contracted measles and died of the disease in July 1824. This misfortune left Kamehameha III, the king's 11-year-old brother, to rule. Power, however, was wielded by the formidable regent, Queen Ka'ahumanu. By the time of her death eight years later, Ka'ahumanu had engineered the peaceful conversion of the entire kingdom to Christianity.

The Rise of American Business

Generally speaking, the missionary children showed a greater appetite for commerce than for religion. They and other Western entrepreneurs began to experiment with agribusiness ventures, particularly plantation-style production of sugar. In 1832, Kamehameha III leased land in Kōloa, Kaua'i for this purpose.

The king's unenviable job was to push ancient Hawai'i into the Western-dominated world. Guided by his *haole* (Western) advisors, he developed a constitution in 1840. Then, needing an infusion of revenues for the monarchy and maintaining that the *maka'āinana* (commoners) deserved to own land, he announced the Great *Mahele*

Kamehameha III (1814–54)

1809 Kaua'i joins united Hawaiian Kingdom

1820 First missionary party arrives in Kailua-Kona

1840 Kamehameha III proclaims Hawai'i's first constitution

1825 Kamehameha III becomes king, with Ka'ahumanu as regent

1800	1810	1820	1830	1840

A blubber pot used in the whaling trade

1819 Kamehameha I dies; Kamehameha II discards *kapu* system. Whaling commences

1825 Sugar and coffee plantations begun on O'ahu

1842 US recognizes independence of Hawaiian Kingdom

Sugar plantation workers gathered around a steam plow in the mid-19th century

(land division) in 1848. This released millions of acres for sale to private owners. Ironically, the *maka'āinana* possessed a weak understanding of "owning" land, and most of the deeds went to Western planters. For the next 100 years, sugar ruled the Hawaiian economy.

Large plantations required a labor force willing to endure long hours, poor pay, and cruel treatment, and native Hawaiians, demoralized by social change and crippling foreign plagues, largely declined. Instead, the planters began importing contract laborers, first from China in 1852. Later recruitments drew from the Portuguese islands of Madeira and the Azores, Japan, Puerto Rico, Korea, and the Philippines. As workers finished their contracts, a great number assimilated into island life. Many Chinese married into Hawaiian families. The Portuguese came, with their families, intent on settling. Other workers, particularly Japanese men, saw little incentive for returning to their former lives of hardship; they opted to pioneer lands leased in the Hawaiian

Queen Kapi'olani and Princess Lili'uokalani, wife and sister of Kalākaua, visiting the White House in 1887

wilderness, eventually writing home for brides and family members to join them. By 1900, over half the population of Hawai'i was of Japanese origin.

The Endangered Monarchy

After Kamehameha III's death in 1854, a succession of short-lived rulers did what they could for the rapidly dwindling native population. Kamehameha IV and his wife Queen Emma established Queen's Medical Center to help stave off the effects of contagious disease on Hawaiians. Kamehameha V issued a new constitution in 1864 that strengthened the power of the monarchy, and introduced laws to protect the rights of foreign laborers. Lunalilo ruled only a year. By 1873, high tariffs on sugar were causing the planters to talk openly of annexation to the US. In 1874, David Kalākaua took the throne. Called the "Merrie Monarch," he initiated a cultural renaissance by promoting a revival of the *hula* and ancient chants, spending lavishly to build 'Iolani Palace *(see p59)*, and planning a Polynesian empire with Hawai'i as its capital. The tide of history, however, had turned against him. Pressure applied by armed *haole* planters forced the king to secure a reciprocity treaty with the US. It eliminated tariffs on Hawaiian sugar, creating an economic dependency on agribusiness and US imports. In 1887, a league of planters forced Kalākaua to sign the Bayonet Constitution, which restricted the power of the monarchy.

Father Damien (1840–89)

1848 Kamehameha III proclaims Great *Mahele*. Imported diseases kill 10,000 Hawaiians

1866 Leprosy patients taken to Moloka'i's Kalaupapa Peninsula

1876 H.P. Baldwin completes Hāmākua Ditch, bringing wide-scale sugar production to Maui. Reciprocity Treaty with US

1850	1860	1870	1880	1890

1863 Kamehameha IV dies

1864 Kamehameha V issues constitution strengthening the monarchy

1874 Kalākaua ascends the throne

1887 Royal power curtailed by Bayonet Constitution

1845 Seat of government moves om Lahaina to Honolulu

1873 Lunalilo reigns for a year

The king's sister Lili'uokalani took the throne in 1891 and attempted to broaden constitutional powers, but was deposed in 1893 by the all-white "Committee of Safety" backed by illegally requisitioned American troops. Queen Lili'uokalani turned to the United States government for justice. President Grover Cleveland examined the facts and demanded that the queen be restored. However, the Provisional Government, led by missionary son Sanford P. Dole, refused.

Hula dancers accompanied by musicians at Waikīkī, with Diamond Head in the background (c.1920)

The Stolen Kingdom

The Provisional Government established itself as the Republic of Hawai'i in 1894, but its clear intention was to be absorbed into the United States. Cleveland refused to annex the pirated kingdom, but his successor McKinley did so gladly in 1898. In 1900, Hawai'i became a US territory. The territorial government was largely an oligarchy of white Republicans who controlled every aspect of island life from their positions as directors of Hawai'i's five main agribusiness companies. Attempts to unionize plantation labor in the 1930s were firmly

A meeting to celebrate the US annexation of Hawai'i in 1898

squelched. Ironically, it took the threat of Japanese invasion to force democracy on the nearly feudal institutions of territorial Hawai'i.

On December 7, 1941, Japanese bombers crippled US military installations on O'ahu, sinking or severely damaging 18 battleships at rest in Pearl Harbor, destroying or disabling nearly 200 aircraft, and killing more than 2,000 officers and men. Within 24 hours, Hawai'i's government was replaced by a military one that stayed in power throughout World War II. Five years of direct federal involvement forced territorial leaders to adopt more democratic methods. After the war, a strike – violent, but ultimately effective – shut down the plantations for 79 days. At the same time, Hawai'i's underclass began wielding the power of the ballot, and soon the children of the plantation camps were being swept into positions of political power. In 1959 the US Congress offered to make Hawai'i the 50th state of the union, and a majority of citizens voted to accept, led by a strong endorsement from the Japanese population.

The invention of air travel has changed Hawai'i perhaps more than any other imported technology, not only because it

1893 Monarchy is overthrown

1894 Hawai'i is declared a republic

1917 Lili'uokalani dies

1922 Dole creates world's largest pineapple plantation on Lāna'i

1936 *Hawai'i Clipper* flies from San Francisco to Honolulu, initiating commercial air traffic to Hawai'i

1949 Strikes cripple Hawai'i, shifting political power away from "Big Five" companies

| 1890 | 1900 | 1910 | 1920 | 1930 | 1940 | 1950 |

1898 Hawai'i annexed by US

1895 Citizens attempt an armed insurrection

US Territory seal

1927 Royal Hawaiian Hotel is built, catering to cruise liner trade

1941 Japan attacks Pearl Harbor; many Japanese-Americans sent to mainland internment camps

1954 Labor-backed Democrats swamp Republicans in Territorial elections

Japanese bombing of US naval base at Pearl Harbor in 1941, bringing the United States into World War II

turned O'ahu into the center of US military defense in the Pacific but also because it opened the door for mass tourism. Commercial flights had begun in the 1930s with Pan Am's *Hawai'i Clipper*, but it was the introduction of jet travel in 1959 that brought the world to the islands. Suddenly, Hawai'i, especially Waikīkī, was an affordable four-and-a-half hour flight from the US mainland. Hotel development and population growth hit O'ahu first; by 1959 more than half the people in the state lived in Honolulu. Soon the large agribusiness landholders on all islands began diversifying. During the 1960s, the development of West Maui's Kā'anapali as a resort community signaled a new era for island economy. Whereas the plantations were once the driving economic force, many of the great sugar and pineapple fields now lay fallow, and Hawai'i's fortunes began to rise and fall with the moods of tourism and the price of real estate.

At the same time, some 140,000 resident Hawaiians have started taking political action to reclaim autonomy in their ancient homeland. During the 1970s, Hawaiians began demanding the release of Kaho'olawe from the grip of the US military, which had been using the island for target practice for 50 years. A renewed interest in Hawaiian culture, language, and crafts culminated in 1976 with the building of the *Hōkūle'a* – the first authentic voyaging canoe to be built in over 500 years *(see p61)*. In 1993, the US government apologized for any complicity in the wrongful overthrow of the monarchy, and the "nation of Hawai'i" began a movement to reestablish its own sovereignty.

Anniversary of the monarchy's overthrow (1993)

Today the Hawaiian islands support a population of over 1 million, with Hawaiians accounting for 12.5 per cent, and each year over 6 million tourists visit. The island chain accommodates one of the most ethnically diverse and tolerant populations in the world, where over 15 entrenched cultures jostle for position with an embattled heritage. No matter where you go in the islands, however, Polynesian roots grow very close to the surface.

The crowded golden sand of Waikīkī Beach, Hawai'i's most popular visitor destination

"Statehood" newspapers

Hawai'i ...mes US state

1982 Hurricane Iwa devastates Kaua'i

1983 Kīlauea begins present eruption

1992 Closure of Hāmākua Sugar, Hawai'i Island's last plantation. Hurricane Iniki devastates Kaua'i

2006 The US Government announces the Northwestern Hawaiian islands as a national monument; it is the largest marine sanctuary in the world

| 0 | 1970 | 1980 | 1990 | 2000 | 2010 | 2020 |

1977 Activists George Helm and Kimo Mitchell die while trespassing on Kaho'olawe

1986 John Waihe'e becomes first Hawaiian governor

1996 Citizens vote to convene on the issue of sovereignty

2008 Hawai'i-born Barack Obama elected president of the US

2002 Linda Lingle is elected as the first woman governor of Hawai'i

HONOLULU
AND WAIKĪKĪ

Honolulu and Waikīkī at a Glance

Hawai'i's capital city has two focal points, the historic and business district of Downtown Honolulu and the world-famous resort of Waikīkī. The downtown area first gained prominence as a trading port in the early 19th century. Waikīkī, by contrast, was still a swamp when its first luxury hotel went up in 1901. With Honolulu's best beach, however, the resort's success was guaranteed.

Chinatown *(see pp62–3)* is a lively district. The streets are lined with exotic shops, religious shrines, and lei stands.

'Iolani Palace *(see p59)* was built in 1882 and served as home for Hawai'i's last two monarchs, King Kalākaua and Queen Lili'uokalani.

Mission Houses Museum *(see p58)* preserves three mission buildings from the early 1800s.

DOWNTOWN HONOLULU *(see pp54–63)*

0 meters 500
0 yards 500

The Aloha Tower *(see p60),* built in 1926 to a height of 184 ft (56 m), was at the time Honolulu's tallest building. A street-level marketplace contains shops and restaurants.

Hawai'i Theatre *(see p61)* closed in 1984 after years of decline. Reopened in 1996, this historic Art-Deco theater has been beautifully renovated. Its neon sign has become a Honolulu landmark.

◀ Statue of Duke Kahanamoku, the father of modern-day surfing, on Waikiki Beach in Honolulu, Hawai'i

Royal Hawaiian Hotel (see p66), "Pink Palace," affords tranquil respite from Waikīkī's incessant bustle. This landmark hotel, opened in 1927, has played host to Roosevelts and Rockefellers.

Honolulu and Waikīkī

O'AHU

DOWNTOWN HONOLULU

WAIKĪKĪ

0 kilometers 2
0 miles 1

International Market Place (see p68), a huge open-air shopping center with eateries and entertainment.

King's Village (see p69) is a Victorian–theme shopping mall.

WAIKĪKĪ (see pp64–69)

Kūhiō Beach (see p69) features a statue of Duke Kahanamoku, the "Father of Surfing."

The Waikīkī Beachfront (see pp66–7) is lined by high-rise hotels, restaurants, and nightclubs, with the distinctive Diamond Head crater at the far end. Every day of the year, this 2-mile (3-km) stretch of golden sand attracts sun-seekers by the thousands.

The Moana Surfrider, A Westin Resort & Spa (see p68) dates from the early 20th century. The seaside Banyan Court bar is the perfect spot for sipping cocktails while watching glorious sunsets over the ocean.

DOWNTOWN HONOLULU

Once a fishing village called Kou, Honolulu was described in the 1820s as "a mass of brown thatched huts looking like haystacks." In the course of that century, however, it became a vital port of call for fur traders and whaling vessels visiting O'ahu, and in 1866, the novelist Mark Twain commented that every step in the city revealed a new contrast. This is no less true today. In a relatively small and compact area, downtown Honolulu manages to squeeze together towering skyscrapers, Japanese shrines, New England-style missionary houses, a cathedral, a royal palace, former opium dens, strip joints, and fish markets.

This bustling capital has a strong ethnic mix, and the downtown streets mirror the diversity. Hawaiian businessmen in three-piece suits, children in school uniforms, and Samoans in bright sarongs mingle in harmony.

Sights at a Glance

Historic Streets and Buildings
4 'Iolani Palace
5 State Capitol
7 Fort Street Mall
8 Aloha Tower Marketplace
9 Hawai'i Theatre
11 *Chinatown pp62–3*

Museums and Galleries
3 Mission Houses Museum
10 Hawai'i State Art Museum

Cathedrals and Churches
2 Kawaiaha'o Church
6 St. Andrew's Cathedral

Monuments
1 King Kamehameha Statue

See also Street Finder, map 1

0 meters 400
0 yards 400

◀ The King Kamehameha Statue in front of Ali'iōlani Hale, Honolulu

For map symbols see back flap

Street-by-Street: Capitol District

The architectural contrasts in this compact area mirror Hawai'i's cultural medley and trace its fascinating history. A short walk takes you from clapboard missionary homes to a sophisticated, Victorian-style palace where Hawaiian kings hosted lavish parties and the last queen of the islands was imprisoned. This majestic survivor of the island monarchy soon gives way, though, to a nearby symbol of 20th-century democracy – one of the few domeless state capitol buildings in the United States.

The 'Iolani Barracks were built in 1871 to house royal soldiers.

Chinatown (see pp62–3)

Hawaii State Art Museum

❹ ★ 'Iolani Palace
The only royal residence in the United States, 'Iolani ("Royal Hawk") Palace was completed in 1882. The interior has an elegant *koa*-wood staircase.

Hawaiian Electric Company building

The Royal Bandstand, set in the shaded grounds of 'Iolani Palace, was built for the coronation of King Kalākaua in 1883. It is still used for official functions.

Post Office

❶ King Kamehameha Statue
The king's bronze statue stands proudly in front of Ali'iōlani Hale.

Key
— Suggested route

Ali'iōlani Hale ("House of the Heavenly King") was designed as a palace and built in 1874. It now houses the Supreme Court and the Judiciary History Center.

For hotels and restaurants see pp182–4 and pp192–4

6 St. Andrew's Cathedral
Built in 1867, this cathedral features a large window of vivid stained glass.

Washington Place, a Georgian-style frame house built in 1846, is now a museum for Hawai'i's last queen, Lili'okulani.

Locator Map
See Street Finder, Map 1

Eternal Flame War Memorial

5 State Capitol
The design of this unique building represents the formation of Hawai'i's volcanic islands.

The Statue of Queen Lili'uokalani commemorates Hawai'i's last monarch, who took the throne in 1891 but was deposed by the "Committee of Safety" just two years later (see p48).

LILI'UOKALANI

2 ★ Kawaiaha'o Church
Prior to the completion of this New England-style church in 1842, missionaries used to preach from thatched huts on the same site. Sunday services are conducted here in both English and Hawaiian.

Kawaiaha'o Cemetery

3 ★ Mission Houses Museum
This excellent museum is housed in three buildings, including a printing house, erected by missionaries between 1821 and 1841.

0 meters 100
0 yards 100

Bronze statue of the king, his hand extended in a gesture of welcome

❶ King Kamehameha Statue

Corner of King St & Mililani St.
Map 1 B3. 🚌 2, 13.

Kamehameha the Great, who ruled the islands from 1795 to 1819, is Hawai'i's most revered monarch. This Hawai'i Island chief turned the islands from chiefdoms riddled by internecine warfare into a respected monarchy. As a young warrior, Kamehameha met illustrious foreigners, including Captain Cook in 1778. He soon grasped the importance of Western technology and incorporated ships and cannons into his conquest of the warring chiefs. After consolidating the kingdom, Kamehameha I turned his attention to looking after his people.

With its gold-leaf feathered helmet and cloak, the bronze statue in front of Ali'iōlani Hale is one of the most famous sights in Hawai'i. The original statue was lost in a storm, and this replica was unveiled by King Kalākaua in 1883. The original was recovered by divers the same year and erected in Kapa'au (see p145).

❷ Kawaiaha'o Church

957 Punchbowl St. **Map** 1 B3. **Tel** (808) 522-1333. 🚌 2. **Open** 8:30am–4pm daily. **Closed** public hols. ♿ 🅿 by appt. 🌐 **kawaiahao.org**

This imposing edifice is a monument to Hawai'i's missionary days. With the collapse of the old Hawaiian religion around 1820 – shortly after Kamehameha I's death –

the missionaries soon gained influential converts, including the formidable Ka'ahumanu, the king's favorite wife. In earlier thatched churches on the site, the Reverend Hiram Bingham preached to as many as 2,000 penitent Hawaiians, who would attend in what one missionary wife described in 1829 as "an appalling state of undress." With their first exposure to Western clothing, some wore just a shirt or a top hat. By the time the present church was built in 1842, the women wore decorous *mu'umu'u* (long dresses), and most worshipers sported shoes due to the planting of thorn-shedding *kiawe* trees.

The church's New England-style architecture is softened by the coral-block construction. The upper gallery has 21 portraits of the Hawaiian monarchs and their families, most of whom were baptized, married, and crowned here.

King Lunalilo's Gothic-style mausoleum

Outside are two cemeteries for missionaries and their early converts, and a mausoleum where King Lunalilo is buried. Apart from Kamehameha I, whose bones were hidden so that no one could steal his *mana* (spiritual power), most of the other royalty lie in the Royal Mausoleum (see p74).

❸ Hawaiian Mission Houses Museum

553 South King St. **Map** 1 C3. **Tel** (808) 531-0481. 🚌 2, 13. **Open** 10am–4pm Tue–Sun. **Closed** public hols. 🖼 ♿ first floor only. 📷
🌐 **missionhouses.org**

This bucolic enclave of the past contains the oldest timber frame house in Hawai'i, a testament to the persuasive powers of the New England missionaries. In 1821, one year after their arrival, Kamehameha II allowed Reverend Bingham to build a Christian house and to establish Hawai'i's first printing press. A more elegant house followed, part of which contains a replica press. The interiors have been lovingly preserved. Especially interesting are the clothes worn by the missionaries, including long underwear. The missionaries were so good at converting the rowdy whalers and Sandwich Island heathens that in 1825, a Russian visitor described Honolulu as follows: "streets deserted, games prohibited [and] singing, dancing [and] riding horseback on Sundays all punishable offenses."

Elegant coral-block house at the Hawaiian Mission Houses Museum

South façade of 'Iolani Palace, with steps up to the main entrance

❹ 'Iolani Palace

King St & Richards St. **Map** 1 B3.
Tel (808) 522-0832. 🚌 2, 13.
Open 8:30am–4pm Mon–Sat.
Closed Jan 1, Jul 4, Thanksgiving & Dec 25. 🎦 📷 ♿ 📷 recommended (except at gallery). 🅦 iolanipalace.org

King David Kalākaua was inspired by English Victorian architecture when he commissioned this royal residence on the site of an earlier palace. Drawing heavily on sugarcane profits, Hawai'i's "Merrie Monarch" tried to recreate the pomp and circumstance of the English court in the palace's luxurious interiors.

The only royal palace in the US, 'Iolani ("Royal Hawk") Palace served that function for just 11 years. Kalākaua took up residence in 1882, followed by his sister, Lili'uokalani, who reigned for only two years before the monarchy was overthrown in 1893 *(see p48)*.

The palace became the seat of government, and in 1895, Lili'uokalani was imprisoned here for nine months. The first governor used Kalākaua's bed-room as his office, and the legislature met in the chambers downstairs. After the govern-ment moved to the Capitol building, the palace became a set for Jack Lord's office in the television series *Hawaii Five-0*. Fans will recognize the arched floor-to-ceiling windows. Children under five are not admitted to the palace.

The grounds make a pleasant place for a stroll. The barracks of Kalākaua's royal guard, which date from 1871, serve as a gift shop and visitor center. The

grass near Kalākaua's coronation bandstand makes an ideal picnic spot, and every Friday at noon – except in August – the Royal Hawaiian Band gives a free concert.

❺ State Capitol

Beretania St & Richards St. **Map** 1 B2.
Tel (808) 586-0221. 🚌 2, 13.
Open 7:45am–4:30pm Mon–Fri.
Closed public hols. ♿ 📷 by appointment. Washington Place: 📷 Mon–Fri; reservations required: (808) 586-0248.

Crossing beneath the canopy of banyans from 'Iolani Palace to the back of Hawai'i's State Capitol is a trip from old to new, from Victorian monarchy to contemporary crossroads of the Pacific.

America's youngest state boasts the most imaginative statehouse, its architecture symbolizing Hawai'i's majestic environment. The building rises from a reflecting pool just as the islands rise from the blue Pacific.

Fluted columns, suggesting lofty palms, circle the veranda, and two volcano-shaped chambers contain the houses of the legislature. At the rear, by the Capitol veranda, stands a statue of Queen Lili'uokalani, holding the music to "Aloha 'Oe," a famous ballad she composed. The words mean "may you be loved or greeted." The statue is often decked with flower *lei*. In front of the building is a modern statue of Father Damien *(see p105)* by Marisol Escobar.

Across Beretania Street ("British" street in Hawaiian) is the **Eternal Flame**, a memorial to World War II soldiers. Farther down the street is **Washington Place**, formerly the governor's mansion and Hawai'i's oldest continuously occupied dwelling. This Georgian-style frame house was built by John Dominis, Queen Lili'uokalani's father-in-law, in 1846. After release from imprisonment in the palace, the queen lived out her days in this house and it is now a museum in her honor.

The Eternal Flame, a war memorial across from the State Capitol

Statue of St. Andrew outside the cathedral in Downtown Honolulu

6 St. Andrew's Cathedral

229 Queen Emma Square. **Map** 1 B2.
Tel (808) 524-2822. 2, 13.
Open 9am–5pm daily.
W saintandrewscathedral.net

The oldest Episcopal edifice in Hawai'i, St. Andrew's was built as an Anglican cathedral in 1867. (It turned Episcopalian in 1898, when Hawai'i became an American territory.) Alexander Liholiho (Kamehameha IV), Hawai'i's most Anglophile king, brought Anglicanism to Honolulu following a trip to England during which he was enchanted by English church rituals. His wife Queen Emma, the granddaughter of Englishman John Young, an advisor of Kamehameha the Great, was baptized by the first Anglican clergymen to arrive in the islands.

After the death of the king in 1863, Emma traveled to England to raise funds and to find an architect for the cathedral. Her husband's brother and successor, Kamehameha V, laid the cornerstone four years later. Much of the stone was imported from England, although the arched walkways are more suggestive of Gothic churches in France.

The cathedral was not consecrated until 1958, when the final phase of construction,

Detail of stained glass at St. Andrew's

including a huge stained-glass mural, was completed. Outside, a statue of St. Andrew appears to preach to fish rising from a surrounding pool. The carved message reads "Preach the Gospel to every creature."

7 Fort Street Mall

Fort St. **Map** 1 A3. 2, 13.

This street was named after the former Kekuanohu fort. Kamehameha I decided to build a harbor fort after he fought off a Russian bid to colonize the islands in 1816. John Young, the king's advisor, supervised the work, and the whitewashed walls stood until 1857. According to early documents, the stronghold also functioned as a prison. By the 1860s, the adjacent street was a thriving business center, with a dressmaker, milliner, hardware store, and lumberyard. Some small shops remain today, but the four-block street has been turned into a pedestrian mall. At the *mauka* end (toward the mountains) is **Our Lady of Peace**, an austere Catholic cathedral built of coral in 1843. Father Damien (*see p105*), the "Martyr of Moloka'i," was ordained here in 1864. Opposite is the contemporary **Hawai'i Pacific University** building. Eating places nearby reflect the university's international student body – Vietnamese,

Korean, Chinese, French gourmet, and even a Filipino-Polish restaurant. Midway down the mall, the benches are often occupied by retired Filipino grandpas who spend their time people watching, strumming *'ukulele*, and chatting away in Tagalog. The mall affords interesting views both *mauka* and *makai* (toward the sea).

View down Fort Street Mall, lined with diverse eating establishments

8 Aloha Tower Marketplace

Pier 9, Honolulu Harbor. **Map** 1 A3.
Tel (808) 528-5700. 19, 20, 47.
Open 10am–7pm Mon–Sat, 10am–6pm Sun; observation deck: 9:30am–sunset daily.
W alohatower.com

Originally known as the "Gateway to Fort Street," the Aloha Tower was constructed in 1926, in the days when tourists arrived by steamship. Locals flocked to the tower and terminals to sell *lei* to the

View of Aloha Tower Marketplace and the Honolulu Harbor

arriving passengers, dance the *hula*, dive for coins, and partake vicariously of the excitement of travel only few could afford. Departing passengers threw multi-colored streamers from the decks while the Royal Hawaiian Band played the famous and much loved ballad, "Aloha 'Oe" *(see p59)*.

Standing ten stories high, with four clocks facing the four points of the compass, what was once Honolulu's tallest building is now dwarfed by gleaming skyscrapers. An elevator carries visitors to an observation deck, which delivers a 360° view of Honolulu Harbor and the mountains.

Today, the tower is the hub of a tasteful complex that houses upscale stores, and restaurants offering sheltered outdoor seating, perfect for sunset-watching. Local musicians play throughout the complex. Cruise liners still pull up at the pier, as do working ships from all over the world. Some naval vessels welcome visitors free of charge during designated hours. Sightseeing vessels run harbor tours, and **Navatek I** offers whale-watching cruises from January to April.

Clock face at the top of the Aloha Tower

❾ Hawai'i Theatre

1130 Bethel St. **Map** 1 A2. **Tel** (808) 528-0506. 🚌 2, 13. **Open** 9am–5pm Tue–Sat (box office). **Closed** most public hols. 🚻 Ⓦ hawaiitheatre.com

Opened in 1922 to present vaudeville, musicals, plays, and silent movies, the Hawai'i Theatre was dubbed "The Pride of the Pacific". Hawaiian architects Walter Emory and Marshall Webb created a Neo-Classical exterior with a variety of decorative elements – Byzantine, Corinthian, and Moorish – and a lavish interior with plush carpets, ornate columns, marble statuary, and a gilded dome. When talking pictures took off in the 1930s, the Hawai'i became an upscale movie theater, but eventually it went into decline, finally closing down in 1984. A local campaigning group raised funds to save the building and restore it to its former glory. It reopened in 1996 as a multi-purpose venue offering films, concerts, and stage performances. Exterior renovations were completed in 2005. In recognition of its historic importance, the theater is listed on the US National Register of Historic Places.

Model of a sailing canoe in Hawai'i State Art Museum

❿ Hawai'i State Art Museum

2nd floor, No.1 Capitol Building, 250 South Hotel St. **Map** 1 A2. **Tel** (808) 586-0900. **Open** 10am–4pm Tue–Sat. **Closed** public hols. 📷 🏛 🚻 Ⓦ hawaii.gov/sfca

This museum, housed in a handsome Spanish-Mission-style building, is dedicated to Hawaiian art, including bark cloth items, embroidery, quilts, and pottery. Many items blend Western forms and traditional folk art. The museum is also home to Art in Public Places, which brings together over 5,000 works of art by more than 1,400 Hawaiian artists.

The Hōkūle'a

Hawai'i's first modern reconstruction of an ancient sailing canoe, the *Hōkūle'a* sailed to Tahiti and back in 1976 without radar or compass. This feat proved that the first Hawaiians arrived in these islands thanks to their mastery of celestial navigation, rather than by chance, and helped to spark off a full-blown renaissance of Hawaiian culture.

Ancient navigators were carefully chosen as infants for a lifelong training to read the stars, ocean currents, and flights of birds. Because this knowledge had been lost to modern Hawaiians, the *Hōkūle'a* relied on a Micronesian, Mau Pialug, to steer that first voyage. Over the years, he has passed on his wisdom to a young Hawaiian, Nainoa Thompson, who, with Hawai'i's Polynesian Voyaging Society, is training new generations in the ancient arts of canoe building and navigation. Since 1976, the society has sponsored further voyages of rediscovery.

The *Hōkūle'a* ("Star of Joy") at sea with billowing sails

Street-by-Street: Chinatown

Hawai'i's first Chinese arrived on merchant ships in 1789, followed in 1852 by large numbers who came to work on O'ahu's sugar plantations. On completion of their contracts, many gravitated to downtown Honolulu to build restaurants, herb shops, and clubhouses. Chinatown also developed a flourishing opium trade. A fire in 1886 destroyed the area, and in 1900 another was started by health officials to wipe out bubonic plague. By this time, Chinese immigration was a divisive political issue, and some believe the fire was intended to ruin the area. However, Chinatown rose from the ashes and today is a thriving community.

★ **Izumo Taisha Shrine**
The oldest Japanese Shinto shrine in Hawai'i, this was built in 1923 without nails. Facing the Nu'uanu Stream is a traditional gate.

Footbridge

Nu'uanu Stream

COLLEGE WALK

RIVER S

Dr. Sun Yat-sen (1866–1925), the Chinese statesman who became the first president of the Republic of China, is honored with this statue next to the Nu'uanu Stream. On the other side of the stream is a statue of Jose Rizal (1861–96), a Filipino hero.

Maunakea Market Place

RIVER STREET

PAUAHI STREET

NORTH

The Wo Fat building, with its pagoda-style roof, was once a landmark Chinese restaurant. Mr. Wo Fat, a baker, opened the original establishment in the 1880s. The present pink building dates from 1936.

NORTH KING STREET

KEKAULIKE STREET

HOTEL

MAUNAKEA STREET

STREET

At O'ahu Market, you can haggle for fresh fish, exotic fruits and vegetables, and delicacies such as pigs' heads.

SMITH STREET

0 meters   100
0 yards   100

★ **Open-Air Markets**
Chinatown's abundant open-air markets sell everything from duck and salmon heads to fresh ginger.

Waterfront

For hotels and restaurants see pp182–4 and pp192–4

⓫ Chinatown

Map 1 A2. 🚌 2, 13. 🛈 HVCB, Waikiki, (808) 924-0266. 🎎 Chinese New Year (early Jan–Mar). Foster Botanical Gardens: 50 N Vineyard Blvd.
Map 1 A1. **Tel** (808) 522-7066. 🚌 4.
Open 9am–4pm daily. **Closed** Jan 1 & Dec 25. 🚗 🛗 🎫

Locator Map
See Street Finder, map 1

The Lum Sai Ho Tong Temple is a small Taoist temple above a store, where members of the Lum clan worship.

Chinese Cultural Plaza contains shops and a stage where Chinese dances and plays are performed.

★ **Hawai'i Theatre**
This lovingly renovated Art Deco theater on the edge of Chinatown has elaborate plasterwork on the exterior and also boasts an elegant interior.

At the entrance to Chinatown sit two marble lions. They were donated by Honolulu's sister city, Kaohsiung in Taiwan, in honor of the 200th anniversary of Chinese settlement in Hawai'i.

This exotic neighborhood is full of colorful flower *lei* (garlands worn around the neck) stands, open markets with hanging ducks and tropical fish, herbal medicine shops displaying dried snakes and rats, trendy art galleries, and acupuncture and tattooing emporia. There are also less salubrious saloons with topless dancing, especially on Pauahi and North Hotel streets, downtown Honolulu's red light district – the legacy of World War II soldiers on leave.

The twin lions on Bethel and North Hotel streets, the gateway to Chinatown from the adjacent business district, are symbols of a major rejuvenation project. Many buildings, such as the Hawai'i Theatre, have been beautifully restored.

Visitors to Chinatown may be lucky enough to witness a Chinese wedding with full percussion orchestra and a prancing lion dance. At the Maunakea Market Place, you can sample food from all over Asia, and the noodle shops along River Street are much favored by local residents.

At the edge of Chinatown, the **Foster Botanical Gardens** are an oasis of tranquillity in the heart of a fast-paced city. They contain some protected trees and a prehistoric plant exhibit. The gift shop sells plants that can be sent home.

Chinese herbalist in a North King Street shop weighing his goods

Key

— Suggested route

WAIKĪKĪ

Waikīkī was a nondescript place of taro patches and fish ponds when Kamehameha I, the chief who united the Hawaiian islands, landed here to launch an invasion in 1795 *(see p45)*. After conquering the chiefs of O'ahu, he built a bungalow facing the ocean, not far from the present Royal Hawaiian Hotel. Now Waikīkī has one of the world's famous beaches, a sliver of people-packed sand against the backdrop of Diamond Head crater.

Waikīkī's "golden mile" of glass and concrete skyscrapers is a hectic hodge-podge of Western, Asian, and Pacific cultures bustling with some 65,000 tourists a day. The streets are packed with T-shirt vendors, sunburned honeymooners, Japanese matrons with Christian Dior bags, and barefoot boys carrying surfboards on their bikes. Local people strum 'ukulele at beachfront bars, music throbs from nightclubs, and a band of performers roams the streets.

The turquoise water is dotted with swimmers and multicolored inflatables. Beyond them, outrigger canoes cut swaths through the ranks of surfers, and farther out, red and yellow sailboats bob on the horizon.

Sights at a Glance

Historic Hotels
1 Royal Hawaiian Hotel
3 Moana Surfrider

Shopping Areas
2 International Market Place
4 King's Village

Beaches
5 Kūhiō Beach

See also Street Finder, map 3

0 meters 300
0 yards 300

◀ An array of watersports take place in Waikīkī's beach lagoon

For map symbols *see back flap*

Beachfront façade of the Royal Hawaiian Hotel, known to countless tourists as the "Pink Palace"

❶ Royal Hawaiian Hotel

2259 Kalākaua Ave. **Map** 4 D5.
Tel (808) 923-7311. 🚌 many buses.
w royal-hawaiian.com

An oasis in the high-rise surroundings of Waikīkī, the Royal Hawaiian Hotel occupies 10 acres of land in a former coconut grove where Kamehameha V built a summer cottage in the 1870s. Some of the hotel's palms are thought to survive from that period. Paths meander across emerald green lawns under cathedral-size banyan trees to arrive at this Spanish-Moorish-style gem, known affectionately as the "Pink Palace." Almost everything here is coral pink, from the rooftop cupolas to the telephones, and carpets.

When it opened in 1927, the Royal Hawaiian Hotel was hailed by the *Honolulu Star-Bulletin* as "the finest resort hostelry in America." It soon became famous for its rollicking parties and was patronized by the

Waikīkī Beachfront

This world-famous sandy beach actually encompasses several individually named, smaller beaches stretching 2.5 miles (4 km) from the Hilton Hawaiian Village (*see p183*) to Diamond Head. The whole beach is open to the public.

Thousands of tourists flock to Waikīkī Beach daily to sunbathe on the golden sand, swim in the sheltered water, and surf the gentle waves.

The coral-pink Royal Hawaiian Hotel is a pocket of luxury at the west end of the beach (*see p184*).

The Sheraton Waikiki Hotel's Hanohano Room, on the 30th floor, offers stupendous views, especially at sunset (*see p183*).

Royal Hawaiian Shopping Center

Hawai'i Visitors and Convention Bureau

The International Market Place reopens in 2016. It will be home to a shopping center (*see p68*).

Outrigger Waikīkī on the Beach (*see p183*).

Moana Surfrider, a Westin Resort and Spa (*see p183*).

wealthy and fashionable. Some guests even brought along their own servants and Rolls Royces.

The Depression of the 1930s slowed business down, and during World War II the hotel was leased to the US Navy as a center for rest and recreation for sailors in the Pacific Fleet. After refurbish-ment, the hotel was reopened in 1947. It was closed again in 2008 for a $110 million restoration that includes a new lobby, new pools, renovated guest rooms, and the addition of spa suites.

The aura of Hollywood glitz still lingers. On the beach, the "beautiful people" can be seen tanning and attracting all sorts of local commerce.

Behind the hotel, covering three city blocks, is the **Royal Hawaiian Shopping Center**. This modern arcade contains dozens of upscale shops, boutiques, and fast-food places.

Early Tourism in Waikīkī

Prior to the development of tourism, Waikīkī was a swampy marshland, consisting mainly of taro patches *(see p129)* and rice paddies. The land was reclaimed in the early part of the 20th century; large areas were filled in and the Ala Wai Canal was dug to drain the area by diverting streams from the hills above Waikīkī to the sea. Tourism began gradually around 1901 with the building of the Moana Hotel (now the Sheraton Moana Surfrider), which included a wooden pier that extended 300 ft (90 m) into the sea. Tourism accelerated in the 1920s with the opening of the Royal Hawaiian Hotel, which was host to movie stars and millionaires.

A view toward the gracious Moana Hotel in April 1920

Kūhiō Beach and the waves of Waikīkī make a fitting backdrop for this statue of Duke Kahanamoku, the beloved Father of Surfing who pop-ularized the royal pastime *(see p69)*.

Hyatt Regency Waikīkī *(see p183)*.

The ancient Wizard Stones are believed to possess sacred powers *(see p69)*.

Tourists enjoying canoeing and swimming

The Moana Hotel, Waikīkī's first luxury hotel, was built in 1901 *(see p68)*. Today it is part of the Moana Surfrider, A Westin Resort & Spa .

King's Village *(see p69)*.

Aston Waikīkī Beach Tower *(see p182)*.

Waikīkī Beach Marriott *(see p183)*.

The Damien Museum is dedicated to the priest of Kalaupapa *(see pp104–5)*.

St. Augustine's is a small Catholic church.

Police Station

Kalākaua Avenue

The façade of the Moana Surfrider, the "First Lady of Waikīkī," restored to its original splendor in 1989

❷ International Market Place

2330 Kalākaua Ave. **Map** 4 E5.
Tel (808) 971-2080. 🚌 many buses.
Closed for renovations until 2016. ♿

Situated across the street from the Royal Hawaiian Shopping Center *(see p67)*, the open-air International Market Place previously occupied a city block between Kalākaua and Kūhiō Avenues. For more than five decades, it served as a shopping destination for countless visitors. The theme-park shopping plaza included a labyrinth of food stalls (on the Kūhiō Avenue side) and souvenir-crammed carts. Everything from funky cigarette lighters, shell sculptures and "island" candles,

Typically vivid Hawaiian shirt on sale at a gift shop in the International Market Place

to racks of identical chains and watches, often manufactured in China, were available here. The complex closed at the end of 2013 for renovations, and is due to reopen in 2016. The new structure is a 360,000 sq ft, state-of-the-art shopping destination, featuring more than 75 stores, including international chains such as Saks Fifth Avenue. The complex will remain open-air, with additional dining and entertain-ment options. The site's well-known banyan tree has been left untouched to serve as a focal point in the area.

❸ Moana Surfrider, A Westin Resort & Spa

2365 Kalākaua Ave. **Map** 4 E5.
Tel (808) 922-3111. 🚌 many buses. **Open** daily. ♿ 📷
🌐 moana-surfrider.com

The colonial-style Moana, Waikīkī's oldest hotel, opened in 1901 to cater to an international steamship crowd. It became famous for gala events attended by movie stars. In 1920, the Prince of Wales

stayed at the hotel and was given outrigger canoe and surfing lessons from local hero Duke Kahanamoku.

An award-winning restoration project, begun in 1986, returned the hotel to something approaching its original look. Restorers used original drawings and templates that were found in the hotel basement. Memorabilia now on display through-out the hotel include a 1905 guest register, photos of famous visitors, and mono-grammed woolen swimsuits that were issued to guests in the 1930s. There are free daily tours.

Although nowadays the Moana is part of the Starwood Group's Westin Resort and Spa chain *(see p183)*, the hotel's quiet luxury still seems a world away from brash and bustling Kalākaua Avenue, just outside the grand entrance. On a front porch bedecked with rocking chairs, visitors are greeted with *lei* by South Seas beauties dressed in Victorian attire. The nostalgic lobby is decorated with period furniture and huge vases of anthuriums, while over on the ocean side, guests are served high-tea on the airy veranda.

Souvenir plate at a shop in Waikīkī

❹ King's Village

131 Kaʻiulani Ave. **Map** 4 E4.
Tel (808) 237-6344. 🚌 many buses.
Open 9am–10pm daily. ♿

King's Village is a cobblestone shopping mall that recreates the period of David Kalākaua, ruler of the islands from 1874–91. Kalākaua was the last Hawaiian king and is known as the Merrie Monarch, thanks to his revival of the *hula*, which had been banned by the missionaries as a "lewd and lascivious dance." As the first Hawaiian monarch to travel the world, Kalākaua was particularly impressed with the British Empire and modeled 'Iolani Palace *(see p59)* and his guards' uniforms on what he saw in Victorian London.

King's Village itself consists of mock 19th-century shops selling souvenirs, clothing, jewelry, and fabrics. There are various food stalls and themed restaurants. Local street artists gather here at night to provide impromptu entertainment.

Every day at 6:15pm, the center puts on a changing-of-the-guard ceremony, set against the backdrop of a Victorian-style Burger King! This is followed three nights a week by a *hula* show that demonstrates both ancient and modern styles *(see pp30–31)*. The area where King's Village and

Locals unwind in the waters of Kūhiō Beach, Waikīkī

the Princess Kaʻiulani and Hyatt hotels now stand was once a royal estate called ʻĀinahau, famous for its lush gardens and flocks of peacocks. Here, in a grass hut, Robert Louis Stevenson told tales of England and Scotland to Kaʻiulani, a half-Scottish, half-Hawaiian princess who was next in line to the Hawaiian throne. Later, distressed by the US annexation of Hawaiʻi *(see p48)*, Stevenson left the islands, heading farther into the Pacific, to Samoa. Princess Kaʻiulani died in 1899 at the age of 23, some say from a broken heart caused by the loss of her beloved land.

Changing of the guard at King's Village

❺ Kūhiō Beach

Map 4 F5. 🚌 many buses.

Wide Kūhiō Beach stretches eastward from Duke Kahanamoku's statue in central Waikīkī. Near the statue are four sacred boulders, known as the **Wizard Stones**, that represent healers who came from Tahiti before the 16th century. The healers are said to have passed their powers to the stones before returning home. The beach is a calm haven amid Waikīkī's swirling crowds. It is often rich in local color – grandmas in *muʻumuʻu* (long, loose dresses) string *lei* garlands and weave coconut fronds, locals play backgammon, and *hula* schools entertain in the evenings.

Duke Kahanamoku

Duke Kahanamoku (1890–1968) first swam into fame at the 1912 Olympics, when he broke the world record for the 100-yard freestyle. It was as the father of modern surfing, though, that "the Duke" really made his name. He popularized the Hawaiian pastime, called *heʻe nalu* (wave sliding), by giving demonstrations in the US, Europe, and Australia, and has been credited with putting Hawaiʻi on the map almost single-handedly. Back home, the popular hero was sheriff of Honolulu and unofficial goodwill ambassador. When he danced the *hula* with Queen Elizabeth, the photos were captioned "royalty dancing with royalty." At his funeral in 1968, 10,000 people turned out to see his ashes scattered in the seas off Waikīkī. His statue on Kūhiō Beach, always draped with *lei* from devoted fans, stands with its back to the sea. Some say it should be turned around so that the Duke can face his beloved ocean.

Sports hero Duke Kahanamoku receiving an award from Mayor Hylan of New York in 1920

GREATER HONOLULU

The landscape around Honolulu and Waikīkī is dominated by the peaks of the Koʻolau Range. Here, wild boar roam freely and hiking trails lead to waterfalls splashing into mountain pools. Set in these wooded hills, the Lyon Arboretum offers the chance to marvel at Hawaiʻi's botanical heritage, while nearby, the Queen Emma Summer Palace provides respite from the city heat, just as it did for the Queen herself back in the 1850s.

Closer to the city, the extinct craters of Diamond Head and Punchbowl stand guard. Kapiʻolani Park, which sprawls beneath Diamond Head's famous profile, is home to the Honolulu Zoo and Waikīkī Aquarium. The National Memorial Cemetery of the Pacific, in Punchbowl Crater, contains the graves of thousands of US war dead, and the horror of war is also remembered to the west, at Pearl Harbor. Here, on the site of the infamous 1941 attack, visitors tour the memorials and pay their respects to those who died.

Many of Honolulu's museums and galleries are situated on the outskirts of the city. Most significant among them is Bishop Museum, which houses the world's finest collection of Hawaiian and Polynesian artifacts.

Sights at a Glance

Museums and Galleries
1 Bishop Museum pp72–3
6 Honolulu Museum of Art
7 Honolulu Museum of Art Spalding House

Historic Buildings
4 Queen Emma Summer Palace

Parks and Gardens
8 Lyon Arboretum
9 Kapiʻolani Park

Cemeteries and Memorials
2 Oʻahu Cemetery
3 Royal Mausoleum

5 National Memorial Cemetery of the Pacific
10 Pearl Harbor

Key
▦ Main Sightseeing Areas
▨ Urban Areas
▨ Military/Restricted Areas
▭ Freeway
▬ Major road
▭ Minor road

0 kilometers   5
0 miles   3

◄ The Diamond Head, an extinct volcano located close to Kapiʻolani Park   **For map symbols** see back flap

● Bishop Museum

Considered the world's finest museum of Polynesian culture, Bishop Museum was created as an American businessman's farewell to his beloved wife. When Princess Bernice Pauahi, the last royal descendant of Kamehameha the Great *(see p45)*, died in 1884, she left all her family heirlooms to her husband, Charles Bishop. Her cousin, Queen Emma, died shortly afterward and bequeathed her own Hawaiian artifacts to Bishop. He immediately set about building a home for the priceless collection, and Bishop Museum opened in 1902. Designated the "State Museum of Natural and Cultural History," it has over a million Pacific artifacts, plus millions of specimens of regional fauna and flora.

Third floor

Three tiers of galleries overlooking the heart of the impressive Hawaiian Hall

Museum Guide

The Hawaiian Hall has three floors: the first covers pre-contact Hawaiian culture, including a replica heiau; the second illustrates the importance of nature to Hawaiians in daily life and culture; and the third deals with Hawaiian gods, ali'i and history. Artifacts from the whole Pacific region can be seen in the Polynesian Hall, while the Kāhili Room displays the treasures of Hawai'i's monarchy. Other parts of the complex include a Science Adventure Center, planetarium, a library, and the Castle Building, which usually houses contemporary traveling exhibitions.

★ Tamate Costume
Worn in dances involving a mock chase of women, this Melanesian shredded-fiber costume is a very rare artifact, as most are burned after the dance.

Entered from outside only, this vine-covered pavilion leads to a shell collection.

Traditional Hawaiian Quilts

The Hawaiians' style of quilting reflects both their own tradition with *kapa* (bark cloth) and the quilting methods of missionaries. The designs, which are said to have been inspired by the shadows cast by breadfruit leaves on a piece of cloth, often honor the Hawaiian monarchy or depict the natural beauty of the islands. The habit of stitching Hawaiian flags into quilts began in 1843, when a British admiral ordered all flags to be destroyed. The Bishop Museum has a fine collection of old and contemporary quilts.

Traditional Hawaiian quilt

Key

▫ Hawaiian Hall
▫ Polynesian Hall
▫ Picture Gallery
▫ J.M. Long Gallery
▫ Kāhili Room
▫ Non-exhibition space

★ Pili-grass Hale
The timbers of this fullsized *hale* (traditional house), thatched with *pili* grass, were brought from Kaua'i in 1902. It sits on a platform to discourage dampness, has woven floor mats and a low doorway.

Second floor

Fern Stem Top Hat
A Hawaiian adaptation of Western fashion, this top hat was made in the early 19th century from local ferns.

First floor

Planetarium and Science Adventure Center

Kū, the War God
This large sacred image of the war god Kū, carved from 'ōhi'a wood, dates from the early 19th century. It probably came from a *heiau* (temple) on Hawai'i Island.

Moai
This Moai looms large on the lawn at the museum. It is a life-size replica of an Easter Island *Rapanui*, and was a gift from Japan.

Kāhili Room
Feather standards, or *Kāhili*, which accompanied high chiefs, are exhibited here in this room. They were made from feathers of forest and sea birds.

Castle Building

Main entrance

Tombstones at O'ahu Cemetery, established in 1844

❷ O'ahu Cemetery

2162 Nu'uanu Ave. **Tel** (808) 538-1538. 🚌 4. **Open** 7am–6pm daily. 📷 only 5 or 6 times a year. 🅦 oahucemetery.org

O'ahu Cemetery (1844) was one of the first cemeteries established in Hawai'i. It was created to bury foreigners who did not belong to Kawaiaha'o Church *(see p58)*, including members of prominent 19th-century missionary and merchant families. The cemetery is still in use, and many notable people of Asian, European, and Hawaiian descent are buried here. Among them are A.J. Cartwright, the "father of baseball"; Martha Root, spokesperson for the Baha'i faith; and several of Hawai'i's governors. Veterans of the Civil War are laid to rest here, as are casualties of the bombing of Pearl Harbor on December 7, 1941 *(see p48)*.

❸ Royal Mausoleum

2261 Nu'uanu Ave. **Tel** (808) 587-0300. 🚌 4. **Open** 8am–4pm Mon–Fri. **Closed** public hols, except Mar 26 & Jun 11.

A few hundred yards from O'ahu Cemetery is the Gothic-influenced Royal Mausoleum, enclosed by a wrought-iron fence with gold crowns on

each post. The final resting place of the kings and queens of Hawai'i, and their families, their bodies lie in tombs placed about the lawns.

Only two royal names are missing from this sanctuary: Kamehameha the Great (1758–1819), who was buried in the traditional way – in secret, his whereabouts unknown to this day – and Lunalilo (1835–74), who is buried in the grounds of Kawaiaha'o Church *(see p58)* in downtown Honolulu.

Other people buried at the Royal Mausoleum include John Young, the English advisor to Kamehameha the Great, and Charles Bishop, the founder of the Bishop Museum *(see pp72–3)*. The original mausoleum building (1865) is now a chapel. The interior is made entirely of rich, dark *koa*-wood.

❹ Queen Emma Summer Palace

2913 Pali Highway (Hwy 61). **Tel** (808) 595-3167. 🚌 4, 55, 56, 57. **Open** 9am–4pm daily. **Closed** public hols. 📷 📷 📷 🅦 queenemma summerpalace.org

Built in the 1840s, this airy retreat in the Nu'uanu Valley was used as a summer home by Queen Emma and her husband, Kamehameha IV. More modest than its name implies, it is a unique combination of Greek Revival architecture and local touches, such as the long *lānai* (porch). Emma's uncle, John Young II, left the palace to her in 1850.

Set in extensive gardens, it is still a cool oasis surrounded by huge trees, some planted by the royal family over 100 years ago. The mango trees planted at their wedding in 1856 are now 100 ft (30 m) tall and still bear fruit. The tamarind tree was planted by the couple's only son, Prince Albert, who died soon afterward, at the age of four.

The building houses many of the royal couple's personal belongings, including valuable period pieces, jewelry, household items, and artifacts from their Hawaiian heritage. Among the beautiful *koa*-wood furniture is the couple's large bed and their son's cradle, famous for its wave design.

The gift shop is run by the Daughters of Hawai'i, a group of women descended from missionary families, who rescued the house from demolition in 1913, restored it and then reopened it two years later. They also give daily tours to groups of ten or more.

The elegant façade of Queen Emma Summer Palace

The Honolulu Memorial at the National Memorial Cemetery of the Pacific

❺ National Memorial Cemetery of the Pacific

2177 Pūowaina Dr. **Map** 1 C1.
Tel (808) 532-3720. 🚌 15, then short walk. **Open** 8am–5:30pm daily. 📷

Looming above downtown Honolulu is Punchbowl, an extinct volcanic crater. Within it lies a 116-acre US military cemetery, dedicated in 1949. By 1991, the plot was filled to capacity with over 33,000 graves, nearly half of them for World War II dead, including victims of the Pearl Harbor attack in 1941 *(see p48)*. There are also casualties from the Korean War (1950–3) and the Vietnam War (1964–75).

Dominating the grounds is the **Honolulu Memorial** (dedicated in 1966), which consists of a chapel, marble slabs bearing the names of over 28,000 soldiers missing in action, and a staircase topped by **Columbia**, a huge memorial statue. South of here, a short walk leads to a great viewpoint over the city.

❻ Honolulu Museum of Art

900 S Beretania St. **Map** 2 D2.
Tel (808) 532-8700. 🚌 2, 13.
Open 10am–4:30pm Tue–Sat, 1–5pm Sun. **Closed** public hols. 📷 ♿ Ward Ave Gate. 📷 🖥 11:30am–2pm Tue–Sat. 🌐 honolulumuseum.org

In 2012, the Honolulu Academy of Art, founded by Mrs. Charles Montague Cooke in 1922, and The Contemporary Museum combined to form the Honolulu Museum of Art. The galleries are located in two of Honolulu's most beautiful buildings. Visitors can enjoy the cafés, gardens, concerts, and films in both locations for a single admission fee.

The permanent collection includes more than 20,000 works of Asian art, with the highlight being the James A. Michener Collection of more than 10,000 Japanese *ukiyo-e* woodblock prints.

The collection also features European art, notably Italian Renaissance paintings and works by Van Gogh, Monet, and Picasso. American works on display include pieces by Mary Cassatt and Winslow Homer among others.

A tour to the Shangri La, home of American heiress Doris Duke, starts at the museum. This architectural landmark houses an extensive Islamic art collection from Iran, India, Morocco, and Syria.

❼ Honolulu Museum of Art Spalding House

2411 Makiki Heights Dr.
Tel (808) 532-8700. 🚌 15.
Open 10am–4pm Tue–Sat; noon–4pm Sun. **Closed** public hols. 📷 ♿ 📷 🖥 🌐 honolulumuseum.org

Honolulu's only museum dedicated to modern art was formerly known as The Contemporary Museum. It started life in the downtown News Building and moved to the present site in 1988, when the now defunct daily newspaper, the *Star-Advertiser*, donated the luxurious estate as a permanent home.

Housing a permanent collection of sculptures, ceramics, paintings, prints, photos, and videos by national and international artists, spanning the years from 1940 to the present. There are also numerous temporary exhibitions. The **Cades Pavilion** displays *L'Enfant et les Sortilèges* (1983), David Hockney's walk-through installation based on his set for Ravel's opera, staged by New York's Metropolitan Opera.

The estate that surrounds the museum has innovative sculpture, huge trees, sloping lawns, orchids, bromeliads, and a path that encourages meditation as it winds among grottoes designed by a local minister turned gardener.

The Spalding House Café, set in a secluded corner, has delicious food *(see p193)*.

Hockney's *L'Enfant et les Sortilèges* at Honolulu Museum of Art Spalding House

❽ Lyon Arboretum

3860 Mānoa Rd. **Tel** (808) 988-0456.
🚌 5. **Open** 8am–4pm Mon–Fri,
9am–3pm Sat. **Closed** public hols.
Donation: 🅿 ♿ 🆆 hawaii.edu/
lyonarboretum

Only a short drive from busy
Waikīkī, this retreat is an ideal
tonic for the weary sightseer.
Short, verdant trails wind
through the trees and reveal
botanical delights at every turn.

Founded in 1918 in an effort
to reforest land made barren by
cattle grazing, the Lyon Arboretum is now home to over 5,000
plant species, both native and
introduced. It is nationally
recognized as a center for the
conservation of Hawaiian plants,
and its 194 acres support over
80 endangered and rare species.
These include the state flower,
ma'o hau hele (a yellow hibiscus),
and the tree gardenia, *nānū*,
whose scientific name, *Gardenia*

brighamii, honors
W.T. Brigham, the first
director of the Bishop
Museum *(see pp72–3)*.
The arboretum now
features around 600
varieties of palm, more
than any other botani-
cal garden in the world.

A substantial part of
the arboretum is open
to the public; the rest is
set aside for research. The
on-site hybridization program
has resulted in more than 160
new cultivars, including hybrids
of hibiscus and rhododendron.

There are three quiet memorial gardens and an aromatic
spice and herb patch near
the main building. A little
farther away, the Beatrice H.
Krauss Ethnobotanical Garden
displays plants that have been
used by native Hawaiians
as medicine, food, and
building materials.

View of Kapi'olani Park from Diamond Head

❾ Kapi'olani Park

Map 4 F5. 🚌 4, 8, 19, 20, 47.
Open daily. ♿ Zoo: 151 Kapahulu
Ave. **Tel** (808) 971-7171. **Open** 9am–
4:30pm daily. **Closed** Dec 25. 🅿 ♿
🆆 honoluluzoo.org. Aquarium:
2777 Kalākaua Ave. **Tel** (808) 923-9741.
Open 9am–5pm daily. **Closed** Dec 25.
🅿 ♿ 🆆 waquarium.org

This 300-acre expanse of green
offers a 2-mile (3-km) jogging
path, tennis courts, barbecues,
and special areas for softball,

Honolulu's Makiki-Tantalus Trails

Forming a loop around lush Makiki Valley 3 miles (5 km) north of Waikīkī,
Round Top Drive and Tantalus Drive offer fine views of the city. The trails that
lace between the roads delve deep into the rain forest and teem with bird
life and exotic flora. Weekday mornings are quietest, but weekend hikes run
by the Sierra Club or Nature Conservancy *(see pp220–21)* are informative and
tackle the more challenging areas. On any hike, be well prepared: dress for
comfort, wear sturdy shoes, bring a flashlight and plenty of water and food,
and stick to the main trails. Most importantly, never hike alone. The Hawai'i
Nature Center, off Makiki Heights Drive, provides maps and good advice.

View from Pu'u 'Ōhi'a Trail

Key

═══ Road

• • Hiking trail

0 meters 750
0 yards 750

archery, and kite-flying. It is also the site of crafts fairs and many celebrations.

The north end of the park is devoted to **Honolulu Zoo**, whose highlight is an extensive African savanna section. On Sunday mornings, local artists display their works on the zoo fence facing Monsarrat Avenue.

The **Waikiki Aquarium**, on the southwest side, features the usual sea life as well as a special exhibit on the endangered Hawaiian monk seal and a hands-on tide pool. The aquarium also organizes reef walks, some specially for children.

The park acts as a gateway to **Diamond Head**. To see the extinct volcano, either take the scenic circle drive to Diamond Head lighthouse, whose lawn is a favorite spot for tourist weddings and sunset watching, or you can hike to the summit from a parking lot in the crater. Entrance to the crater is marked by a sign on Diamond Head Road, the continuation of Monsarrat Avenue. The trail is quite steep, but the sweeping view is worth the hour-long ascent. Part of the hike involves climbing a staircase in a tunnel; take a flashlight if you are claustrophobic.

A huge Galapagos tortoise at Honolulu Zoo

❿ Pearl Harbor

7 miles (11 km) NW of downtown Honolulu. 🚌 20, 42. USS *Arizona*: 1 Arizona Memorial Dr. **Tel** (808) 422-0561. **Open** 7am–5pm daily. **Closed** Jan 1, Thanksgiving & Dec 25. ♿ 📷 📶 **nps.gov/usar**. USS *Bowfin*: 11 Arizona Memorial Dr. **Tel** (808) 423-1341. **Open** 8am–5pm daily. **Closed** Jan 1, Thanksgiving & Dec 25. 📷 ♿ museum only. 📶 **bowfin.org**. USS *Missouri* and Battleship *Missouri* Memorial: 11 Arizona Memorial Dr. **Tel** (808) 423-2263. **Open** 8am–4pm daily. **Closed** Jan 1, Thanksgiving, Dec 25. 📷 📷 📶 **ussmissouri.com**

When Honolulu was made capital of Hawai'i in 1845, a major reason was its proximity to one of the world's best

The white-marble USS *Arizona* Memorial in Pearl Harbor

natural harbors – Pearl Harbor. In the time of Kamehameha the Great, the inlet supported oysters that were farmed for their pearls. Later, the port was crucial for whalers, trade with China, and both the sugar and pineapple industries. Leased to the US in 1887 as part of a trade treaty, it was first used militarily in the Spanish-American War of 1898. Today it houses modern warships, military museums, and memorials. Most significant among these is the **USS *Arizona* Memorial**, perched above the sunken ship of that name. The ship went down with hundreds of its crew during the Japanese attack on December 7, 1941 that brought the US into World War II. For many people, the visit to this site is a pilgrimage, so appropriate dress is requested.

On busy days, tickets may all be allocated by 1pm, and there is often a wait of up to 2 hours for the boat to the offshore memorial. It is best to get your ticket first and then browse in the museum, which features details of the attack and histories of the ships, planes, and personnel involved, both US and Japanese. It offers a balanced and personal view of the participants. Near the ticket desk is a panel describing the volunteers for the day. They are usually Pearl Harbor survivors and are available to answer questions and share their stories. Ceremonies are held here on important days.

Another place to visit during a day at Pearl Harbor is the nearby award-winning **USS *Bowfin* Submarine Museum and Park**, a tribute to the role of the submarine in war and peacetime security. The museum covers the history of submarines, beginning with the first attempt to build one in 1776. Visitors can view the inner workings of a Poseidon missile, and they can also inspect control panels from retired submarines and see how the crew whiled away their time in cramped quarters.

The USS *Bowfin* submarine is moored nearby and is open for public viewing. The park itself contains a memorial to the crews of the 52 US submarines lost in World War II.

The **USS *Missouri***, opened to the public in 1999 as the **Battleship *Missouri* Memorial**. On September 2, 1945, General MacArthur, aboard this ship, accepted the Japanese surrender that ended World War II. Check the website for additional information and images from the ship's history: (www.ussmissouri.com).

The crew's tightly packed bunks inside the USS *Bowfin* submarine

STREET FINDER

The map references given for sights, shops, and entertainment places in Honolulu and Waikīkī refer to the four pages of maps in this section. The key map below shows the area of the city that is covered, with the two major sightseeing districts color-coded red. All the principal sights mentioned in the text are marked as well as useful information such as transit stations, parking lots, tourist offices, and post offices; a full list is given in the key. Map references are also given in the Travelers' Needs section for the hotels (see pp182–4) and restaurants (see pp192–4) in Honolulu and Waikīkī.

Key

▦ Major sight	▣ Police station
▢ Other building	✝ Church
🚌 Bus terminal	🏛 Temple
⛴ Ferry terminal	⛳ Golf course
🛈 Tourist information	▤ Freeway
✚ Hospital with emergency room	▨ Pedestrianized street

0 kilometers 1
0 miles 1

Scale of Maps 1–4

0 meters 250
0 yards 250

HAWAI'I ISLAND BY ISLAND

The Hawaiian Islands at a Glance

The Hawaiian Islands offer an outstanding array of natural beauty spots and places of cultural interest. The landscape is incredibly diverse, from beach-fringed coastal shores to lush, grassy uplands and alpine summits. Visitors may experience volcanic eruptions, see world-class surfing, explore the fascinating cultural heritage of Polynesia, or simply relax in the sea and sun.

Princeville *(see p169)*, a resort community on Kaua'i's lush North Shore, is a favorite with golfers for its excellent courses.

KAUA'I
(see pp160–77)
Anahola

NI'IHAU

Līhu'e

Kaua'i's Nā Pali Coast
(see pp172–3) features stunning, sharply incised cliffs, slender beaches, and deep blue seas. Enthusiastic hikers can see the scenery up close by following the rugged Kalalau Trail.

O'AHU
(see pp88–97)
Kān

Hon

Waimea Bay on O'ahu's North Shore *(see p35)* is home to some of the world's biggest waves. Expert surfers flock here from around the world to demonstrate their skill and courage in front of appreciative onlookers.

The Polynesian Cultural Center *(see p96)* in Lāʻie on O'ahu's windward shore displays Polynesian heritage. Through dances and craft demonstrations, visitors witness the traditional cultures of Tonga, Hawai'i, Samoa, Tahiti, Fiji, the Marquesas, and New Zealand.

◄ Panoramic view of Hawai'i Kai and Kuapa Pond, O'ahu

Kalaupapa National Historical Park
(see pp104–5) commemorates the more than 8,000 victims of leprosy who suffered and died on this remote Moloka'i peninsula, and the saintly work of Father Damien who tended the sick. He was buried in the garden of St. Philomena.

Wailea Beach is one of a string of beautiful sheltered beaches on South Maui's leeward coast *(see p131)*. Visitors flock here to relax on the golden sands and in the calm coastal waters, and to take advantage of the ideal swimming, snorkeling, and diving conditions.

0 kilometers 50

0 miles 25

Kaunakakai

**MOLOKA'I
AND LĀNA'I**
(see pp98–109)

Lāna'i City

Kahului • Wailua

MAUI
(see pp110–33) Hāna

KAHO'OLAWE

Hawai'i Volcanoes National Park
(see pp156–7), with its active East Rift Zone, is the site of both spectacular fire cones and lava flows. Billowing steam plumes, such as this one at Lae'apuki at sunrise, form when fiery lava enters the ocean.

Maui's sheltered coastal waters are home to wintering whales.

Mauna Kea, snow-capped for part of the year, is Hawai'i's tallest mountain.

Waimea
Honoka'a
Wailea
Kailua-Kona
Hilo

HAWAI'I ISLAND
(see pp134–59)

Pāhoa

Nā'ālehu

Pu'uhonua o Hōnaunau National Historical Park *(see pp142–3)*, an ancient place of refuge, provides a unique glimpse into traditional Hawaiian culture and its laws.

O'AHU

The third largest island in the archipelago with an area of 600 sq miles (1,550 sq km), O'ahu was born of two volcanoes that formed the Wai'anae Mountains to the west and the Ko'olau Range to the northeast. Three-quarters of Hawai'i's million residents live here, mostly in the Greater Honolulu area or nestled in the deep valleys that cut between the mountains. This island also receives the largest number of visitors.

O'ahu was conquered in 1795 by Kamehameha the Great, whose forces chased rival chiefs Kai'ana and Kalanikūpule and their men back into Nu'uanu Valley, forcing them off a precipice at the top. Kai'ana was killed outright, and though Kalanikūpule escaped, he was later captured and sacrificed by the great king. The battle was an important victory in Kamehameha's campaign to unify the islands (see pp45–6).

In the 1800s, farmers began growing pineapples in the highlands, and by the middle of the century, sugarcane plantations had become big business. Workers came from China, Japan, Portugal, and elsewhere – the origin of Hawai'i's ethnic diversity. But increasingly, as both the sugar and pineapple industries have declined, much of central O'ahu has been given over to malls and nondescript housing complexes, crammed together on expensive acreage. Some residents now link tourism with overdevelopment and the resultant threat to ancestral lands. Many local people live in relative poverty.

Beautiful scenery, however, is never far away. From Wahiawā, the road rolls through undulating fields of pineapple down to the bohemian North Shore surfing town of Hale'iwa. From here to Makapu'u Point on O'ahu's southeast corner, the narrow highway skirts a chain of green velvet, mist-draped mountains. Islets dot the turquoise sea as you pass seaside villages and one deserted beach after another. Along the way are fruit stands, sparkling waterfalls, and Buddhist temples. In the west, the old town of Waipahu is a living museum of plantation history, and the arid Wai'anae Coast offers perfect sunsets and a chance to see an unspoiled slice of Hawaiian life.

Traditional dancing at the Polynesian Cultural Center in Lā'ie, a popular tourist attraction

◀ A turtle lies on the sands of Lanikai Beach, O'ahu

Exploring O'ahu

Hawai'i's most visited island, O'ahu has much to offer besides the clamor of humanity in Honolulu, Waikīkī, and the central 'Ewa plain. The rest of the island is amazingly rural, with large areas of sugar-cane fields and rain forest where wild boar still roam. It is easy to escape into O'ahu's spectacular scenery as jungle-clad roads and trails transport you from the high-rises of Honolulu. The Wai'anae Mountains and the Ko'olau Range form the backbones of the island, while tropical beaches line the shimmering coast. The snorkelers' paradise of Hanauma Bay and the world-class surf breaks on the North Shore draw the crowds, but the Wai'anae Coast is peaceful. Cultural attractions range from the popular Polynesian Cultural Center to the tranquil Byodo-In Temple.

Byodo-In Temple, a Buddhist Shrine

Sights at a Glance

1. Hanauma Bay
2. Makapu'u Point
3. Byodo-In Temple
4. Hau'ula Trails
5. Polynesian Cultural Center
6. Waimea Valley
7. Hale'iwa
8. Dole Plantation
9. Hawai'i's Plantation Village
10. Wai'anae Coast
11. Ka'ena Point

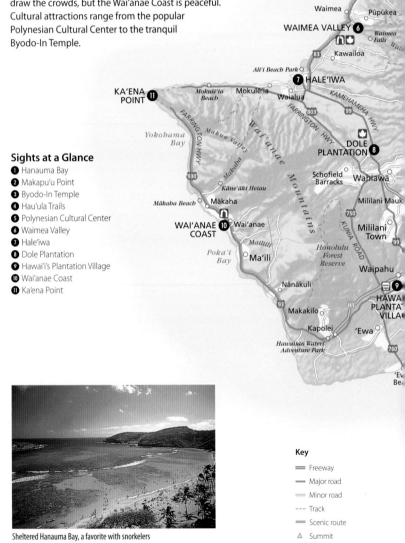

Sheltered Hanauma Bay, a favorite with snorkelers

Key

═══ Freeway
──── Major road
═══ Minor road
- - - Track
──── Scenic route
△ Summit

Top Recreational Areas

The places shown here have been selected for their recreational activities. Conditions, especially those of the ocean, vary depending on the weather and the time of year, so exercise caution and, if in doubt, stay out of the water or seek local advice.

	Swimming	Snorkeling	Diving	Body-Surfing	Windsurfing	Hiking	Horseback Riding	Golf
Ala Moana Beach County Park	●	▨		▨				
Ali'i Beach Park	●			▨				
Diamond Head				▨	●	▨		
Hanauma Bay		▨	●					
Hau'ula Trails						▨		
Ka'ena Point						▨		
Kahuku And Kuilima	●						●	▨
Kailua Beach County Park	●				●			
Koko Head Crater						▨		
Makapu'u Point				▨				
Mānoa Falls						▨		
Maunawili					●		●	
Mokulē'ia	●							
North Shore	●	▨	●	▨	●	▨	●	
Tantalus						▨		
Wai'anae Coast	●	▨	●	▨	●			▨
Waikīkī	●	▨		▨				
Waimānalo	●			●			●	

Getting Around

O'ahu is served by Honolulu International Airport. There is a good road network, and the best way to get around is by rented car. Three freeways radiate out from Honolulu: H1 takes you to the Wai'anae Coast, H2 veers north toward Hale'iwa, and H3 crosses to the windward (northeast) coast. *TheBus* company runs two routes (52, 55) that link Honolulu with central O'ahu, the windward coast, and the North Shore *(see inside back cover)*.

0 kilometers 5

0 miles 5

For keys to symbols *see back flap*

Trained dolphins performing graceful maneuvers at Sea Life Park

❶ Hanauma Bay

Honolulu Co. Kalaniana'ole Highway
(Hwy 72), 10 miles (16 km) E of Waikiki.
Tel (808) 396-4229. 🚌 **Open** 6am–
6pm Wed–Mon. **Closed** Dec 25. ♿☐☕🏪

Snorkeling in this sheltered bay
is like swimming in a gigantic
aquarium with more than 400
species of fish, some of which
exist only here. A sandy-
bottomed hole in the reef is
perfect for first-time snorkelers.
Fish-feeding, once a popular
tourist activity, is no longer
allowed since this is a
conservation district. A Marine
Education Center presents an
orientation video and offers
restrooms, a snack bar, and
a tram service to the beach.
To avoid the crowds, visit
early in the morning.

❷ Makapu'u Point

Honolulu Co. Kalaniana'ole Highway
(Hwy 72), 14 miles (23 km) E of Waikiki.
🚌 Sea Life Park.

It is worth stopping at the
lookout below the Makapu'u
lighthouse for humbling views
of sky and sea, with rock islets
artistically arranged. You can
watch the action on nearby
Makapu'u Beach, a pocket
cove that boasts the island's
best body-surfing waves. Local
kids make the wave-hopping
look easy, but it requires precise
timing to avoid being dragged
onto the rocks.
    Hiking trails lead upward
into black mountains, but you
do not need to climb beyond
the first 100 ft (30 m) or so for
spectacular photos. Hikers can

continue to the hang-glider
launch site at 1,250 ft (380 m)
and watch the intrepid fliers.
    Facing Makapu'u Beach,
the educational **Sea Life Park**
features a huge Hawaiian reef
tank and regular performances
by penguins, sea lions, and
dolphins. The park has
spectacular views of O'ahu's
breathtaking coastline.
Buses link up with Waikīkī.

🐟 **Sea Life Park**
41-202 Kalaniana'ole Hwy
(Hwy 72). **Tel** (808) 259-7933.
Open 10:30am–5pm daily. ♿ 🚻
🏪 W sealifeparkhawaii.com

❸ Byodo-In Temple

Honolulu Co. 47-200 Kahekili Highway
(Hwy 83), Kāne'ohe. **Tel** (808) 239-
8811. 🚌 on Kahekili Hwy (Hwy 83),
then 10-min walk. **Open** 9am–5pm
daily. **Closed** Dec 25. ♿🚻
W byodo-in.com

This replica of a 900-year-
old Japanese temple cannot
be seen from the highway.
The only marker is a Hawai'i
Visitors and Convention
Bureau sign for a historic
sight. Once you turn into
the Valley of Temples –
a non-denominational
cemetery – the road winds
into the valley to reach this
hidden treasure, its walls
red against fluted, green
cliffs. After crossing the
curved vermilion foot-
bridge, you can ring a
three-ton bell to assure
long life and to receive the
blessings of the Buddha.
Remove your shoes before
entering the shrine, where

a 9-ft (3-m) gold and lacquer
Buddha presides.
    Visiting the temple just
before sunset provides a
tranquil experience. You will
not be able to see the Buddha
(the temple closes at 4pm),
but the profound silence will
be punctuated only by the
singing of birds. The sun
setting behind the cliffs gives
off pink and mauve hues, and,
if you are lucky, you may have
the scene all to yourself.

❹ Hau'ula Trails

Honolulu Co. Kamehameha Highway
(Hwy 83), 20 miles (30 km) NW of
Kāne'ohe, approximately 2 miles
(3 km) past Punalu'u. **Tel** (808)
973-9782. **Open** weekends and
holidays. W hawaiitrails.
ehawaii.gov

The three trails that make up
the Hau'ula Trails area – Hau'ula
Loop Trail, Ma'akua Ridge
Trail, and Ma'akua Gulch Trail –
provide everything that hikers
love best about Hawai'i's finest
trails. They are wide with
excellent footing and offer
spectacular mountain, valley,
and ocean views. You should
allow approximately two hours
for a round-trip of any of the
trails, all of which begin beyond
the end of Ma'akua Road, off
Hau'ula Homestead Road
which is just beyond the
tiny town of Hau'ula.

The beautifully crafted Buddha, centerpiece of the
Japanese Byodo-In Temple

Beaches of Southeast O'ahu

From Makapu'u Point at the southern tip to the commuter suburbia of Kāne'ohe, O'ahu's southeast coast features a range of delightful beaches, with free access to the public. Waimānalo Beach offers lazy swimming in calm seas, Lanikai Beach is exclusive and quiet, and the tree-lined community of Kailua has extensive beach facilities. To discourage break-ins, do not leave items of value in your car.

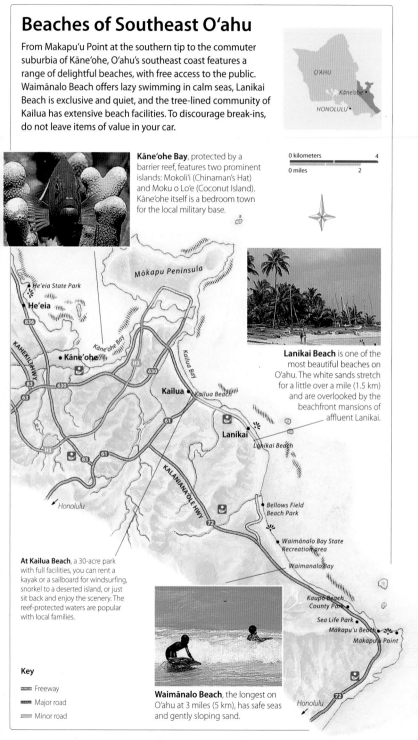

Kāne'ohe Bay, protected by a barrier reef, features two prominent islands: Mokoli'i (Chinaman's Hat) and Moku o Lo'e (Coconut Island). Kāne'ohe itself is a bedroom town for the local military base.

0 kilometers 4
0 miles 2

Lanikai Beach is one of the most beautiful beaches on O'ahu. The white sands stretch for a little over a mile (1.5 km) and are overlooked by the beachfront mansions of affluent Lanikai.

At Kailua Beach, a 30-acre park with full facilities, you can rent a kayak or a sailboard for windsurfing, snorkel to a deserted island, or just sit back and enjoy the scenery. The reef-protected waters are popular with local families.

Waimānalo Beach, the longest on O'ahu at 3 miles (5 km), has safe seas and gently sloping sand.

Key

- Freeway
- Major road
- Minor road

➎ Polynesian Cultural Center

Honolulu Co. 55-370 Kamehameha Highway (Hwy 83), Lā'ie. **Tel** (808) 293-3333. 🚌 **Open** noon–9pm Mon–Sat. **Closed** Thanksgiving & Dec 25. 🅿 ♿ 🅆 polynesia.com

The village of Lā'ie was founded by Mormon missionaries in 1864 after a failed attempt to settle on the island of Lāna'i. Lā'ie now contains a Mormon temple, a branch of Brigham Young University, and a 42-acre educational theme park known as the Polynesian Cultural Center.

At the Center, students from all over the Pacific demonstrate crafts and dancing in seven Polynesian "villages": Tongan, Hawaiian, Samoan, Tahitian, Fijian, Maori, and Marquesan. The instruction, whether it be Tongan drumming or Samoan fire-making, is delivered in almost continuous mini-shows, and audience participation is encouraged. The afternoon show, **Rainbows of Paradise**, presents legends from all the islands with singing, dancing, and martial arts performed on double-hulled canoes.

The Center is worth the hefty admission fee. However, some critics question the authenticity of the exhibits and shows – not all the "islanders" in the villages are the real thing. Despite this, the PCC remains Hawai'i's most popular paid attraction, with almost a million visitors a year. Regular shuttle buses connect with Waikīkī.

➏ Waimea Valley

Honolulu Co. 59-864 Kamehameha Highway (Hwy 83), Waimea. **Tel** (808) 638-7766. 🚌 52, 55. **Open** 9am–5pm daily. **Closed** Jan 1, Thanksgiving & Dec 25. ♿ 🅿 🅆 waimeavalley.net

One of a few intact examples of an *ahupua'a* – a Hawaiian land division from mountain to sea – Waimea Valley is a beautiful, unspoilt environment, a sacred place for native Hawaiians, and an important educational resource. After periods as an attraction, with glitzy *hula* shows and cliff divers, and as a facility run by the Audubon Society, it is now operated by the Office of Hawaiian Affairs. The 1,875-acre (759-hectare) area includes a waterfall, a 5,000-plant botanical collection, a refuge for endangered wildlife, and archaeological sites, including a 15th-century *heiau* (temple) dedicated to Lono, god of peace, agriculture, and music. Walking tours and cultural activities such as *lei* making, *hula* lessons, and story-

Matsumoto's shave ice

telling are included in the cost of admission. Bring binoculars, as the park has great opportunities for bird-watching. After your visit, enjoy a swim or a snorkel at **Waimea Beach Park** across the street.

Environs

Set above Waimea Bay at an elevation of 300 ft (90 m), **Pu'u O Mahuka Heiau State Monument** offers fine views. Here the ruins of three sacred rock terraces make up the largest *heiau* (temple) on O'ahu.

Ironically called "hill of escape" in Hawaiian, this was once a site of human sacrifice.

🏛 Pu'u O Mahuka Heiau State Monument

Off Pūpūkea Rd, half a mile (800 m) E of Kamehameha Highway (Hwy 83), just N of Waimea.

Hale'iwa Beach Park on the North Shore, a sheltered spot for a swim

➐ Hale'iwa

Honolulu Co. 👥 4,000. 🚌 *i* HVCB, Waikīkī, (808) 924-0266. 🎎 Obon Buddhist Festival (Jul or Aug).

Once a plantation town and more recently a hippie hangout, Hale'iwa is now the hub for the North Shore surfing community. Graced by local color from these subcultures, the town has a single main street with art galleries, boutiques, general stores, restaurants, and coffee shops. Tin-roofed **Matsumoto's** is the best place to try a Hawaiian specialty known as shave ice (thinly shaved ice flavored with exotic syrups and top-pings, such as adzuki beans).

Flanking a picturesque boat harbor are well-appointed public beaches. **Ali'i Beach Park** is famous for big waves and surfing contests (*see p35*), but the adjacent **Hale'iwa Beach Park**, protected by a breakwater, is one of the few North Shore spots where it is usually safe to swim in winter.

The town's biggest event, the Obon Festival, is held every summer at a seaside Buddhist temple. It involves folk dancing and the release of thousands of floating lanterns into the sea, a truly enchanting sight.

Dancers performing aboard a canoe at the Polynesian Cultural Center

Environs

Driving west from Hale'iwa, you pass a former sugar plantation at Waialua and arrive at **Mokulē'ia**, where polo fields border on empty, white-sand beaches. Here you can spend a pleasant afternoon watching parachutists from nearby Dillingham Airfield float down across the surf like clouds of colorful butterflies.

❽ Dole Plantation

Honolulu Co. 64-1550 Kamehameha Highway (Hwy 99), 2 miles (3 km) N of Wahiawā. **Tel** (808) 621-8408. 🚌 Wahiawā. **Open** 9:30am–5:30pm daily. **Closed** Dec 25. 🔌 💻 🔲 dole-plantation.com

The Dole Cannery, built by James Dole in 1903 next to his Wahiawā pineapple plantation, was at that time the world's largest fruit cannery. In 1907, operations moved to Honolulu, eventually closing in 1991 due to increasing competition from Asia. The original Dole Cannery in Wahiawā now functions as a distribution warehouse.

Dole's famous company logo

Across from the warehouse is Dole Plantation, a gift shop selling a range of pineapple products and a demonstration garden showing the different stages of the fruit's growth.

The Plantation is also home to the **Pineapple Garden Maze**, which is the largest maze in the world, with 1.7 miles of paths and covering more than two acres.

🌀 Pineapple Garden Maze

Open 9:30am–5pm daily. **Closed** Dec 25. 🔲

❾ Hawai'i's Plantation Village

Honolulu Co. 94-695 Waipahu St, Waipahu. **Tel** (808) 677-0110. 🚌 Waipahu. **Open** 10am–2pm Mon–Sat. **Closed** public hols. 🔲 🔌 🔲 hawaiiplantationvillage.org

This $3 million restored village portrays over 100 years of sugar plantation culture. It shows how plantation owners segregated

Interior of the Chinese Cookhouse at Hawai'i's Plantation Village

workers along strict ethnic lines and how, in spite of this, a common pidgin language developed *(see p29)*.

The village contains some recreated buildings from the major ethnic groups that worked the plantations, from the Korean, Puerto Rican, and Japanese homes to a Japanese bathhouse and a Shinto shrine. Personal objects placed in the houses give the impression that the occupants have just left.

❿ Wai'anae Coast

Honolulu Co. 🚌 Nānākuli, Wai'anae and Mākaha Beach. 🚹 HVCB, Waikīkī, (808) 924-0266.

With no souvenir stands and very few restaurants, O'ahu's sunny leeward coast is home to a population of native Hawaiians and other Pacific islanders. One of the coast's

prettiest beaches is **Pōka'ī Bay**, where a breakwater shelters an aquamarine lagoon with sand as soft as cloth under your feet.

Farther northwest is **Mākaha Beach**, famous for its 30-ft (9-m) waves. In Mākaha Valley is **Kāne'ākī Heiau**, with thatched houses and *ki'i* (carved idols). It was used as a war temple by Kamehameha I. Mākaha means "ferocious," and the valley was once notorious for bandits. The area still has a reputation for car break-ins; camping is not advised.

🏠 Kāne'ākī Heiau

Off Mākaha Valley Rd. **Tel** (808) 695-8174. **Open** Tue–Sun.

⓫ Ka'ena Point

Honolulu Co. Beyond end of Farrington Highway (Hwy 930), 7 miles (11 km) N of Mākaha.

O'ahu's western extremity, Ka'ena Point has a stark, mountainous coastline and spectacular sunsets. A hot but relatively easy 2-mile (3-km) trail leads to the point.

Legend tells that the rock off the point is a chunk of Kaua'i that the demigod Maui pulled off when he was trying to unite the two islands. On clear days, Kaua'i can be spotted to the north. You may also see rare monk seals, green turtles, and humpback whales *(see p119)*. The world's highest waves slam against the rocks here. So far, no one has been suicidal enough to surf them. The point can also be reached from the road's end in Mokulē'ia. The two roads do not connect.

Ka'ena Point, reached by the exposed trail in the foreground

MOLOKA'I AND LĀNA'I

The small island of Moloka'i tends to be overlooked by vacationers scurrying between O'ahu and Maui. Far less developed for tourism than its neighbors, Moloka'i is the place to get away from it all, and most visitors are enchanted by its gentle pace. Across the Kalohi Channel to the south lies the smaller island of Lāna'i. This former pineapple plantation is now an exclusive tourist destination.

Moloka'i is formed from two extinct volcanoes that were once, along with Lāna'i and Kaho'olawe, attached to Maui. Its higher eastern peak, at some 5,000 ft (1,500 m), is topped by dense rainforest. The north shore is lined by the world's highest, steepest sea cliffs and indented by vast green valleys. The sheltered southern slopes traditionally held the bulk of the inhabitants, who planted crops along the coastline and raised fish in artificial enclosures just offshore. The western volcano, Mauna Loa, has been eroded to a smooth, rounded monolith, which receives so little rain that it is technically desert. Until recently, this end of Moloka'i was barely populated, but since the 1970s, thanks to guaranteed sun and beaches like vast Pāpōhaku, it has been the site of what little development Moloka'i has seen. Despite

repeatedly falling to invading armies from O'ahu, Maui, and Hawai'i Island, Moloka'i acquired a reputation for great spiritual power. Partly thanks to that sense of mystery and isolation, the Kalaupapa Peninsula was set aside in the 1860s as a leprosarium. The work of the Belgian priest Father Damien (canonized in 2009) in tending its exiled patients became famous, and pilgrims now flock to the peninsula from all around the world.

Lying in the rainshadow of Moloka'i and Maui, Lāna'i is now almost entirely owned by the tech magnate, Larry Ellison, and the island's luxury resorts have shifted the economy from agriculture to tourism. Visitors will find an open, sun-baked terrain, spectacular sea cliffs, unpopulated beaches, and the haunting remains of ancient native Hawaiian settlements.

Moloka'i's isolated Kalaupapa Peninsula, backed by the world's highest sea cliffs

◀ St. Philomena Church, located in the Kalaupapa National Historical Park, Moloka'i

Exploring Moloka'i and Lāna'i

Most of Moloka'i's accommodations are in the resort of Kaluako'i at the island's sunnier west end. Kaluako'i offers wonderful beaches. Kaunakakai, on the south coast, has a few charming hotels and most of the island's restaurants. No visitor should miss a drive along the flower-decked south coast to Hālawa Valley or a trip to Kalaupapa National Historical Park, backed by the north shore's huge sea cliffs. Lāna'i, Moloka'i's smaller and drier neighbor to the south, has luxury hotels, deserted beaches, and ancient ruins. Most residents live in the island's one small town, Lāna'i City.

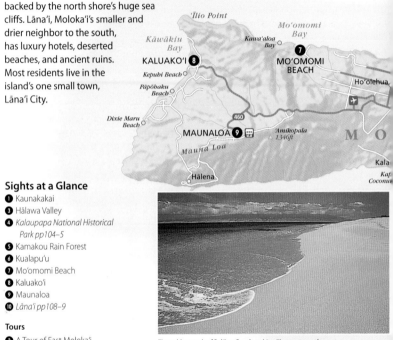

Sights at a Glance

1 Kaunakakai
3 Hālawa Valley
4 Kalaupapa National Historical Park pp104–5
5 Kamakou Rain Forest
6 Kualapu'u
7 Mo'omomi Beach
8 Kaluako'i
9 Maunaloa
10 Lāna'i pp108–9

Tours

2 A Tour of East Moloka'i

The golden sands of Polihua Beach on Lāna'i's remote north coast

Top Recreational Areas

The places shown here have been selected for their recreational activities. Conditions, especially those of the ocean, vary depending on the weather and the time of year, so exercise caution and, if in doubt, stay out of the water or seek local advice.

	Swimming	Snorkeling	Diving	Body-Surfing	Windsurfing	Hiking	Horseback Riding	Golf
GolfDixie Maru Beach	●	■						
Hālawa Valley	●			■				
Hulopo'e/Mānele Bay (Lāna'i)	●	■	●					■
Kalaupapa Nat'l Historical Park						■	●	
Kamakou Rain Forest						■		
Kawa'aloa Bay	●			■				
Kawākiu Bay	●	■						
Kepuhi Bay	●				●		●	■
Kō'ele (Lāna'i)						■	●	■
Mo'omomi Beach	●	■						
One Ali'i Beach Park	●							
Pāpōhaku Beach						■		
Twenty-Mile Beach	●	■						

Key

— Major road
═══ Minor road
--- Track
— Scenic route
△ Summit

For hotels and restaurants see p184 and pp197–8

The road to Kalawao on Kalaupapa Peninsula, with 'Ōkala Island and Moloka'i's northern cliffs behind

KALAUPAPA NATIONAL HISTORICAL PARK ❹

Kalaupapa Peninsula

Kalaupapa

'i Musuem ltural Center

Kala'e

APU'U

K A _ A _ I

KAUNAKAKAI

Mōkapu Island

Kalawao

Waikolu Lookout

KAMAKOU RAIN FOREST ❺

Kamakou △ 4961ft

'Ili'ili'opae Heiau

Our Lady of Sorrows Church

Pukoo

Kalua'aha

'Ualapu'e

'Ualapu'e Fishpond

HĀLAWA VALLEY ❸

Moa'ula Falls

Pu'u o Hōkū Ranch

Cape Hālawa

Twenty Mile Beach

450

Pailolo Channel

450

Kawela

One Ali'i Beach Park

TOUR OF EAST MOLOKA'I

St Joseph's Church ❷

Kamalō

Kalohi Channel

Shipwreck Beach

hua ch

Garden of the Gods

LĀNA'I ❿

Pu'u Mahana 4714ft △

Kane Pu'u Forest Preserve

Keone Bay

L Ā N A ' I

Kō'ele

Lāna'i City

nalapau Harbor

440

Pālāwai Basin

Luahiwa Petroglyphs

Kaunolū

Hulopo'e Bay

Mānele Bay

Federation Camp

'Au'au Channel

430

Hauola Gulch

MUNRO TRAIL

Keōmuku

Lāna'ihale 3370ft

Lōpā

Pōka'i

Naha

Mākole Point

440

Getting Around

Neither Moloka'i nor Lāna'i has public transportation, so renting a car is essential. Car rental firms operate at Moloka'i's Ho'olehua airport and in Lāna'i City. A 12-mile (19-km) drive west of Ho'olehua gets you to Kaluako'i, while Hālawa Valley is 35 miles (56 km) east, on a road that steadily narrows beyond Kaunakakai. Lāna'i is best explored in a four-wheel-drive vehicle, since the island has only 30 miles (48 km) of paved road and more than 100 miles (160 km) of red-dirt "pine roads" and rocky trails to the sea.

0 kilometers   10

0 miles   5

For keys to symbols *see back flap*

❶ Kaunakakai

Maui Co. 🏕 3,500. ℹ️ Ala Malama St and Kamehameha V Highway (Hwy 450), (808) 553-3876. 🎉 Ka Moloka'i Makahiki (cultural festival; late Jan).

The main town on Moloka'i, Kaunakakai was built at the end of the 19th century as an administrative center and port for the local sugar plantations. During the 1920s, pineapple production took over from sugar, but these days commercial agriculture has all but

disappeared from the island, and Kaunakakai looks its age. The wooden boardwalks of its principal thoroughfare, Ala Malama Street, are lined with false-fronted stores, such as the **Kanemitsu Bakery** (see p197), famous throughout the islands for its sweet Moloka'i bread. Dotted along the same street, homey diners reflect Moloka'i's broad ethnic mix. At the eastern end, tiny **St. Sophia's Church** is all but obscured behind an African tulip tree with its orange blossoms.

About half a mile (800 m) from the town center, the long stone jetty of of **Kaunakakai Harbor** juts out into the ocean. It was built in 1898 with rocks taken from a destroyed *heiau* (temple). To the ancient Hawaiians, this place was known as Kaunakahakai, or "beach landing." A break in the

coral reef made it a natural place from which to launch canoes. The harbor is often busy with local fishermen and divers.

During the 1860s, Chief Kapuāiwa, who later became King Kamehameha V, had a home near here. Its remains can still be seen just west of the road leading to the jetty.

Environs
Chief Kapuāiwa was also responsible for planting the soaring palms of the **Kapuāiwa Coconut Grove**, sandwiched between the highway and the ocean 2 miles (3 km) west of Kaunakakai. Well over 1,000 in number, the trees are a majestic sight when silhouetted against the setting sun. Visitors should take care, however, not to stand in the way of falling nuts. Opposite the grove is Kaunakakai's **Church Row**, a set of small wooden chapels belonging to different sects.

Ala Malama Street, Kaunakakai's main street

❷ A Tour of East Moloka'i

The coastal highway that nestles beneath the peaks of eastern Moloka'i is among the most beautiful drives in Hawai'i. Ancient sites and picturesque churches lie tucked away amid tropical flowers and luxuriant rainforest, while the slopes of West Maui are visible across the water. Few people live here now, so the villages often feel like ghost towns. The road finally twists to a halt at ravishing Hālawa Valley, one of Hawai'i's most stunning "amphitheater" valleys.

Fishing boats and yachts in Kaunakakai Harbor

Key

▦ Tour route

● Kaunakakai

KAMEHAMEHA V HIGHWAY

①

450

②

Tips for Drivers

Tour length: 55 miles (88 km) round trip.
Stopping-off points: Allow a full day to visit the ancient fish ponds and pretty churches, to have a picnic at Twenty-Mile Beach or One Ali'i Beach Park, and even to fit in a hike through Hālawa Valley.

① One Ali'i Beach Park
At One Ali'i Beach Park, the small expanse of lawn, scattered with coconut palms, is ideal for picnics and also provides a perfect launching point for kayak trips. One Ali'i is a modern misspelling of the ancient Hawaiian name Oneali'i, meaning "Royal Sands."

② St. Joseph Church
Built in 1876 by Father Damien (see p105), this tiny church was painted a dazzling white in 1995 to celebrate the return of the priest's right hand to Kalaupapa. His statue, permanently garlanded with fresh *lei*, stands in the colorful garden.

❸ Hālawa Valley

Maui Co. End of Kamehameha V Highway (Hwy 450), 27 miles (43 km) E of Kaunakakai. *i* Kaunakakai, (808) 553-3876.

Hawai'i's original Polynesian settlers were established in beautiful Hālawa Valley by AD 650, and for over 1,000 years they grew taro *(see p129)* in an elaborate network of terraced fields. The ruins of nearly 20 ancient *heiau* (temples), including two dedicated to human sacrifice, lie hidden in the undergrowth on both sides of the valley. Hālawa was all but abandoned after the 1946 tsunami, but new generations of farmers grow taro now.

Visitors get their first glimpse of Hālawa from an overlook near mile marker 26. Though its farthest reaches are often obscured by mountain mists, the dramatic shoreline lies spread out 750 ft (230 m) below. The placid,

Waterfall in Hālawa Valley, seen from a roadside overlook

unhurried meanderings of the main stream as it approaches the ocean are in sharp contrast to the roaring surf just ahead.

The highway switchbacks down the hillside, reaching the valley floor at a quaint wooden chapel. A little farther along, the road ends at a low ridge of dunes, knitted together by *naupaka*, a white-flowered creeper. Surfers launch themselves into the waves from the small gray beach just beyond.

In summer, visitors wade across the river mouth to reach a nicer beach on the far side; in winter, it's safer to follow the dirt road that curves from beside the chapel. Shaded by imposing palm trees and sheltered from the full force of the sea by a stony headland, the beach is idyllic for swimming.

An intermediate, spectacular two-hour trail, which involves wading through the stream, leads through the rainforest to the 250-ft (75-m) **Moa'ula Falls**. Hawaiians claim that the pool at its base is home to a *mo'o* or giant lizard. Hikers traditionally throw a *ti* leaf onto the water before swimming; if it sinks, the *mo'o* is lying in wait. The trail is accessible only by guided hikes. Contact the Moloka'i Visitors Bureau (808) 553-3876 for information.

---

⑦ Hālawa Valley
With its soaring walls, lush vegetation, and shimmering waterfalls, Hālawa Valley is regarded as the most scenic spot on Moloka'i.

0 kilometers 5
0 miles 3

⑥ Twenty-Mile Beach
This thin strip of pristine sand at mile marker 20 is shaded by overhanging trees. Sheltered from the open ocean, it's great for snorkeling, but beyond the reef, the sea can be dangerous.

⑤ 'Ili'ili'ōpae Heiau
This huge structure, Hawai'i's second largest *heiau* (temple), witnessed human sacrifices in the 18th century. It is on private land, but hikers can follow the five-minute trail that runs inland halfway between mile markers 15 and 16.

④ Our Lady of Sorrows
Father Damien took his first short break from Kalaupapa in 1874, to build the church of Our Lady Of Sorrows at 'Ualapu'e. Below lush mountain slopes, its red-tiled roof is shaded by the tousled coconut palms that surround it.

③ 'Ualapu'e Fish Pond
Of the 50 or so ancient fish ponds that line Moloka'i's southeast coast, 'Ualapu'e, just after mile marker 13, is one of the largest. Created by erecting a stone wall on top of a submerged reef, it encloses a vast area of shallow ocean and was used to raise mullet for the chief's table.

❹ Kalaupapa National Historical Park

Millions of years after Moloka'i emerged from the sea, a volcanic afterthought created the remote Kalaupapa peninsula (see pp22–3). In 1865, when the imported disease of leprosy seemed to threaten the survival of the Hawaiian people, the peninsula was designated a leprosy colony. Bounty hunters rounded up those with even minor skin blemishes to be exiled at the original settlement of Kalawao. In the beginning, food and medicine were in short supply, and condemnation to the peninsula was seen as a death sentence. The settlement eventually relocated to the more sheltered Kalaupapa. The last patients arrived in 1969, when the policy of enforced isolation ended. The park now serves as a permanent memorial.

View from Pālā'au State Park
Sealed off from the rest of Moloka'i by a mighty wall of cliffs, this remote peninsula was an obvious choice for a leprosy colony.

★ Kalaupapa
All of the peninsula's residents, consisting of aging patients who chose to live out their lives here and state and federal employees, live on its sheltered western side in the village of Kalaupapa. It has three churches and a bar – Elaine's Place.

★ Kalaupapa Trail
Hikers and mule riders alike pick their way down the 26 switchbacks of this precipitous trail, enjoying stupendous views during the 3-mile (5-km) journey.

KEY

① **Pālā'au State Park** (see p106)

② **The Damien Monument**, a Celtic cross, was paid for by public donations in England (1890) and erected in 1893.

③ **SS Kā'ala**, wrecked in 1932, remains a rusting hull stranded on the reef just offshore.

④ **Kalaupapa airstrip**

⑤ **The Moloka'i Light**, from Kalaupapa Lighthouse, was one of the most powerful in the Pacific when it was built in 1908.

⑥ **Kauhakō Crater**, what's left of the volcano that formed the peninsula, has an 800-ft (245-m) deep lake at its center.

⑦ **Kalawao**, the original settlement, had a peak population of 1,174 in 1890, but it was abandoned in 1932.

⑧ **Judd Park**

⑨ **Ancient Hawaiians** used to jump off Leinaopapio Point for fun, with palm leaves as parachutes.

Offshore Islands

From the peninsula's exposed eastern side, small islands can be seen poking out of the sea next to staggering 2,000-ft (600-m) cliffs – the tallest sea cliffs in the world.

★ St. Philomena Church

The church was shipped from Honolulu in 1872 and later modified by Father (now Saint) Damien, whose grave lies nearby. In 1936, his body was returned to Belgium, but his right hand was later reinterred here.

VISITORS' CHECKLIST

Practical Information
Maui Co. Reached by foot or mule on Kalaupapa Trail: trailhead on Highway 470, 3 miles (5 km) N of Kualapu'u, between the mule stables and Kalaupapa Overlook. 🚶 🛖 compulsory. Book well in advance. Visitors must be 16 or older. Moloka'i Mule Ride, (808) 567-6088, book well in advance. **Closed** Sun. **w** nps.gov/kala

Transport
✈ from Ho'olehua, Moloka'i or Honolulu.

0 kilometers   1

0 miles   1

⑦ ⁂ ⑧

⑨

St. Damien of Moloka'i (1840–89)

Joseph de Veuster, born in Belgium, went to Hawai'i as a Roman Catholic missionary in 1864, and was ordained as Father Damien at Our Lady of Peace (see p60) in Honolulu. In 1873, he volunteered to serve the original leprosy colony of Kalawao, on the isolated Kalaupapa Peninsula. Hailed as a hero by the Honolulu press, he embraced his destiny willingly. He built hospitals, churches, and homes with his bare hands and nursed patients without fear for his own life. Father Damien finally succumbed to leprosy in 1889. The dedication of the "Martyr of Moloka'i" won him universal acclaim. His beatification as the "Blessed Damien" in 1995 preceded his canonization by Pope Benedict XVI in 2009.

Father Damien statue in Honolulu

Key

═══ Minor road

══ Dirt or four-wheel-drive road

■ ■ Hiking trail and mule track

For keys to symbols see back flap

Path through the dense vegetation of the Kamakou Rain Forest

❺ Kamakou Rain Forest

Maui Co. Reached by four-wheel-drive road E of Maunaloa Highway (Hwy 460), 4 miles (6.5 km) NW of Kaunakakai. 🛈 Kaunakakai, (808) 553-3876.

The remote mountain-top ridges of eastern Moloka'i preserve one of the least spoiled tracts of rainforest in Hawai'i. It is reached by four-wheel-drive vehicle or mountain bike on a rutted dirt road.

This region saw its one brief flurry of activity early in the 1800s, when native Hawaiians were sent up here in search of sandalwood to sell to foreign merchants (see p46). Near the top of the island's central ridge is a grooved depression in the shape of a ship's hold. This so-called **Sandalwood Boat** was where the cut logs were piled.

The higher you climb, the wetter and lusher the forest becomes, and the more the road deteriorates. Native fauna and flora increasingly predominate, with colorful 'ōhi'a trees erupting amid vivid green foliage. Ten miles (16 km) in, superb views open out all the way to the north shore valleys. Here, Waikolu Lookout stands above the 3,700-ft (1,150-m) drop of Waikolu Valley.

Just beyond, the Pēpē'ōpae Trail climbs along a wooden walkway through otherwise impenetrable rainforest. Every tree is festooned with hanging vines and spongy moss, while orchids glisten in the undergrowth. This misty wonderland is the last refuge of endangered birds like the Moloka'i thrush (oloma'o) and Moloka'i creeper (kākāwahie). After crossing an eerie, windswept bog, the trail traverses a series of gulches to emerge at an astonishing overlook above Pelekunu Valley.

❻ Kualapu'u

Maui Co. 🗻 1,900. 🛈 Kaunakakai, (808) 553-3876.

The former plantation village of Kualapu'u is now home to Moloka'i's first coffee plantation, whose products can be tasted at the friendly, roadside espresso bar. Two miles (3 km) northeast of town, the **RW Meyer Sugar Mill** preserves the remains of the area's short-lived dabble in the sugar business. The mill machinery, now beautifully restored, was in use for just 11 years from 1878 to 1889. It now forms part of the adjoining

RW Meyer Sugar Mill, the smallest in Hawai'i

Moloka'i Museum and Cultural Center, an interesting little collection of artifacts that illustrates the island's varied history.

Environs

Four miles (6.5 km) northeast of Kualapu'u, Kala'e Highway (Hwy 470) comes to an end at **Palau'au State Park**, which combines superb views over the Kalaupapa Peninsula (see pp104–5) with a legendary site. Stop at the viewpoint to gaze eastward along the awesome cliffs to Kalaupapa village and beyond. From the vista's parking lot, a hiking trail leads through the forest to **Phallic Rock**. As ancient legend has it, women who sleep beneath this outcrop will wake up pregnant. Its lifelike appearance is in part the work of human hands.

🏛 **Moloka'i Museum and Cultural Center**
Kala'e Highway (Hwy 470). **Tel** (808) 567-6436. **Open** 10am–2pm Mon–Sat. **Closed** public hols. 🅿 ♿

Legendary Phallic Rock at the Pālā'au State Park, Moloka'i

❼ Mo'omomi Beach

Maui Co. At the end of Mo'omomi Rd, 5 miles (8 km) NW of Ho'olehua.

Mo'omomi Beach, the only stretch of Moloka'i's north shore accessible to casual visitors, belongs very much to the drier western end of the island. The coastline here is made up of ancient sand dunes that have become lithified (turned to rock). The area is rich in the bones of flightless birds, which may have been hunted to extinction by the early Polynesian settlers. A 5-mile

The dirt road serving Mo'omomi Beach

(8-km) dirt road from Ho'olehua leads to Mo'omomi Bay, a surfing and fishing beach popular with local residents.

❽ Kaluako'i

Maui Co. Off Maunaloa Highway (Hwy 460), 5 miles (8 km) NW of Maunaloa. 🛈 Kaunakakai, (808) 553-3876. 🎏 Moloka'i Ka Hula Piko (May).

The gentle slopes of Mauna Loa, Moloka'i's western volcano, have always been far too arid to sustain a significant human presence. The island's west coast was known to the ancients as Kaluako'i, "the adze pit," for its valuable basalt deposits. This area had a population of just one person in the 1970s. Since then, it has become Moloka'i's only resort, home to a large hotel and condo complexes.

Environs
The island's most spectacular expanse of sand, broad **Pāpōhaku Beach** starts about a mile (1.5 km) down the coast. Colossal waves render the beach unsafe for swimming, so it is often empty, with a splendid sense of romantic isolation.

Every May, **Pāpōhaku Beach County Park** hosts the Moloka'i Ka Hula Piko festival, which celebrates the birth of *hula* with music and dance. There are *hālau hula* (*hula* schools), contemporary musicians, and local crafts. Lectures and storytelling take place across the island in the week before the festival.

Beyond Pāpōhaku's southern end, secluded **Dixie Maru Beach** offers sheltered swimming and good snorkeling.

❾ Maunaloa

Maui Co. 🗺 400. 🛈 Kaunakakai, (808) 553-3876.

When the Moloka'i Ranch specialized in cattle and pineapples, tiny Maunaloa, on the flanks of the mountain, was the quintessential Hawaiian plantation village. From wooded groves, the timber-frame houses of its farm workers and *paniolo* (*see p147*) faced right across the ocean to Waikiki.

In the 1970s, the ranch switched to tourism, offering luxury camping, an upscale hotel, and outdoor activities. However, it was not successful and shut down in 2008. Today, a few homespun businesses still survive on the main street, including the **Big Wind Kite Factory**. Owner Jonathan Socher is happy to show visitors around his manufacturing area and discuss the many kite designs. He also offers kite-flying lessons in the adjacent park.

Moloka'i was renowned in ancient times as *Moloka'i pule o'o* (Moloka'i of strong prayers), the home of powerful priests and sorcerers. Dreaded "poisonwood gods" lived in the forests above Maunaloa; a sliver of wood cut from their favored trees could kill any foe. However, the *'ōhi'a* woods nearby played a more benign role in Hawaiian legend. Here the goddess Laka learned the *hula* and taught it to humans. This claim to be the birthplace of *hula* is disputed. Kē'ē Beach on Kaua'i boasts the same distinction (*see p171*).

Big Wind Kite Factory
120 Maunaloa Highway (Hwy 460). **Tel** (808) 552-2364. 🌐 bigwindkites.com

Colorful kites at the Big Wind Kite Factory in Maunaloa

⑩ Lāna'i

Sun-baked Lāna'i was once the world's largest pineapple plant-ation, owned by the Dole Company. In 1991, Lāna'i's new owner, the Castle & Cooke Corporation, opened two luxury resorts and re-employed the island's farm workers as hotel staff. This identity shift left the island open for an exploration of its many beaches, cliffs, and ancient ruins. In 2012, the tech magnate Larry Ellison purchased the island and made several eco-friendly changes.

Colorful Lāna'i City house backed by Cook Island Pine trees

Exploring Lāna'i

This relatively low island is topped by the Lāna'ihale ridge. The heart of the island, rural Lāna'i City, is perched below the ridge at an elevation of 1,600 ft (490 m). Roads, more often dirt than paved, radiate outward to reach the coast at a few remote, beautiful spots.

Lāna'i City

Home to virtually all of the island's 3,200 residents, Lāna'i City offers a first-hand experience of the classic Hawaiian plantation town. Built in the early 1920s to house Dole's mostly Filipino laborers, this friendly town centers on rectangular **Dole Park**. The park is lined with frontier-style shops and the **Hotel Lāna'i**, a vintage wooden inn (see p184). At the northeast corner of the town, on the site of the former

headquarters of Lāna'i Ranch (1874–1951), is **Four Seasons Resort Lāna'i, The Lodge at Kō'ele** (see p184). This award-winning resort offers respite from the island's coastal heat. The attractions here include an 18-hole golf course, an orchid house, stables, and manicured grounds. The fine restaurant is open to the public.

🚶 Luahiwa Petroglyphs

Off Hō'ike Rd, 2 miles (3 km) S of Lāna'i City, near the water tower on the ridge.

The broad, softly hazy expanse of Pālāwai Basin is actually the remains of Lāna'i's extinct and worn-down volcanic crater. Its eastern wall bears one of Hawai'i's richest collections of petroglyphs. Visible from quite a distance, a cluster of 34 black boulders stands out against a steep red hillside dotted with dry white patches of *pili* grass. Some of these stones were thought to possess the *mana* (sacred power) of the rain gods Kū and Hina. Starting at least 500 years ago, Hawaiians decorated them by carving enigmatic figures representing humans and dogs. More recent images of horses, surfers, and leashed dogs were carved by students from Maui's Lahainaluna School during the 1870s. The petroglyphs are best viewed early or late, when the sun is not overhead.

🌊 Mānele and Hulopo'e Bays

End of Mānele Rd (Hwy 440), 8 miles (13 km) S of Lāna'i City.

Together, these adjacent bays form a marine life conservation district, home to Hawaiian spinner dolphins. Mānele Bay is Lāna'i's only small boat harbor. The misleadingly named **Four Seasons Lāna'i at Mānele Bay** (see p184) spreads over the hillside above Hulopo'e Bay, the island's best swimming and snorkeling spot. The resort, even with its interior opulence and fragrant gardens, harmonizes with its savage location. The bay is off-limits to all boats except those of Maui's oldest sailing excursion company, **Trilogy**. Camping is permitted here.

Between the bays lies **Pu'u Pehe**, or Sweetheart Rock. According to legend, lovely Pehe was kept by her jealous husband in a nearby cave until one day, while he was away, she drowned in a storm. He buried her on this rock island and then jumped to his death.

Pu'u Pehe, or Sweetheart Rock, in the waters off Mānele Bay

🚶 Kaunolū

Kaunolū Trail, a dirt track off Kaupili Rd, which leaves Mānele Rd (Hwy 440) 4.5 miles (7 km) S of Lāna'i City.

Few sites evoke the drama of ancient Hawaiian life like the ruins of this seldom-visited fishing village, abandoned in the mid-19th century. The rough drive to this naturally fortified clifftop, with its dizzy-ing views of Lāna'i's southern coast, takes a full hour from Lāna'i City and requires a four-wheel-drive vehicle.

The early Hawaiians excelled in the art of building with

The beautifully maintained grounds of The Lodge at Kō'ele in Lāna'i City

Lāna'i's Cook Island Pine Trees

Groves of Cook Island Pine, which give the island its characteristic look, were planted in the early 1900s by New Zealander George C. Munro, the manager of what was then the Lāna'i Ranch. Freshwater is Lāna'i's most precious resource, and Munro realized that these trees increase the island's water-drawing capacities. Mountain mists collect in the trees' tightly leaved branches and drip onto the thirsty ground – on a good day, as much as 40 gallons (150 liters) of water per tree.

An impressive row of Cook Island Pines at The Lodge at Kō'ele stables

unmortared stone, and here at Kaunolū you can see several well-preserved examples, including the stone platform of the large **Halulu Heiau** on Kaunolū Bay's west side. On the east side there is a cliff-side platform that was once the home and fishing retreat of Kamehameha the Great. There are also ruins of a canoe house and a large fishing shrine.

One way in which ancient Hawaiians showed their bravery was by cliff-jumping, and just west of Kaunolū Bay, there is a suicidal diving platform. At **Kahekili's Leap**, the former chief of Maui, Kahekili, proved his mettle by hurling himself more than 60 ft (18 m) down – clearing a 15-ft (4.5-m) wide outcrop of rocks – into water just 10 ft (3 m) deep.

🌲 The Munro Trail
Turn off Mānele Rd (Hwy 440) 5 miles (8 km) S of Lāna'i City.

This pine-studded drive along the volcanic ridge of Lāna'ihale, whose summit reaches 3,370 ft (1,050 m), offers sensational views of five of the Hawaiian islands. Because the Kō'ele end of the road can be alarmingly muddy, best taken downhill, the drive should begin at the other end. At the concrete stripe on Mānele Road just after the Pālāwai Basin, turn left onto a dirt road and then follow the most worn track up the hill. Allow at least two hours by jeep for this rugged 20-mile (32-km) jaunt.

🌲 Garden of the Gods
Polihua Rd, 6 miles (10 km) NW of Lāna'i City.

The Garden of the Gods is a visual oddity, a reddish lunar landscape dotted with boulders made of compacted sand. They range in color from reds and oranges to browns and blues, and the effect is most intense at sunset, when the rocks seem to glow. This peculiar dry and rocky landscape is reached by an easy 30-minute drive along a dirt road from Kō'ele, which passes through

a hunting zone for axis, or spotted, deer and native dryland forest.

Continuing on, the road to the island's northern tip gets rougher, ending at long, wild **Polihua Beach**. At this remote strand, one hour from Kō'ele, a visitor's footprints may be the only ones of the day. The ocean currents can be dangerous.

Strange rust-red rock formations at the Garden of the Gods

🌲 Shipwreck Beach
Keōmuku Rd (Hwy 430), 8 miles (13 km) NE of Lāna'i City.

Lāna'i's northern shore is lined with an 8-mile (13-km) stretch of beach that takes its name from the rusting hulk of a World War II supply ship that is wrecked on the reef. Many other ships have come to harm in these shallow, hazardous waters, including an oil tanker that is visible 6 miles (10 km) up the beach. To reach the beach, follow Keōmuku Road (Hwy 430) until the asphalt ends; then take the dirt road on the left that rambles over sandy ground for about a mile (1.5 km). From here, a beachcomber's trek offers isolation and beautiful views of Maui and Moloka'i – a day's hike northward will bring you to Polihua Beach. Off Shipwreck Beach is an extensive reef, but swimming is dangerous here.

Shipwreck Beach, with the hulking 1940s wreck in the distance

MAUI

The second largest Hawaiian island, Maui is sparsely populated, supporting less than a tenth of the state's population. The land is verdant with sugarcane and pineapple, sprawling cattle ranches, and rainforests that descend mountain slopes to the sea. The 120 miles (195 km) of shoreline invite a host of ocean activities, from swimming, snorkeling, and diving, to world-class windsurfing.

Maui was formed by the convergence of two volcanoes at the isthmus known as the Central Valley. The green 5,788-ft (1,764-m) West Maui Mountains are the eroded slopes of a single extinct volcano, while East Maui is composed of Haleakalā, an enormous 10,023-ft (3,055-m) dormant volcano crowned by a lunar landscape.

The earliest inhabitants are thought to have arrived from the Marquesas Islands around the 4th century AD. The areas around Lahaina and Hāna were the first to be settled. Maui was split into rival chiefdoms until the 14th century, when Pi'ilani conquered the island. This Maui chief built the massive temple of Pi'ilanihale Heiau, whose ruins are near Hāna. In 1795, Kamehameha I conquered Maui in his quest to unite the Hawaiian Islands, and in 1800, established his royal seat at Lahaina. Jean-François de Galaup, Comte de La Pérouse, was the first European to set foot on Maui, in 1786. Other foreigners followed during the 1800s, including missionaries, whalers, and contract laborers from Europe and Asia who came to work the growing sugar plantations. The communities they established retained the character of their homelands and created a multicultural heritage that is celebrated today in local holidays, customs, and food.

Visitors will see a varied landscape, from Kula's farmland, where proteas and sweet onions are grown, to the arid, eroded crater of Haleakalā and the lush, tropical vegetation on the windward coast. If you want to soak up the sun, the leeward coast offers white-sand beaches and calm waters that are the winter home of humpback whales.

Windsurfers at Ho'okipa Beach County Park near Pā'ia, on Maui's north shore

◀ View of the Haleakala Crater, located in the Haleakala National Park, Maui

Exploring Maui

Maui is composed of two volcanoes connected by the Central Valley, the island's population hub and the site of several attractions. The West Maui Mountains (Kahalawai) are actually a single, extinct volcano that time has carved into steep canyons, accessible at just a few places, such as 'Iao Valley. A road skirting the mountain's southern flank leads to historic Lahaina and the coastal resorts of Kā'anapali and Kapalua. Haleakalā, a dormant volcano capped by a huge crater, makes up the larger region of East Maui. Its outer slopes are covered with cattle ranches and fields of sugarcane and pineapple. The lush windward coast in the north features the plantation town of Pā'ia, Ho'okipa Beach – a windsurfers' mecca – and the little town of Hāna. The popular leeward coast enjoys a sunnier climate and calmer ocean.

Top Recreational Areas

The places shown here have been selected for their recreational activities. Conditions, especially those of the ocean, vary depending on the weather and the time of year, so exercise caution and, if in doubt, stay out of the water or seek local advice.

	Swimming	Snorkeling	Diving	Body-Surfing	Windsurfing	Hiking	Horseback Riding	Golf
Haleakalā National Park						◉	◉	
Hāmoa Bay	◉	◉		◉				
Hāna	◉					◉	◉	
Ho'okipa Beach County Park					◉			
Hosmer Grove						◉		
'Iao Valley						◉		
Kā'anapali and Keka'a Point	◉	◉	◉		◉			◉
Kahana				◉				
Kanahā Beach County Park	◉				◉			
Kapalua and Honolua Bay	◉	◉	◉				◉	◉
Ke'anae Peninsula						◉		
Kihei	◉	◉	◉				◉	◉
La Pérouse Bay		◉	◉			◉	◉	
Lahaina	◉	◉	◉					
Mākena	◉	◉	◉				◉	◉
Molokini		◉	◉					
'Ohe'o Gulch and Kipahulu	◉			◉		◉		
Olowalu		◉	◉					
Pā'ia	◉		◉	◉	◉			
Polipoli Springs Recreation Area						◉		
Spreckelsville	◉				◉			
Ukumehame	◉	◉	◉			◉		
'Ulupalakua							◉	
Wai'ānapanapa State Park	◉	◉				◉		
Waihe'e	◉					◉	◉	◉
Waikapū						◉		
Wailea	◉	◉	◉					◉

Key

— Major road
═ Minor road
--- Track
— Scenic route
△ Summit

0 kilometers 10
0 miles 5

For hotels and restaurants see pp185–6 and pp198–202

Getting Around

Maui's main airport is in Kahului, but smaller airports serve Hāna and Kapalua. Major resorts offer guests free shuttle services to and from the airport and around the resort, but most people explore Maui with a rental car or by tour. There is a county bus with limited routes. Some roads are tortuous, and progress can be slow. Many highways have bicycle lanes, and tour companies will take you up the slope of Haleakalā to bike back down. Stables offer horseback tours all over the island. Ferry services run between Maui and the islands of Lāna'i and Moloka'i.

'Īao Needle, marking the confluence of two streams in the lush 'Īao Valley

Sights at a Glance

A secluded swimming spot on the rocky coast of the Ke'anae Peninsula

For keys to symbols see back flap

❶ Street-by-Street: Lahaina

Stroll the streets of Lahaina, and you follow in the footsteps of scoundrels and kings. Until 1845, this small harbor town was the capital of the Kingdom of Hawai'i. By the mid-19th century, during the peak of the whaling era, it had a reputation as a rowdy port-of-call. Missionaries sometimes struggled to maintain control over the town and the souls of its inhabitants. Today, it is one of the most popular visitor attractions on Maui. Front Street, lined with pioneer-style homes and storefronts, is evocative of Lahaina's past. The Lahaina Restoration Foundation has restored a number of historic sites, and a wealth of history can be found within a small area.

Front Street, once the haunt of boisterous sailors after women and whiskey, now offers souvenir shops and colorful street stalls.

Wo Hing Temple

Masters' Reading Room

DICKENSENI STREET

FRONT ST

MARKET ST

PAPELEKANE ST

MISSIONARY HOME
&
THE REV. DWIGHT BALDWIN
1834
Museum Open Daily

★ **Baldwin Home**
Maui's oldest Western-style dwelling, dating from the 1830s, has been faithfully restored with period furnishings, including several original pieces.

The Hauola Stone was believed by ancient Hawaiians to calm and heal.

★ **Pioneer Inn**
Built in 1901 by an Englishman, the Pioneer Inn was the first hotel to open in Lahaina. It remains a hotel to this day and is a favorite landmark in the town.

Key

— Suggested route

The Old Lahaina Courthouse was built in 1859 and was intended to be a palace for King Kamehameha III, but was used instead as a post office, a courtroom and jail. It now serves as a Visitor Center and Art Society where local artists' pottery and paintings are displayed.

Lahaina's Tragic Princess

Hawaiian culture once sanctified royal marriages between siblings; such alliances kept bloodlines pure and ensured offspring great *mana* (power). Ancient custom was cast aside with the arrival of Christianity, however. When Nahi'ena'ena and her brother Kauikeaouli (later Kamehameha III) fell in love, they were separated. Nahi'ena'ena still managed to bear their son, who lived only hours. Sick in body and soul, she died soon afterward.

Nahi'ena'ena, who died at 21

VISITORS' CHECKLIST

Practical Information
Maui Co. 🗺 11,700.
ℹ 648 Wharf St, (808) 667-9193.
🎭 Ocean Arts Festival (Mar);
4th of July Fireworks; Halloween
in Lahaina (Oct 31); Holiday
Lighting of the Banyan Tree (Dec).
🌐 **visitlahaina.com**

Transport
🚢 Lahaina Harbor.

0 meters	100
0 yards	100

HALE STREET

LUAKINI STREET

FRONT STREET

PRISON STREET

CANAL STREET

Chapel in the
prison grounds

Lahaina Fort was built
in the 1830s to jail rowdy
whalers, but dismantled
20 years later. A small part
has been reconstructed.

Hale Pa'ahao, or "Stuck-in-Irons
House," was the new prison built
in the 1850s with bricks from
the Lahaina Fort.

★ **Banyan Tree**
The tree is over a century old
and is so large that special
events, including arts and
crafts fairs, are held beneath
its many branches. The
square is named after it.

Exploring Lahaina

Front Street is the hub of Lahaina. A low seawall opens up nearly a block of the street to scenic views of the sea and nearby islands, and makes strolling an old-fashioned pleasure. Whether you visit the historic Baldwin Home, the Old Lahaina Courthouse, or shop in the town's colorful stores, Lahaina offers a variety of interesting diversions. On most evenings, live music spills into the street from restaurants and bars.

Lahaina Harbor, against a backdrop of the West Maui Mountains

🏠 Baldwin Home

696 Front St. **Tel** (808) 661-3262.
Open 10am–4pm daily. **Closed** Jan 1 & Dec 25. 🅿 🔼 🎫 compulsory.
🆆 lahainarestoration.org

The four original rooms of this historic home were built in 1834 by the Reverend Ephraim Spaulding. The coral and stone walls were 24 in (60 cm) thick, perhaps a measure to minimize the sounds of revelry outside. At the height of the Pacific whaling trade, tensions often ran high between the seamen who frequented the port's brothels and grog shops and the missionaries who sought to establish Christian faith and law in the islands.

The Reverend Dwight Baldwin and his wife came to Hawai'i from the US in the early 1830s and were assigned to Lahaina's Waine'e Church. When Spaulding fell ill around 1836, the Baldwins moved into his house. As the family grew – to an eventual total of eight children – so did their home. A second-story dormitory was added in 1849, apparently to protect the daughters from the town's rowdier elements.

The first floor is open to the public. Many of the furnishings, which were donated by the Baldwin family, date from the 1850s. Original pieces include an 18th-century sewing box, rocking chairs, and a four-poster bed made out of *koa* wood. Among the acquisitions is a quilt with a Hawaiian-flag design (*see p72*), a gift to a Captain Born from Hawai'i's last queen, Lili'uokalani.

The two-story house next door was built around 1834 – the same time as the Baldwin Home. It takes its name, the **Masters' Reading Room**, from the second floor, which was designed to offer "suitable reading rooms for the accommodation of Seamen who visit Lahaina, as well as a convenient place of retirement from the

The Baldwin Home, set in a shady garden

heat and unpleasant dust of the market."

The Reading Room, once housing the Lahaina Restoration Foundation, has been preserved in its original state but is closed to the public.

🌳 Banyan Tree

Canal St or Front St.

The Banyan Tree (*ficus benghalensis*) was all of 8 ft (2.4 m) tall when it was planted by Maui sheriff William O. Smith in 1873 to mark the 50th anniversary of the founding of Lahaina's first Christian mission. Lahaina was once the capital of the Hawaiian kingdom and the whaling capital of the world, and as the town grew and developed, the tree continued to grow – and grow. Today, it measures almost one-fourth of a mile (402 m) in circumference, stands 60 ft (18 m) high and covers two-thirds of an acre (2,700 sq m) in the courtyard outside the Lahaina courthouse. There are many celebrations and festivities held underneath its branches, such as the weekly He U'i Cultural Arts Festival and the annual holiday tree lighting ceremony in December. The Banyan Tree attracts hundreds of people every day who come to take its picture and catch a glimpse of history. It has also been designated as a National Historical Landmark.

🏠 Pioneer Inn

658 Wharf St. **Tel** (808) 661-3636. 🔼

Lahaina's best-known hotel was built by an Englishman called George Freeland. He had originally emigrated to Canada, where he joined the Mounties, but ended up in Lahaina in 1900, having pursued a criminal all the way to Maui. Freeland did not catch the fugitive, but stayed here, fell in love with a Hawaiian woman, and, in 1901, built a hotel.

Pioneer Inn is a hotel to this day, on land still owned by the Freeland family. It has been renovated but retains many of the original features. These include whaling memorabilia and a list

Scrimshaw – the Whalers' Art

Life aboard a 19th-century whaling ship had its moments of excitement, but these were the exception. For the average sailor, whaling meant months of boredom, bad food, and low pay. To pass the time, sailors made scrimshaw from whale ivory – carving and etching into the surface of whale teeth and bones. Their "dot-to-dot" technique involved puncturing the surface with a knife or sail needle, applying a mixture of soot and oil, and polishing the ivory with shark's skin. The results were often exquisite works of art. A scrimshander might just decorate the ivory, or else carve it into something useful, such as spoons or gun handles. Scrimshaw fetched a high price then and still does today, in stores along Lahaina's Front Street and at Kā'anapali's Whalers Village (see p118).

Decorative scrimshaw made from whale bones

formed mutual aid societies to maintain ties with China. One such was the Wo Hing Society, founded in 1909, which built the Wo Hing Temple in 1912.

As a museum, the temple provides a good insight into the local Chinese community. There are artifacts as well as a shrine; the altar is replenished with fresh offerings every day.

A separate cookhouse serves as a theater, showing old films about Hawai'i made by American inventor Thomas Edison in 1898 and 1906.

⊞ Hale Pa'i

End of Lahainaluna Rd. **Tel** (808) 667-7040. **Open** 10am–4pm Mon–Fri. **Closed** Jan 1 & Dec 25. ♿ 🖼

The "house of printing" is situated on the grounds of the oldest high school west of the Rocky Mountains – the former Lahainaluna Seminary. When missionaries arrived in Hawai'i, they lost no time in trying to convert the locals to Christianity, as well as teaching them to read.

The Lahainaluna Seminary was set up in 1831, and in 1834 the missionaries added the Hale Pa'i. Originally a thatched hut, the printing house was later replaced with a sturdier building made of stone and timber.

In 1982, the Hale Pa'i became a museum, tracing the history of the written word in Hawai'i. There is a working replica of the original printing press and facsimiles of early Hawaiian printing.

of house rules in the rooms, forbidding tenants from burning the beds and womanizing. You do not need to be a guest to explore the shopping arcade or enjoy the popular bar and grill overlooking the harbor.

⊞ Lahaina Courthouse

649 Wharf St. **Tel** (808) 667-9193. **Open** 9am–5pm daily. **Closed** Jan 1 & Dec 25. ♿

Completed in 1859, the Lahaina Courthouse on Wharf Street originally contained a governor's office, a customs house, a post office, a courtroom, and a jail. It was built with stones from the earlier courthouse and palace that were destroyed by gale-force winds in 1858.

Here too is the Lahaina Visitor Center, which sells souvenirs. Archive photos in the hallway give a glimpse of how the place once looked. The galleries of the Lahaina Arts Society are located in the old jail in the basement.

⊞ Hale Pa'ahao

Prison St & Waine'e St. **Tel** (808) 667-1985. **Open** 10am–4pm Mon–Fri. **Closed** Jan 1 & Dec 25. ♿

Sailors and missionaries who arrived in the islands in the 18th and 19th centuries introduced Hawaiians to a host of new vices – and to codes of conduct unfamiliar to them.

This jail, whose name means "Stuck-in-Irons House," was built by convicts in the 1850s, using coral stone taken from the town's

demolished fort. It was used to incarcerate foreigners and natives alike for crimes ranging from murder to riding horses on the Sabbath or violating fish taboos.

A high stone wall encloses a grassy yard and the jailhouse. Visitors can peek into one of the cells, where a "convict" (actually a mannequin lying on a straw mattress) talks about 19th-century prison life.

Hawaiian papers in Hale Pa'i

⊞ Wo Hing Temple

858 Front St. **Tel** (808) 661-5553. **Open** 10am–4pm Sat–Thu, 1–8pm Fri. **Closed** Jan 1 & Dec 25.

The Chinese were among Hawai'i's earliest immigrants. They came to work on the plantations and many moved into commerce. They often

Taoist altar in the shrine room of the Wo Hing Temple

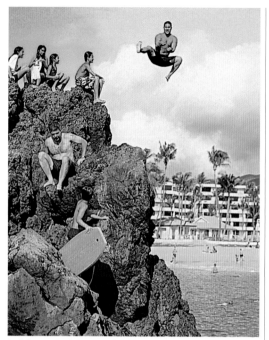
Locals demonstrating their courage at Pu'u Keka'a (Black Rock)

❷ Kā'anapali

Maui Co. 🏔 1,400. 🛈 Suite 1B, 2530 Keka'a Drive, (808) 661-3271. 🎨 Maui Onion Festival (early Aug), Na Mele O Maui (Dec). 🌐 **kaanapaliresort.com**

Nestled between a 3-mile (5-km) beach and the West Maui Mountains, Kā'anapali is Maui's largest resort. It includes six beachfront hotels, five condominiums, two golf courses, 35 tennis courts, and a large shopping center.

Despite all the hotels, the resort maintains a sense of community by staging events like Na Mele O Maui ("the songs of Maui"), a celebration of Hawaiian culture, and the Maui Onion Festival, which honors the local crop.

Through the ages, Kā'anapali was a special place, the site of a *heiau* (temple), a taro patch, and a royal fishpond. In the early 20th century, it became a playground for Hawaiian royalty, complete with a horse-racing track. Free tours of sites throughout the resort are conducted by hotel employees each week.

Pu'u Keka'a, better known as Black Rock, towers above long,
white Kā'anapali Beach and overlooks one of the best snorkeling spots in Maui. Two centuries ago, when Maui chief Kahekili sought to encourage his troops, he would leap into the ocean from Black Rock. This involved spiritual, not physical, danger since it was believed that the dead jumped into the spirit world from here.

At the heart of Kā'anapali is **Whalers Village**, an upscale shopping center with many stores and restaurants.

In addition, the **Whalers Village Museum** explores in unhappy detail the demise of the whale through the whaling trade. Displays include tools and weapons used for whaling, old photographs, models of whaling ships, and products made from the carcasses. Even more fascinating is the insight given into a young whaler's life by letters, diaries, and official accounts.

West Maui's most unusual means of transportation is the **Lahaina Kā'anapali & Pacific Railroad**, whose steam locomotives chug the 6 miles (10 km) between Lahaina and Kā'anapali. Steam engines were used in Hawai'i from the late 1800s until the 1950s to carry both sugarcane and plantation workers. Now the "Sugarcane Train" rides again, taking passengers along the same route as that used in earlier times. The scenic ride passes fields of cane and rises to cross the impressive Hahakea Trestle for a view of the ocean and the West Maui Mountains.

🏛 **Whalers Village and Whalers Village Museum**
2435 Kā'anapali Parkway. **Tel** (808) 661-5992. **Open** 9:30am–10pm daily. ♿ 🌐 **whalersvillage.com**

Lahaina Kā'anapali & Pacific Railroad
Lahaina Station: Limahana Place. Ka'anapali (Pu'ukoli'i) Station: off Pu'ukoli'i Rd.**Tel** (808) 661-0080. **Open** daily. 🚂 ♿
🌐 **sugarcanetrain.com**

Steam "Sugarcane Train", Lahaina Kā'anapali & Pacific Railroad

For hotels and restaurants see pp185–6 and pp198–202

One of the pristine bays that line the coast at Kapalua

❸ Kapalua

Maui Co. 🏔 350. ✈ 🚗 ℹ Lahaina, (808) 669-0244. 🍷 Kapalua Wine & Food Symposium (Jul), Celebration of the Arts (March/April).
W kapaluamaui.com

Twenty minutes' drive north of Kā'anapali lies Kapalua, West Maui's second planned resort, whose luxury rooms and 54 championship fairways are surrounded by a series of exquisite crescent bays and a pineapple plantation that carpets the lower slopes of the West Maui Mountains.

Two of the bays, **Honolua** and **Mokulē'ia**, have been designated marine life conservation districts, where divers and swimmers keep company with reef fish and sea turtles. The golf courses are Audubon Society-approved bird sanctuaries, and the environmentally sensitive lands above the resort are under the stewardship of the Nature Conservancy. The resort also hosts a PGA golf championship in January, with prize money in excess of $1 million, and a wine and food symposium that attracts vintners, chefs, and connoisseurs from around the world. The resort also offers a wedding package, complete with a cake and Hawaiian performers.

Built in 1929 as a plantation general store, **Honolua Store** looks much the same today as it did when it opened. Now the merchandise is more upscale and clothing here sports the Kapalua Resort butterfly logo. A deli counter serves breakfast and lunch.

🏠 **Honolua Store**
502 Office Rd. **Tel** (808) 665-9105. **Open** 6am–8pm daily.

❹ Nākālele Point

Maui Co. Highway 30. ℹ Maui VB, Wailuku, (808) 244-3530.

This is the most northerly point on Maui and the site of Hawai'i's first lighthouse. Vivid red-hued cliffs drop to the ocean and the trails along the bluffs offer terrific ocean views. When the surf is right here, sea water is forced as high as 100 ft (30 m) into the air through a hole in the shoreline lava tube. The blowhole is a short walk down the hill from the road, though you can see it from the top. Be careful if you approach it, as both the waves and the geysers are unpredictable.

❺ Kahakuloa Village and Head

Maui Co. 🏔 25. ℹ Maui VB, Wailuku, (808) 244-3530.

For nearly 1,500 years, families have inhabited Kahakuloa, growing taro (see p129) on stone terraces and using aqueducts to irrigate their crops from mountain streams. One of the most isolated villages on Maui, it has no gas stations or restaurants, and the most prominent building is a lovely small church. East of the village, the monolithic 636-ft (194-m) Kahakuloa Head rises majestically from the water's edge.

Humpback Whales

Once the hub of the Pacific whaling trade, Maui County is today an official sanctuary for humpbacks. The whales spend the winter here, bearing their young in the warm, shallow waters. Newborns are 10–12 ft (3–4 m) long and weigh a svelte 1–2 tons. Adults may reach 45 ft (14 m) in length and weigh 30 to 40 tons. In the mating season, males produce a hauntingly beautiful "song" – a series of whistles, groans, creaks, and screeches that are thought to help establish territory or attract females. Although regulations forbid boats from moving too close, these intelligent creatures may approach a boat, as passengers on Maui's whale-watching cruises (see p220) are often thrilled to discover.

The unforgettable sight of a humpback whale breaching

Plants cultivated at Maui Tropical Plantation and Country Store

❻ Wailuku

Maui Co. 🏘 15,000. ✈ 🏢 MVB, 1727 Wili Pā Loop, (808) 244-3530.

Tucked into the foothills of the West Maui Mountains, Wailuku was in ancient times a royal center and the scene of many important battles. Today, it is a county seat and a thriving community. It has an intriguing mix of architectural styles, with several notable buildings along High Street. These include Wailuku Library, whose main structure was designed by noted Hawaiian architect C.W. Dickey, the old Wailuku Courthouse, the Territorial Building, and Wailuku Union Church. Also of interest is Market Street, with its antique stores, art galleries, cafés, boutiques, and the historic 'Iao Theater.

🏛 Bailey House Museum
2375A Main St. **Tel** (808) 244- 3326. **Open** 10am–4pm Mon–Sat. **Closed** Jan 1, Thanksgiving & Dec 25. 📷
🌐 mauimuseum.org

Headquarters of the Maui Historical Society, this museum is a time capsule of mission life in 19th-century Hawai'i. From 1837 to 1849, the building housed the Wailuku Female Seminary, where New England missionary Edward Bailey and his wife, Caroline, taught. When the seminary closed, Bailey bought the house. Today, the museum contains a large collection of local artifacts, including *kapa* (tree bark) cloth, stone utensils, carvings, *lei (see p33)*, and Bailey's own paintings of Maui.

🏠 Ka'ahumanu Church
103 S. High St. **Tel** (808) 244-5189. 🏠 9am Sun.

This Wailuku landmark was originally constructed in 1832 and is listed on the National Register of Historic Places. After several attempts at rebuilding, the New England-style structure and steeple we see today were erected in the 1880s. It is named for an important early convert to Christianity, Queen Ka'ahumanu, the powerful wife of Kamehameha I. The church was designed by the Protestant missionary Edward Bailey, whose home next door is now the Bailey House Museum. At this church, the Sunday services are conducted in the Hawaiian language and visitors are welcome to attend.

🌴 Maui Tropical Plantation and Country Store
1670 Honoapi'ilani Highway (Hwy 30), 2 miles (3 km) S of Wailuku. **Tel** (808) 244-7643. **Open** daily. 🚃 tram only. ♿

Some of the tropical plants displayed here, such as banana, coconut, breadfruit, and taro, were brought to the Hawaiian islands by the ancient Polynesians. Others were introduced more recently, such as orchids from Africa, papaya from South America, starfruit from Southeast Asia, and macadamia nuts from Australia. An informative open-air tram tour circles about half of the plantation's 112 acres. Various plants are sold in the shop.

Carving at Bailey House Museum

🏛 Haleki'i-Pihana Heiau State Monument
Hea Place, off Kūhiō Place, accessed from Waiehu Beach Rd. **Tel** (808) 984-8109. **Open** daily.

Important religious and civic affairs were conducted here, at the most significant pre-contact *heiau* (temple) in the Central Valley. Haleki'i ("the House of Images") was probably a compound for chiefs. During religious ceremonies, *ali'i* (royalty) would reside in thatched houses whose walls are still visible on the temple's eastern face. A reconstructed section of wall is all that remains of Pihana ("Fullness"), a *luakini heiau* (temple used for human sacrifices). Kamehameha I conducted a sacrifice here in order to give thanks for his victory in 'Iao Valley in 1790.

❼ Kahului

Maui Co. 🏘 26,000. 🏢 MVB, Wailuku, (808) 244-3530.

Kahului is the commercial and industrial center of Maui. The island's biggest airport and principal shipping harbor are located here. It also offers beaches, large parks, historic sites, and cultural attractions.

The **Alexander and Baldwin Sugar Museum** is located 2 miles (5km) west of Kahului. Across from the Pu'unēnē Sugar Mill, built in 1902 by Alexander and Baldwin *(see p127)*, the old supervisor's residence has been transformed into a museum about the industry that dominated Hawai'i's economy for more than half a century. It features historical exhibits, narrated

Aerial view of Kahului harbor

displays, and a model of a cane-crushing mill.

The **Kanaha Pond State Wildlife Sanctuary**, once a royal fish pond, is home to many migratory and native birds. These include two endangered species, the slender, pink-legged Hawaiian stilt (ae'o) and the gray-black, ducklike Hawaiian coot ('alae keoke'o). To access the walking trails, visitors must obtain a permit from the **State Department of Natural Resources**. There is an observation pavilion on the ocean side of Hāna Highway.

Statue of Japanese workers at Kepaniwai Heritage Gardens

🏛 Alexander and Baldwin Sugar Museum
3957 Hansen Rd. **Tel** (808) 871-8058. **Open** 9:30am–4:30pm daily. **Closed** Jan 1, Thanksgiving & Dec 25. 🐾 ♿ 🅦 sugarmuseum.com

🐦 Kanaha Pond State Wildlife Sanctuary
Off Hāna Highway, between Kahului Airport and Kahului town. **Tel** (808) 984-8100.

State Department of Natural Resources
Division of Forestry and Wildlife, 54 S High St, Room 101. **Tel** (808) 984-8100.

❽ ʻĪao Valley
Maui Co. 🅸 MVB, Wailuku, (808) 244-3530.

The ʻĪao Valley Road leads into the West Maui Mountains, winding beneath sheer cliffs as it follows a river hidden by trees. As the road begins to climb, the air becomes cooler, and traffic noise is replaced by the green of ʻĪao Valley, one of Maui's most sacred and historic sites. At one time, the bones of kings were buried here. In this valley in 1790, equipped with Western knowledge and weaponry, the forces of Kamehameha the Great trapped and annihilated those of Kahekili, the last independent chief of the island.

In a beautiful setting, about 2 miles (3 km) up the valley from Wailuku, you will find **Kepaniwai Heritage Gardens**, a lovely

county park with shaded picnic tables used by local families. Scattered about the park are smaller-than-life models showing the architectural styles brought to the islands by various ethnic and racial groups. A thatched Hawaiian hale (house), a Portuguese dwelling with its outdoor oven, a simple Japanese home, and a prim New England cottage are some of the structures that reflect Hawai'i's people – immigrants who come from the four corners of the world.

Adjacent to the gardens, the **Hawai'i Nature Center** offers hikes and other outdoor activities for young and old. "Mud Scientists," "Tremendous Trees," and "Slugfest" are a few of the hands-on educational offerings for budding scientists as young as three years old. In 1997, the center opened a new building called the ʻĪao Valley Interactive Science Arcade, an innovative museum featuring games and displays that serve to educate visitors about the plant and animal life that has reached these islands.

The paved road ends at ʻĪao **Valley State Park**, at the foot of ʻĪao Needle, a pinnacle of rock that towers 1,200 ft (365 m) above the valley floor. The Needle is a hard, volcanic rock that remained when softer rocks around it eroded away. Trails continue into the valley, but this is one of the wettest places on earth, and hiking here can be dangerous when heavy rains create flash-flood conditions.

🌳 Kepaniwai Heritage Gardens
ʻĪao Valley Rd. **Tel** (808) 270-7230. **Open** daily. ♿

🐾 Hawai'i Nature Center
ʻĪao Valley Rd. **Tel** (808) 244-6500. **Open** 10am–4pm daily. **Closed** Jan 1, Thanksgiving & Dec 25. 🐾 ♿ 🅦 hawaiinaturecenter.org

🏞 ʻĪao Valley State Park
ʻĪao Valley Rd, 3 miles (5 km) W of Wailuku. **Open** 7am–7pm daily.

❾ Māʻalaea
Maui Co. 🅜 400. 🅸 MVB, Wailuku, (808) 244-3530.

Nestled along the shoreline off Honoapiʻilani Highway, Māʻalaea has oceanfront condominiums, several restaurants, a shopping plaza, a few attractions, and a small boat harbor. Many snorkel and fishing boat charters depart from Māʻalaea Harbor and facilities here include an activity booth and a US Coast Guard station. Māʻalaea Bay is a favorite of surfers and windsurfers. In the winter, humpback whales (see p119) frequent the bay and can easily be seen from shore.

On the seafront, **Maui Ocean Center**, a huge aquarium and marine park, has more than 60 indoor and outdoor displays, where it is possible to see marine life up close without getting wet. Exhibits include the Living Reef, Turtle Lagoon, and the Open Ocean. The Discovery Pool is an interactive exhibit, where visitors can handle creatures that inhabit tide pools, like sea stars and sea cucumbers. For a thrilling experience, try The Underwater Journey, on which visitors walk through a transparent tunnel set inside a 750,000-gallon tank that is teeming with colorful fish, sharks, rays, and other marine life.

🐠 Maui Ocean Center
192 Māʻalaea Rd. **Tel** (808) 270-7000. **Open** 9am–5pm daily. 🐾 🅦 mauioceancenter.com

Diving with spotted eagle rays, Maui Ocean Center

⑩ Kīhei

Maui Co. 🚉 17,000. 🚌 ℹ MVB, Wailuku, (808) 244-3530.

One of the most populated areas on Maui, Kīhei lies on the island's sunny southern shore and boasts a vast stretch of sparkling white-sand beaches. Some of the island's best beaches for swimming, windsurfing, and snorkeling are found here, including Kalama Park and Kama'ole I, II, and III Parks. Just south of Kama'ole III, there is a boat ramp from which many ocean activity charters depart.

The **Hawaiian Islands Humpback Whale National Marine Sanctuary** encompasses most of the ocean around Hawai'i, but its administrative center is located in Kīhei, at the edge of an ancient fishpond. Here there is an observation deck with a large viewing scope, allowing visitors to enjoy whale watching at a safe and non-intrusive distance.

Covering 1.1 sq miles (2.8 sq km) of some of the last remaining natural wetland habitat in Hawai'i, **Kealia Pond National Wildlife Refuge** has wet and dry periods. It is home to more than 30 species of birds. Neighboring it is Kealia Beach, a nesting ground for the endangered hawksbill turtle.

🕸 **Hawaiian Islands Humpback Whale National Marine Sanctuary** 726 S Kīhei Rd. **Tel** (808) 879-2818. **Open** 10am–3pm Mon–Fri. 🌐 hihwnms.nos.noaa.gov

🕸 **Kealia Pond National Wildlife Refuge** Off Mokulele Highway near Mile Marker 6. **Tel** (808) 875-1582.

⑪ Mākena

Maui Co. 🚉 5,700. ℹ MVB, Wailuku, (808) 244-3530.

At Mākena, Big Beach is separated from Little Beach by a rock outcropping that you have to climb over. When conditions are right, both beaches are good spots for body surfing, boogie boarding, snorkeling, swimming, and sunbathing. Big Beach

An alluring stretch of golden sand at Little Beach, Mākena

is the nickname of the long, white-sand, crescent-shaped Oneloa Beach, which lies to the south of Wailea Marriott Resort *(see p186)*. Facilities in the area are few so arrive prepared. Unofficially, Little Beach is known as a "clothing optional" beach.

The white, steepled **Keawala'i Church** stands beside the ocean in a tranquil, palm-tree-fringed cove. The spectacular setting of this quaint church make it a popular venue for weddings. Built in 1855, it has had a continuous and active congregation, which has lovingly renovated the building over the years. The church welcomes visitors, but asks that they remove their shoes before entering. Sunday services are held in the Hawaiian language.

🏠 **Keawala'i Church** 190 Makena Rd. **Tel** (808) 879-5577. 🌐 keawalai.org

⑫ Ahihi-Kina'u Natural Area Reserve

Maui Co. At the end of Mākena Alanui, 5 miles (8 km) past Wailea. **Tel** (808) 873-3506. **Open** daily.

About a mile and a half south of the Makena Beach and Golf Resort *(see p186)*, this preserve is unique in Hawai'i in that it protects both land and sea environments. To that end, some areas are closed to the public. The section on dry land is a dramatic lava landscape created by the last eruption of

Haleakalā *(see pp132–3)* in 1790. Underwater, fantastic snorkeling and diving is on offer. Because this area is protected, it is illegal to damage or remove any of the natural habitat.

⑬ La Pérouse Bay

Maui Co. ℹ MVB, Wailuku, (808) 244-3530.

South of Mākena, this bay was named for the first European to set foot on Maui, French explorer Jean Francis Gallup Comte de La Pérouse, who arrived in 1786. There is a monument marking the spot on the *mauka* (mountain) side of the road. When La Pérouse returned in 1790, he found that the communities he had visited before were abandoned and covered with lava. Today the bay is known for its fantastic kayaking, snorkeling, and diving.

Kayaking in the crystal clear waters of La Pérouse Bay

For hotels and restaurants see pp185–6 and pp198–202

⑭ Kaho'olawe

Maui Co. No general access.

A dry, uninhabited island less than 11 miles (18 km) long, Kaho'olawe has at different times been host to exiled convicts, sheep and goats who eroded the soil, and the United States Navy, who used it for target practice. In the 1970s, native Hawaiians began a campaign to regain the island, and in 1994 the US ceded it to the state of Hawai'i. Hundreds of ancient sites have been found here, and although access is strictly limited, Hawaiians have begun to reclaim their heritage.

The tiny island of Molokini, popular for underwater exploration

⑮ Molokini

Maui Co. 🚢 from Mā'alaea Harbor. 🅸 MVB, Wailuku, (808) 244-3530.

An almost completely sub-merged volcano, Molokini rises just 160 ft (50 m) above the sea. The exposed rim is rocky and barren, but below the surface, this marine reserve teems with pelagic (open-sea) fish that are comfortable with people, thanks to the many boats that anchor here for snorkeling and scuba diving.

⑯ 'Ulupalakua Ranch and Tedeschi Winery

Maui Co. Highway 37. Tel (808) 878-6058. **Open** 10am–5pm daily. 🅦 ulupalakuaranch.com & 🅦 mauiwine.com

High up on the slopes of Haleakalā, where this ranch and winery are located, the air is cooler and the scenery is panoramic. In the 19th cen-tury, this area was known as Rose Ranch because of the many rose gardens planted here by the then owner's wife. Some of the trees that she planted still stand shading the grounds today. What is today known as 'Ulupalakua Ranch is a working ranch and the site of Maui's only winery, at the Tedeschi Vineyards. The winery's tasting room is located in King's Cottage, which was built in 1874 for King David Kalakaua, a frequent visitor. Here you can sample and purchase the fruits of the winery's labor. Two free tours of the winery are offered daily.

⑰ Upcountry Farms

Maui Co. Kula District. 🅸 MVB, Wailuku, (808) 244-3530.

Upcountry is the term used to describe the verdant western slopes of Haleakalā. At these higher elevations, the views are breathtaking, the scenery is magnificent, the cool and misty air is invigorating, and the volcanic soil is fertile. Here you will find most of the island's farms and ranches, where an intriguing array of flowers, vegetables, fruits, and livestock flourish. Many welcome visitors to enjoy their beauty and their bounty.

O'o Farm is run by the owners of two leading Lahaina restaurants, Pacific'O and I'o (see p200), who are the first in the state to own and operate a farm for the sole purpose of supplying their restaurants. Their farm features orchards where citrus fruits, tropical fruits, stone fruits, and apples are cultivated, as well as extensive herb and vegetable gardens. Visitors may tour the farm with a culinary specialist, handpicking items for a one-of-a-kind lunch, with a choice of fresh fish or vegetarian fare. You are welcome to bring wine to enjoy with your lunch.

Fragrant and pastoral, **Ali'i Kula Lavender** farm cultivates 45 different varieties of lavender. Stroll through the gardens or take a 90-minute guided tour that offers information about the history, health benefits, and culinary attributes of lavender. In addition to the walking tour, a visit to this farm can include lunch and various seasonal tours, some with wreath-making and others with cooking demonstrations.

So named because there are surfboards in the pens and the goats stand on them, the **Surfing Goat Dairy** produces more than 20 different varieties of goat's cheese. The dairy offers daily tours that include information about cheese making and cheese sampling. During the "Evening Chores and Milking" tour, you can help bring in the herd, feed them, and even try out your skills at hand milking the goats.

O'o Farm
651 Waipoli Rd, Kula. **Tel** (808) 667-4341. 🇧🇧🇧 🅦 oofarm.com

Ali'i Kula Lavender
1100 Waipoli Rd, Kula. **Tel** (808) 878-3004. **Open** 9am–4pm daily. 🇧🇧 🅦 aklmaui.com

Surfing Goat Dairy
3651 Omaopio Rd, Kula. **Tel** (808) 878-2870. 🇧🇧 🅦 surfinggoatdairy.com

Fertile upcountry farmland on the misty western slopes of Haleakalā

⑱ A Tour of Upcountry Maui

Between Maui's coastal towns and the mountaintop wilderness of Haleakalā, the air is cool, scented by eucalyptus groves that give way to the rolling hills of 'Ulupalakua and Haleakalā ranches. Here, roads wind through long stretches of countryside and often ascend into cloud banks, meanwhile offering stupendous views of Central Maui, the West Maui Mountains, and the surrounding island-dotted seas. While the scenery alone is worth the drive, any bend in the road can reveal a surprising bit of history – a European-style winery, a park paying homage to Chinese immigrants, or a church shaped like the Queen of Portugal's crown.

⑧ Baldwin Avenue
From Makawao to the coast at Pā'ia, this scenic road makes a pleasant drive and is used by bicycle tours descending from Haleakalā National Park *(see pp132–3).*

① Church of the Holy Ghost
Built in the mid-1890s by Maui's Portuguese community, this Catholic church has an octagonal shape based on a crown worn by Queen Isabella of Portugal. Inside, opposite an exquisite wood and gold altar, sits a replica of a crown given to the church by Portugal.

② Kēōkea
Little Kēōkea has a colorful church and charming country stores. Beyond it, the road twists through pastureland offering expansive views of West Maui and the islands of Lāna'i, Moloka'i, Kaho'olawe, and tiny Molokini.

③ Sun Yat-sen Memorial Park
In this now overgrown park, stone lions guard the statue of the revolutionary Dr. Sun Yat-sen, first president of the Republic of China (1911), whose brother was among the many Chinese immigrants who settled in Kēōkea. Sun Yat-sen hid his family here during the Chinese Revolution (1911–12).

Tedeschi Winery ④
Set in the heart of 'Ulupalakua Ranch, this winery has picnic tables under grand old trees. The tasting room is in a cottage once used by King Kalākaua.

Wailuku

• Pā'ia

HANA HIGHWAY

HALEAKALĀ HIGHWAY

Pukalani •

KULA HIGHWAY

Rolling hills and open spaces, typical upcountry landscape

Tips for Drivers

Tour length: 48 miles (77 km).
Stopping-off points: Plan half a day to accommodate a tour of Tedeschi Winery, a walk through Kula Botanical Gardens, and a stroll around Makawao. There are good restaurants in Makawao and Hāli'imaile (north of Makawao) *(see p201 & p198)*; alternatively, there are various good picnic spots along the way.

⑦ Hui No'eau Visual Arts Center

Set in charming grounds, the Arts Center occupies a 1917 mansion designed for the Baldwin family by C.W. Dickey. A gallery and gift shop feature pieces by local artists, and the various art classes welcome visitors on a drop-in basis.

Key

▨ Tour route

═ Other roads

0 kilometres — 5
0 miles — 3

⑥ Small Upcountry Farms

Proteas and sweet Maui onions are the principal crops here. Several walk-through farms and gardens admit visitors and sell cut proteas.

Haleakalā National Park

⑤ Kula Botanical Gardens

These lush, cool gardens display hydrangeas, proteas, and other delights. There is also a collection of the world's most poisonous plants.

Henry Perrine Baldwin

Maui's verdant "lawn" of cane fields is due largely to the vision of H.P. Baldwin (1842–1911), the son of prominent Lahaina missionaries.

In 1876, he and his partner S.T. Alexander trumped their sugar competitors by digging the Hāmākua Ditch, an innovative 17-mile (27-km) irrigation system that carried up to 40 million gallons (150 million liters) of upcountry water a day to their dry fields east of Pā'ia. "HP" went on to develop a highly profitable sugar company and build modern Maui's top business power (Alexander & Baldwin). In effect, he ruled Maui during its transition from monarchy to annexation *(see pp47–8)*.

"HP" (right) and associate at Hāmākua Poko Mill in 1898

Bronco-riding at the Makawao Rodeo, an annual extravaganza

⑲ Makawao

Maui Co. ▨ 7,184. ℹ MVB, Wailuku, (808) 244-3530. ᴹ Makawao Rodeo (Jul 4).

The false-front wooden buildings, the annual rodeo, and the cattle ranches that surround the town give Makawao a distinctly Old West flavor. It has been a cowboy town since the mid-19th century, but gradually the *paniolo (see p147)* have made way for an "alternative" culture catering to a growing artistic community.

Trendy art galleries showing local creations cluster around the crossroads at the town center. Glassblowing can be seen throughout the day at **Hot Island Glass** on Baldwin Avenue. Alternatively, you can sit in a café to watch town life go by, or stroll into **Komoda Store and Bakery** (also on Baldwin Avenue) for pastries and old-Maui ambience.

A glassblower demonstrating his skills at Hot Island Glass

Windsurfers at Ho'okipa Beach County Park

⑳ Pā'ia

Maui Co. 🏛 2,700. 🛈 MVB, Wailuku, (808) 244-3530.

Today, Pā'ia is a bohemian beach town with offbeat stores, an international surfing reputation, and good, rustic restaurants. Back in the 1930s, though, this little sugar town was the island's biggest population center. No longer in use, the sugar mill that once supported the town is located on Highway 390, a mile (1.5 km) southeast of Pā'ia's only traffic light. The **Mantokuji Buddhist Temple**, just east of town beside Hāna Highway (Hwy 36), speaks eloquently of those who came to work the plantations.

Environs
To the west of town, **HA Baldwin Beach County Park** is good for bodysurfing and popular with locals. Ten minutes east of Pā'ia on Hāna Highway is the world-famous windsurfing spot, **Ho'okipa Beach County Park**. Unique conditions allow windsurfers to perform spectacular aerial maneuvers over the breaking waves. This is not a swimming beach, but with five surf breaks it is certainly a spectators' spot, especially in the afternoon when the wind blows strongly.

㉒ Ke'anae Peninsula and Wailua Valley

Maui Co. 🛈 MVB, Wailuku, (808) 244-3530.

Between Mile Markers 16 and 20, drivers cross an area deemed by the state a "cultural landscape." The star attraction, the ancient *lo'i* or taro ponds, can be seen from overlooks at mile markers 17 and 19. It is said that the Ke'anae Peninsula was just lava rock until the local chief, jealous of his neighbors in Wailua, sent people to bring soil down from the hills.

Wailua's Coral Miracle Church, site of **Our Lady of Fatima** shrine, was built in 1860 with sea-coral. A freak storm deposited the coral on a nearby beach. The locals gathered what they needed to build the church; later, another storm swept the unused coral back out to sea.

㉑ The Road to Hāna

Not until 1926 did the "Hāna Belt Road" connect the rest of Maui to its rain-forested eastern shores. The drive itself is pure fun, somehow being as suited to Jeeps as to convertible BMWs. The road is notoriously twisting and narrow, and road-handling commands every second of your attention. At the same time, the scenery demands that you stare in awe. This is one of the earth's rainiest coasts; the terrain is sliced with waterfalls and gulches choked with tropical vegetation.

① **Waikamoi Ridge Trail**
An unmarked but obvious rest stop between mile markers 9 and 10 offers a picnic area, barbecues, and an easy nature walk. On the trail, labels identify the flora, which includes species of eucalyptus and bamboo.

Pā'ia • Ke'anae • Wailua • HANA HIG

② **Honomanū Bay**
This dramatic bay with its rocky, black-sand beach is a popular surfing spot, but swimming in the turbulent waters can be risky.

0 kilometers 5
0 miles 5

Key
▦ Tour route
═ Other road

③ **Ke'anae Arboretum**
These public gardens just before mile marker 17 provide a close-up look at working taro fields as well as a pleasant trail amid a variety of tropical flora from around the world.

㉓ Hāna

Maui Co. 🏛 1,200. ✈ 🛈 MVB, Wailuku, (808) 244-3530. 🎭 East Maui Taro Festival (Mar/Apr).

Often called Hawai'i's most Hawaiian town, Hāna continues to lag lazily behind the tempo of modernity, and everyone here seems to think that this is just fine. Its perfect round bay and dreamy climate have made Hāna a prized settlement since time immemorial. Kings of Maui and Hawai'i Island fought to possess the district, using **Ka'uiki Head**, the large cinder cone on the right flank of the bay, as a natural fortification. A cave at the base of the cone was the birthplace of Queen Ka'ahumanu (see p46).

Tiny **Hāna Cultural Center and Museum** presents a *kauhale* (residential compound) in the pre-contact style once unique to this area. Exhibited artifacts give a sense of local history. **Wānanalua Church**, beside Hāna Highway (Hwy 360), was constructed from blocks of

Taro in Hawai'i

The purplish-gray root (corm) of *Colocasia esculenta* was the staff of life in ancient Hawai'i. It was believed that taro and humans had the same parents and that the gods had ordered the plant to care for humans, its siblings. This it did by providing nutrition, mostly in the form of *poi*, a pounded paste. It also acted as a symbol of the ideal *'ohana* (family): the plant grows in clumps of *'ohā* (stems), with the younger stems, like children, staying near the older core.

The taro plant, a traditional source of food in Hawai'i

coral in 1838. Missionaries built it on top of an existing *heiau* (temple), thus symbolizing the triumph of Christianity over paganism.

Sugar cultivation took root in Hāna in the 1860s and continued until 1944, when San Francisco capitalist Paul Fagan closed the mill and converted the area to cattle. Three years later, he built Hotel Hāna-Maui on a plot once

used by early missionaries. Today, Fagan's influence is still felt, and his large memorial cross looms on the hillside above the bay.

🏛 Hāna Cultural Center and Museum
Uakea Rd. **Tel** (808) 248-8622. **Open** 10am–4pm daily. **Closed** Jan 1 & Dec 25. 🅿 ♿ 🌐 hanaculturalcenter.org

---

Pi'ilanihale Heiau
beautifully preserved anihale Heiau is vai'i's largest ancient ple. It is well worth aking your journey a closer look.

⑤ Wai'ānapanapa State Park
Plan a stop here to explore sea caves, rocky cliffs, the black-sand beach, and the ancient "King's Trail," which follows the spectacular coastline from here to Hāna.

⑥ Ka Iwi o Pele
This large cinder cone beyond mile marker 51 is the site of mythical struggles involving Pele, the goddess of volcanoes. Nearby, the excellent Kōkī and Hāmoa beaches face the waters where Maui the demigod is said to have fished the islands out of the sea.

⑦ 'Ohe'o Gulch
The pools in this lovely stream are perfect for swimming, but beware of sudden flooding. A 2-mile (3-km) trail leads through a forest to Waimoku Falls, one of Maui's highest waterfalls.

⑧ Palapala Ho'omau Congregational Church
The famous US aviator Charles Lindbergh is buried at this beautifully preserved 1864 church, along with fellow flyer Sam Pryor.

Tips for Drivers

Tour length: 70 miles (110 km) round trip.

Stopping-off points: Start early, allowing a day for the drive. There are no gas stations from Pā'ia to Hāna, where most facilities close at dusk. Hāna has a few restaurants (see p198); there are camping facilities at Wai'ānapanapa State Park (permit required) and 'Ohe'o Gulch (very basic). For tours of Pi'ilanihale Heiau, phone (808) 248-8912.

Breathtaking waterfall at Kīpahulu

㉔ Kīpahulu

Maui Co. Highway 31. ℹ Haleakalā
National Park, (808) 248-7375.
🌐 nps.gov/hale

Reached on the winding Hāna
Highway, in the Kīpahulu
District of Haleakalā National
Park (see pp132–3), is 'Ohe'o
Gulch, popularly but incorrectly
called The Seven Sacred Pools.
In Hawai'i, all water is considered
sacred and there are many
more than seven pools here,
all formed by the waterfalls
rushing seaward from the
top of Haleakalā.

About 10 miles (16 km) past
Hāna, you will drive over a small
concrete bridge that spans the
pools. A few curves after the
bridge is a parking lot on your
left, which is the site of the
ranger station. An admission fee
($10 per car) is charged. There
are restrooms, but no food, gas,
or drinking water are available.

This lush, tropical area is great
for hiking, swimming, and
camping. The pools below the
road are easy to reach along the
short Kuloa Point Loop Trail that
begins in the parking area. More
adventurous visitors can search
out the upper pools along the
Waimoku Falls Trail. This trail
begins across the road from the
ranger station, climbs through
a meadow and winds along the
stream through the rainforest.
After ascending for a while, it
passes the magnificent Falls
at Makahiku, an 181-ft (55-m)
waterfall, where you can stop

for a breathtaking view
down the cascading
falls and pools to the
ocean. Continuing for
another 2 miles (3 km),
beyond a fantastic
bamboo forest, the trail
ends at a shallow pool
at the base of Waimoku
Falls, which spill 400 ft
(120 m) over the high
cliff ledge. It is possible
to swim or wade in the
refreshing water here.
Always be alert to the
weather as flash
flooding is common
throughout this area.

A mile (1.5 km)
past 'Ohe'o Gulch, on
the ocean side of the road,
stands the small, white **Palapala
Ho'omau Congregational
Church**, built in 1857. It is the
final resting place of the famed
American aviator Charles
Lindbergh (1902–74), the
first person to fly a plane
solo across the Atlantic. He
spent his last days in peaceful
Hāna. Next to the cemetery is
**Kīpahulu Lighthouse Point
County Park**, perched on the
edge of the cliff. There are
shaded picnic tables here.

㉕ Kaupo

Maui Co. 8 miles (13 km) past 'Ohe'o
Gulch on Highway 31. ℹ Maui VB,
(808) 244-3530.

From 'Ohe'o Gulch, the Hāna
Highway winds in and out of
valleys with steep rock walls
and on blind curves hugging
the ocean cliffs, to arrive at
Kaupo. Kaupo means "Landing
at Night" and could refer to
travelers from other islands,

who arrived by canoe at night.
Established in the mid-1920s,
the quaint **Kaupo Store** was the
last of the Soon family stores.
These were set up by the son of
an indentured Chinese laborer,
Nick Soon, who also built the
first electric generator in the
area. The store sells cold
beverages and local snacks
like marlin jerky and shave ice.
Opening times are erratic but if
it is closed, stop and peruse the
bulletin board by the door,
which is plastered with business
cards from all over the world.

Before the first Europeans
arrived on Maui, thousands
of people lived in the villages
along this coast, sustaining
themselves through farming
the fertile land and fishing
in the bountiful sea. The
missionary churches that still
stand here, such as **St. Joseph's
Church** (built in 1862), give
a clue to the large Hawaiian
population they once served.
Built in 1859, **Huialoha Church**
fell into disrepair during the last
century. However, volunteers
worked to renovate the building
and it was reopened in 1978,
adding extra meaning to its
name Huialoha, "meeting
of compassion".

From Kaupo, the landscape
turns into dry desert as this
area is in the lee of Haleakalā
and gets little rain. The impressive **Kaupo Gap** is visible
from the road. It was created
when an erupting Haleakalā
blew away a large section of
the mountain's rim.

Eventually, the highway
leads to the verdant uplands
of 'Ulupalakua (see p125),
offering spectacular scenery
and serenity.

Spectacular scenery surrounding Huialoha Church, Kaupo

Beaches of South Maui

From the small harbor town of Māʻalaea to the solidified lava flows of La Pérouse Bay, South Maui's leeward coast is a playground for activities in, on, and near the water. Haleakalā's towering bulk shelters the region from trade winds and rain, while the proximity of neighboring islands and shallow waters create generally mild ocean conditions. All the beaches on Maui are public, and these along South Maui's leeward coast are particularly fine for swimming, snorkeling, scuba diving, and kayaking.

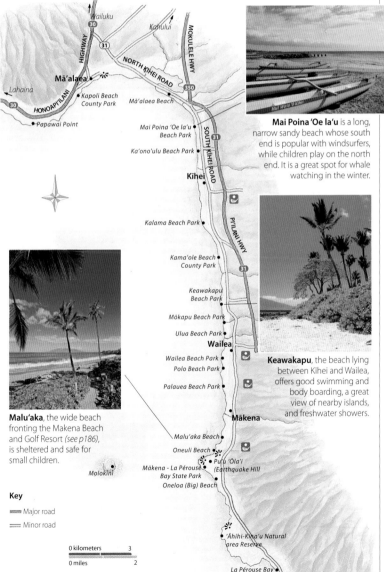

Mai Poina ʻOe laʻu is a long, narrow sandy beach whose south end is popular with windsurfers, while children play on the north end. It is a great spot for whale watching in the winter.

Keawakapu, the beach lying between Kīhei and Wailea, offers good swimming and body boarding, a great view of nearby islands, and freshwater showers.

Maluʻaka, the wide beach fronting the Makena Beach and Golf Resort *(see p186)*, is sheltered and safe for small children.

Key

▬▬▬ Major road

══ Minor road

0 kilometers   3

0 miles   2

㉖ Haleakalā National Park

The land mass of East Maui is really the top of an enormous shield volcano that begins more than 3 miles (5 km) below sea level. Haleakalā ("House of the Sun") is thought to have last erupted some 200 years ago and is still considered to be active, although not currently erupting. Its summit depression is 7.5 miles (12 km) long and 2.5 miles (4 km) wide, formed by erosional forces acting on volcanic rock. This natural wonder is preserved as part of the national park, which includes Kīpahulu valley and 'Ohe'o Gulch on the coast (*see p130*). In under two hours, motorists drive from sea level to the 10,023-ft (3,055-m) summit, rising from one ecosystem to the next while temperature and oxygen levels fall dramatically.

Makawao

★ Pu'u'ula'ula Summit
Standing on Pu'u'ula'ula (Red Hill) is a breathtaking experience because of both the altitude – this is the highest point on Maui – and the view of the entire volcano. A glassed-in shelter provides relief from the bitterly cold winds.

Haleakalā Observatories
This off-limits, science fiction-style cluster of research stations is set in the summit's lunar landscape. Data from here help scientists map movements of the Earth's crust.

Visitor center

HALEAKALĀ CRATER ROAD

KEY

① **Park headquarters**

② **Hosmer Grove**, campground has an easy, informative nature hike.

③ **At Leleiwi Overlook**, it may be possible to see your shadow on the clouds in the valley below, encircled by a rainbow.

④ **Hōlua Cabin**

⑤ **Pele's Paint Pot**, is a surreal landscape of brightly colored ashes.

⑥ **Palikū Cabin**

0 kilometers 2
0 miles 1

Summit Depression
At one time, Haleakalā was much higher than it is now. Water eroded the peak, formed the basin you see today, and drained away through two huge gaps in the rim. Later volcanic activity filled in the valley floor and created the cinder cones.

Halemau'u Trail
This trail incorporates switchbacks and sharp drops, plus fine views, often to the ocean. The hike from the trailhead on Haleakalā Crater Road to Hōlua Cabin and back is a good but tough day trip.

★ Silversword Loop
The Haleakalā Silversword, one of the world's rarest plants, thrives here under the most hostile conditions the volcano can offer: hot days, cold nights, and porous ash soil. The soft silvery hairs on its incurved leaves protect the plant from sunlight and draft. It takes up to 50 years to flower, when it raises a spectacular spike of purplish flowers.

Ko'olau Gap

HALEMAU'U TRAIL

⑤

TRAIL

SLIDING SANDS TRAIL

NG SANDS TRAIL

⑥

KAUPŌ TRAIL

Kaupō Gap

Key
═══ Minor road

▪ ▪ Hiking trail

★ Sliding Sands Trail
The only way to really appreciate the scale and varied terrain here is to descend 3,000 ft (900 m) into the volcano. The 10-mile (16-km) Sliding Sands Trail takes you from the visitor center through scenery that ranges from a barren cinder desert to an alpine shrubland.

Kapalaoa Cabin
One of three primitive cabins in the volcano – so popular that you must reserve well in advance.

For keys to symbols *see back flap*

HAWAI'I ISLAND

To understand fully the culture and spirit of the Hawaiian islands, travelers must venture to the island of Hawai'i itself – commonly called "the Big Island." This is the site of some of the earliest Polynesian settlements as well as the last heiau (temple) to be built. Here, Captain Cook met his demise, Kamehameha the Great rose to power, and the first Christian missionaries set foot on Hawaiian soil.

Being a relatively young island (a million years old, compared with Kaua'i's five million) not yet ringed with sandy beaches, Hawai'i has wisely placed its tourist-industry focus on the preservation of cultural sites. An amazing number of these are accessible to the traveler.

Spreading over 4,035 sq miles (10,450 sq km), Hawai'i Island is more than twice the size of all the other islands combined. Its bulk includes the earth's most massive mountain, Mauna Loa, which rises over 30,000 feet (9,150 m) from its base on the sea floor and is still growing. It also includes the state's tallest peak, the often snow-capped Mauna Kea, and three other mountains: Hualālai, which blocks the moist trade winds from dry north Kona; Kohala, the soft hump of the Waimea area's northern ranch lands;

and Kīlauea, the most active volcano on earth. A new mountain called Lō'ihi, currently forming 20 miles (32 km) off the southeast coast, should emerge from the sea thousands of years from now. Hawai'i Island's great bulk offers travelers the chance to see a variety of ecosystems, from alpine heights to barren desert.

Today, with only ten percent of the state's population, the Big Island is one of Hawai'i's sleepiest, most scattered communities. Hilo, its main town, was pushed into the economic background by devastating tsunamis in 1946 and 1960, and in the 1990s, the island's sugar industry collapsed. Now tourism plays a big role, especially in sunny Kona. Visitors will find a land of open space, quiet towns, and a population that is friendly in the traditional Hawaiian way.

Paniolo (Hawaiian cowboys) at the Parker Ranch in the Waimea area

◄ Carved, wooden Ki'i stand in the Pu'uhonua O Hōnuaunau National Historical Park

Exploring Hawai'i Island

Both East and West Hawai'i Island provide good bases for touring. Hilo is well situated for excursions to the Hāmākua Coast, Mauna Kea, the Puna district, and Hawai'i Volcanoes National Park – a highlight on any visitor's itinerary, with Kīlauea Caldera and its active lava rifts. Hilo itself is charming but very rainy, averaging 130 in (330 cm) per year. Travelers who prefer their days bone dry head for Kailua-Kona on the island's burgeoning west side. From here there is access to the South Kohala resorts to the north, the Parker Ranch country of Waimea, Kona coffee country to the south, and many well-preserved ancient sites, including Pu'uhonua O Hōnaunau.

Traditional canoe at Pu'uhonua O Hōnaunau National Historical Park

Top Recreational Areas

The places shown here have been selected for their recreational activities. Conditions, especially those of the ocean, vary depending on the weather and the time of year, so exercise caution and, if in doubt, stay out of the water or seek local advice.

	Swimming	Snorkeling	Diving	Body-Surfing	Windsurfing	Hiking	Horseback Riding	Golf
Ahalanui Beach Park	●							
'Anaeho'omalu Bay	●	●	●	●	●			
Hāpuna Bay	●	●	●	●				●
Hawai'i Volcanoes National Park						●		
Hilo	●	●	●	●			●	●
Honoka'a								●
Ho'okena	●	●						
Ka Lae						●		
Kahalu'u Beach County Park	●	●	●					
Kailua-Kona	●	●	●	●			●	●
Kalōpā State Recreation Area						●		
Kapa'au						●		
Kawaihae Harbor				●				
Kealakekua Bay	●	●	●				●	
Kekaha Kai State Park	●	●	●			●		
Kolekole Beach County Park	●							
Lapakahi State Historical Park	●	●						
Mauna Kea						●	●	
Mauna Lani	●	●		●			●	●
Pāhala								●
Pepe'ekeo Scenic Drive						●		
Puakō		●						
Punalu'u Beach County Park	●	●	●					
Pu'uhonua O Hōnaunau	●	●						
Spencer Beach County Park	●	●	●	●				
Volcano Village								●
Waikoloa							●	●
Waimea							●	
Waipi'o Valley	●					●	●	

Mo'ok... Heiau
HĀWĪ 13
KAPA'A
LAPAKAHI STATE HISTORICAL PARK 12
250
KOHALA MOUNTAIN ROAD
270
Kawaihae
PU'UKOHOLĀ HEIAU NATIONAL HISTORIC SITE 11
HĀPUNA BAY 10
MAUNA LANI 8
WAIKOLOA COAST 7
Wai... Vil...
Kīlolo Bay
19 190
Makalawena
KEKAHA KAI STATE PARK 6
Huaiā 8,271...
Honokōhau
180
KAILUA-KONA 1
Kailua Bay
HŌLUALOA 2
Keauhou
Honalo
Kealakekua
Captain C...
KEALAKEKUA BAY 3
PU'UHONUA O HŌNAUNAU NATIONAL HISTORICAL PARK 5
HO'OK... 4
Kauhakō Bay
11
Miloli'i
Hawaii O... View Es...

0 kilometers 25
0 miles 20

For hotels and restaurants see pp186–7 and pp202–4

Key

— Major road
=== Minor road
--- Track
— Scenic route
△ Summit

Sights at a Glance

1. Kailua-Kona
2. Hōlualoa
3. Kealakekua Bay
4. Ho'okena
5. *Pu'uhonua O Hōnaunau National Historical Park pp142–3*
6. Kekaha Kai State Park
7. Waikoloa Coast
8. Mauna Lani
9. Waimea
10. Hāpuna Bay
11. Pu'ukoholā Heiau National Historic Site
12. Lapakahi State Historical Park
13. Hāwī
14. Kapa'au
15. Kohala Mountain Road
16. Waipi'o Valley
17. Honoka'a
18. Hāmākua Coast
19. World Botanical Gardens
20. Saddle Road
21. Mauna Kea
22. 'Akaka Falls State Park
23. Pepe'ekeo Scenic Drive
24. Mauna Loa
25. *Hilo pp152–3*
26. Pāhoa
27. Kapoho
28. Puna Lava Flows
29. Volcano Village
30. Ka'ū District
31. Ka Lae
32. *Hawai'i Volcanoes National Park pp156–9*

Ka Lae, the southernmost point in the United States

Getting Around

Travelers can fly into Hilo International Airport or Kona International Airport, north of Kailua-Kona. From there, a rented car is essential as bus services are minimal. The island is encircled by the Hawai'i Belt Road. Its northern stretch (Hwy 19 and continuing on Hwy 190) crosses from Hilo via Waimea to Kailua-Kona, taking about two hours. The southern route (Hwy 11) crosses the Ka'ū district in around three hours. Saddle Road, a shorter middle route passing between Mauna Kea and Mauna Loa, has narrow stretches that make progress slow. Lava flows have split Highway 130 into two sections: an eastern route into the Puna area, and Chain of Craters Road, which offers a close-up view of Kīlauea's eruptions.

For keys to symbols *see back flap*

Aerial view of the coastline south of Kailua-Kona

❶ Kailua-Kona

Hawai'i Co. 🏔 33,000. ✈ 🚌 ℹ Big
Island VB, (808) 961-5797. 🏃 Ironman
Triathlon (Oct: Sat closest to full moon).

Referred to locally as "Kona",
this town is the center of the
island's "Gold Coast". Within a
two-block span along oceanfront Ali'i Drive are sites that
played a role in some of the
most important moments
in Hawai'i's history, from the
unification of the islands to
the advent of Christianity.
Kailua-Kona's tourist strip does
little to obscure these vivid
reminders of Hawaiian history.

Built out into Kailua Bay is
Ahu'ena Heiau, an ancient
temple dedicated to the
god Lono. It was restored
by Kamehameha the Great,
whose residence was next
to the temple. Adjoining it is
**King Kamehameha Kona
Beach Hotel** (see p186) – the
lobby has Hawaiian artifacts:
tools, handicrafts, and
a feather cape.

Idyllic Kahalu'u Beach

In 1820, the first party of
missionaries landed at Kailua-
Kona. They built the original
Moku'aikaua Church on Ali'i
Drive. The present lofty, granite
church dates from 1837. A
modest museum at the rear
offers a scale model of the
missionaries' brig, *Thaddeus*.
Across the street, **Hulihe'e
Palace** was built at the same
time of similar rough-stone
construction. In 1885, King
Kalākaua beautified
the little building,
which now serves
as a museum. It takes
a candid look at the
lifestyle of the mon-
archy in its heyday.

Kailua-Kona, so
named to distinguish
it from Kailua on
O'ahu, is synonymous
with sportfishing.
Charter boats
offer year-round
opportunities to fish
for marlin and other ocean
giants. In October, the town
is overrun by endurance
athletes who compete in
the grueling Ironman Triathlon.
The sunny coastline is dotted
with small beaches good for
swimming, snorkeling, and
diving. **Kahalu'u Beach**, 4.5
miles (7 km) south of Kailua,
provides snorkelers with the
island's finest natural aquarium.

🏛 **Moku'aikaua Church**
75-5713 Ali'i Dr. **Tel** (808) 329-0655.
Open daily. ♿

🏛 **Hulihe'e Palace**
75-5718 Ali'i Dr. **Tel** (808) 329-
1877. **Open** 10am–3pm Tue–Sat.
Closed public hols. 📷

Kona Coffee Cultural
Festival poster

❷ Hōlualoa

Hawai'i Co. 🏔 6,100. ℹ Big Island VB,
West Hawai'i, (808) 885-1655.
🎨 Kona Coffee Cultural Festival
(2nd week of Nov).

A 15-minute drive up the
winding and scenic Hualalai
Road from Highway 19, on the
slopes of Mount Hualalai, lies
Hōlualoa. Set in the heart of
the Kona coffee belt, coffee is
its main focus, as attested by
the annual Kona Coffee Cultural
Festival. Artists also add their
flavor to the town.

Long before tourism took hold,
many immigrants settled here to
work on the coffee plantations
and vegetable farms and
Hōlualoa was a thriving town
full of hotels, restaurants, and
general stores to provide for their
needs. Some of these stores still
operate today. **Kimura Lauhala
Shop** began as a general store in
1915, but became famous for its
lauhala hats woven from the
leaves of the pandanus tree.

The Kimura family
still runs the store.
Hōlualoa's main street
is lined with galleries
that present works
by many of the
island's most well
known artists.
Studio 7 showcases
the creations of
Hiroki and Setsuko
Morinoue. He is
known for his large
watercolors and
woodblock prints;
she is a ceramist. The studio also
displays works by other artists,
including turned bowls, wooden
bracelets, and silk-screen prints.
The pottery and paintings of
Matthew and Mary Lovein are on
show at their **Hōlualoa Gallery**,
along with jewelry, sculptures,
and glass works by other artists.

🏛 **Kimura Lauhala Shop**
Mamalahoa Highway and Hualalai
Road. **Tel** (808) 324-0053.

🏛 **Studio 7**
76-5920 Mamalahoa Highway.
Tel (808) 324-1335.

🏛 **Hōlualoa Gallery**
76-5921 Mamalahoa Highway.
Tel (808) 322-8484.

Kona Coffee

For over a century, the upward slopes of the Kona district have been home to the most prolific coffee-growing region in the United States'. The massive bulk of Mauna Loa, an enormous shield volcano *(see p151)*, creates a localized weather pattern that favors the crop. Sunny mornings are followed by cloudy, humid afternoons that often drench the rich, volcanic soil with rain. Over 500 independent small farms cultivate this world-class, gourmet coffee, producing a crop of about 2 million pounds (900,000 kg) a year. Roadsides are dotted with cafés, mills, and farms, and the Hawai'i Visitors and Convention Bureau in Kailua-Kona offers a driving map of the area. Every year, in the second week of November, the district celebrates its coffee with the Kona Coffee Cultural Festival.

How Coffee is Harvested

Coffee beans grown in the rich soil of the Kona district are picked by hand, ensuring only the best beans go into making coffee.

"Kona snow" is the local term for the white, fragrant spring flowers. The first Coffea arabica plants were introduced to the area in 1828 by the American missionary Samuel Ruggles.

Coffee cherries ripen in waves, from August until March, so they must be laboriously hand-harvested. The cherries start out green in color and turn red as they ripen.

A kuriba (pulping mill) separates the flesh of the cherry from its hard, parchment-covered bean. After soaking and washing, beans in the "wet parchment" stage are left to dry in the sun.

A hoshidana is a drying deck with a wheeled cover that is rolled over the beans whenever the mountain rains move in. Beans are raked three or four times a day for up to two weeks.

Milling removes two outer layers from the hard beans - the tough parchment and the filmy "silver skin." Raw beans, called green coffee, are then graded and ready for roasting.

Immigrant Workers

The success of Kona's coffee owes as much to its people as to its weather. In the late 19th century, after decades of control by the large plantations, the crop began to be cultivated tenaciously on small-scale family farms. Many of these farmers were Japanese immigrants who fled slavelike conditions on the plantations to work their own farms. Today, their descendents continue the coffee tradition.

Kona coffee beans are known throughout the gourmet coffee world for their rich, highly aromatic flavor. The roasting process brings out the flavor: beans that are roasted longer and at higher temperatures are darker with a more intense taste. Additional flavorings, such as chocolate or macadamia nuts, may be added immediately after roasting.

Roasted coffee beans

The colorful interior of St. Benedict's Painted Church in Hōnaunau

❸ Kealakekua Bay

Hawai'i Co. Nāpō'opo'o Rd,
4 miles (6 km) S of Captain Cook.
🚌 Captain Cook. ℹ️ Big Island VB,
(808) 961-5797.

In 1778, Captain Cook sailed
into this deep, protected bay,
"discovering" Hawai'i. He was
honored as the returning
Hawaiian god Lono, but less
than a month later was killed
here (see p45). Hikiau Heiau,
where Cook was honored, is at
the road's end. A monument
marks where he died.
    The bay, a State Marine Life
Preserve with an abundance of
fish, sea turtles, and spinner
dolphins, offers excellent diving,
snorkeling, and kayaking.

Environs
The bay sits at the heart of Kona
coffee country, with its rustic
farms and mills. In the town of
Kealakekua, the **Kona Historical
Society** gives interpretive tours
of its headquarters in the 1870s-
vintage Greenwell Store and
of neighboring Uchida Farm,
a restored 1930s coffee farm.
The entire district invites
exploration, from Hōnaunau
in the south up to Hōlualoa
(see p138) in the north. In
Hōnaunau, **St. Benedict's
Painted Church** is brightly
illuminated with biblical scenes
executed by a Belgian priest
in the early 20th century.

🏛 **Kona Historical Society**
81-6551 Māmalahoa Highway (Hwy 11).
Tel (808) 323-3222. **Open** 9am–3pm
Mon–Fri. **Closed** public hols.
🎫 donation requested. ♿

🔼 **St. Benedict's Painted Church**
Painted Church Rd, off Highway 160
near mile marker 1. **Tel** (808) 328-2227.
Open daily. ♿

❹ Ho'okena

Hawai'i Co. ℹ️ Big Island VB, West
Hawai'i, (808) 885-1655.

In 1889, when author Robert
Louis Stevenson
asked to see a classic
Hawaiian village,
King Kalākaua sent
him to Ho'okena. In
those days, the town
could boast
churches, a school, a
court-house, and a
pier from which
cattle were shipped
to market in
Honolulu. Today,
besides weather-
beaten houses and
beach shacks, only lava walls and
the ruined pier survive as reminders of its more prosperous past.

Ho'okena's Kauhakō Bay, which is
lined with a beach of gray sand

The center of life, then as
now, is beautiful **Kauhakō Bay**,
with its gray-sand beach backed
dramatically by long cliffs. The
water teems with sea life, and
there is excellent snorkeling
and diving. However, the surf
can be rough, and wearing foot
protection is recommended.

❺ Pu'uhonoua O Hōnaunau National Historic Park

See pp142–3.

❻ Kekaha Kai State Park

Hawai'i Co. Off Queen Ka'ahumanu
Highway (Hwy 19), 9 miles (14 km)
N of Kailua-Kona. **Tel** Division of State
Parks, (808) 961-9540. **Open** Thu–Tue.

North of Kailua, the road runs
through barren lava fields, the
aftermath of an 1801 eruption
of Mount Hualālai.
In places, road and
landscape are
distinguishable
only by their
relative smooth-
ness. The state
park, with its
picnic shelters and
sinuous beach of
salt-and-pepper
sand, is an oasis in
this distorted
wasteland. It is an
excellent spot for
swimming, snorkeling, diving,
and, when the conditions are
right, surfing.

Green sea turtle swimming in the waters off the beach at Makalawena

Just before the park entrance, a dirt road on the right leads 1.5 miles (2.5 km) to isolated Makalawena, a beautiful beach with dunes and coves for snorkeling. Turtles, dolphins, and seals frequent these waters, as well as whales.

❼ Waikoloa Coast

Hawai'i Co. W of Queen Ka'ahumanu Highway (Hwy 19), 24 miles (39 km) N of Kailua-Kona. 🛈 Kohala Coast Resort Association, (808) 885-6414.

Waikoloa Beach Resort has built itself around one of this coast's best family recreational areas, coconut-rimmed 'Anaeho'omalu Bay. The beach at "A-Bay" is calm, with a gradual, sandy bottom. Water sports equipment, including kayaks and sailboats, can be rented from the beach hut, and lessons in windsurfing and scuba diving are offered. Boat dives and cruises are also available. From the beach, coastal trails lead to fish ponds, caves, and natural pools in which salt and fresh water mix to form unique ecosystems. A short walk north of the beach is Hilton Waikoloa Village Resort, a 62-acre fantasy resort built in 1988 at a cost of $360 million. Silent monorails and canal boats provide transportation around the resort. Visitors can view the impressive art collection and explore the artificial beach, lagoon, and waterfall. At the dolphin pool, both guests and visitors can swim with the resort's trained dolphins. Also within the resort, the Waikoloa Beach Marriott Resort (see p186) fronts ancient fishponds along A-Bay and is a short walk from a restored heiau (temple).

Hilton Waikoloa Village Resort
69-425 Waikoloa Beach Dr.
Tel (808) 886-1234. **Open** daily. 🚻
🆆 hiltonwaikoloavillage.com

Vacationers enjoying the lagoon at Hilton Waikoloa Village Resort

❽ Mauna Lani

68–1400 Mauna Lani Dr. **Tel** (808) 885-6622. **Open** daily. 🚻
🆆 maunalani.com

The vast resort at Mauna Lani includes two luxury hotels, a couple of award-winning golf courses, several tennis courts, and small, white-sand beaches. It also encloses sites of cultural importance. **Kalāhuipua'a Trail** – a 20-minute hike, usually through blazing sunshine – winds past petroglyphs, lava tubes, and ancient habitation sites, ending at several ancient fish ponds. A coastal trail from here leads about a mile (1.5 km) south to **Honoka'ope Bay**, a sheltered swimming and snorkeling spot.

Petroglyph figure

At the northern end of the resort, a shorter shady trail leads to the **Puakō Petroglyphs**. These are an expanse of crusty red lava plates that were engraved with more than 3,000 symbols between AD 1000 and 1800. Wear sturdy shoes.

❾ Waimea

Hawai'i Co. 🏠 9,200. ✈ 🚌
🛈 Waimea Visitor Center, Main St, (808) 885-6707. 🎪 Parker Ranch Rodeo (Jul 4).

Waimea's setting amid sprawling pasture land at a cool elevation of 2,700 ft (820 m) is a startling contrast to Hilo's rainforest and the Kona Coast's lava flats. By Hawai'i Island standards, Waimea is a large, modern town. On the edge of town is the **Keck Observatory Center**, with the world's most powerful telescopes (see p151).

In the middle of town, the **Parker Ranch Visitor Center** offers a short video and an eloquent collection of artifacts that tells the history of *paniolo* (cowboy) culture and provides an insight into the tempestuous and influential Parker family.

The **Historic Parker Ranch Homes** include Puopelu, a ranch house with a Regency interior and a respectable collection of European art, and Mānā Hale, the Parkers' original home, which has a display of family photographs.

🏛 Keck Observatory Center
65-1120 Māmalahoa Highway (Hwy 19). **Tel** (808) 961-2120.
Open 8am–4:30pm Mon–Fri.
Closed public hols. 🚻
🆆 keckobservatory.org

🏛 Parker Ranch Visitor Center
Parker Ranch Shopping Center, Māmalahoa Highway (Hwy 19).
Tel (808) 887-1046. **Open** 9am–5pm Mon–Sun. **Closed** public hols. 🚻

🏛 Historic Parker Ranch Homes
Off Māmalahoa Highway (Hwy 190).
Tel (808) 885-5433. **Open** 10am–5pm Mon–Sat. **Closed** Sun, public hols.
🚻 (partial access only.)
🆆 parkerranch.com

The façade of Puopelu, one of the Historic Parker Ranch Homes

❺ Pu'uhonua O Hōnaunau National Historical Park

From the 11th century on, social interactions were regulated by the *kapu* (taboo) system *(see p44)*. Violent death was the consequence of infractions, which ranged from stepping on a chief's shadow to women eating bananas. Lawbreakers could escape punishment, however, by reaching a *pu'uhonua* (place of refuge). The greatest of these was at Hōnaunau, a six-acre temple compound dating from the 16th century that offered absolution to all who managed to run or swim past the chief's warriors. The sanctuary was stripped of power in 1819, after the fall of the *kapu* system. Partially restored, it now provides a glimpse into precontact Hawai'i.

Heleipālala Fish Ponds
These two ponds were stocked with fish reserved for the royal table.

Hālau
Thatched A-frame structures were used for storage and as work sheds.

Papamū
This carved stone board was used to play *kōnane*, a Hawaiian game similar to checkers.

★ Hale O Keawe Heiau
The *pu'uhonua's* spiritual power resided in this temple compound, built in 1650. Now reconstructed, the *heiau* (temple) once held the bones and therefore the *mana* (sacred power) of great chiefs.

A Reconstruction

This is an artist's impression of the pu'uhonua when the ruling chief of the district lived here along with his court and attendants. Some elements have been reconstructed by the National Park Service, and visitors may see artisans at work.

Wooden Ki'i
These carved images of gods outside Hale O Keawe Heiau are copies based on drawings and descriptions of the originals.

A reconstructed sailing canoe with passengers

VISITORS' CHECKLIST

Practical Information
Hawai'i Co. Highway 160,
off Hawai'i Belt Rd (Hwy 11).
Tel (808) 3282326. **Open** 7am–
sunset. 🅿️ ♿ Visitor Center:
Open 8am–4:30pm.
Ⓦ nps.gov/puho

★ **The Great Wall**
This superb example of a dry-
stone wall, built around 1550,
separated the *pu'uhonua*
from the palace area
inland. It is 10 ft (3 m)
high and 17 ft
(5 m) wide.

⑤

⑦

| 0 meters | 50 |
| 0 yards | 50 |

KEY

① **Outrigger canoes**

② **Keone'ele Cove** was the royal canoe landing, making it *kapu* to all commoners.

③ **Animals in enclosure**

④ **Worker in a field**

⑤ **'Āle'ale'a Heiau** predates the 16th-century Great Wall. It served as the focus of spiritual power until the construction of Hale O Keawe.

⑥ **The Keōua Stone** was a favorite resting spot of Keōua, a high chief of Kona district.

⑦ **The old *heiau*** may have been built by the Tahitian priest Pā'ao in the 13th century *(see p44)*. It is now in ruins, destroyed by either tsunamis or large storm waves.

Exposed Peninsula of Black Lava
The peninsula's jagged shoreline made it difficult for
kapu-breakers to approach from the sea.

The popular white-sand beach at Hāpuna Bay, on Hawai'i Island's Kohala Coast

⑩ Hāpuna Bay

Hawai'i Co. Off Queen Ka'ahumanu Highway (Hwy 19), 7 miles (11 km) N of Waikoloa Coast.

An expanse of white sand, both broad and deep, makes Hāpuna Bay the most popular beach on Hawai'i Island. With its clean, sandy bottom, the bay offers excellent swimming, snorkeling, and diving conditions. When the waves are active, surfers and body-boarders flock here, and it is generally a good spot for beginners to acquire some wave-riding skills. The water should be approached with caution, however; strong currents have resulted in several drownings. On the beach, there are places to rent snorkel sets and boogie boards, and posts staffed by life guards throughout the day.

Hāpuna Beach State Recreation Area, which surrounds the beach, provides cabins for overnight stays, as well as a snack bar and picnic tables at which visitors can enjoy their own food.

About 1 mile (1.5 km) north of the bay, accessed via the Mauna Kea Beach Hotel (see p187), is the lovely, crescent-shaped **Kauna'oa Beach**, with fine conditions for swimming and snorkeling most of the year. One of the most photographed beaches on the island, this stretch of sand was once the playground of *ali'i* (Hawaiian royalty).

🗺 Hāpuna Beach State Recreation Area
Around Hāpuna Beach. **Tel** Division of State Parks, (808) 882-6206. **Open** daily.

⑪ Pu'ukoholā Heiau National Historic Site

Hawai'i Co. Off Akoni Pule Highway (Hwy 270), 1 mile (1.5 km) S of Kawaihae. **Tel** (808) 882-7218. **Open** 7:30am–4pm daily. 🚻 visitor center only. 🆆 nps.gov/puhe

In 1790, Kamehameha I had reached an impasse in his drive to unify the island chain. On the advice of an oracle, he undertook the construction of **Pu'ukoholā Heiau**, dedicated to Kūkā'ilimoku, his family war god, which was destined to become the last such temple ever built. For the dedication ceremonies, the crafty king invited his rival Keoua, the chief of Ka'ū. As Keoua stepped out of

his canoe, he was slaughtered and carried to the new altar to serve as its first sacrifice.

Today, the massive monument stands undamaged on a hilltop overlooking Kawaihae Bay. Below it are the ruins of **Mailekini Heiau**, built for Kamehameha's ancestors. A third *heiau*, **Haleokapuni**, dedicated to shark gods, is believed to lie submerged in the waters below. Sacrifices left here would soon have become shark fodder. An easy trail runs down past the first two *heiau* from the visitor center.

Immediately south of the *heiau* is **Spencer Beach County Park**, a popular spot for camping, snorkeling, and diving. The clean beach and calm waters make it a great area for children. Operated by the National Park Service, it includes a visitor center where park rangers provide information and you can pick up a map of points of interest.

Traditional ceremony at Pu'ukoholā Heiau National Historic Site

⑫ Lapakahi State Historical Park

Hawai'i Co. Off Akoni Pule Highway (Hwy 270), 12 miles (19 km) N of Kawaihae. **Tel** (808) 961-9540. **Open** daily. **Closed** public hols.

The ruins of this large settlement provide a glimpse into the daily life of an old Hawaiian fishing village. Established in the 14th century, the village was inhabited for 500 years – until a falling water table and changing economic conditions caused the natives to abandon their homes.

Some thatched walls and roofs are gone; others have been restored to their original appearance. The lava foundations, *hālau* (canoe sheds), *kū'ula ko'a* (fishing shrines), and a *kōnane* stone board-game remain undamaged.

⑬ Hāwī

Hawai'i Co. ⛰ 950. 🛈 Big Island Visitors Bureau, (808) 961-5797.

The town of Hāwī had its heyday during the era of "King Cane," when five sugar plantations brought prosperity to Kohala, the island's northern district. After the mills closed in 1975, Hāwī was left to dwindle to its present size.

A traditional *hale* (grass hut) at Mo'okini Heiau

These days it is a pleasant town to wander through, with its wooden sidewalks and brightly painted storefronts. Hāwī's grassy, windswept surroundings and relaxed charm now attract

Restored thatched dwelling, Lapakahi State Historical Park

a new breed of citizen – the town currently offers a health-food store and a handful of trendy eateries.

Environs

Reached by a rutted dirt road, lichen-covered **Mo'okini Heiau** is one of the oldest temples on the islands, possibly dating from the 5th century AD. In 1250, it was re-dedicated as a *luakini heiau* (for human sacrifice). Legend says the temple was built in one night using stones that were passed hand to hand by a human chain of 18,000 men from Pololu Valley 14 miles (23 km) away. In 1963, Mo'okini Heiau was the first Hawaiian site to be listed in the National Historical Site Registry. Today, visitors to this massive *heiau* will discover a remote and peaceful ruin.

🏠 Mo'okini Heiau

Off Akoni Pule Highway (Hwy 270) at mile marker 20, then left at airfield.

⑭ Kapa'au

Hawai'i Co. ⛰ 1,300. 🛈 Big Island Visitors Bureau, (808) 961-5797.

The small town of Kapa'au contains the original statue of Kamehameha the Great, a much-photographed replica of which stands in front of Ali'iōlani Hale in Honolulu (*see p58*). King Kalakaua commissioned the bronze sculpture in 1878. Cast in Paris, France, the statue was thought lost when the ship carrying it to Hawai'i sank. A new statue was commissioned and cast and this is the one that now stands in Honolulu. However, the original statue was found and arrived in the islands a few weeks after the first was installed on O'ahu. So it was brought to Kapa'au, historically known as the birthplace of Kamehameha I. A large boulder labeled **Kamehameha Rock** can be found on the roadside heading east of town. Legend has it that the big chief once carried it to prove his strength; whole road crews have failed to move it since! Nearby, the intricately painted **Tong Wo Society** building is the last of its kind on Hawai'i Island. Immigrant Chinese communities once relied on clubs like this to provide social cohesion.

Environs

At the end of Highway 270, a lookout focuses the gaze on idyllic **Pololū Valley**. Isolated by lush canyon walls, the valley's wide floor meets the ocean at a black-sand beach. It is a 20-minute walk down the steep trail to the beach.

Kapa'au's Tong Wo Society building, part of Hawai'i's immigrant heritage

Some of the dramatically varied terrain along Kohala Mountain Road

⑮ Kohala Mountain Road

Hawai'i Co. Highway 250. ℹ️ BIVB, East Hawai'i, (808) 961-5797.

The 20-mile (32-km) drive from Hāwī to Waimea follows the western ridge of low, worn Kohala Mountain. It is a beautiful, cool and breezy drive. This narrow, twisting, tree-lined road provides breathtaking vistas and constantly changing scenery. The landscapes range from lush green hills and rolling pastures to black lava rock and distant beaches. A good place to stop and enjoy the dramatic panoramic views of the entire North Kohala coastline is at the Kohala Mountain Road lookout, which gives a sense of the awesome size of Hawai'i island. This is ranch land, and the scenic drive gives views of elegant ranch houses, cattle and horses grazing in deep grass, and occasional vistas of the north Kohala Coast.

Parker Ranch is the largest operation in this area, and, in fact, the largest privately owned cattle ranch in the United States. Its origins date right back to the early years of Western discovery and a young American adventurer named John Palmer Parker. In 1809, Parker befriended Kamehameha I and eventually married one of the king's granddaughters. He established a small dynasty that shaped the history of the Kohala district. Today, the ranch covers a tenth of the island and supports 35,000 head of cattle.

⑯ Waipi'o Valley

Hawai'i Co. ℹ️ Big Island Visitors Bureau, (808) 961-5797.

If any particular spot could be designated the spiritual heartland of ancient Hawai'i, it would have to be Waipi'o, or the "Valley of the Kings." The largest of seven enormous amphitheater valleys that punctuate this windward stretch of coast, Waipi'o measures 1 mile (1.5 km) wide at the sea and extends nearly 6 miles (10 km) inland. Its steep walls, laced with waterfalls, including the stupendous Hi'ilawe cascade, rise as high as 2,000 ft (600 m). Waipi'o Stream slices the lush valley floor, courses through fertile taro fields, and empties into the rough sea across a wide black-sand beach.

The road from the stunning lookout at the end of Highway 240 down to the valley floor is only a mile (1.5 km) long, but its steepness limits access to four-wheel-drive vehicles; on foot, the trip takes about 30 minutes. Shuttle tours, even one in a mule-drawn surrey, are available at the tiny village of Kukuihaele, and nearby stables offer horseback trips.

In precontact days, Waipi'o supported a population of over 10,000. A sacred place, the valley contained important *heiau*, including a *pu'uhonua* (place of refuge) equal to that at Hōnaunau *(see pp142–3)*. The valley was Kamehameha the Great's boyhood playground. It was here that he received the sponsorship of his terrifying war god Kūkā'ilimoku, and that he defeated his cousin and rival Keoua. Today, Waipi'o's few inhabitants cultivate taro, lotus, avocado, breadfruit, and citrus, and earnestly protect Hawai'i's ancient spirit.

Isolated Waipi'o Valley, historically a sacred site and now a favorite of hikers and nature lovers

⓱ Honoka'a

Hawai'i Co. ⬚ 🏔 3,400. ℹ️ Big Island VB, East Hawai'i, (808) 961-5797.

A 15-mile (24-km) drive from Waipi'o Valley, this quaint rural town is actually one of the largest on the Hāmākua Coast. It has one hotel, bed and breakfast accommodations, shops, boutiques, and restaurants. The town also boasts art galleries, antique stores, a macadamia nut factory, a movie theater, and a nine-hole golf course.

This small community is home to the **Honoka'a People's Theater**. Built in 1930 on the town's main thoroughfare, Mamane Street, the renovated theater now shows movies on a big screen and also hosts the Hawai'i Inter-national Film Festival *(see p214)* and the **Hāmākua Music Festival**. Held each fall, the music festival features renowned Jazz, Classical, and Hawaiian folk musicians such as Eric Marienthal, Gene Harris, Ray Brown, and Kenny Burrell.

🎵 **Hāmākua Music Festival**
PO Box 1757, Honoka'a. **Tel** (808) 775-3378. W hamakuamusicfestival.com

Honoka'a People's Theater
Mamane St, Honoka'a.
Tel (808) 775-0000.
W honokaapeople.com

⓲ Hāmākua Coast

Hawai'i Co. (Hwy 19), Waipi'o Valley to Hilo. ⬚ Honoka'a, Laupāhoehoe, Honomū, and Pepe'ekeo. ℹ️ BIVB, East Hawai'i, (808) 961-5797.

The verdant cliffs lining the island's windward coast are stunning company on the drive along the Hawai'i Belt Road (Hwy 19). With dozens of side roads begging investigation, you can easily spend a day traveling the 55 miles (89 km) between Waimea and Hilo.

This stretch has been designated the Hilo-Hāmākua Heritage Coast due to the area's historic and cultural significance. Look out for brown-and-white signs on the Hawai'i Belt Road as these indicate specific points of interest situated along the way.

High in the hills south of Honoka'a is **Kalōpā State Recreation Area**. This has a native forest nature trail and a small arboretum of Hawaiian and introduced plants. Twelve miles (19 km) farther on is Laupāhoehoe Point, a lush lava outcrop that juts into the pounding sea, providing stupendous views along the coast. A sizable village once existed here but was destroyed by the 1946 tsunami *(see p153)*.

At **Kolekole Beach County Park**, south of mile marker 15, a delightful stream tumbles into the ocean, making this a popular picnic and swimming spot.

🏕 **Kalōpā State Recreation Area**
Off Hawai'i Belt Rd (Hwy 19), 2 miles (3 km) S of Honoka'a. **Tel** (808) 961-9540. **Open** daily. ⛺

Paniolo Culture

When George Vancouver brought eight cattle to Hawai'i Island in 1794, the sight of the huge beasts sent the natives running in terror. Fifty years later, herds of wild cattle had become such a scourge that Kamehameha III hired three Mexican *vaqueros* (cowboys) to control them. The *vaqueros* introduced their own customs, which evolved into the tradition of the *paniolo* (from *español*). They also brought the guitar and the fundamental sound of popular Hawaiian music. There are now ranches all over the state. Hawai'i Island has annual rodeos at Honoka'a, Waimea, Nā'ālehu, and Waikoloa. Maui's *paniolo* host a parade and rodeo on July 4 in Makawao *(see p127)*.

A paniolo astride his horse

⓳ World Botanical Gardens

Hawai'i Co. Off Highway 19 near mile marker 16. Tel (808) 963-5427. **Open** 9am–5:30pm daily. 📷 W wbgi.com

World Botanical Gardens, just north of Hilo on an expanse of former sugarcane fields, is Hawai'i's largest botanical garden. Featuring 5,000 species, it includes the spectacular three-tiered 300-ft (90-m) Umauma Falls. The viewing area for Umauma Falls is reached by a short walk through the rainforest along a flower-lined path that follows a stream.

Although only in development since 1995, the site is abundant with fruits, flowers, trees, medicinal plants, and lush greenery. There is also a large children's maze.

The sheer, green cliffs of the stunning Hāmākua Coast

The picturesque Pololū Valley on the coast of Kapa'au, Hawai'i Island ▶

The route serving Mauna Loa weather station, off Saddle Road

⑳ Saddle Road

Hawai'i Co. Highway 200 from Waimea to Hilo. ⓘ BIVB, East Hawai'i, (808) 961-5797.

To drive the 55-mile (89-km) Saddle Road linking Hilo and Waimea is to drive along the shoulders of giants. The jumbled peaks of **Mauna Kea** rise to the north, while broad **Mauna Loa** looms to the south, the road following the trough where the two mountains collide. Some car rental companies ban drivers from taking the Saddle Road, an "unimproved" two-lane highway, but the road is better than they make out. As long as you drive at a reasonable speed, and in daylight, this is not a hazardous trip.

Drivers get a close-up look at the ecological forces at work on the island's interior – the cool rainforests of Hilo district,

dominated by *'ōhi'a* trees, *koa*, and huge ferns; the subalpine lava fields at the road's 6,500-ft (2,000-m) summit; and the vast, parched grasslands on the Waimea side. Much of the traffic is generated by two sizable military installations.

The highest vantage point from which to view the imposing terrain is a weather station situated 11,000 ft (3,350 m) above sea level. It is reached along a narrow paved road that begins near the summit of Saddle Road and climbs for 17 miles (27 km) up Mauna Loa. The 45-minute drive is hard work (loosening the gas tank cap helps to prevent vapor lock at this altitude), but the reward is the spectacular view across Saddle Road to Mauna Kea. Starting at the weather station, an extremely rugged trail – a four- to six-hour hike – leads to the crater on the summit of Mauna Loa, at 13,677 ft (4,169 m).

㉑ Mauna Kea

Hawai'i Co. Off Saddle Rd (Hwy 200) at mile marker 28. ⓘ BIVB, East Hawai'i, (808) 961-5797.

Midway between Hilo and Waimea, an unmarked but well-paved road climbs up Mauna Kea, winding through a native *māmane* forest that has been severely damaged by the predations of wild goats and sheep. The road rises so steeply that most cars crawl up the 15-minute drive to the **Onizuka Center for International Astronomy**. Here, a small visitor

center, named after the Kona-born astronaut who died in the 1986 explosion of the space shuttle *Challenger*, offers the solace of shelter with refreshments. It also has informative displays about the ecology of Mauna Kea and a video about its observatories. There are impressive views, too, but the panorama is better still from the summit. Driving to the very top of Mauna Kea is impossible, however, without a four-wheel-drive vehicle. The alternative is to go on foot. The 4,600-ft (1,400-m) climb is a tough 6-mile (10-km) hike.

The route to the summit takes in several remarkable sites: the **Mauna Kea Ice Age Natural Area Reserve**, with a quarry where the ancient Hawaiians obtained the rock used for making their axlike tools, or adzes; **Moon Valley**, where *Apollo* astronauts practiced driving their lunar rover in the 1960s; **Lake Waiau**, the third-highest lake in the US; and **Pu'u Poli'ahu**, the legendary abode of Pele's sister Poli'ahu, the goddess of snow.

Mauna Kea is crowned with a cluster of astronomical domes, including the **W.M. Keck Observatory**. Research teams from the US, Canada, France, and the UK are based here, collecting new information about the cosmos.

🏛 **Onizuka Center for International Astronomy**
6 miles (10 km) N of mile marker 28 off Saddle Rd (Hwy 200). Visitor Center: **Tel** (808) 961-2180. **Open** 9am–10pm daily. ♿ 📷

Mauna Kea, a giant post-shield stage volcano *(see pp22–3)*, viewed from Mauna Loa weather station

The W.M. Keck Observatory

Mauna Kea, due to its elevation, the clear air, and the absence of light and air pollution, is the best observatory site in the world – enabling the telescopes at its summit to observe the universe with minimal distortion. Keck I (built in 1992) and Keck II (1996), sitting like a pair of huge eyes on the mountaintop, have four times the imaging power of the world's next largest telescope in California. Instead of just one monolithic mirror, each observatory has a mosaic of flexible mirror segments computer-guided to focus in unison.

The twin globes of the W.M. Keck Observatory on Mauna Kea

㉒ 'Akaka Falls State Park

Hawai'i Co. Highway 220, 3.5 miles (5.5 km) W of Honomū. ⊞ Honomū. **Tel** Division of State Parks, (808) 961-9540. **Open** daily.

Two of the state's most hypnotic waterfalls have been packaged for easy viewing at 'Akaka Falls State Park, in the hills above the Hāmākua Coast. A loop trail, taking less than half an hour, links the 400-ft (120-m) **Kahūnā Falls** to **'Akaka Falls**, an unbroken cascade of 420 ft (130 m). At the main lookout, the roar of water almost drowns out the incessant clicking of cameras. At the edge of the path, you can see the entire length of the falls from top to bottom, including the pool below, yet not get wet from the spray.

The waterfalls apart, the breezy 66-acre park alone is worth the visit. Paths wind through a rich blend of trees, vines, bamboo, ginger, orchids, and other exotic plants, accompanied by the cooling sounds of rushing streams.

The access road veers off Highway 19 at the welcoming old sugar town of **Honomū**, which has dwindled from its 1930s population of 3,000 to just over 500 today. The residents have kept the small main

street alive, with the **Ishigo General Store and Bakery** (established 1910) and several other weathered wooden buildings serving as cafés and gift shops. The **Honomū Henjoji Mission**, a temple of the Buddhist Shingon Esoteric sect, was founded in the 1920s and has a sanctuary richly ornamented in black lacquer and gold. The signs inviting visitors to come in are sincerely meant.

⊞ Honomū Henjoji Mission

28-1668 Government Main Rd, Honomū. **Tel** (808) 963-6308. **Open** call ahead for details.

Gracefully cascading 'Akaka Falls, set back above the Hāmākua Coast

㉓ Pepe'ekeo Scenic Drive

Hawai'i Co. Off Hawai'i Belt Rd (Hwy 19), 4 miles (6.5 km) N of Hilo. ⊞ Pepe'ekeo. 🛈 BIVB, East Hawai'i, (808) 961-5797.

This 4-mile (6.5-km) scenic detour off the Hawai'i Belt Road plunges into tropical growth, crossing waterfall-fed streams and shaded by vine-draped palms and mango, banana, and *hala* trees.

Halfway along the drive, at beautiful Onomea Bay, the **Hawai'i Tropical Botanical Garden** has trails meandering through a patch of rainforest that includes a lily pond and a vast array of tropical plants.

🛈 Hawai'i Tropical Botanical Garden

2 miles (3 km) from either end of the drive. **Tel** (808) 964-5233. **Open** 9am–5pm daily. **Closed** Jan 1, Thanksgiving & Dec 25. 🗷 🖳 htbg.com

㉔ Mauna Loa

Hawai'i Co. 🛈 BIVB, East Hawai'i, (808) 961-5797.

Mauna Loa, or "Long Mountain", is the largest volcano on earth and one of the most active. One of five volcanoes that form Hawai'i Island, it covers the entire southern half of the island. It is 60 miles (95 km) long and 30 miles (50 km) wide and rises to 13,677 ft (4,169 m) above sea level. Mauna Loa's summit is protected as part of Hawai'i Volcanoes National Park (see pp156–9).

Since its first documented eruption in 1843, Mauna Loa has erupted more than 33 times, most recently in 1984. It is a shield volcano, with gently sloping inclines that have been created from successive lava flows oozing from the earth's crust. The caldera at the summit, Moku'aweoweo, is more than 3 miles (5 km) long and 1.5 miles (2.5 km) wide, with 600-ft (180-m) walls.

Kilauea (see pp156–9), an extremely active volcano with areas of continually moving lava, lies on Mauna Loa's southeast flank.

㉕ Hilo

With 43,000 residents, significant shipping and fishing industries out of its large bay, and a campus of the University of Hawai'i, Hilo rightfully deserves its designation as the state's second city. In spirit, though, "rainy old Hilo" couldn't be more different from sunny, urban Honolulu. The downtown buildings, many of them beautifully restored, were mostly constructed in the early 1900s; the streets are quiet, the pace is slow, and the atmosphere is low-key. Local attractions include gardens, waterfalls, beach parks, and fish ponds.

Exploring Hilo

Nature itself has checked the city's progress in two ways: the fact that rain falls 278 days of the year has not endeared Hilo to sun-worshiping vacationers; and, as though even more water were needed, the sea pounded Hilo with two destructive tsunamis in 1946 and 1960.

The Hawaiian Telephone Company building

The city has since retreated from the sea, turning the waterfront area into enormous green parks.

Hilo has a friendly, relaxed, and ethnically diverse personality. The population is largely Japanese and Filipino in ancestry, and the stores and eating places reflect that heritage. The Merrie Monarch Festival, the state's most prestigious *hula* competition, takes place here every year in the week following Easter. The plentiful rain makes Hilo a natural garden, suited to orchids and anthuriums. This is a city not so much for "tourists" as for visitors.

Downtown

Many of the brightly colored, restored buildings of the old business district, clustered next to the Wailuku River, are listed with the National Register of Historic Places. Look out for the **Hawaiian Telephone Company building**, which combines aspects of the traditional Hawaiian house *(hale)* and Californian mission architecture; its designer, C.W. Dickey, is credited with developing Hawaiian Regional Architecture. Hilo Downtown Improvement Association offers visitor information.

🜲 Farmers' Market

Corner of Mamo St and Kamehameha Ave. **Open** Wed & Sat. 🆆 hilofarmersmarket.com

On two mornings a week, the junction of Mamo Street and Kamehameha Avenue turns into a multilingual open-air marketplace. Farmers bring exotic produce such as squash blossoms, ice cream bananas, cut orchids, and mats woven from *lauhala* (leaves of the pandanus plant). Stroll around and pick up a fresh breakfast.

�� Pacific Tsunami Museum

130 Kamehameha Ave. **Tel** (808) 935-0926. **Open** 9am–4pm Mon–Sat. **Closed** public hols. 🆆 tsunami.org

This museum is located in the historic First Hawaiian Bank Building, designed by C.W. Dickey. Built in 1930, it survived both the 1946 and 1960 tsunamis and was donated to the museum in 1970. Exhibits focus on how tsunamis (often called tidal waves) are formed.

⊞ Mokupāpapa Discovery Center

308 Kamehameha Ave, Suite 109. **Tel** (808) 933-8181. **Open** 9am–4pm Tue–Sat. **Closed** public hols. 🆆 papahanaumokuakea.gov

The natural science, culture and history of the remote northwest Hawaiian islands, and that of the surrounding marine environment, is explained at this free exhibition center. A 2,500-gallon salt-water aquarium provides a home for some of the fish that inhabit the region's coral reef.

⊞ Wailoa Center

In Wailoa River State Park, Piopio St. **Tel** (808) 933-0416. **Open** 8:30am–4:30pm Mon–Fri, noon–4:30pm Wed. **Closed** public hols. 🦽

This octagonal gallery sits on a wide lawn where the Japanese quarter used to be – the town refused to rebuild here after the tsunami of 1960. Downstairs, there is a photographic display showing the appalling destruction caused by the giant waves. The rest of the gallery hosts temporary exhibitions.

⊞ Lyman Museum and Mission House

276 Haili St. **Tel** (808) 935-5021. **Open** 10am–4:30pm Mon–Sat. **Closed** Jan 1, Jul 4, Thanksgiving & Dec 25. 🜲 🦽 museum only. 🆆 lymanmuseum.org

Once the home of the Reverend David and Sarah Lyman, missionaries who settled in Hilo in the early 1830s. It is well preserved with household items like a

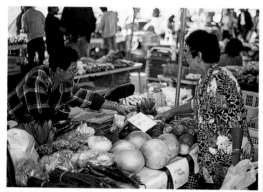

People and produce at the lively Farmers' Market

For hotels and restaurants see pp186–7 and pp202–4

Tsunamis in Hilo

In 1946, an Alaskan earthquake triggered a tsunami that hit the unsuspecting Hawaiian Islands on the morning of April 1. Waves 56 ft (17 m) high tore Hilo's bayfront buildings off their foundations and swept them inland, killing 96 people. In 1960, another tsunami struck with a vengeance. Originating off the coast of Chile, it slammed Hilo on May 23 with three successive waves, causing damage worth $23 million. In spite of warnings, many locals refused to retreat, and 61 died.

Great devastation in the aftermath of the 1946 tsunami

🌺 Rainbow Falls
Waiānuenue Ave, 2 miles (3 km) W of Downtown.
Rainbow ("Waiānuenue") Falls earns its name when the morning sun filters through the mist generated by the 80-ft (24-m) waterfall, creating rainbows. The hollow at its base is the legendary home of Hina, Maui's mother. The nearby trails provide many lookouts.

🏖 The Eastern Beaches
Kalaniana'ole Ave.
Kalaniana'ole Avenue, which follows the east side of Hilo Bay, passes a number of beach parks interlaced with large fish ponds. **James Kealoha Beach Park** (also called Four Mile Beach) offers excellent snorkeling and swimming on its sheltered eastern side; fishermen often cast their nets on the Hilo side, which is also a popular but challenging winter surfing hangout. Another good swimming spot is **Richardson Ocean Park**, which nature has sculpted into protected, lagoon-like pools.

cradle and quilts. The complex also includes a modern museum housing a varied collection of Hawaiiana, including a display of volcanic geology and artifacts from the years of immigration, such as a *braginha* – the Portuguese precursor to the 'ukulele.

🎵 Waiākea Peninsula
Banyan Dr.
Jutting into Hilo Bay, Waiākea Peninsula supports a nine-hole golf course, a row of high-rise hotels, and the 30-acre **Lili'uokalani Gardens**. The latter is a Japanese park that blends fish ponds with small pagodas and arched bridges. A footbridge crosses to tiny **Coconut Island**, now a park and popular fishing spot but once a place of healing; the Hawaiians called it Moku Ola (Island of Life). **Banyan Drive** loops the peninsula under the dense shade of huge banyans planted by celebrities such as Amelia Earhart and Babe Ruth.

A fisherman throwing his net into the rough waters off James Kealoha Beach Park

Pāhoa's old Akebono Theater, now a popular spot for concerts

❷❻ Pāhoa

Hawai'i Co. 🏔 1,100. 🚌 🛈 BIVB, East Hawai'i, (808) 961-5797.

The main strip of Pāhoa, the central town of the Puna district, offers a double surprise – "Wild West"-style buildings with raised boardwalks and low awnings that have been reinterpreted along psychedelic themes. Shops sell hemp products, espresso coffee, and New Age books. The popular **Akebono Theater** (built in 1917) has been kept alive to host a busy schedule of rock and reggae concerts.

Three miles (5 km) southeast of Pāhoa, a state-sponsored geothermal energy project has attempted to derive electricity from the heat of the world's most active volcano. However, a public outcry over environmental damage has embroiled the project in legal controversy.

❷❼ Kapoho

Hawai'i Co. 🛈 BIVB, East Hawai'i, (808) 961-5797.

In 1960, the town of Kapoho was destroyed by lava that spewed from a fire fountain 2,600 ft (795 m) wide. Today, the eerie devastation can be crossed on a 2-mile (3-km) cinder road leading to **Cape Kumukahi**, where a light-tower was inexplicably spared when the flow parted. Volcanic activity in Kapoho is a source of local legends: one tells of a local chief

who challenged a beautiful young woman to a sled race down Kapoho Crater and found to his shock that he was competing with the volcano goddess, Pele, riding on a wave of lava.

In 1790, one such wave surged through a nearby forest, leaving *'ōhi'a* trunks sheathed in black stone. Today, only the hollowed-out casts, or "lava trees," remain, but new trees have grown back. Together they make up the **Lava Tree State Monument**, a shady park with a trail around the casts. This serene spot will be best enjoyed if you bring your mosquito repellent.

🌺 **Lava Tree State Monument**
Highway 132, 2.5 miles (4 km) E of Pāhoa. **Tel** Division of State Parks, (808) 961-9540. **Open** daily. ♿

Clidemia hirta (Koster's curse) growing in a lava tree cast

❷❽ Puna Lava Flows

Hawai'i Co. Highway 137 SW of Kapoho for 14 miles (23 km). 🛈 County Parks & Recreation, (808) 961-8311.

Narrow highway 137 traces the Puna coastline along the base of Kīlauea's East Rift Zone. Here, the dense foliage occasionally breaks into solidified lava flows, mute reminders that Puna residents live by the grace of Madam Pele's fury.

At **Ahalanui Beach Park**, a natural thermal spring in a coconut grove has been adapted into a 60-ft (18-m) wide seaside swimming pool. With a sandy bottom and waves crashing against the pool's edge, this is the best place to swim in the district.

Isaac Hale Beach Park features camping, a small boat ramp, and a rugged beach with a respectable surf break. **MacKenzie State Recreation Area**, a clifftop campsite set in an ironwood forest, gives access to an old Hawaiian coastal trail and a long lava tube. Southwest of here the Puna coastal road ends with shocking abruptness where the roadway, and indeed the entire countryside, has been obliterated by congealed piles of lava. In 1990, this flow erased the town of Kalapana and a much-loved black-sand beach called Kaimū.

Lava tree cast

🏖 **Ahalanui Beach Park**
Highway 137, 1 mile (1.5 km) NE of junction with Pāhoa-Pohoiki Rd. **Open** daily.

🏖 **Isaac Hale Beach Park**
Junction of Highway 137 and Pāhoa-Pohoiki Rd. **Open** daily.

🌺 **MacKenzie State Recreation Area**
Highway 137, 2 miles (3 km) S of junction with Pāhoa-Pohoiki Rd. **Open** daily.

❷❾ Volcano Village

Hawai'i Co. 🏔 2,200. 🚌 🛈 BIVB, East Hawai'i, Hilo, (808) 961-5797.

Cut into the *'ōhi'a* rainforest of Mauna Loa's high windward slopes, this village lies just a mile (1.5 km) outside the entrance to **Hawai'i Volcanoes National Park**

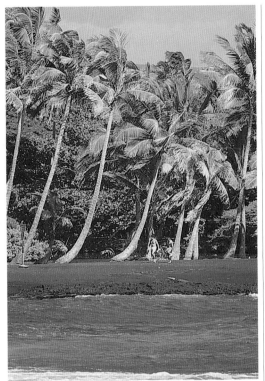
The beautiful black beach at Punalu'u Beach Park, southwest of Pāhala

from shoots. The gem of the south coast is **Punalu'u Beach Park**, where a pure black-sand beach is crowded with coconut trees. Visitors may camp here and at **Whittington Beach Park**, 5 miles (8 km) farther south.

🏕 **Punalu'u Beach Park**
Off Hwy 11, 5 miles (8 km) SW of Pāhala. **Open** daily. **Tel** Dept of Parks and Recreation, Hilo, (808) 961-8311.

❸❶ Ka Lae

Hawai'i Co. S Point Rd, off Highway 11, 6 miles (10 km) W of Wai'ōhinu. ℹ BIVB, East Hawai'i, Hilo, (808) 961-5797.

Also known as South Point, Ka Lae is as far south as you can travel in the United States. Constant fierce winds drive against a battered grassland that gives way finally to a rocky shoreline. Halfway along the 11-mile (18-km) access road, three rows of enormous, propeller-driven electricity generators emit a repetitive music of almost maddening whistles. It all feels suitably like the ends of the earth.

Although the powerful waves are daunting, these have long been prime fishing grounds. The mooring holes that ancient Hawaiians drilled into the coastal rocks so that they could keep their canoes safe while they went fishing are still visible – providing some of the earliest recorded evidence of Polynesian settlement.

A four-wheel-drive road runs 2.5 miles (4 km) northeast, to **Green Sands Beach**, which is composed of olivine sand.

Wind-powered electricity generators along the road to Ka Lae

(see pp156–9). The village has a general store and a gas station (the only one in the area) and makes a good provisioning stop before entering the park.

Environs
Just 2 miles (3 km) west of the park entrance, a small road leads northwest to **Volcano Golf and Country Club**, which has an 18-hole public golf course and an inexpensive restaurant. At the end of the road, a winery (see p207) gives tastings of its unique wines, which include a guava Chablis.

A short drive east of Volcano Village are **Akatsuka Orchid Gardens**, where visitors can take a self-guided tour.

🌺 Akatsuka Orchid Gardens
Hawai'i Belt Rd (Hwy 11), 5 miles (8 km) E of Volcano Village. **Tel** (808) 967-8234. **Open** 9am–5pm daily. **Closed** public hols. ♿

❸⓪ Ka'ū District

Hawai'i Co. 🚌 Pāhala, Punalu'u, Nā'ālehu and Wai'ōhinu. ℹ County of Hawai'i, (808) 961-8311.

The long southern arc of the Hawai'i Belt Road (Hwy 11) between Volcano Village and Kailua-Kona traverses the vast and sparsely populated Ka'ū district. Three very small towns are located here. Agricultural **Pāhala**, where macadamia nuts, sugarcane, and oranges are grown, is a quiet place where the only commotion might be the occasional crowing of roosters. **Nā'ālehu**, the most southerly town in the United States, is Ka'ū's largest town, with a few small shops. Tiny **Wai'ōhinu** is known for a monkeypod tree that Mark Twain planted in 1866. The original tree fell in a storm in 1957 but has since grown again

NAALEHU
SOUTHERNMOST COMMUNITY
IN THE U.S.A.
Road sign in Nā'ālehu

❷ Hawai'i Volcanoes National Park

The national park encompasses about a quarter of a million acres, including the 13,677-ft (4,169-m) summit of Mauna Loa, 150 miles (240 km) of hiking trails, and vast tracts of wilderness that preserve some of the world's rarest species of flora and fauna. But it is Kīlauea Caldera and the lava flows of its furious East Rift Zone that draw most visitors. Two roads – Crater Rim Drive, which loops around the caldera, and Chain of Craters Road, which descends through the recent outpourings – form a gigantic drive-through museum. The present eruption started in 1983. Check for viewing conditions before you visit; since lava flow, sulfur dioxide gas, and other hazards may restrict access. You should also stay out of closed areas. It is unknown how long the flow will continue or when it will next erupt.

Lava fountains spewing from Kīlauea during the 1983 eruption

★ **Halema'uma'u Overlook**
Once a boiling lake of lava, the crater below still steams with sulfurous fumes. This is the home of Pele, the volcano goddess (see p28).

Kipuka
Puaulu

HAWAI'I BELT ROAD

CRATER RIM DRIVE

CRATER RIM DRIVE

Mauna Loa

Nā'ālehu

Kīlauea Caldera

Halema'uma'u Crater

HALEMA'UMA'U TRAIL

CRATER RIM DRIVE

Professor Jaggar (1871–1953)

Thomas A. Jaggar was a pioneer in the young science of volcanology. A professor of geology at Massachusetts Institute of Technology, he founded the Hawaiian Volcano Observatory (now part of the Jaggar Museum) at Kīlauea Caldera in 1912. Four years later, he and Honolulu publisher Lorrin Thurston persuaded Congress to preserve the area as a national park. Professor Jaggar developed techniques for collecting volcanic gases and measuring ground tilt, seismic activity, and lava temperatures. The work he initiated has made Kīlauea one of the best understood volcanoes in the world.

Professor Jaggar working at his desk in 1916

KEY

① Jaggar Museum

② Kīlauea Overlook

③ Kīlauea Military Camp

④ Steam Vents

⑤ Kīlauea Visitor Center and Volcano Art Center

⑥ Volcano House Hotel

Kīlauea Iki Overlook

In 1959, the crater below this overlook filled with bubbling lava, shooting fire fountains 1,900 ft (580 m) into the air. Today a hiking trail crosses the cool crater floor to give a close-up view.

VISITORS' CHECKLIST

Practical Information
Hawai'i Co. Hawai'i Belt Rd (Highway 11), 30 miles (48 km) SW of Hilo, 96 miles (155 km) SE of Kailua-Kona. **Tel** (808) 985-6000. Open 24 hours daily. 🚌 ⛺ ♿ **w** nps.gov/havo
Jaggar Museum: **Tel** (808) 985-6049. **Open** 8:30am–5pm daily. ♿ Volcano House Hotel: **Tel** (808) 967-7321. ♿ ✏️

★ Thurston Lava Tube
This huge tunnel was left behind when a subterranean river of lava drained away. An easy trail runs through the tube and a grove of giant ferns.

Key

▬▬ Major road

═══ Minor road

■ ■ Hiking trail

Devastation Trail
This short walk passes through the ghostly remains of a rainforest wiped out by ash falling from Kīlauea Iki's 1959 eruption.

Southern Extent of the Park

For keys to symbols *see back flap*

Exploring Hawai'i Volcanoes National Park

The impressive volcanic terrain of Hawai'i Volcanoes National Park supports diverse climates and eco-systems that range from sea level to the summit of Mauna Loa, the largest volcano on earth. The park is also the site of Kilauea – the world's most active volcano. This dramatic volcanic landscape, including sulfur banks, steam vents, lava tubes, fern forests, lava deserts, and endangered plants and animals, attracts millions of visitors each year. Numerous hiking paths and scenic drives lead visitors from one awe-inspiring panoramic scene to another. Over half of the park is designated wilderness and, in recognition of its outstanding natural wonders, the area has been recognized as an International Biosphere Reserve and as a World Heritage Site.

Lava fountain erupting from Kilauea

Kilauea Visitor Center building

Kilauea Visitor Center

Highway 11. **Tel** (808) 985-6000. **Open** 7:45am–5pm daily.

The visitor center presents an informative overview of the environmental, historical, and cultural features of the park. Exhibits give information about island formation, ecosystems, invasive species, and resource protection. A 25-minute film about geology and volcanism, "Born of Fire, Born of the Sea", is shown throughout the day. Trail and lava viewing conditions can change rapidly, so check with the park rangers at the center for the latest information. Overnight visitors must register here and permits are issued on a first-come basis.

Volcano Art Center

Crater Rim Dr. **Tel** (808) 967-8222. **Open** 9am–5pm daily. **Closed** Dec 25.
W volcanoartcenter.org
The Volcano Art Center preserves and promotes Hawaii's rich culture and traditions through *hula* performances, exhibitions, and concerts. The center's Volcano Art Center Gallery is housed in the nearby 1877 Volcano House Hotel, listed in the National Register of Historic Places as Hawai'i's oldest visitor accommodation. The gallery features works by over 300 prominent local artists inspired by Hawaii's environmental and cultural heritage. The displays embrace a variety of media including paint, glass, metal, ceramic, fiber, wood, and photography. The center also offers classes and workshops on Hawaiian music, dance, crafts, writing, and language as well as sponsoring a performing arts season.

Earthquake Trail (Waldron Ledge)

A section of the Crater Rim Loop Trail along Waldron Ledge, this is an easy trail that is wheelchair and stroller accessible over a paved road surface. It begins to the left of the Volcano House Hotel and follows a section of the road that was cracked and destroyed by a devastating magnitude 6.6 earthquake in 1983 on Mauna Loa. The earthquake caused many rockfalls along the caldera walls and damaged trails and roads in the park. It takes approximately 45 minutes to complete the one mile (1.6-km) round-trip. The trail features interesting earthcracks, a rich variety of plants, birds, and insects, and spectacular views of Kilauea Caldera and Mauna Loa.

Panorama of Kilauea Caldera from Waldron Ledge

For hotels and restaurants see pp186–7 and pp202–4

Halema'uma'u Crater

On the floor of the enormous expanse of the Kilauea Caldera, Halema'uma'u Crater is 3,000 ft (914 m) across and 300 ft (90 m) deep. The many fumaroles found both in the crater and along the rim continue to spew a large quantity of sulphur dioxide daily so those with respiratory problems should beware. The challenging 7-mile (11-km) Halema'uma'u Trail that leads to the crater can take three to six hours to complete. It begins by the Volcano House Hotel, descends 400 ft (120 m) through lush rainforest to the barren floor of the caldera, and crosses old lava flows to the southern edge of the crater. The trail passes Halema'uma'u Overlook which offers direct views of the crater pit.

Ancient Hawaiian petroglyph depicting a human figure

Pu'u Loa Petroglyphs

This coastal trail crosses old lava flows to reach an extensive petroglyph field located on the southern flank of Kilauea. It is an easy to moderate 2-mile (3.2-km) round-trip hike, beginning at mile marker 16 on Chain of Craters road, that takes about one and half hours to complete. Hikers walk across rough basaltic lava to reach a wooden boardwalk that surrounds in excess of 23,000 petroglyph images etched on to the abundant lava surface. The majority of the images in this extensive field depict stylized human forms, but there are also representations of the moon, canoes, ships, insects, fish, and spears. Circles, spirals, dots, and other geometric designs are also common features.

Thurston Lava Tube Trail

Thurston Lava Tube can be accessed via an easy 15-minute loop trail. The paved trail begins with a steep descent into the rainforest, dense with towering green ferns. The trail then leads visitors in to a pit crater where it is possible to enter the lava tube. Formed when the exterior of a lava flow cooled to a crust while the still-molten interior magma flowed out, the tube resembles a giant tunnel. Walking through the 600-ft (180-m) winding passage takes about ten minutes. Signs posted along the trail provide information about plants and animals that can be seen in the area.

Kilauea Iki Trail

Descending 400 ft (120 m) through tropical rainforest, this trail crosses the Kilauea Iki Crater floor, passes Pu'u Pua'i cinder cone, and returns along the crater's rim. It is a moderate to challenging 4-mile (6.4-km) loop that takes two to three hours to hike. The trail allows visitors to explore features resulting from the 1959 Kilauea Iki eruption, such as steam vents and cinder cones. Beginning at the Thurston Lava Tube parking lot on Crater Rim Drive, it takes 2-3 hours to complete. The contrast between the lush vegetation found on the crater rim and the barren rocky terrain of the crater floor is striking.

Native *elepaio* bird

Devastation Trail

This easy paved trail winds through a forested area recovering from the devastating effects of the 1959 eruption of Kilauea Iki. The eruption produced huge fountains of lava that shot up to 1,900 ft (580 m) in the air and covered the densely forested area with black pumice and falling cinder. In addition to the ghostly remains of the trees, the one-mile (1.6-km) trail features a variety of native plants, birds, tree molds, and cinder and spatter cones.

Kipuka Puaulu

A kipuka is a forested island untouched by surrounding lava flow. Vegetation has been spared by the lava flows and is therefore older and richer here. The lush green woodlands of Kipuka Puaulu bird park are home to one of the richest concentrations of rare native plants and birdlife in Hawai'i. The 1-mile (1.6-km) loop trail takes about one hour to complete. It begins with a gentle hike on an unpaved forest path, surrounded by recent lava flows from Mauna Loa. Native *koa* and *'ōhi'a lehua* trees *(see p24)* grow here. It is possible to glimpse endemic birds such as the 'elepaio or 'apapane as well as other species including finches and Japanese white eyes. A bulletin board at the start of the trail provides descriptions of the diverse birds and plants species that are found here.

Kipuka Puaulu, dense forest land on the barren slopes of Mauna Loa

KAUA'I

It is no coincidence that the oldest of the major Hawaiian islands is also the most beautiful. Wind and water have had six million years to carve Kaua'i into a stunning array of pleated cliffs and yawning chasms, while the rich topsoil of the "Garden Island" is cloaked in a spectacular mantle of emerald green vegetation. With its sandy beaches and large coral reefs, Kaua'i is Hawai'i's most irresistible destination.

The outline of the volcano that created Kaua'i has all but vanished, leaving a roughly circular island on which no place is more than a dozen miles (19 km) from the ocean. Although its highest point barely exceeds 5,000 ft (1,500 m), the interior remains a forbidding, waterlogged wilderness, and Kaua'i's 55,000 inhabitants are distributed fairly evenly around the coastal lowlands.

Settled by a separate wave of Polynesian voyagers – possibly the small, legendary Menehune *(see p165)* – and never conquered by the other islands, Kaua'i has its own proud history. It was here that Captain Cook first landed, and here too that the sandalwood and sugar industries were established. A trail of ancient temples can still be seen along the Wailua River on the east shore, and former plantation towns from Hanalei in the north to Hanapēpē

in the south lend the island a small-town charm. The capital Līhu'e is surprisingly sleepy, while resorts such as Princeville and Po'ipū are rare pockets of modern luxury in an otherwise timeless rural landscape.

Scenery is Kaua'i's greatest attraction. The North Shore, in particular, is stunning, with a succession of gorgeous beaches to the east and the soaring Nā Pali Coast to the west. High above lies Kōke'e State Park, where trails command views of the valleys and lace through the rain-soaked Alaka'i Swamp, home to rare flora and fauna. The road to the park climbs the flanks of mighty Waimea Canyon, an ever-changing panoply of colors.

Visitors are both intrigued by Kaua'i's fascinating history and awed by the vast array of scenic beauty that it offers. Exotic, enchanting, and welcoming, the "Garden Isle" is a memorable place to stay.

Workers picking taro, a traditional Hawaiian crop cultivated in Kaua'i's Hanalei Valley

◄ Canoeing is a popular sport on the Wailua River, Kaua'i

Exploring Kaua'i

Tourist facilities on Kaua'i are concentrated in three main areas. Po'ipū in the south is a classic family resort, with beautiful beaches and modern hotels. On the east coast, from Līhu'e to Kapa'a, the beaches are equally stunning, and the hotels are cheaper and well placed for sightseeing. Līhu'e also has a couple of grand plantation-era mansions, while the back roads behind Kapa'a offer glimpses of both ancient history and scenic wilderness. Finally, the lush North Shore is a playground for active travelers, with surfing and golf at Hanalei and Princeville, plus hiking and canoeing on the magnificent Nā Pali Coast. No visitor should leave Kaua'i without taking in the dramatic splendor of Waimea Canyon and the breathtaking views from Kōke'e State Park.

Ni'ihau Locator Map
See p177

Top Recreational Areas

The places shown here have been selected for their recreational activities. Conditions vary depending on the weather and the time of year, so exercise caution and, if in doubt, stay out of the water or seek local advice.

	Swimming	Snorkeling	Diving	Body-Surfing	Windsurfing	Hiking	Horseback Riding	Golf
Anahola Bay	●			■				
'Anini Beach	●				●			
Hanalei Bay	●			■				
Kalapaki Beach	●	■		■	●			
Kalihiwai Beach	●			■				
Keālia Beach				■				
Kē'ē Beach	●	■						
Kōke'e State Park						■		
Lumaha'i Beach						■		
Lydgate State Park	●	■						
Nā Pali Coast State Park		■				■		
Pali Ke Kua (Hideaways) Beach		■						
Po'ipū Beach County Park	●	■	●	■				■
Princeville	●	■					●	■
Pu'upōā Beach	●	■						
Salt Pond Beach County Park	●				●			
Secret Beach						■		
Tunnels Beach	●	■	●					

Getting Around

Kaua'i's major highway is prevented from completing a loop around the island by the Nā Pali cliffs. Known as Kūhiō Highway (Hwy 56) north of Līhu'e, and Kaumuali'i Highway (Hwy 50) to the west, it is served by the regular, inexpensive Kaua'i Bus (large suitcases and backpacks not allowed). To explore the island in detail, however, rent a car at either Līhu'e or Princeville airport. You can drive anywhere in Kaua'i in three hours or less, so you can see the whole island from a single base.

Mount Wai'ale'ale, one of the wettest places on earth

NCEVILLE
'Anini
Beach
Secret
Beach

ᴬLEI
9 KILAUEA POINT
10 Kilauea
KALIHIWAI
Larsen's
Beach
Moloa'a
Bay
Anahola Mtn
Anahola
Bay
8 ANAHOLA
Donkey Beach
Keālia
MOUNT
WAI'ALE'ALE
Keahua
Arboretum
aikini
45ft
SLEEPING
GIANT
5
7 KAPA'A
Waipouli
Wailua
580
4 KING'S HIGHWAY
WAILUA FALLS 2 3
FERN GROTTO
Lydgate State Park
583
56
Hanamā'ulu
Kilohana
Puhi
50 58 1 LĪHU'E
Nāwiliwili Bay
Hule'ia National
Wildlife Reserve
Ōma'o
a'i
Kōloa
ALLERTON
GARDEN
Māhā'ulepū Beach
PO'IPŪ 23
Ha'upu Ridge
Kauai Channel

Sights at a Glance

Remote Polihale Beach, with the soaring Nā Pali cliffs behind

0 kilometers 10
0 miles 5

Key
— Major road
═ Minor road
--- Track
━ Scenic route
△ Summit

For keys to symbols see back flap

❶ Līhu'e

Līhu'e is the administrative and business center of Kaua'i and is also the site of the island's main air and sea ports. It was built in the mid-19th century to serve the Līhu'e Sugar Mill, whose rusting machinery is being dimantled and removed from the area. Līhu'e's multi-ethnic heritage, which stems from plantation days, is reflected in some of the shops and restaurants here. Located within a few miles of central Līhu'e are several more attractive areas. The oceanfront district is especially appealing. Though the Kaua'i Marriott Resort dominates Kalapakī Beach, visitors can also enjoy a safe swim or a surfing lesson.

The Kaua'i Museum relates the history of indigenous people of Kaua'i and Ni'ihau

Exploring Līhu'e

The outskirts of town offer hidden delights. To the west, Hulē'ia Stream is a wildlife sanctuary, overlooked by a splendidly forbidding ridge of green mountains. To the east lies the barely distinct community of Hanamā'ulu, where a pleasant little beach lines a sweeping crescent bay.

🏛 Kaua'i Museum

4428 Rice St. **Tel** (808) 245-6931.
Open 10am–5pm Mon–Sat.
Closed Jan 1, Labor Day, Jul 4,
Thanksgiving & Dec 25. 🅿 🅔
🖵 kauaimuseum.org

This two-part museum relates the history of the island and its indigenous people. The Wilcox Building centers on a collection of traditional artifacts gathered by the missionary Wilcox family, including huge *koa*-wood bowls and *kāhili*, feathered standards once used as a sign of royalty in Hawai'i. The newer Rice Building tells *The Story of Kaua'i*, with displays ranging from ancient weapons to videos on geology. Dioramas show how the island might have looked before European contact, and the arrival of immigrants from

around the world is chronicled, with an emphasis on the harsh conditions endured by early plantation workers. A gift shop sells books, jewelery, and crafts.

🏠 Grove Farm Homestead

Nāwiliwili Rd. **Tel** (808) 245-3202.
Open Mon, Wed & Thu. **Closed** public
hols. Donation. 🗐 by appointment.
🖵 grovefarm.net

No settlement existed on the site of modern Līhu'e until 1864, when George Wilcox, the son of early missionaries, established the Grove Farm Plantation. Hawai'i's sugar business was then in its first boom, and although water was scarce, Wilcox prospered by developing a network of irrigation channels that reached deep into the mountains.

He lived on until the 1930s, content with a humble cottage. His heirs built the imposing mansion, paneled throughout in dark, heavy *koa*-wood, that now forms the centerpiece of

the Grove Farm Homestead. As well as the rather formal house and cramped servants' quarters, the two-hour guided tour takes in Wilcox's private orchard. Phone a week in advance for a place on the tour; you will not be let in without a reservation.

🏖 Kalapakī Beach

Off Wa'apā Rd (Hwy 51), at Kaua'i
Marriott Resort & Beach Club.

Līhu'e became Kaua'i's main port during the 1920s, when a new deepwater harbor was dredged in Nāwiliwili Bay. While the breakwaters and harbor installations appeal only to avid fishermen, the gently sloping white sands of Kalapakī Beach just to the east are highly inviting.

This is one of the safest beaches in the area, making it a good choice for families, and it is also home to the top-class Kaua'i Marriott Resort & Beach Club (*see p187*) and a handful of restaurants. Expert surfers swirl right out into the bay, but the inshore waters are sheltered enough for children. The western limit of the beach is marked by the mouth of Nāwiliwili Stream. On the far side, the palm-fringed lawns of Nāwiliwili Beach County Park are ideal for picnics.

🏠 Kilohana Plantation

3-2087 Kaumuali'i Highway (Hwy 50),
1.5 miles (2.5 km) W of Līhu'e. **Tel** (808)
245-5608. **Open** 9:30am–9:30pm
daily. 🅔 ground floor. 🅿
🖵 kilohanakauai.com

The grand house known as Kilohana Plantation was, like

The shady *koa*-wood veranda at Grove Farm Homestead

Kilohana Plantation Railway

Grove Farm Homestead, built by the Wilcoxes. Dating from the 1930s, its resemblance to an English country estate makes it the perfect home for one of Kaua'i's most elegant restaurants (see p205), as well as a small mall of expensive craft shops and galleries. The train offers a comfortable way of exploring the vast plantation, and allows visitors to discover Kilohana's agricultural past and present. The conductor will point out the various fruits and vegetables that grow alongside the track; this produce is used in the restaurant.

🔲 Menehune Fish Pond

Lookout Hulemalū Rd, 1.5 miles (2.5 km) S of Līhu'e. **Closed** to the public.

West of Nāwiliwili Harbor, a minor road ascends a small headland to enter an idyllic pastoral landscape that comes as a surprise so close to Līhu'e. Beneath a highway lookout, the tranquil Hulē'ia Stream makes a sharp right-angle turn. Ancient Hawaiians exploited this natural bend by constructing a 900-ft (275-m) dam of rounded boulders to create the Alekoko ("Rippling Blood") Fish Pond. Skilled fish farmers, the Hawaiians used it to fatten mullet for the royal table; as the fish grew, they could no longer pass through the

VISITORS' CHECKLIST

Practical Information
Kaua'i Co. 🔼 5,600. 🚹 KVB, 4334 Rice St, Suite 101, (808) 245-3971. 🎭 Kaua'i-Polynesian Festival (mid-Aug).
🔳 gohawaii.com/kauai

Transport
✈️ 2 miles (3 km) E. 🚌 Rice St, (808) 241-6410.

latticed sluices that had allowed them to enter the enclosure.

This ancient structure is more commonly referred to as the Menehune Fish Pond, its prehistoric stonemasonry being credited, as so often in Hawai'i, to the little *Menehune*. These mythical figures are described by popular legend as a magical people already hard at work in Hawai'i when the first Polynesian settlers arrived. Now privately owned, the fish pond can be seen only from afar.

Unless you rent a kayak, the same goes for the **Hulē'ia National Wildlife Refuge** just upstream, where former taro and rice terraces are set aside for the exclusive use of a raucously grateful population of waterbirds.

❷ Wailua Falls

Kaua'i Co. Mā'alo Rd (Hwy 583), 5 miles (8 km) N of Līhu'e. 🚌 Līhu'e.

The one winding road through the old sugarcane fields, which branches from the main highway a mile (1.5 km) north of Līhu'e, leads directly to the 80-ft (24-m) Wailua Falls.

From the roadside parking lot, you can admire the white cascade as it tumbles from a sheer ledge. After heavy rain, the river also bursts from a couple of natural tunnels hollowed into the rock wall below. Reaching the pool below the falls is forbidden. The walk down is difficult and dangerous because the hillside is all but vertical and very muddy.

The best time to visit is in the morning when the sun is glistening off the water and you are likely to be the only people viewing the falls.

The twin cascade of Wailua Falls, seen from a roadside overlook

The ruins of Poli'ahu Heiau, a sacrificial temple on the King's Highway

beach. Only vestiges survive here of the mighty stone walls of the **Hikinaakalā Heiau** (the name means "Rising of the Sun"), where worshipers would greet the dawn. Across the highway farther inland, Kaua'i's largest temple, **Malae Heiau**, lies buried beneath a tree-covered mound.

North of the river, a short way up Kuamo'o Road (Hwy 580), **Holoholokū Heiau** was, by contrast, so small that it could be entered only on all fours. Even so, it was the site of Kaua'i's first human sacrifices. Farther up the road lies a pair of boulders known as the **Birthing Stones**; only chiefs whose mothers gave birth while wedged between them could ever rule Kaua'i. A mile (1.5 km) farther up Kuamo'o ("lizard") Ridge, on a flat promontory with wide views, the stone walls of **Poli'ahu Heiau** remain in place, guarded by swaying coconut palms.

Half a mile (800 m) more and the ground to the right drops away to swift 'Ōpaeka'a ("rolling shrimp") Stream, which tumbles over the broad **'Ōpaeka'a Falls**. It is a fine spectacle, but do not go closer than the roadside lookout.

Lydgate State Park
Leho Dr, off Kūhiō Highway (Hwy 56), just S of Wailua River.

❺ Sleeping Giant

Kaua'i Co. 1.5 miles (2.5 km) NW of Wailua. Waipouli.

The east shore's principal residential district nestles 3 miles (5 km) in from the ocean, behind the undulating ridge of Nounou Mountain. This long, low hillock is

❸ Fern Grotto

Kaua'i Co. Wailua River. Smith's Motor Boat Service, (808) 821-6895.
Waipouli. **Open** daily.
W smithskauai.com

Although a bridge makes it impossible to sail up the Wailua River from the ocean, a constant procession of pleasure barges sets out from a marina upstream for the 2-mile (3-km) excursion to the Fern Grotto. This large cave behind a fern-draped rock face is famous for its beauty. A paved path, lined with lush foliage, leads up to the grotto, where you may end up being serenaded with the *Hawaiian Wedding Song* – about three couples per day get married here. The hour-long narrated cruise up the longest navigable river in Hawai'i gives you a chance to enjoy some attractive scenery; the riverbanks are covered in palm-like pandanus plants and piri grass. There's a singalong on the return trip.

❹ King's Highway

Kaua'i Co. Waipouli. KVB, Līhu'e, (808) 245-3971.

The Wailua Valley was the seat of power in ancient Kaua'i, and the nearby shoreline remains the island's main population center. A trail of sacred sites known as the King's Highway ran from the ocean to the remote peak of Mount Wai'ale'ale. It started just south of the Wailua River in what is now **Lydgate State Park**, a deservedly popular

Sleeping Giant ridge, its profile reminiscent of a reclining figure

more commonly known as Sleeping Giant, thanks to an outline resembling a huge human figure lying flat on its back.

Three distinct hiking trails climb from its east, west, and south sides. They are reached from Kūhiō Highway (Hwy 56), Kāmala Road (Hwy 581), and Kuamo'o Road (Hwy 580) respectively. They converge to follow the alarmingly narrow crest, arriving at a meadow-like clearing in the forest at the top. This prime picnic spot offers panoramic views up and down the coastline, as well as westward to the sequence of parallel ridges that stretch inland. You can continue up the giant's head from here, but be extremely careful; the ridge is very steep in places and prone to rock slides.

❻ Mount Wai'ale'ale

Kaua'i Co. 11 miles (18 km) W of Wailua.

Within spitting distance of Kapa'a's sunny beaches lies one of the wettest places on earth – Mount Wai'ale'ale, or "overflowing water." An average of 440 in (1,100 cm) of rain each year cascades in huge waterfalls down its green-velvet walls. The summit, wreathed in almost perpetual mists, was the last call on the sacred King's Highway; the ancients would follow knife-edge ridges to reach a mountain-top *heiau* (temple).

These days, unless you take a helicopter tour, you can glimpse Wai'ale'ale only from below. Follow Kuamo'o Road (Hwy 580) past 'Ōpaeka'a Falls and the Keahua Forestry Arboretum, and if the clouds clear you will be confronted by astonishing views of a sheer, pleated cliff face. Dirt roads lead through the forest to its base, where the Wailua River thunders down from the 5,148-ft (1,570-m) peak. These roads are dangerous, if not impassable, after heavy rain.

The curving expanse of Donkey Beach, popular with nudists and surfers

❼ Kapa'a

Kaua'i Co. 🛣 10,700. 🚌 *i* KVB, Lihu'e, (808) 245-3971.

Tourist development along Kaua'i's East Shore, also known as the Coconut Coast, is mostly concentrated into the 5-mile (8-km) coastal strip that stretches north of the Wailua River. Maps mark distinct communities at Wailua and Waipouli, but the only real town here is Kapa'a, farther north, home of the Coconut Festival *(see p39)*. Most of the false-front buildings that line its wooden boardwalks now hold tourist-related businesses such as restaurants, souvenir stores, or equipment rental outlets, but Kapa'a still maintains the look of a late 19th-century plantation village. The fringe of sand at the ocean's edge is divided into a number of beach parks.

1920s rain gauge once used on Mt. Wai'ale'ale

Environs

The first of the more appealing beaches north of Kapa'a is tucked out of sight half a mile (800 m) from the highway and is reached by a forest trail that drops to the right not far past mile marker 11. This uncrowded, pretty stretch of sand is known as **Donkey Beach**, thanks to the beasts of burden that used to work in the adjacent sugar fields and were turned loose to graze along the beach's edges in the evenings. In their absence,

wildflowers have flourished. There are no trees to provide shade for sunbathers, many of whom take advantage of this remote spot to go entirely naked. The surf is generally too rough to allow swimming, but is a rendezvous for expert surfers.

❽ Anahola

Kaua'i Co. 🛣 2,200. 🚌 *i* KVB, Lihu'e, (808) 245-3971.

The small, scattered village of Anahola overlooks the sweeping, palm-fringed curve of Anahola Bay, an ancient surfing site. North of town, just inland of the highway, is the picturesque **Anahola Baptist Church**. Set against a beautiful mountain backdrop, the church makes a lovely photograph.

Nearby Anahola Beach is often relatively empty, despite its combination of beautiful setting, safe swimming, and convenient access. Reached by a spur road that loops down from Kūhiō Highway (Hwy 56) shortly after mile marker 13, the beach faces the most sheltered section of Anahola Bay. The area nearest the showers is reserved for family swimming, while the slightly more turbulent waters farther north are enjoyed by local surfers.

Hawaiian activists have sometimes staged protests on the beach, arguing that the state has failed to meet its obligation to provide native Hawaiians with affordable housing in the area. However, their campaigns have not been directed against tourists.

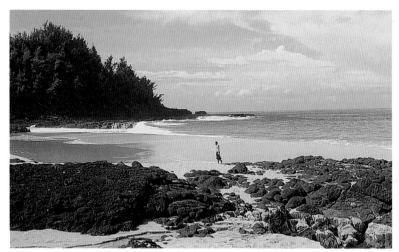

An inviting stretch of golden sand at secluded Secret Beach, near Kīlauea Point

⑨ Kīlauea Point

Kaua'i Co. Kīlauea Rd, off Kūhiō Highway (Hwy 56), 10 miles (16 km) NW of Anahola. 🚌 Kīlauea.
ℹ️ KVB, Līhu'e, (808) 245-3971.

The Hawaiian name Kīlauea ("much spewing") applies not only to the southernmost volcano on Hawai'i Island but also to the northernmost spot on the Hawaiian archipelago, Kaua'i's Kīlauea Point. Here the name refers not to spouting lava, but rather to the raging waves that foam around the base of this rocky promontory.

Together with a couple of tiny off-shore islets, the splendidly windswept cliff-top has been set aside as the **Kīlauea Point National Wildlife Refuge**, a sanctuary for Pacific seabirds. Displays in the refuge's well-equipped visitor center enable amateur birdwatchers to pick out frigatebirds, Laysan albatrosses, and various tropic birds.

A short walk beyond the visitor center leads to the red and white **Kīlauea Lighthouse**, which marks the beginning of Kaua'i's North Shore. When erected in 1913, the lighthouse held the largest clamshell lens in the world, but that has now been supplanted by a much smaller and barely noticeable structure on its far side. As you approach the tip of the headland, extensive views open up to the west beyond Secret Beach and Princeville to the Nā Pali cliffs. The exposed oceanfront slopes to the east, meanwhile, are flecked with thousands of white seabirds and can be explored on ranger-led walking tours.

Environs: The most dramatic views of Kīlauea Lighthouse and, in winter especially, of the mighty waves that pound northern Kaua'i, are from the vast but little-visited shelf of glorious yellow sand known as **Secret Beach**. To reach it, turn right onto Kalihiwai Road, half a mile (800 m) west of the Kīlauea turn-off, then follow a red-dirt track that cuts away almost immediately to the right. From its far end, a narrow trail zig-zags through the woods, coming out after ten minutes at a luscious tropical cove. Even in the summer, when the mile (1.5 km) of coarse sand at least doubles in width, the sea tends to be too rough for swimming. However, it is worth walking the full length of the beach to see the white surf as it crashes against the black lava rocks that poke from the sand, and the glorious waterfall at the far end, nearest the lighthouse.

🦅 **Kīlauea Point National Wildlife Refuge**
Kīlauea Point. **Tel** (808) 828-1413.
Open 10am–4pm Mon–Fri. **Closed** Jan 1, Thanksgiving & Dec 25. 🅿️ ♿

⑩ Kalihiwai

Kaua'i Co. 🏛 1,000. ℹ️ KVB, Līhu'e, (808) 245-3971.

From Kūhiō Highway (Highway 56), two successive turnings, a mile and a half (2.5 km) apart, are called Kalihiwai Road. The two parts of the road through this small settlement were connected until a tsunami washed away the bridge over the Kalihiwai River in 1957. The last few hundred yards of the eastern segment, just before the mouth of the river, run alongside the lovely **Kalihiwai Beach**. Shielded behind a grove of ironwood trees, this beach offers fine surfing and body-surfing as well as swimming. Kūhiō Highway crosses the river about half a mile (800 m) back from the ocean; glance inland from the bridge at this point to spot the beautiful, wide **Kalihiwai Falls**.

HAWAII VISITORS BUREAU MARKER

KILAUEA LIGHTHOUSE
Colorful official marker for the lighthouse

Environs

The second (western) segment of Kalihiwai Road quickly dead-ends at the Kalihiwai River, with no beach on this side. However, an unmarked spur road to the left, halfway down this segment, leads to quiet **'Anini Beach**. Here, between 3 miles (5 km) of golden sand and the coral reef that lies 200 yds (180 m) offshore, shallow turquoise waters provide the safest swimming on Kaua'i's North Shore. There is also excellent snorkeling on the coral reef itself, as well as an idyllic campsite set among the trees. The large lawns on the inland side of the road host polo matches on summer Sunday afternoons, often with boisterous crowds cheering on the players.

The mouth of the Kalihiwai River at the Kalihiwai Beach

The Westin Princeville, set amid golf courses and ocean views

⓫ Princeville

Kaua'i Co. 🗺 2,200. 🚗 🚌 ℹ KVB, Līhu'e, (808) 245-3971.

The former sugar plantation and livestock ranch of Princeville, set on the rolling meadows of a headland above Hanalei Bay, was sold off in the 1960s to be developed as Kaua'i's most exclusive resort. Its centerpiece, the opulent **Westin Princeville**, occupies a prime site near the remains of an earthwork fort built by the German adventurer George Schäffer in 1816 (see p176). Its long-range views of the North Shore mountains are now shared by two golf courses, as well as several more hotels, condominiums, vacation homes, and a small shopping mall.

Below the bluffs, Princeville boasts some delightful little beaches. The best of the bunch, **Pu'upōā Beach**, is reached by trails that drop from both the Princeville Hotel and the Hanalei Bay Resort next door. Its wide sands offer dramatic views across Hanalei Bay, as well as over the wetlands to the peaks that tower behind Hanalei (see p170), and there's excellent family swimming in the shallow waters. Pu'upōā Beach stretches as far as the mouth of the Hanalei River, so rented kayaks can easily be paddled upstream. Princeville-based surfers and snorkelers flock to **Pali Ke Kua Beach**, also known as Hideaways Beach, by way of a trail down from the tennis courts of the Pali Ke Kua condominiums.

Kaua'i in the Movies

The fabulous scenery of Kaua'i has served as an exotic backdrop in countless Hollywood blockbusters, from a Caribbean paradise in *Islands in the Stream* (1977) to South America in *Raiders of the Lost Ark* (1981) and Vietnam in *Uncommon Valor* (1983). Ever since Esther Williams performed one of her trademark aquatic ballets in Hanalei Bay in *Pagan Love Song* (1950), the island has starred alongside the big screen's biggest names. Frank Sinatra's war-torn Pacific-island beach in *None but the Brave* (1965) was Pīla'a Beach, east of Kīlauea. Meanwhile, Elvis Presley's greatest box-office hit, *Blue Hawaii* (1961), climaxed with a gloriously kitsch wedding ceremony at the Coco Palms Resort. The remote Honopū Valley on the Nā Pali coast stood in as Skull Island in the 1977 remake of *King Kong* and, before Hurricane Iniki put an abrupt end to proceedings, much of *Jurassic Park* (1993) was shot in Hanapēpē Valley. Kaua'i is probably best remembered, however, for its role in the smash-hit Rodgers and Hammerstein musical *South Pacific* (1958). Of the movie's show-stopping songs, *Some Enchanted Evening* was filmed at Hanalei Bay, and, most famous of all, Mitzi Gaynor sang *I'm Gonna Wash That Man Right Out of My Hair* at Lumaha'i Beach.

Publicity poster of Elvis Presley in *Blue Hawaii*

⑫ Hanalei

Kaua'i Co. ⚏ 500. 🚌 ℹ️ KVB, Līhu'e, (808) 245-3971.

Only one spot in all the islands bears the name Hanalei, or "crescent bay." Nowhere deserves it more than the placid half-moon inlet, fringed with golden sand and cradled by soaring green cliffs, that lies just west of Princeville.

The flat valley floor of the Hanalei River was in ancient times a prime area for growing taro. Later turned into a patchwork of rice paddies by Chinese settlers, it is once again dominated by taro, planted under the auspices of the **Hanalei National Wildlife Refuge** to re-create the preferred habitat of the state's increasingly endangered waterbirds. Criss-crossed by irrigation channels and scattered with inaccessible islands that poke from the mud, it is home to an ever-changing population of coots, herons, stilts, and transient migratory birds. The valley's lush, green landscape is best seen from a lookout on Kūhiō Highway (Hwy 56), just west of the Princeville turn-off.

The slender bridge across the Hanalei River is the first of a series of one-lane bridges that slow North Shore traffic to a virtual crawl, thereby helping to protect the region from the ravages of overdevelopment. The village of **Hanalei** on the far side is a relaxed place, still recognizably a plantation set-tlement but kept busy these days catering to the needs of a year-round community of surfers and Nā Pali adventurers. A trio of

The taro fields of Hanalei Valley, seen from a highway overlook

awe-inspiring mountains forms a magnificent backdrop – Hīhīmanu to the east, Māmalahoa to the west, and, in the center, the sublime Nāmolokama, furrowed with over 20 waterfalls that combine to form Wai'oli Stream.

At first glance, **Hanalei Bay** might look like an ideal harbor, but so many ships have come to grief on its submerged reefs that only shallow-draft pleasure yachts now use the old jetty on its eastern side. Conditions for swimmers using the 2-mile (3-km) strand west of the jetty depend on the state of the reef; although there are several attractive spots for sunbathing or camping, swimming is only really advisable from Waikoko Beach at the western end, beyond the mouth of the Wai'oli Stream. Expert surfers, untroubled by these issues, set off from Wai'oli Beach, or "Pinetrees Park," nearer the center of the bay, to practice their art amid the waves that break at the bay's entrance.

Hanalei's most visible relic of the past is the missionary complex, set on landscaped lawns west of the town center and backed by high, tree-clad mountains. The town's earliest Christian edifice, **Wai'oli Church**, was put up in 1841. Dwarfed beneath a tall, sloping roof, this large wooden structure now functions as a social hall, set back to the right of its successor, the 1912-vintage **Wai'oli**

The striking façade of Wai'oli Hui'ia Church

Hui'ia Church. With its vivid green shingles, shimmering stained glass, and gray-capped belfry, all nestled beneath a spreading palm tree, Wai'oli Hui'ia is without a doubt the loveliest building on Kaua'i. Tucked away behind it, the **Wai'oli Mission House** was home to several generations of two missionary families, including the Wilcoxes (see p164), whose descendants lived here until the late 1970s. Although some of the original furnishings have gone, period replacements provide a sense of 19th-century Hanalei.

🏠 **Wai'oli Mission House**
Kūhiō Highway (Hwy 56). **Tel** (808) 245-3202. **Open** 9am–3pm Tue, Thu & Sat. **Closed** public hols. Donation. ♿ ground floor only.

⑬ Lumaha'i Beach

Kaua'i Co. Off Kūhiō Highway (Hwy 56), 2 miles (3 km) W of Hanalei. 🚌 Hanalei.

Immediately beyond Hanalei Bay, a small roadside pull-off marks the top of a steep, muddy trail down to the spell-binding Lumaha'i Beach. Thanks to its appearance in the movie South Pacific (see p169), this has a reputation as the most romantic beach in all Hawai'i. Its golden sands always seem to hold at least one pair of lovers, but the beaches are long and broad enough to maintain the illusion of privacy. Except on very calm days, rolling in the surf is not a good idea.

The mountain peak of Bali Hai may have dominated the beach on screen, but that was due to technical trickery; in fact, it's a tiny outcrop called Makana at the end of a ridge, 4 miles (6.5 km) farther west.

⓮ Limahuli Garden

Kaua'i Co. Kūhiō Highway (Hwy 56), 6 miles (10 km) W of Hanalei. **Tel** (808) 826-1053. **Open** 9:30am–4pm Tue–Sat. **Closed** Jan 1, Thanksgiving & Dec 25. 🅿️ 📷 **W** ntbg.org

The lush Limahuli Garden is located a quarter of a mile (400 m) before the end of Kūhiō Highway, in a steep, high valley. In ancient times, the Limahuli Valley was part of a self-sufficient *ahupua'a* (a wedge-shaped division of land running from mountain to sea). Since then, it has barely been occupied, with the exception of the notorious "Taylor Camp," an oceanfront commune that survived from 1969 to 1977 on land owned by Elizabeth Taylor's brother.

Part of the valley remains in sufficiently pristine condition to have been set aside as a botanical sanctuary, protecting both indigenous Hawaiian plants and species brought to the islands by early Polynesian settlers. The preserve is run by the National Tropical Botanical Garden, whose aim is to preserve the native species and increase their numbers.

Visitors can explore only a 17-acre portion that begins at the road and stretches inland,

Hibiscus at Limahuli Garden

supporting reconstructed ancient taro terraces that climb the hillside. A network of trails allows one to meander through a mixed forest of unusual trees, such as the Polynesian-introduced *kukui* or candlenut, once prized for its oil, and the native *'ōhi'a 'ai* or mountain apple. The higher slopes command wonderful views of the coastline below, as well as giving glimpses of the jagged Nā Pali cliffs to the west. Inland, the strangely eroded mountains loom above slender Limahuli Stream, overshadowing the off-limits Limahuli Preserve.

⓯ Hā'ena and Kē'ē Beaches

Kaua'i Co. Off Kūhiō Highway (Hwy 56), 7 miles (11 km) W of Hanalei.

Two separate beach parks with similar names are located near the end of the highway along the North Shore. The first one, **Hā'ena Beach County Park**, offers a pleasant campsite in a coconut grove where the shoreline is too exposed for safe swimming. Ten minutes' walk east from here is **Tunnels Beach**, whose extensive reef is one of Kaua'i's most popular snorkeling sites. The name refers not to the beautiful coral formations but to the tubular waves that lure the surfers here in winter.

Immediately west of here, the second park, **Hā'ena State Park**, is mostly inaccessible to casual visitors, having been set aside

Snorkeling at Tunnels Beach

more to spare this section of coast from development than to make it available for public use. **Kē'ē Beach**, at the end of the road but still within the state park, is one of the most beautiful of all the North Shore beaches, its glowing yellow sands all but engulfed by rampant tropical vegetation. The turquoise inshore lagoon provides an irresistible cooling-off spot for hikers back from the Kalalau Trail *(see pp172–3)*, as well as a much-loved swimming and snorkeling site. However, the often-turbulent waters around and beyond the reef hold perils for the unwary.

Many legends attach themselves to this remote beach, including one that identifies it as the original birthplace of *hula*. Pele the volcano goddess *(see p28)* is said to have been enticed in a dream by the sweet music of the young Kauaian warrior Lohi'au. Upon waking, she sent her sister Hi'iaka to bring Lohi'au to her, but these two promptly fell in love. Beneath the undergrowth, near the start of the Kalalau Trail, crumbling walls mark the site of Lohi'au's home, while the raised headland just west of the beach holds the remains of Hawai'i's first *hālau hula* (hula school). Here, Hi'iaka passed on the art of *hula* to eager devotees from all the islands.

Limahuli Garden's taro terraces, where the crop is grown in the traditional way

⓰ Kalalau Trail

The precipitous cliffs of the Nā Pali Coast make it impossible for the road to continue west of Kē'ē Beach, but hardy hikers can follow the narrow Kalalau Trail 11 more miles (18 km) to isolated Kalalau Valley. One of the most dramatic hikes in the world, it threads its way through a landscape of almost primeval vastness and splendor. While this is not an expedition to undertake lightly, a half-day round trip to Hanakāpī'ai Valley is within most capabilities and provides an unforgettable wilderness experience. The trail gets progressively drier as it heads west, so the initial stretches are the muddiest, with the densest vegetation. Negotiating this tangled forest of *hala* (pandanus) trees often requires scrambling over rock falls, or picking your way among slippery tree roots.

① Start of the trail
The trail climbs steeply from the trailhead at the end of Kūhiō Highway, affording spectacular views of the rugged coastline.

② Makana Peak
On special occasions, the ancient Hawaiians tossed flaming logs into the night sky from this peak. Crowds would gather in boats on the sea below to watch this early form of fireworks.

③ Ke Ahu A Laka
This was once Hawai'i's most celebrated *hālau hula* (hula school), where students could spend several years learning their art. The ancient temple nearby is thought to have been used for graduation ceremonies.

④ Hanakāpī'ai Valley
In summer, a pristine sandy beach replaces the pebbles found in winter at the mouth of Hanakāpī'ai Valley. Swimming and wading are not recommended due to dangerous rip currents.

⑨ End of the trail
For the last 5 miles (8 km), the trail clings perilously to a sandstone cliff that turns to dust at every step, thanks to the goats that have eaten the vegetation that should bind the soil together. The view of Kalalau Valley is the reward for the long hike.

Tips for Hikers

There is no food or safe drinking water along the trail. To camp in Hanakāpi'ai, Hanakoa, or Kalalau valleys, you must obtain permission in advance from the State Parks office, 3060 'Eïwa St, Līhu'e, HI 96766, (808) 274-3444, www.hawaiistate parks.org. It is also possible to enjoy the North Shore coastline by boat or helicopter. For a full list of tour operators, contact the KVB, Līhu'e, (808) 245-3971, www.gohawaii.com.

Kē'ē Beach

56

② **KŪHIŌ HWY**

⑤ **Hanakāpi'ai Falls**
An energetic hour's hike inland, through a long-abandoned coffee plantation, ends up at this towering waterfall.

⑥ **Pā Ma Wa'a**
This vertical 800-ft (240-m) cliff stands above a protected little cove welcomed by weary canoers. The boulder at the top marks the highest point on the Kalalau Trail.

⑦ **Hanging Valleys**
Between Hanakāpi'ai and Hanakoa, the trail dips into a number of "hanging valleys," where the streams have yet to cut their way down to sea level.

⑧ **Hanakoa Valley**
The campsite here is set amid the ruins of ancient taro terraces (see p129), with no access to the sea. The mighty 2,000-ft (600-m) cascade at the head of the valley is just 600 yds (550 m) away – a short but muddy climb.

0 kilometers — 2

0 mile — 1

Key

▪ ▪ Hiking trail

▬ Road

Ko'olau the Leper (far right) with his family

⑰ Kalalau Valley

Kaua'i Co.

ℹ KVB, Līhu'e, (808) 245-3971.

Unless you persevere through the last difficult stretch of the Kalalau Trail, the majestic amphitheater of Kalalau Valley can be seen only from afar. Most visitors view it by boat or helicopter tour, or from the two lookouts at the end of Kōke'e Road (see pp174–5).

For well over 1,000 years, this isolated valley was home to a thriving community of taro farmers. In the years after European contact, however, disease and the lure of the city thinned out the population, the last permanent inhabitant leaving in 1919. Later, Kalalau became a cattle ranch and was then briefly colonized by hippies who sneaked in during the 1960s. Attempts to evict them resulted in the creation of the Nā Pali Coast State Park, which now controls access and limits places at Kalalau's idyllic camp site.

The valley's pinnacles made a perfect refuge for the infamous Ko'olau the Leper, as immortalized by Jack London (see p29) in his story of the same name. Ko'olau, a cowboy from Waimea, fled into the valley in the 1890s rather than face exile and death at Moloka'i's dreaded leper colony (see pp104–5). Ko'olau's wife eventually left Kalalau alone, after both her husband and son had died of leprosy.

Birds of Kaua'i

The innermost recesses of the Nā Pali valleys, and the bogs and ravines that stretch across the top of Kaua'i, are cloaked with dense rainforest. This unique environment is the last natural sanctuary for the island's native flora and fauna. Before human contact with Hawai'i, only a handful of bird species lived here – probably descendants of wind-blown stragglers lucky to find dry land. Encountering endemic plants with curved flowers, many birds developed curved bills for sipping nectar; others acquired short, strong beaks for crushing seeds and nuts.

The tiny 'anianiau

Forest birds extinct elsewhere in the state still cling to life in the 'ōhi'a forests of the Alaka'i Swamp. Honeycreepers abound here, the most common being the bright-red 'i'iwi, with its black wings and salmon-colored sickle-shaped bill; the 'apapane, similarly colored but with a short, black bill; and the diminutive yellow 'anianiau. Also conspicuous is the gregarious rust-colored 'elepaio, which follows hikers through the forest.

Red-billed tropicbird

Most prominent on the Nā Pali Coast are the soaring tropicbirds, while in the drier Kōke'e State Park, honking nēnē appear at the lookouts together with Kaua'i's most ubiquitous bird, the moa, or red jungle fowl – a showy wild chicken.

Moa, red jungle fowl

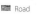

⑱ Waimea Canyon and Kōke'e State Park

Waimea Canyon, known as the "Grand Canyon of the Pacific," was created by earth movements that almost split Kaua'i in two. Over time, heavy rains have helped form a gorge 3,000 ft (915 m) deep that is still being eroded today, as occasional landslides slash away layers of rich green vegetation and the Waimea River carries the red mud into the ocean. Most visitors see the canyon from the lookouts dotted along the rim, along Kōke'e Road, but hiking trails enable the more adventurous to explore in greater depth. At the north end of Waimea Canyon is Kōke'e State Park, laced through by more hiking trails and including the most accessible part of the daunting Alaka'i Swamp. The road finally ends at two stunning overlooks 4,000 ft (1,220 m) above the Nā Pali Coast.

View from Waimea Canyon Drive showing eroded, exposed earth

Kōke'e Natural History Museum
Displays on wildlife and local history are featured in the museum, while the shop has hiking information, books, and trail maps.

★ Waimea Canyon Lookout
Despite being the lowest of the lookouts, this offers the definitive canyon views: north into the gorges cut by the Waiahulu and Po'omau streams, and south to Waimea itself on the distant shoreline.

KEY

① **Kalalau Lookout**

② **Kalalau Trail** (see pp172–3)

③ **Pihea Trail** switchbacks down for 4 miles (6.5 km) to emerge at an exposed headland high above Nu'alolo Valley.

④ **Alaka'i Swamp Trail** is a makeshift boardwalk leading to the cliffs above Wainiha Valley, with views to Hanalei.

Iliau Nature Loop
Reached from mile marker 9, this road-side trail is named after the *iliau* plant, which is endemic to this part of Kaua'i. Native plants along the loop are labeled.

Waimea

★ **Pu'u O Kila Lookout**
The main body of the magnificent Kalalau
Valley (see p173) opens out at this
spectacular lookout. The shore is
inaccessible from here.

KALALAU TRAIL ②

VALLEY TRAIL

PIHEA TRAIL ①

ALUAPUHI TRAIL

PIHEA TRAIL ③

ALAKA'I SWAMP TRAIL

PIHEA TRAIL ④

Kilohana Lookout

DITCH TRAIL

MOHINI TRAIL

KOHUA RIDGE TRAIL

KOAI'E CANYON TRAIL

WAIMEA CANYON TRAIL

↓ *Waimea*

0 kilometers 2
0 miles 1

★ **Alaka'i Swamp**
This bowl-like depression is drenched by up to 500 in
(1,270 cm) of rain per year. Much of that water goes to
feed Kaua'i's myriad waterfalls, but the rest is trapped
by an underlying layer of nonporous volcanic rock.
Part rainforest, part mist-draped bog, the Alaka'i
Swamp boasts some of Hawai'i's rarest birds, such
as the 'i'iwi, or honeycreeper.

Kukui Trail
An extension of the Iliau
Nature Loop, this trail
heads sharply down into
the canyon as far as the
Waimea River – a relatively
easy, rewarding trip.

Key

▬▬▬ Major road

═══ Minor road

══ Dirt or four-wheel-drive road

■ ▪ Hiking trail

For keys to symbols see back flap

⑲ Polihale Beach

Kaua'i Co. 5 miles (8 km) beyond the end of Kaumuali'i Highway (Hwy 50).

The westernmost region of Kaua'i, shielded from the ocean winds in the rain shadow of the central mountains, is characterized by long, flat expanses of sand. A sizable chunk has been taken over by the US military, whose sophisticated installations include systems that would give early warning of another attack on Pearl Harbor.

Skirt the security fences by following the dirt roads inland, and 15 miles (24 km) northwest of Waimea you come to the vast expanse of Polihale Beach. The surf is far too ferocious for swimming, but it's a wonderful place for a walk, with the cliffs of the Nā Pali Coast rising to the north. Head west from the end of the road and you'll reach the dunes known as the **Barking Sands**, whose hollow grains are said to groan and howl when disturbed by wind or a heavy footfall.

⑳ Waimea

Kaua'i Co. 1,700. KVB, Lihu'e, (808) 245-3971.

Waimea is among Kaua'i's more historic towns. It was here in 1778 that the crewmen of Captain Cook's third Pacific voyage – after pausing to shoot a Hawaiian – became the first Europeans to set foot on Hawaiian soil. Cook stated that "I never saw Indians so much astonished," while he himself was amazed to find the natives speaking a Polynesian language similar to those in the far-off South Seas. A statue of Cook graces the town center.

However, perhaps mindful of the mixed results of Cook's visit, including rampant venereal disease, the beach where he landed is named not in his honor but after Lucy Wright, Waimea's first native teacher. Situated west of the Waimea ("reddish water")

River, it is made up largely of mud washed down from Waimea Canyon. A plaque marks the site of Cook's first landfall.

Just across Waimea River, a headland holds what's left of **Russian Fort Elizabeth**. This star-shaped edifice was built by an adventurer, George Schäffer, in 1816. A German doctor, pretending to be a naturalist but working as a spy for the Russian-American Company, he had gained the confidence of Kaumuali'i, the chief of Kaua'i, and decided to double-cross his employers. He and Kaumuali'i hatched a plot to conquer the archipelago and divide it between the Tsar of Russia and the chief. Within a year, fooled into thinking that the US and Russia were at war, Schäffer fled the islands. His fort served the government for 50 more years but is now dilapidated.

Statue of Captain Cook in Waimea

㉑ Hanapēpē

Kaua'i Co. 2,500. KVB, Lihu'e, (808) 245-3971.

Halfway between Waimea and Po'ipū, Hanapēpē makes an intriguing detour off Kaumuali'i Highway (Hwy 50). Although taro was once grown in the valley, the village owes its late 19th-century look to the Chinese laborers who farmed rice here after serving out their

contracts on sugar plantations. Later Hanapēpē was all but abandoned, but several of its timber-frame buildings have now reopened as galleries and craft shops, and there are several attractive restaurants.

㉒ Allerton Garden

Kaua'i Co. **Tel** (808) 332-7324. **Open** 8:30am–5pm daily. **Closed** public hols. with prior notification. by appointment, at visitor center across from Spouting Horn parking lot, Lāwa'i Rd, Po'ipū. **ntbg.org**

Lāwa'i Valley stretches back from the pretty little cove of Lāwa'i Kai, 2 miles (3 km) west of Po'ipū Occupied in antiquity by taro farmers and later used by Chinese immigrants to grow rice, the valley became Queen Emma's favorite retreat in the 1870s. In the 1930s, it was bought by the Allertons, a Chicago banking family, and a plot near the sea was exquisitely landscaped to create Allerton Garden.

Bequeathed to the National Tropical Botanical Garden by the last of the Allertons in 1987, the valley was devastated by Hurricane Iniki in 1992. Both the Allertons' oceanfront home and Queen Emma's cottage have been fully restored, and the Allerton Garden is once more a showpiece. Unlike its counterpart at Limahuli (see p171), it aims to delight the eye rather than concentrate on native plants.

Visitors are transported from the visitor center near Po'ipū to the otherwise inaccessible site

The pool and pavilion of the Diana Fountain at Allerton Garden

via a mandatory 15-minute tram ride, and from there, tour the garden on foot. The Allertons conceived the design as a series of separate "rooms," and each section, such as the serene Diana Fountain or the Italianate Art Deco Mermaid Fountain, has its own character. The plants are the real stars, however, from heliconias and bromeliads to assorted tropical fruits in the orchards. Species familiar as house plants in chillier climes run riot, while graceful palms line the placid stream that glides through the heart of the valley.

Serious botanists will appreciate the chance to see rare species in the nursery, including *Kanaloa kahoolawensis*, a woody shrub whose only two known wild specimens were first identified on Kaho'olawe (*see p125*) during the 1980s. Prior reservation is required for the tour, and children under five are not admitted. A visitor center, surrounded by ten acres of gardens near the parking lot, was opened in 1997.

❷ Po'ipū

Kaua'i Co. 🏠 1,000. 🚌 2 a day.
ℹ️ KVB, Līhu'e, (808) 245-3971.

Sprawling to either side of the mouth of the Waikomo Stream, at the southern tip of Kaua'i, Po'ipū remains the island's most popular beach resort. In 1992,

Spouting Horn sending up a jet of water

Hurricane Iniki ripped the roofs off its plush oceanfront hotels and filled their lobbies with sand and ruined cars. Give or take the odd derelict property, Po'ipū is now back to normal: a strip of hotels, condos, and restaurants.

The prime spot in the center of the beach is **Po'ipū Beach Park**, complete with vigilant lifeguards and a kids' playground. There's safe swimming directly offshore, and great snorkeling around the rocks at its western end. To the east, **Brennecke's Beach** is more of a haunt for young surfers, while farther along, beyond Makahū'ena Point, the shoreline becomes a wilderness of sand dunes. The fossilized bones of long-extinct

flightless birds known as Māhā'ulepū have been found in this area, and several native plant species survive here and nowhere else.

Environs
Po'ipū itself is a modern creation, but the rudimentary jetty at the mouth of Waikomo Stream has been in use since the mid-19th century. Known as Kōloa Landing, it was built to serve Hawai'i's first sugarcane plantation, established 2 miles (3 km) inland at **Kōloa** in 1835. Kōloa now plays second fiddle to Po'ipū, but with its wooden boardwalks and false-fronted stores, it's a pleasant place for a stroll. A huge sugar mill dominates the area a mile (1.5 km) east of town. Built in 1913, it finally shut down in 1996.

The coastal road west of Po'ipū ends after only a mile (1.5 km) at **Spouting Horn**, a natural blowhole in a ledge of black lava a few steps back from the sea. The waves that break against the rock are channeled underground and then forced up in fountains of white spume that can reach a height of 50 ft (15 m) before raining down onto the usual crowd of spectators. It is very dangerous to approach closer than the roadside lookout.

Ni'ihau, the "Forbidden Island"

Lying 15 miles (24 km) southwest of Kaua'i, but just visible from the coast at Waimea, Ni'ihau is the smallest populated island in the chain, with 250 inhabitants. Owned by the Robinson family – descendants of Elizabeth Sinclair, who paid Kamehameha V $10,000 for the island in 1864 – it is little affected by tourism. You can visit only by a costly helicopter tour that avoids the inhabited areas (*see p239*). It has no hotel, airport, or cars.

Although Ni'ihau's original inhabitants were furious at the sale of their homeland to an outsider, the isolation has since turned the island into the last stronghold of Hawaiian culture – Hawaiian is still the first language here. When not tending cattle for the Ni'ihau Ranch, locals support themselves with fishing, farming, and threading necklaces of the delicate *pūpū* (shells) that wash up on the beaches.

With annual rainfall of just 12 in (300 mm), Ni'ihau is able to support only minimal agriculture. The only town, Pu'uwai ("heart"), is on the west coast, a grid of dirt roads dotted with bungalows and colorful gardens.

Ni'ihau's west coast and the tiny town of Pu'uwai

TRAVELERS' NEEDS

WHERE TO STAY

From large, oceanfront resorts to a treehouse for two in Hawai'i Island's Waipi'o Valley, the accommodation possibilities in Hawai'i are as numerous and diverse as their price ranges are vast. As the beach is the main attraction for most visitors, hotels closest to the ocean are considered most desirable and are the most pricey. Air conditioning is standard, though some smaller and older properties provide ceiling fans instead. Many rooms across all price levels offer a small balcony or private *lanai* (veranda), the better to enjoy the lovely weather. In addition to resorts, there are many smaller hotels, condominiums, inns, and bed & breakfasts, all with lower rates. Many of the inns and B&Bs are charming and distinctive and stress personalized service; some, like the Old Wailuku Inn at Ulupono on Maui, are historic properties.

Chain and Boutique Hotels

Most of Hawai'i's large resorts are run by well-known chains such as **Hilton**, **Hyatt**, and **Sheraton**. Some are so self-contained and offer such a variety of activities that many visitors choose never to leave the property. If you prefer elegance and gracious service, however, head for gems such as the Halekūlani in Waikīkī (*see p183*) or the Four Seasons Resort at Mānele Bay (*see p184*).

Less expensive options include local chains such as **Aqua Hotels**, **Aston Hotels**, **Outrigger Hotels Hawai'i**, and **Castle Resorts**, as well as smaller, individual establishments that focus on service over amenities. The latter are often popular with inter-island travelers.

Condominiums

A condominium or apartment is an ideal choice for a family or travelers who prefer to spend their money on sightseeing and other activities rather than on accommodation and dining. On O'ahu, they are mostly in high-rise buildings *mauka* (inland) of Waikīkī. On the neighboring islands, they are generally in low-rise complexes often located on or near the beach.

Condos range in size from studios to multi-bedroom units suitable for up to eight adults or a family. They have kitchens and are often stocked with everything from china to beach towels. Housekeeping service varies, but is normally provided every few days.

Inns and B&Bs

A few inns in Hawai'i are worth seeking out as an alternative to big hotels. Because they are small and do not offer the amenities of resorts, their staff pride themselves on service and attention to detail. Maui's Lahaina Inn, a restored Victorian-era masterpiece, is a stunning example (*see p185*). B&Bs (bed &

Twist Lounge, Sheraton Waikīkī (*see p183*)

breakfasts) can be found all over Hawai'i. Many are just a room in someone's home; others are charming cottages.

Camping and Hostels

Campsites range in setting from beachfront park to volcanic crater. All county and state parks require permits, available for a small fee from County Departments of Parks and Recreation or the State Department of Land and Natural Resources. Some parks have basic cabins, which are inexpensive, but usually booked months in advance, especially on weekends.

Prices and Booking

Hawai'i has accommodations to match every desire and wallet. Prices are usually highest from December to April, and lowest in May, June, September, and October. One of the more economical options is to stay in a condo. A one-bedroom unit, which can easily fit a family of four, might cost between $150 and $250 per night. Some inns and B&Bs have double rooms for under $100 a night.

The **Hawai'i Visitors and Convention Bureau** can help

Aston Waimea Plantation Cottages (*see p187*)

◀ The fabulous view from the Manele Clubhouse, Four Seasons Lānai at Manele Bay

Idyllic seaside camp site at 'Anini Beach on Kaua'i's North Shore

in booking accommodation, as can resort and B&B reservation services. You can usually book directly over the Internet; check for good deals and packages.

Hidden Extras

All accommodations are subject to a combined sales and room tax of over 13 percent. Most places allow children to stay with parents at no extra charge, but ask beforehand. Phone calls and faxes from hotel rooms are more expensive than normal rates, and many hotels charge a daily rate for parking. Tipping is not mandatory, but $2–3 a day for housekeepers and $1–2 for bellmen and parking attendants are average tips for staff.

Cabin in Haleakalā National Park

Visitors with Disabilities

All hotels and many smaller properties have at least some rooms with disability access; many ensure access to public areas as well. The Disability and Communication Access Board website *(see p233)* provides an up-to-date list of the most accessible hotels.

Oceanfront bungalow at the Four Seasons Resort Hualalai *(see p222)*

Recommended Hotels

The accommodation options featured in this guide have been selected across a wide price range for their excellent facilities, good location, and value. From rustic, family-owned inns and relaxing coastal resorts to stylishly modern boutique hotels, these hotels run the gamut across all price levels and environments. Luxury options abound, offering the very best in service and amenities. Style-conscious, trendy types feel most at home in the state's numerous hip boutique hotels. For a more intimate experience, consider a cozy, atmospheric B&B. Value destinations - from out-of-the-way hidden gems to clean yet nondescript motels - help to keep vacation costs down. If traveling with a family, consider the islands' numerous world-class resorts, several of which include noteworthy activity packages. Large groups or families can also choose to stay in a rental unit, or condo. For the best of the best, look out for options featured under "DK Choice". These establishments have been highlighted in recognition of an exceptional feature – a stunning location, notable history or an inviting atmosphere. The majority of these are exceptionally popular among local residents and visitors, so be sure to inquire regarding reservations or you may be left on the outside looking in.

DIRECTORY

Hotel Chains

Aqua Hotels and Resorts
Tel (808) 924-6543.
W aquaresorts.com

Hilton Hotels
Tel (800) 445-8667
W hilton.com

Hyatt Hotels & Resorts
Tel (800) 233-1234
W hyatt.com

Castle Resorts
Tel (800) 367-5004
W castleresorts.com

Outrigger Hotels Hawai'i
Tel (866) 956-4262
W outrigger.com

Aston Hotels
Tel (877) 997-6667
W astonhotels.com

Sheraton Hotels & Resorts
Tel (800) 325-3535
W sheraton.com

Bed & Breakfast Booking Services

Bed & Breakfast Hawai'i
Tel (808) 822-7771.
W bandb-hawaii.com

Hawai'i's Best Bed & Breakfasts
Tel (800) 262-9912
W bestbnb.com

Camping

County Departments of Parks and Recreation
Hawai'i Co.
Tel (808) 961-8311
W hawaiicounty.gov

Camping Honolulu
Tel (808) 768-2267
W camping.honolulu.gov

Kaua'i County
Tel (808) 241-4460
W kauai.gov

Maui County
Tel (808) 270-7230
W co.maui.hi.us/parks

State Department of Land and Natural Resources
Tel (808) 587-0300.
W dlnr.hawaii.gov

Where to Stay

Honolulu and Waikīkī

Greater Honolulu

Hotel Renew $
Boutique **Map** 4 F5
129 Paoakalani Ave, 96815
Tel *(808) 687-7700*
w hotelrenew.com
A short walk from Waikīkī beach, this small and comfortable property has minimalist, Asian-inspired decor. Modern amenities.

Manoa Valley Inn $
B&B **Map** 4 D1
2001 Vancouver Dr, 96822
Tel *(808) 947-6019*
w manoavalleyinn.com
1912 home with beautiful grounds has rooms named after prominent Hawaiian historical figures. Old-world charm and friendly service.

Pagoda Hotel $
Value **Map** 3 A3
1525 Rycroft St, 96814
Tel *(808) 941-6611*
w pagodahotel.com
Comfortable rooms situated near the Ala Moana Center. Floating restaurant and attractive water gardens.

Ala Moana Hotel $$
Value **Map** 3 A4
410 Atkinson Dr, 96814
Tel *(808) 955-4811*
w outrigger.com
Located near Ala Moana Beach Park, Convention Center and Ala Moana Center, with nice rooms and many amenities including restaurants and a nightclub. Fitness center with sauna.

Aqua Ilikai Hotel & Suites $$
Boutique **Map** 3 B4
1777 Ala Moana Blvd, 96815
Tel *(808) 949-3811*
w ilikaihotel.com
Lovely open-air lobby decked with many tropical plants. Some rooms feature lānai and ocean views. The on-site restaurant is popular for its ocean views.

DoubleTree by Hilton Alana Waikiki Hotel $$
Boutique **Map** 3 C4
1956 Ala Moana Blvd, 96815
Tel *(808) 941-7275*
w doubletree.hilton.com
Chic hotel with well-furnished, compact rooms that offer ocean or mountain views. Incorporates luxurious amenities and provides excellent service.

Hawai'i Prince Hotel Waikīkī $$
Luxury **Map** 3 A4
100 Holomoana St, 96815
Tel *(808) 956-1111*
w princeresortshawaii.com
Marina-front hotel with unique architectural elements including a moat and a spectacular five-story water wall. Features award-winning restaurants, tennis courts, and a spa.

Lotus Honolulu at Diamond Head $$
Boutique **Map** 4 F5
2885 Kalākaua Ave, 96815
Tel *(808) 922-1700*
w lotushonoluluhotel.com
Centrally-located, stylish hotel with rooms that have great views of the ocean or Diamond Head.

New Otani Kaimana Beach Hotel $$
Boutique **Map** 4 F5
2863 Kalākaua Ave, 96815
Tel *(808) 923-1555*
w kaimana.com
On Sans Souci beach. The well-appointed rooms boast lovely sunset views. On-site surf school.

Kahala Hotel & Resort $$$
Resort **Map** 4 F1
5000 Kahala Ave, 96816
Tel *(808) 739-8888*
w kahalaresort.com
Modern beachfront hotel with multiple restaurants, an excellent fitness center, and a free spa.

Waikīkī

Aqua Bamboo $
Boutique **Map** 4 E4
2425 Kūhiō Ave, 96815
Tel *(808) 922-7777*
w aquaresorts.com
This stylish property, just a block from the beach, features well-appointed rooms. The spa offers a range of massage services.

Aqua Oasis $
Boutique **Map** 4 D4
320 Lewers St, 96815
Tel *(808) 441-7781*
w aquaresorts.com
Peaceful hotel in the heart of Waikīkī. Rooms feature soaking tubs and private, furnished lānais.

Aqua Queen Kapiolani Hotel $
Value
150 Kapahulu Ave, 96815
Tel *(808) 922-1941*
w aquaresorts.com
Simple and comfortable rooms with elegant decor. Superb views overlooking Kapi'olani Park and Diamond Head.

Aqua Skyline at Island Colony $
Value **Map** 4 E4
445 Seaside Ave, 96815
Tel *(808) 923-2345*
w skylineislandcolony.com
Condo-style units with private lānai and kitchenette. Great views of Diamond Head and the ocean.

Aston Waikīkī Beachside Hotel $
Boutique **Map** 4 E5
2452 Kalākaua Ave, 96815
Tel *(808) 931-2100*
w astonhotels.com
Elegant property offering rooms with luxurious private bathrooms.

Aston Waikīkī Sunset $
Value **Map** 4 F4
229 Paoakalani Ave, 96815
Tel *(808) 922-0511*
w astonwaikikisunset.com
All-suite property with tropical decor at a quiet location near the beach. Suites have private lānais.

Plush interiors of a bedroom at the DoubleTree by Hilton Alana Waikiki Hotel

The tranquil Halekulani hotel, Waikīkī, with its view of the Pacific Ocean

Coconut Waikīkī Hotel $
Boutique   Map 4 D4
450 Lewers St, 96815
Tel *(808) 923-8828*
🌐 jdvhotels.com
A range of rooms, most with kitchenettes, near the scenic Ala Wai waterway.

Ilima Hotel $
Value   Map 4 E4
445 Nohonani St, 96815
Tel *(808) 923-1877*
🌐 ilima.com
Spacious studios with kitchen and lānais in a condo-style property. Lobby features art by local artists.

OHANA Waikiki East $
Value   Map 4 E4
150 Ka'iulani Ave, 96815
Tel *(808) 922-5353*
🌐 ohanahotels.com
Standard rooms and studios with kitchenettes. Good choice for families and has activities for kids.

Pacific Beach Hotel $
Value   Map 4 F5
2490 Kalākaua Ave, 96815
Tel *(808) 922-1233*
🌐 pacificbeachhotel.com
Comfortable rooms with private lānais and great views. The three-story Oceanarium has nearly 400 marine creatures.

Ramada Plaza Waikīkī $
Value   Map 3 B4
1830 Ala Moana Blvd, 96815
Tel *(808) 955-1111*
🌐 ramadaplazawaikiki.com
Reliable hotel offers comfort and multiple amenities including gift shop, pool and sundeck. Free Wi-Fi.

The Breakers Hotel $
Value   Map 4 D4
250 Beach Wlk, 96815
Tel *(808) 923-3181*
🌐 breakers-hawaii.com
Vintage property that offers rooms overlooking a shady courtyard.

Hilton Hawaiian Village Waikīkī Beach Resort $$
Resort   Map 4 E4
2500 Kūhiō Ave, 96815
Tel *(808) 922-0811*
🌐 hiltonwaikikibeach.com
Near the beach and Kapi'olani Park, built on a tropical theme including landscaped gardens, ponds and waterfalls.

Holiday Inn Waikīkī Beachcomber $$
Value   Map 4 E4
2300 Kalākaua Ave, 96815
Tel *(808) 922-4646*
🌐 waikikibeachcomberresort.com
Modern hotel located close to the beach. It hosts the dazzling *Magic of Polynesia* show.

Outrigger Reef on the Beach $$
Resort   Map 4 D5
2169 Kālia Rd, 96815
Tel *(808) 923-3111*
🌐 outrigger.com
Beachfront property with out-standing decor. Live music nightly.

Outrigger Waikīkī Beach Resort $$
Resort   Map 4 E5
2335 Kalākaua Ave, 96815
Tel *(808) 923-0711*
🌐 outrigger.com
Oceanfront property that affords great views and offers a variety of cultural programs and workshops.

Sheraton Princess Kaiulani $$
Resort   Map 4 E4
120 Ka'iulani Ave, 96815
Tel *(808) 922-5811*
🌐 princess-kaiulani.com
Enjoy the popular cocktail-dinner show *Creation – A Polynesian Journey* at this comfortable hotel.

The Modern Honolulu $$
Boutique   Map 3 B4
1775 Ala Moana Blvd, 96815
Tel *(808) 943-5800*
🌐 themodernhonolulu.com
Chic and stylish with sophisti-cated service, spa and nightclub.

Waikīkī Beach Marriott Resort & Spa $$
Resort   Map 4 F5
2552 Kalākaua Ave, 96815
Tel *(808) 922-6611*
🌐 marriott.com
Large property in the heart of Waikīkī, with very attractive rooms.

Waikīkī Parc $$
Boutique   Map 4 D5
2233 Helumoa Rd, 96815
Tel *(808) 921-7272*
🌐 waikikiparc.com
Affordable luxury in a great location. Well-equipped rooms.

Aston Waikīkī Beach Tower $$$
Luxury   Map 4 E5
2470 Kalākaua Ave, 96815
Tel *(808) 926-6400*
🌐 astonhotels.com
Well-furnished suites with views of the Waikīkī Beach. Activities include paddle tennis and billiards.

> ### DK Choice
>
> #### WAIKĪKĪ: Halekulani $$$
> Luxury   Map 4 D5
> *2199 Kālia Rd, 96815*
> **Tel** *(808) 923-2311*
> 🌐 halekulani.com
> The epitome of elegance, this beachfront hotel boasts impeccable service and impressive views. Spacious rooms with a tasteful decor. The hotel has superb dining options as well.

Hyatt Regency Waikīkī Resort & Spa $$$
Resort   Map 4 E5
2424 Kalākaua Ave, 96815
Tel *(808) 923-1234*
🌐 hyatt.com
Impressive, centrally-located, property with an atrium waterfall. Activities for children are available.

Moana Surfrider, A Westin Resort & Spa $$$
Resort   Map 4 E5
2365 Kalākaua Ave, 96815
Tel *(808) 922-3111*
🌐 moana-surfrider-com
A 1901 property with Victorian elegance and modern comforts. On-site program for kids.

Sheraton Waikīkī Hotel $$$
Resort   Map 4 D5
2255 Kalākaua Ave, 96815
Tel *(808) 922-4422*
🌐 sheraton-waikiki.com
Elegant property at a prime beachfront location. Luxurious rooms with fantastic views.

Elegant interiors of the Sheraton Princess Kaiulani resort, Waikīkī

For more information on types of hotels *see page 181*

The Royal Hawaiian $$$
Luxury   **Map** 4 D5
2259 Kalākaua Ave, 96815
Tel *(808) 923-7311*
w royal-hawaiian.com
A landmark, 1927 property
restored to its original grandeur.
Offers elegant rooms and cabanas.

Trump International
Hotel & Tower $$$
Luxury   **Map** 4 D5
223 Saratoga Rd, 96815
Tel *(808) 683-7495*
w trumphotelcollection.com
Sumptuously-appointed rooms
with floor-to-ceiling windows that
look out to magnificent views.

O'ahu

HALE'IWA: Kē iki Beach
Bungalows $$
Rental Unit
59–579 Kē Iki Rd, 96712
Tel *(808) 638-8829*
w keikibeach.com
Attractive and comfortable
beach cottages on a stretch of
white sand. Lovely sunset views.

KAHUKU: Turtle Bay Resort $$$
Resort
57–091 Kamehameha Hwy, 96731
Tel *(808) 293-6000*
w turtlebayresort.com
The North Shore's only destination
resort features luxury rooms,
suites, cottages, and villas. On-
site spa and sports facilities.

KAILUA: Lanikai Bed
& Breakfast $$
B&B
1277 Mokolua Dr, 96734
Tel *(808) 261-7895*
w lanikaibb.com
Located in a chic neighborhood,
this property offers a kitchenette,
living-dining area, and den. Hosts
are warm and knowledgeable.

KAILUA: LaniKailua Beach
Rentals $$
Rental Unit
P.O. Box 4731 Kaneohe, 96744
Tel *(808) 342-1586*
w lanikailuabeachrentals.com
Choose from a range of properties
including studios, and family-
friendly houses with full kitchens.

KAILUA: Pat's Kailua Beach
Properties $$
Rental Unit
204 S. Kalāheo Ave, 96734
Tel *(808) 261-1653*
w patskailua.com
Island-style homes range from
fully-furnished studios to four-
bedroom units. Great for families.

Charming outdoors of Four Seasons Resort
Lānai at Mānele Bay

KĀNE'OHE: Ali'i Bluffs Windward
Bed & Breakfast $
B&B
46–251 Iki Iki St, 96744
Tel *(808) 235-1124*
w aliibluffshawaii.com
The property overlooks Kāne'ohe
Bay and features two eclectically-
decorated double bedrooms with
private bath. Continental breakfast.

DK Choice

KO OLINA: Aulani,
A Disney Resort $$$
Resort
*92-1185 Ali'inui Dr, Ko Olina
Resort*
Tel *(808) 674-6200*
w resorts.disney.go.com
Synonymous with luxury and
hospitality, this family-friendly
resort blends Hawaiian style
with Disney magic. Comfortable and contemporary rooms.
Multiple-dining options. Water
features include slides, lazy rivers,
and a private snorkelling lagoon.

KO OLINA: JW Marriott Ihilani
Ko Olina Resort & Spa $$$
Resort
92–1001 Olani St
Tel *(808) 679-0079*
w ihilani.com
Sprawling beachfront property
with large and luxurious rooms.

Moloka'i and Lāna'i

KAUNAKAKAI (MOLOKA'I):
Dunbar Beachfront Cottages $$
Rental Unit
*Kamehameha V Hwy, just past Mile
Marker 18, 96748*
Tel *(808) 558-8153*
w molokai-beachfront-cottages.com
Plantation-style two-bedroom
cottages with kitchens, on their

own secluded beach. Large decks
have views of nearby islands.

KAUNAKAKAI (MOLOKA'I):
Hotel Moloka'i $$
Boutique
Kamehameha V Hwy, 96748
Tel *(808) 553-5347*
w hotelmolokai.com
Comfortable and spacious rooms
at this property with nightly
entertainment. Oceanfront dining
room is popular with locals.

KAUNAKAKAI (MOLOKA'I):
Molokai Shores $$$
Rental Unit
*Kamehameha Highway, Star Route,
96748*
Tel *(808) 553-5954*
w castleresorts.com
Centrally-located, oceanfront
condominiums with full kitchens.

LĀNAI CITY (LĀNAI): Dreams
Come True $
Inn/B&B
1168 Lāna'i Ave
Tel *(808) 565-6961*
w dreamscometruelanai.com
This 1925 property on lush
grounds, features comfortable
rooms with Asian decor.

LĀNAI CITY (LĀNAI): Hotel Lāna'i $
Value
828 Lāna'i Ave, 96763
Tel *(808) 565-7211*
w hotellanai.com
Built in 1923, this rustic place offers
neat rooms in plantation-style
Hawaiian architecture.

LĀNAI CITY (LĀNAI): Four
Seasons Resort Lānai,
The Lodge at Ko'ele $$$
Luxury
1 Keomuku Hwy, 96763
Tel *(808) 565-4000*
w fourseasons.com
Up-country resort has elegant
rooms with spacious bathrooms.
Golf courses and stables.

DK Choice

MĀNELE BAY (LĀNAI):
Four Seasons Resort Lānai
at Mānele Bay $$$
Luxury
1 Mānele Bay Rd, 96763
Tel *(808) 565-2000*
w fourseasons.com
Overlooking the crescent beach
at Mānele Bay, this upscale
property has spacious rooms
with lānais and big televisions.
Well-equipped bathrooms with
plush bathrobes, deep-soaking
tub, and separate shower.
Top-notch restaurants tempt
most guests to dine on-site.

Maui

HAIKU: Maui Ocean Breezes $
Rental Unit
240 N Holokai Rd, 96708
Tel *(808) 283-8526*
W mauivacationhideaway.com
Eco-friendly retreat with unique decor. Tropical grounds and a saltwater pool fed by a waterfall.

KĀ'ANAPALI: Kā'anapali Beach Hotel $$
Resort
2525 Kā'anapali Pkwy, 96761
Tel *(808) 661-0011*
W kbhmaui.com
Rooms and suites are furnished Hawaiian style. Garden views.

KĀ'ANAPALI: Hyatt Regency Maui Resort & Spa $$$
Resort
200 Nohea Kai Dr, 96761
Tel *(808) 661-1234*
W maui.hyatt.com
Impressive property that features art, tropical flora, an underwater grotto bar, spa, and nightly lu'au.

KĀ'ANAPALI: Kā'anapali Ali'i $$$
Rental Unit
50 Nohea Kai Dr, 96761
Tel *(808) 667-1400*
W kaanapalialii.com
Condominiums with spacious bedrooms and full kitchens.

KĀ'ANAPALI: Marriott's Maui Ocean Club $$$
Resort
100 Nohea Kai Dr, 96761
Tel *(808) 667-1200*
W marriott.com
Fully-equipped apartments ideal for families. Great beach location.

KĀ'ANAPALI: Sheraton Maui $$$
Resort
2605 Kā'anapali Pkwy, 96761
Tel *(808) 661-0031*
W sheraton-maui.com
Comfortable, ocean-facing rooms with lānai, and furnishings reminiscent of the plantation era.

KĀ'ANAPALI: The Westin Maui Resort & Spa $$$
Resort
2365 Kā'anapali Pkwy, 96761
Tel *(808) 667-2525*
W westinmaui.com
Small but luxurious rooms. Asian artworks, pools and lush grounds.

KAHANA: Kahāna Sunset $$
Rental Unit
4909 L Honoapi'ilani Hwy, 96761
Tel *(808) 669-8700*
W kahanasunset.com
Set on the beach amid tropical grounds, the property offers well-furnished units with modern kitchen and lānai.

KAPALUA: Kapalua Villas $$
Rental Unit
200 Village Rd, 96761
Tel *(808) 665-5400*
W kapaluavillasmaui.com
Spacious one- and two-bedroom condominiums with ocean views. Guests have access to Kapalua golf and resort amenities.

DK Choice

KAPALUA: The Ritz-Carlton, Kapalua $$$
Luxury
1 Ritz-Carlton Dr, 96761
Tel *(808) 669-6200*
W ritzcarlton.com
The elegant guest rooms and sumptuous suites benefit from stunning ocean views. The Hawaiian cultural program, including events, seminars, and exhibits are outstanding. A top-notch spa and scenic golf course, bars and restaurants.

KĪHEI: Kama'ole Sands Condominiums $
Rental Unit
2695 S Kīhei Rd, 96753
Tel *(808) 874-8700*
W kamaolesands.com
Studios and suites with kitchens and lānais. Tennis, swimming, and barbecue areas on-site.

KĪHEI: Maui Coast Hotel $
Value
2259 S Kīhei Rd, 96753
Tel *(808) 874-6284*
W mauicoasthotel.com
Well-furnished rooms near a stretch of sandy beach parks.

KĪHEI: Mana Kai Maui Resort $$
Rental Unit
2960 S Kīhei Rd, 96753
Tel *(808) 879-2778*
W crhmaui.com
Simple but comfortable condos on white-sand Keawakapu Beach. Open-air restaurant.

KĪHEI: Punahoa Beach Apartments $$
Rental Unit
2142 Ili'ili Rd, 96753
Tel *(808) 879-2720*
W punahoabeach.com
Fully-equipped oceanfront units with all amenities. Kama'ole and Kalama Parks flank the property.

KUAU: The Inn at Mama's Fish House $$$
B&B
799 Pono Place, off Hana Highway, 96779
Tel *(808) 579-9764*
W mamasfishhouse.com
Well-appointed cottages with retro Hawaiian-style furniture. Oceanfront neighborhood.

KULA: Kula Lodge $
B&B
15200 Haleakalā Hwy, 96790
Tel *(808) 878-1535*
W kulalodge.com
Rustic up-country lodge with scenic views. On-site art gallery. A great romantic getaway.

LAHAINA: Lahaina Inn $
Value
127 Lahainaluna Rd, 96761
Tel *(808) 661-0577*
W lahainainn.com
Comfortable rooms decorated with authentic Victorian furnishings. Centrally located.

LAHAINA: The Plantation Inn $
B&B
174 Lahainaluna Rd, 96761
Tel *(808) 667-9225*
W theplantationinn.com
Charming, plantation-style inn with modern conveniences. Breakfast served around the pool.

LAHAINA: Lahaina Shores Beach Resort $$
Resort
475 Front St, 96761
Tel *(808) 661-4835*
W lahainashores.com
Studios and suites with kitchens. Ocean or mountain views.

The sprawling gardens and pool of the Kā'anapali Beach Hotel, Maui

For more information on types of hotels *see page 181*

LAHAINA: Montage Kapalua Bay $$$
Resort
One Bay Dr, 96761
Tel *(808) 662-6600*
W montagehotels.com
Upscale property offers an authentic Hawaiian experience. Luxury, residential-style suites.

MAKAWAO: Banyan Tree House $
B&B
3265 Baldwin Ave, 96768
Tel *(808) 572-9021*
W banyantreehouse.com
Historic plantation home and cottages with Hawaiian decor.

MAKAWAO: Lumeria Maui $$$
Boutique
1813 Baldwin Ave, 96768
Tel *(855) 579-8877*
W lumeriamaui.com
Intimate rooms with local art and unique, global furnishings.

MĀKENA: Mākena Beach & Golf Resort $$
Resort
5400 Mākena Alanui, 96753
Tel *(808) 874-1111*
W makenaresortmaui.com
Lovely property with simple, stylish rooms. Ocean views.

NAPILI: Outrigger Napili Shores $
Rental Unit
5315 Lower Honoapi'ilani Rd, 96761
Tel *(808) 669-8061*
W www.outrigger.com
Studio and one-bedroom units with lānai and full kitchens. Great site for seasonal whale-watching.

NAPILI: Napili Kai Beach Resort $$$
Resort
5900 Lower Honoapi'ilani Rd, 96761
Tel *(808) 669-6271*
W napilikai.com
Spacious rooms with ocean views. A prime beach location and lush, tropical grounds.

WAILEA: Palms at Wailea $
Rental Unit
3200 Wailea Alanui, 96753
Tel *(808) 879-5800*
W outrigger.com
Spacious condominium units with a kitchen, living and dining areas, and a lānai. Fine dining options.

WAILEA: Paia Inn $$
Boutique
93 Hāna Hwy, 96779
Tel *(808) 579-6000*
W paiainn.com
Small but well-furnished rooms at a former boarding house.

WAILEA: Wailea Beach Marriott Resort & Spa $$
Resort
3700 Wailea Alanui, 96753
Tel *(808) 879-1922*
W marriott.com
Set on a rocky promontory between two white-sand beaches. Most rooms have ocean views.

WAILEA: Andaz Maui at Wailea $$$
Resort
3700 Wailea Alanui Dr, 96753
Tel *(808) 573-1234*
W maui.andaz.hyatt.com
15-acre resort features Hawaiian artifacts and a modern design.

WAILEA: Grand Wailea, A Waldorf Astoria Resort $$$
Resort
3850 Wailea Alanui, 96753
Tel *(808) 875-1234*
W grandwailea.com
Opulent beachfront property with tropical grounds, waterfalls, a saltwater lagoon, and spa.

WAILEA: The Fairmont Kea Lani, Maui $$$
Luxury
4100 Wailea Alanui, 96753
Tel *(808) 875-4100*
W fairmont.com
Suites with sitting rooms and huge bathrooms. Luxurious island ambiance and spa services.

WAILUKU: Banana Bungalow $
Value
310 N Market St, 96793
Tel *(808) 244-5090*
W mauihostel.com
Small yet comfortable hostel with both dorm and private rooms.

WAILUKU: Old Wailuku Inn at Ulapono $
B&B
2199 Kaho'okele St, 96793
Tel *(808) 244-5897*
W mauiinn.com
Restored historic home exudes 1920s Hawaiian ambiance. Well-ventilated and comfortable rooms.

Hawai'i Island

HILO: Hilo Seaside Hotel $
Value
126 Banyan Dr, 96720
Tel *(808) 935-0821*
W seasidehotelshawaii.com
Rooms are basic but comfortable. Tropical gardens with koi ponds.

KAILUA-KONA: Outrigger Royal Sea Cliff Resort $
Rental Unit
75-6040 Alii Dr, 96740
Tel *(808) 329-8021*
W outrigger.com
On a lava rock bluff, with tropical grounds and oceanfront pools.

KAILUA-KONA: Royal Kona Resort $
Resort
75-5852 Ali'i Dr, 96740
Tel *(808) 329-3111*
W royalkona.com
Oceanfront property with large, modern rooms. Saltwater lagoon.

KAILUA-KONA: Holualoa Inn $$$
B&B
76–5932 Mamalahoa Hwy, 96725
Tel *(808) 324-1121*
W holualoainn.com
Nice rooms in a lush coffee estate. Relax at the rooftop gazebo.

KEAUHOU: Sheraton Kona Resort & Spa at Keauhou Bay $$
Resort
78-128 Ehukai St
Tel *(808) 930-4900*
W sheratonkeauhou.com
Modern rooms and many amenities, including children's programs.

KOHALA COAST: Waikoloa Beach Marriott Resort & Spa $$
Resort
69-275 Waikoloa Beach Dr, 96738
Tel *(808) 886-6789*
W marriott.com
Comfortable rooms at an outstanding location. This is a

The lovely pool at Montage Kapalua Bay, Lahaina, with its view of the mountains great spot for swimming, kayaking, and exploring ancient, royal fish ponds.

DK Choice

KOHALA COAST: Fairmont Orchid, Hawaii $$$
Luxury
1 North Kanikū Dr, 96743
Tel *(808) 885-2000*
W fairmont.com
Spacious rooms feature big lānais, sitting areas, and marble bathrooms, each with a double sink and separate shower. Active travelers will love the amenities including the outdoor spa, fitness center, oceanfront pool, and various cultural activities.

KOHALA COAST: Mauna Kea Beach Hotel $$$
Resort
62-100 Mauna Kea Beach Dr, 96743
Tel *(808) 882-72222*
W princeresortshawaii.com
The Big Island's first big resort, houses remarkable collection of museum-quality art and artifacts.

VOLCANO VILLAGE: Chalet Kīlauea – The Inn at Volcano $
Value
Wright Rd & Laukapu Rd, 96785
Tel *(808) 967-7786*
W volcano-hawaii.com
Listen to the rainforest from within the charming rooms, decorated with art and memorabilia.

VOLCANO VILLAGE: Kīlauea Lodge $$
B&B
19–3948 Old Volcano Rd, 96785
Tel *(808) 967-7366*
W kilauealodge.com
Comfortable and well-appointed rooms and cottages, with stained-glass windows throughout.

WAIMEA: Kamuela Inn $
B&B
65-1300 Kawaihae Rd, 96743
Tel *(808) 885-4243*
W thekamuelainn.com
Tranquil property with old-world charm. Modern amenities.

Kaua'i

HANALEI: Hanalei Colony Resort $$$
Rental Unit
5-7130 Kūhiō Hwy, 96714
Tel *(808) 826-9893*
W hcr.com
Quiet, seaside condominium units. Enjoy weekly afternoon Mai tai cocktail parties.

The Hanalei Bay Resort overlooks the breathtaking Hanalei Bay, Princeville

KALĀHEO: Plantation Hale Suites $
Boutique
525 Aleka Loop, 96746
Tel *(808) 822-4941*
W plantation-hale.com
Peaceful property with comfortable suites. Ideal for families.

KAPA'A: Kaua'i Shores, An Aqua Hotel $
Value
420 Papaloa Rd, 96746
Tel *(808) 822-4951*
W kauaishoreshotel.com
Stylish and comfortable beachfront property. Grounds full of native plants and a jogging track.

KAPA'A: Courtyard Kaua'i at Coconut Beach $$
Resort
650 Aleka Loop, 96746
Tel *(808) 822-3455*
W marriott.com
Spacious rooms at this beachfront property amid ancient coconut groves. Traditional torch lighting ceremony at sunset.

KŌKE'E: Kōke'e State Park Lodge $
Value
3600 Kōke'e Rd (Hwy 550), 96796
Tel *(808) 335-6061*
W thelodgeatkokee.net
Rustic cabins well-equipped with utensils and wood for woodstoves.

LĪHUE: Garden Island Inn $
Inn/B&B
3445 Wilcox Rd, 96766
Tel *(808) 245-7227*
W gardenislandinn.com
Comfortable inn located in the heart of the bustling harbor area.

LĪHUE: Kaua'i Marriott Resort & Beach Club $$$
Resort
3610 Rice St, 96766
Tel *(808) 245-5050*
W marriott.com
Large property features a pool, two Jack Nicklaus-designed golf courses, and several restaurants.

PO'IPŪ: Outrigger Kiahuna Plantation $$
Rental Unit
2253 Po'ipū Rd, 96756
Tel *(808) 742-6411*
W outrigger.com
Set in a former sugarcane plantation, the wooden apartments offer spacious units with lānais.

PO'IPŪ: Grand Hyatt Kaua'i Resort & Spa $$$
Resort
1571 Po'ipū Rd, 96756
Tel *(808) 742-1234*
W kauaihyatt.com
Elegant property features tropical grounds, saltwater swimming lagoons, full-service spa, and golf.

PRINCEVILLE: Hanalei Bay Resort & Suites $$
Resort
5380 Honoiki Rd, 76722
Tel *(808) 826-6522*
W hanaleibayresort.com
Well-ventilated rooms with colorful furnishings. Fabulous views.

DK Choice

PRINCEVILLE: St. Regis Princeville Resort $$$
Luxury
5520 Ka Haku Rd, 96722
Tel *(808) 826-9644*
W princeville.com
This elegant resort, built on a bluff above Hanalei Bay, offers exquisite panoramas. Spacious rooms and splendid dining. The buildings terrace down to the beach. Views of cascading waterfalls and sparkling Pacific Ocean.

WAIMEA: Waimea Plantation Cottages $$$
Rental Unit
9400 Kaumuali'i Hwy, 96796
Tel *(808) 338-1625*
W waimea-plantation.com
Seaside plantation cottages set in a coconut grove. Period-inspired furnishings, kitchens and a relaxing front porch.

For more information on types of hotels *see page 181*

WHERE TO EAT AND DRINK

From local-style drive-ins to elegant dining rooms, the opportunities for eating well in Hawai'i are endless. In addition to hundreds of restaurants of every description, there are informal outlets such as street stalls, delis, and coffeehouses that sell tasty, cheap food perfect for a quick bite between sightseeing. Most shopping malls have a food court offering a wide, surprisingly good array of ethnic and American food, and some supermarkets and convenience stores are open all day. There are many open-air restaurants, and indoor places are usually air-conditioned. Unless you stick to the mainstream fast-food outlets, you should have no problem tasting all exotic flavors that influence cooking in Hawai'i.

Beach Bar at the Sheraton Moana Surfrider Hotel *(see p183)*

Meal Times

Some visitors to Hawai'i may be surprised by the state's early meal times. You will find places open for breakfast at 5am; lunch starts at 11am; and dinner begins at 5pm and is often over by 9pm. Many local-style establishments do not serve dinner and close by 2pm.

Cocktail hour begins early too, at around 4pm. Most hotels and restaurants serve *pūpūs* (Hawaiian-style *hors d'oeuvres*) with drinks, sometimes at no additional charge.

Many restaurants are closed on Sunday or Monday, but hours and closing days often change. You should phone if you have your heart set on a particular restaurant.

Hawai'i Regional Cuisine

The days of Hawai'i as a gastronomic wasteland are long gone – thanks, in no small part, to the advent of the Hawai'i Regional Cuisine movement in the early 1990s. Peter Merriman *(see p200 and p204)* is widely acknowledged as the leader of a pack of chefs who were determined to put Hawai'i on the culinary map. Other chefs, including Roy Yamaguchi and Bev Gannon, quickly followed suit – until a core group of 12 chefs formed a nonprofit organization dedicated to the promotion of Hawai'i's regional cuisine. The cuisine takes its ingredients directly from local farms and the surrounding Pacific, but its influences come from the many ethnic groups that make up Hawaiian society. The results have been of benefit to everyone, from local producers to the dining public.

Local Food

Those dishes often referred to as "local food" are as diverse as the population that has created them. This style of cooking is filling, inexpensive, and loved by locals as well as tourists.

The "plate lunch" is the most traditional local-style meal and consists of main course such as garlic chicken or teriyaki beef, two scoops of sticky rice, and a scoop of macaroni or potato salad heaped onto a paper plate or molded tray. These lunches are dispensed from street carts or diners, and there are often dozens of food choices – of Japanese, Chinese, Korean, Filipino, and even American origin. Expect to pay in the range of $5–10.

Poi (a grayish paste made from pounded taro root and definitely an acquired taste); *kālua* pork (from a whole pig baked in leaves, especially at a *lū'au*); sweet potato; *limu* (seaweed); and *laulau* (fish, pork, and taro leaf stems wrapped in *ti* leaves and then steamed) are all easy-to-find Hawaiian staples.

You will see sushi everywhere, and bento is a Japanese version of the plate lunch, served cold. *Saimin*, a Japanese-style bowl of broth brimming with pork, fish cake, green onions, and noodles, is popular for breakfast, lunch, or dinner. Another

Elegant interiors of the renowned American restaurant chain, Spago

The oceanfront Pacific'O in Lahaina *(see p200)*

common dish is *manapua*, the local version of Chinese steamed buns filled with seasoned pork.

Local sweet treats include shave ice (or "snow cones"), shavings of ice flavored with syrup, and crack seed – dried fruits and chewy candies seasoned with Chinese five-spice known as li hing mui.

Fast Food and Take-Out Meals

Hawai'i is part of the United States, after all, so don't be surprised to find Burger King, McDonald's, Pizza Hut, Taco Bell, and other chains. However, you will find things on the menu that are particular to Hawai'i: most notably *saimin*, sticky rice and Portuguese sausage. Local-style fast food is sold at numerous drive-ins through-out Hawai'i; popular chains include Zippy's and L & L Drive-In.

Few restaurants will not give food to take out. Many groceries and supermarkets have delis and salads, Chinese food, or bento bars offering take-out meals. Health food stores often have food bars, too. All these places are good for picnic food – Hawai'i being ideal picnicking territory.

Delivery, on the other hand, is tougher to find in Hawai'i. Your choices will be probably limited to large chains like Pizza Hut and Domino's Pizza.

Coffeehouses

Just like on the US mainland, coffeehouses have opened up all over the islands. The difference in Hawai'i is that they are not chains, and they feature aromatic home-grown Kona coffee *(see p139)*.

Most coffeehouses also sell delicious pastries, mostly home-baked, and many provide light meals as well.

Mock-Victorian Burger King, Waikīkī

Children

Hawai'i is an extremely child-friendly place, and the only restaurants that do not welcome children with open arms are the few very formal dining rooms – mostly located in fancy resort hotels. But even here, children should never be turned away.

Many restaurants provide a children's menu, with small portions of the food kids love, such as pizzas and burgers.

Etiquette

Smoking is prohibited in restaurants in Hawai'i, so those wanting to light up during a meal will have to step outside before doing so.

A standard restaurant tip is 20 per cent of the check. Depending upon

the service and style of restaurant, you may wish to tip more or less than this.

Casual dress is acceptable in all but the most formal of Hawai'i's restaurants, and jackets are usually requested rather than required.

Recommended Restaurants

Befitting one of the world's most popular holiday destinations, Hawaii offers something for everyone when it comes to dining options. The restaurants featured in this guide have been selected across a wide price range for their value, good food, atmosphere, and location. From no-frills snack shacks to pricey temples of gastronomy run by celebrity chefs, these restaurants run the gamut across all cuisine types. Alongside numerous shrimp trucks and poke shops, many of the region's top-rated restaurants focus on fresh, local seafood. Lovers of Asian cuisines (particularly Japanese, Chinese, and Thai) are also well-served; due to the region's proximity, it has become a haven for expats from all corners of the Asian continent. For the best of the best, look for restaurants featured under "DK Choice". These establishments have been highlighted in recognition of an exceptional feature – a celebrity chef, exquisite food, or an inviting atmosphere. The majority of these are exceptionally popular among local residents and visitors, so be sure to inquire regarding reservations or you may be facing a lengthy wait for a table.

Local-style diner on Hawai'i Island

The Flavors of Hawai'i

The diet of ancient Hawaiians consisted of fish, shellfish, pork, fresh fruit – mostly bananas – tubers like sweet potatoes, and, most importantly, taro (kalo). Since the migration of many ethnic groups to Hawai'i in the 1820s, island food has evolved to embrace various new recipes and ingredients. The fusion of these traditional cuisines has brought delicious modern offerings with a Hawaiian twist. Although Hawaiian food is often modified to appeal to Western palates, it is still possible for visitors to experience truly authentic local dishes at a lū'au.

Macadamia nuts

Worker tending plants in a taro field, Maui

Traditional Hawaiian Food

Hawaiians once got everything they needed from ancient land divisions that ran from mountain to sea known as ahupua'a. These plots of land provided them with sweet potatoes, bananas, dozens of types of limu (seaweed), fish and seafood from fresh, brackish, and ocean water, and of course taro, of which there were also dozens of varieties. Many foods were eaten raw, but ancient Hawaiians had several ingenious cooking methods including the 'imu, or underground oven, which is still widely used today. In this, everything from a whole pig to individual sweet potatoes are slow-cooked at a very low temperature. The heat is generated from extremely dry, hot rocks that fill the pit. The rocks are covered with banana stalks and ti leaves onto which the food is laid. It is then covered with more leaves and earth and left to bake. A whole pig takes about nine hours to cook and "the opening of the 'imu" is a ceremony enjoyed to this day by lū'au guests.

Papaya Pineapple Mango Bananas
Coconut Passion fruits
Lychees Kiwi fruits
Lusciously ripe tropical fruits from the Hawaiian islands

The Hawaiian Lū'au

Traditional Hawaiian lū'au (feasts) are still held to mark special occasions with friends and family, as they have been for centuries. It is not unusual to have in excess of 400 guests at a wedding, family reunion, or baby's first birthday. The lū'au was originally a spiritual event when islanders thanked the gods for bountiful harvests whilst enjoying traditional entertainment, such as hula performances. It takes its name from the taro tops served at the feast. The main event is the preparation of the kālua pig, but certain dishes are also central, including laulau, lomi lomi salmon, chicken long rice, haupia, and, most important of all, poi. This thick, purple-gray paste is made from steamed and pounded taro root (kalo). Poi is the absolute staple of the Hawaiian diet and is meant to be eaten with the fingers.

Breadfruit

Laulau Meat or fish, plus taro tops, are wrapped in ti leaves and baked in the 'imu, often served with poi.

Colorful haul of typical Hawaiian fish

Hawaiian Food Today

Mix traditional Hawaiian produce and preparations with foods from Japan, China, Portugal, Korea, the Philippines, Europe, and the mainland United States, and you get what can best be described as today's "local" food. These diverse ethnic groups began arriving in Hawai'i in the mid- to late 19th century, bringing their traditional foods with them.

Perhaps the most obvious example of the resulting combinations is that ubiquitous local staple, the "plate lunch". From lunch wagons to beachside kiosks and neighborhood eateries, plate lunch ingredients are unmistakable – meat or fish, plenty of carbohydrate (usually two scoops of white sticky rice), and a scoop of macaroni salad. However, in the interests of a healthier lifestyle, the protein may now be tofu, the white rice may be replaced by brown, and the macaroni salad by a fresh green salad.

Despite so much culinary integration, there are still many ethnic restaurants, so visitors can sample everything from sashimi and sushi to Portuguese sausage, bean soup, and sweet bread – and even some pretty great all-American hamburgers.

Over the last two decades, top island chefs have gathered to promote the use of locally grown and produced ingredients. They have pioneered modern Hawaiian regional cuisine, emphasizing creative methods and presentation.

Roasted *kālua* pig, the highlight at a traditional *lū'au*

WHAT TO DRINK

From colorful cocktails festooned with orchids and paper parasols, to tropical fruit juices and world-renowned Kona coffee, there are many beverages that are synonymous with Hawai'i. Perhaps the most ubiquitous of the Polynesian cocktails is the Mai Tai. Many claim to have invented this potent rum concoction, the name of which means "good" in Tahitian. Other favorites include the Blue Hawai'i, Chi-Chi, and Banana Daiquiri. Freshly-squeezed tropical juices, like pineapple, papaya, lychee, mango, and coconut, are a perfect start to breakfast on the *lanai* (veranda). In addition to Kona coffee, other islands – notably Maui, Molokai, and Kauai – grow, roast, and sell their own high-end, "estate" coffees. All are rich and delicious, and make an ideal gift or souvenir.

Lomi lomi salmon
Finely sliced raw salmon is marinated with green onions and tomatoes.

Chicken long rice
A cross between a stew and a soup. The "rice" is actually long cellophane noodles.

Haupia
A simple coconut-flavored custard pudding – the dessert of choice at every *lū'au*.

Where to Eat and Drink

Honolulu and Waikīkī

Downtown Honolulu

Palace Saimin $
Asian
1256 N King St, 96817
Tel *(808) 841-9983*
Closed *Sun & Mon*
In operation since 1946, this legendary spot specializes in steaming bowls of *saimin* with fresh wonton and udon noodles. Limited menu. The barbecue beef sticks are a favorite.

Gordon Biersch Brewery Restaurant
American   **Map** 1 A3
1 Aloha Tower Dr, 96813
Tel *(808) 599-4877*
Popular after-work hangout at the iconic Aloha Tower. Afficionados gather to enjoy beer brewed on the premises. The lengthy menu includes pub grub such as chicken wings and garlic fries.

Legend Seafood Restaurant $$
Chinese   **Map** 1 A2
100 N Beretania St, 96817
Tel *(808) 377-6735*
Trolleys stacked with bite-sized delicacies are circulated during the weekend dim-sum service at this popular Chinatown eatery. Extensive lunch and dinner menus also available.

Lucky Belly $$
Fusion   **Map** 1 A2
50 N Hotel St, 96817
Tel *(808) 531-1888*   **Closed** *Sun*
Stylish place in Chinatown frequented by hip locals for modern takes on Asian comfort fare, such as pork belly buns, oxtail dumplings, and steak tartare spiced with Japanese chili powder.

Ruth's Chris Steakhouse $$$
Steakhouse   **Map** 1 B4
500 Ala Moana Blvd, 96813
Tel *(808) 599-3860*
Part of a big-ticket steakhouse chain from the mainland. Guests enjoy top-notch rib eyes and strips alongside an extensive wine list.

Waikīkī

Marukame Udon $
Japanese   **Map** 4 E4
2310 Kūhiō Ave, 96815
Tel *(808) 931-6000*
Casual eatery known for its filling noodle soups. Serves hand-stretched udon noodles and home-made soup stocks featuring imported Japanese ingredients.

Wailana Coffee House $
American   **Map** 3 B4
1860 Ala Moana Blvd, 96815
Tel *(808) 955-1764*
Family-friendly diner serving hearty meals round the clock. Excellent breakfast options. Efficient service. There is also a cocktail lounge with karaoke music in the evening.

Duke's Canoe Club $$
American/Hawaiian   **Map** 4 E5
2335 Kalākaua Ave, 96815
Tel *(808) 922-2268*
Named after famed Hawaiian surfing champion Duke Kahanamoku, the restaurant tempts with a range of fine American and Hawaiian classics. Live Hawaiian music. Pleasant views of the beach.

Gyu-Kaku $$
Japanese   **Map** 4 D4
307 Lewers St, 96815
Tel *(808) 926-2989*
This chain restaurant, specializing in Japanese BBQ, allows diners to

grill their own meat. The menu also includes filling soups as well as rice and noodle dishes.

Hiroshi Eurasion Tapas $$
Fusion   **Map** 1 B4
500 Ala Moana Blvd
Tel *(808) 533-4476*
Traditional Japanese techniques and flavors are merged with modern European twists at this casual eatery. Has an impressive wine list.

Sansei Seafood Restaurant & Sushi Bar $$
Japanese   **Map** 4 F5
2552 Kalākaua Ave, 96815
Tel *(808) 931-6286*
Spectacular views of the world-famous Waikiki Beach. Dozens of signature dishes – from creative sushi with ingredients such as *foie gras* to award-winning contemporary Japanese specialties – draw a steady crowd.

d.k. Steak House $$$
Steakhouse   **Map** 4 F5
2552 Kalākaua Ave, 96815
Tel *(808) 931-6280*
Classic American steakhouse fare with Asian touches. Using the island's first beef dry-aging room, the restaurant's signature is a huge rib eye steak. Incredible ocean views. Top-notch service.

Japengo $$$
Asian   **Map** 4 E5
2424 Kalākaua Ave, 96815
Tel *(808) 237-6180*
Stylish, contemporary restaurant located in the Hyatt Regency Waikiki. The Asian-inspired cuisine is prepared from fresh local produce. The place features a sushi bar and lounge. Innovative cocktails and an extensive wine list.

La Mer at Halekulani $$$
French   **Map** 4 D5
2199 Kālia Rd, 96815
Tel *(808) 923-2311*
Classy, romantic restaurant on the second floor of the opulent Halekulani. Relish impeccably prepared dishes while soaking up magnificent ocean views. Expert servers help navigate the pricey wine list.

Classic French interiors of La Mer at Halekulani, Waikīkī

Morimoto Waikiki $$$
Asian   Map 3 B4
1775 Ala Moana Blvd, 96815
Tel *(808) 943-5900*
Part of chef Masaharu Morimoto's international string of restaurants, this place uses island products as well as imported Japanese seafood. Stylish environs and breezy outdoor patio.

Greater Honolulu

Diamond Head Market & Grill $
Deli
3158 Monsarrat Ave, 96815
Tel *(808) 732-0077*
All-purpose market and take-out counter offering tasty sandwiches and freshly-baked goods. Great place to pick up fresh sashimi, *ahi poke* (raw tuna salad), and scones for a picnic at Diamond Head.

Eggs 'n Things $
American   Map 3 C4
343 Saratoga Rd, 96815
Tel *(808) 923-3447*
This local favorite serves some of the best omelets, pancakes, and waffles on the island. Friendly staff maintain a convivial atmosphere.

Hale Vietnam Restaurant $
Vietnamese   Map 4 F2
1140 12th Ave, 96816
Tel *(808) 735-7581*
No-frills restaurant in the Kaimuki neighborhood, popular with families. Serves authentic Vietnamese vegan and vegetarian dishes, including filling noodle soups. Service is fast and friendly, and the atmosphere, pleasant.

Hank's Haute Dogs $
American   Map 1 C4
324 Coral St, 96813
Tel *(808) 532-4265*
Fun, casual eatery with a variety of expertly-grilled hot dogs and sausages, from chorizo and veggie dogs to deep-fried, bacon-wrapped dogs. Good selection of inviting sides includes truffle mac-and-cheese and beef-fat fries.

Helena's Hawaiian Food $
Hawaiian   Map 1 A1
1240 N School St, 96817
Tel *(808) 845-8044*
Run by Helen Chock since 1946, this is one of the best spots on the island to sample authentic Hawaiian fare such as *pipikaula*-style spare ribs, *kālua* pig, and *lomi lomi* salmon.

Leonard's Bakery $
Bakery   Map 4 F2
933 Kapahulu Ave, 96816
Tel *(808) 737-5591*
Iconic bakery selling sweet treats since 1952. Famous for warm,

The colorful decor of Morimoto Waikiki, popular for its Asian cuisine

made-to-order *malasadas* (Portuguese doughnuts). Fillings include tropical flavors such as coconut, guava, and banana.

Makai Market Food Court $
International   Map 3 A4
1450 Ala Moana Blvd, 96816
Tel *(808) 955-9517*
Massive food hall at the Ala Moana Center with kiosks offering a dizzying range of choices: Japanese *bento*, pizza, salads, ice cream, and even Korean dishes.

Morning Glass Coffee + Café $
Café
2955 E Mānoa Rd, 96822
Tel *(808) 673-0065*
Freshly ground and made-to-order Hawaiian coffee draws crowds to this youthful coffee shop. Breakfast and lunch menus feature simple preparations of mostly local ingredients.

Ono Hawaiian Foods $
Hawaiian   Map 4 F2
726 Kapahulu Ave, 96816
Tel *(808) 737-2275*
One of O'ahu's most sought-after options for authentic Hawaiian dishes such as *poi*, *laulau*, and *lomi lomi* salmon.

Rainbow Drive-In $
Hawaiian/American
3308 Kanaina Ave, 96815
Tel *(808) 737-0177*
This old-school drive-in has been serving authentic "plate lunches" for more than five decades. Tourists and locals alike dig into servings of *loco moco* (rice topped with hamburger patty, fried egg, and brown gravy), chili, and fried rice.

Spalding House Café $
American   Map 2 F1
2411 Makiki Heights Dr, 96822
Tel *(808) 532-8700*
Inviting café housed within the world-class Honolulu Museum of

Art Spalding House. Short menu of soups, salads, and sandwiches. Patrons can either dine indoors surrounded by inspiring artworks or outside in the garden.

Uncle Clay's House of Pure Aloha $
Desserts
820 W Hind Dr, 96821
Tel *(808) 373-5111*
Small, sunny store in the Aina Haina Shopping Center selling all-natural shave ice. The sweet, slushy treats are topped with seasonal ingredients such as pineapple, strawberry, mango, and coconut.

12th Ave Grill $$
American
1120 12th Ave, 96816
Tel *(808) 732-9469*
Award-winning restaurant serving contemporary American cuisine made from locally sourced organic produce, including grass-fed beef. House favorites includes macaroni and cheese, grilled pork chop, and salads.

Akasaka $$
Japanese
1646B Kona St, 96814
Tel *(808) 942-4466*
Tiny sushi bar tucked away on a nondescript street. Patrons sit at diminutive tables or the tiny bar, some opting to leave it to the expert chefs to choose what to prepare for them (omakase style).

Assaggio $$
Italian   Map 3 C4
1450 Ala Moana Blvd, 96814
Tel *(808) 942-3446*
This Ala Moana Center restaurant offers a wide selection of tasty pasta dishes as well as fresh fish and chicken options.

California Beach Rock n' Sushi $$
Sushi   Map 2 D4
404 Ward Ave, 96814
Tel *(808) 597-8000*
Situated near the Ward Center, this eatery invites moviegoers to stop for a bite. The extensive menu mixes traditional and modern sushi. Friendly atmosphere and sociable servers.

California Pizza Kitchen $$
American   Map 4 E1
4211 Wai'alae Ave, 96816
Tel *(808) 737-9446*
Family-friendly chain restaurant in the Kahala Mall. Pizza toppings include everything from barbecue chicken to pears and Gorgonzola cheese. Large, fresh salads and filling sandwiches round out the wide-ranging menu.

For more information on types of restaurants *see page 189*

Chic glass-and-wood decor with luminescent lighting at Chef Chai

Chef Chai $$
Fusion **Map** 2 D4
1009 Kapi'olani Blvd, 96814
Tel *(808) 585-0011*
This stylish place is owned and run by Chai Chaowasaree, one of the city's most beloved chefs. The varied fusion menu bases itself on delicious local ingredients. Designer cocktails are another attraction.

Little Village Noodle House $$
Chinese **Map** 1 A2
1113 Smith St, 96817
Tel *(808) 545-3008*
One of Chinatown's best-known spots, Little Village offers a varied menu full of dishes featuring fresh flavors. Signature dishes include honey walnut shrimp, capital pork chops, and orange chicken.

Mariposa $$
American **Map** 2 F4
1450 Ala Moana Blvd, 96814
Tel *(808) 951-3420*
Sophisticated lunch and dinner spot located on the third level of the Neiman Marcus store in the Ala Moana Center. Outdoor seating provides good views of Ala Moana Beach Park.

Nico's Pier 38 $$
Seafood
1131 N Nimitz Hwy, 96817
Tel *(808) 540-1377*
Top-notch "plate lunches" and a varied dinner menu featuring exceptionally fresh seafood. Amiable staff and family-friendly environs. Breezy outdoor patio.

Side Street Inn $$
Hawaiian **Map** 3 A4
1225 Hopaka St, 96814
Tel *(808) 591-0253*
Legendary late-night hangout with casual ambience. A favorite after-work haunt of Honolulu's best chefs who gather here to enjoy comfort classics like blackened *ahi* and barbecued baby back ribs.

Singha Thai Cuisine $$
Thai **Map** 3 C4
1910 Ala Moana Blvd, 96815
Tel *(808) 941-2898*
Feast on a variety of classic Thai dishes and fusion fare at this award-winning restaurant. Original artwork and fresh orchids adorn the interiors. Silk-clad Thai dancers perform every evening.

Town $$
American **Map** 4 F1
3435 Wai'alae Ave, 96816
Tel *(808) 735-5900*
Trendy, award-winning bistro with seasonal menus full of local and organic ingredients. Crowd favorites include hand-cut pastas, slow-braised meats and fresh seafood. Casual bar area.

Uncle Bo's Pupu Bar & Grill $$
Fusion
559 Kapahulu Ave, 96815
Tel *(808) 735-8311*
Well-known Kaimuki destination serving an assortment of flavorful *pūpū* such as Thai street-style chicken wings and dynamite shrimp with chili garlic *aioli* (sauce). Stylish, well-made cocktails on offer.

3660 on the Rise $$$
Hawaiian **Map** 4 F1
3660 Wai'alae Ave, 96816
Tel *(808) 737-1177*
This simple restaurant in a refurbished building offers diners creative island cuisine with a European twist. Award-winning wine list.

Alan Wong's Restaurant $$$
Hawaiian **Map** 3 B2
1857 King St, 96826
Tel *(808) 949-2526*
Classy restaurant owned by chef Alan Wong, one of Hawai'i regional cuisine's original icons. Innovative dishes prepared using traditional ingredients. The menu changes periodically. Fine service.

DK Choice
Chef Mavro $$$
Fusion **Map** 3 B2
1969 S King St, 96826
Tel *(808) 944-4714*
Originally from France, the namesake award-winning chef is known for his culinary creativity. Guests can dine prix-fixe or à la carte, with or without wine pairings. Try the signature *onaga* (snapper fish) in a salt crust. Menus change to make use of the freshest local seasonal ingredients. Plenty of vegetarian options.

Kincaid's $$$
American **Map** 2 D5
1050 Ala Moana Blvd, 96814
Tel *(808) 591-2005*
Situated near the Ward Center, Kincaid's offer a varied menu of American classics. A popular haunt among local workers. Friendly servers maintain a welcoming environment.

Roy's Restaurant $$$
Euro-Asian **Map** 4 F5
6600 Kalaniana'ole Hwy, 96825
Tel *(808) 396-7697*
The first of celebrity chef Roy Yamaguchi's restaurants in Hawai'i serves his signature Euro-Asian cuisine in a characteristically loud, busy atmosphere. The menus strike a balance between seasonal specials and Roy's classics.

The Pineapple Room $$$
Hawaiian **Map** 3 A4
1450 Ala Moana Blvd, 96814
Tel *(808) 945-6573*
Elegant restaurant at the Ala Moana Center offering delicious regional cooking. A favorite among locals and tourists alike. The menu features Chef Alan Wong's modern twist on island classics.

Entrance to Chef Mavro, a renowned fine dining restaurant in Greater Honolulu

O'ahu

AIEA: Shiro's Saimin Haven & Family Restaurant $
Hawaiian
98-020 Kamehameha Hwy 96701
Tel *(808) 488-8824*
This local, diner-style institution is a great place to try *saimin*, of which dozens of varieties are offered. The lengthy menu also features family-friendly "plate lunches".

AIEA: Champa Thai $$
Thai
98-199 Kamehameha Hwy, 96701
Tel *(808) 488-2881*
Award-winning restaurant in Pearl Kai Shopping Center serving a wide range of curry, with more than 20 vegetarian choices. Spicy dishes can be prepared hot, medium, or mild.

HALE'IWA: Beet Box Cafe $
Vegetarian
66-443 Kamehameha Hwy, 96712
Tel *(808) 637-3000*
A favorite among health-conscious North Shore residents and visitors alike. The inviting menu features sandwiches and salads made from fresh, locally-grown organic produce and grains.

HALE'IWA: Coffee Gallery $
Café
66-250 Kamehameha Hwy, 96712
Tel *(808) 637-5355*
North Shore eatery with classic surf-beach atmosphere. Popular for its legendary breakfasts. The espresso bar features a large selection of fresh-roasted gourmet coffee.

HALE'IWA: Kua Aina $
American
66-214 Kamehameha Hwy, 96712
Tel *(808) 637-6067*
This humble surfer hangout is a local landmark. Juicy chargrilled burgers feature toppings such as avocado and grilled pineapple, and are served with shoestring fries.

HALE'IWA: Matsumoto Shave Ice $
Desserts
66-087 Kamehameha Hwy, 96712
Tel *(808) 637-4827*
Perhaps the island's most sought-after option for shave ice, this outlet dates back to the days when ice was shipped to Hawai'i from Alaska. There are dozens of flavors and toppings to choose from.

HALE'IWA: Opal Thai Food $
Thai
66-197 Kamehameha Hwy, 96712
Tel *(808) 381-8091*
What was once a famous food truck has now become a modest storefront eatery serving exceptionally delectable and authentic Thai fare.

HALE'IWA: Ted's Bakery $
Bakery
59-024 Kamehameha Hwy, 96712
Tel *(808) 638-8207*
Well-known local bakery famous for heavenly cream pies. The chocolate *haupia* pie is the signature variety. There are also fresh pastries, coffee, sandwiches, and "plate lunches" to eat in or take away.

DK Choice

HALE'IWA: Haleiwa Joe's $$
American
66-011 Kamehameha Hwy, 96712
Tel *(808) 637-8005*
A lively North Shore landmark with splendid views of the harbor and glorious sunsets. The kitchen offers an extensive menu with an emphasis on fresh seafood and steaks. There is a full bar and live music on weekends. The outdoor seating area fills up fast; be sure to book ahead.

HALE'IWA: Jameson's by the Sea $$
American
62-540 Kamehameha Hwy, 96712
Tel *(808) 637-6272*
Smart restaurant at the north end of the town. The upstairs dining room serves fresh fish and fine steaks, while the lower level pub does lighter fare. The deck is perfect for watching sunsets.

HAU'ULA: Papa Ole's $
Hawaiian
54-316 Kamehameha Hwy, 96717
Tel *(808) 293-2292*   **Closed** *Wed*
This casual, family-friendly restaurant is a favorite with locals for authentic "plate lunches" of rice and macaroni salad with meat or fish. Freshly baked desserts impress as well.

HAWAI'I KAI: Cha-Cha-Cha Salsaria $$
Mexican
377 Keahole St, 96825
Tel *(808) 395-7797*
Lively spot serving Mexican classics with some Caribbean dishes thrown in. Nightly specials, home-made desserts, and big margaritas are the highlights. Live music is often featured.

HAWAI'I KAI: Kona Brewing Company $$
American
7192 Kalaniana'ole Hwy, 96825
Tel *(808) 396-5662*
This brewpub in the Koko Marina Center offers handcrafted ales and lagers as well as imported and specialty beers. The menu includes hand-tossed pizzas, burgers, and salads.

KAHALA: Hoku's $$$
Fusion
5000 Kahala Ave, 96816
Tel *(808) 739-8760*
The kitchen at this high-end restaurant specializes in contemporary cuisine, blending Hawaiian, Asian and European flavors. Incredible home-made desserts and a varied wine list. Gorgeous ocean views.

KAHUKU: Giovanni's Shrimp Truck $
Seafood
56-505 Kamehameha Hwy, 96731
Tel *(808) 293-1839*
Iconic North Shore shrimp truck that is actually a stationary outdoor food stand with covered seating. Draws in masses daily to devour plates of garlicky local shrimp.

The Coffee Gallery, located in the North Shore marketplace, O'ahu

For more information on types of restaurants *see page 189*

KAHUKU: Kahuku Grill $
American
56-565 Kamehameha Hwy, 96731
Tel *(808) 852-0040*   **Closed** *Sun*
Welcoming eatery located in
the historic Old Kahuku Sugar
Mill. The menu includes burgers
and plates of shrimp made
with fresh ingredients.

**KAILUA: Cinnamon's
Restaurant** $
American
315 Uluniu St, 96734
Tel *(808) 261-8724*
Casual spot for breakfast and
lunch in the heart of Kailua.
The kitchen uses natural ingredients free from chemicals,
preservatives and additives to
whip up a variety of wholesome
dishes. Courteous servers.

KAILUA: Uahi Island Grill $
Hawaiian
131 Hekili St, 96734
Tel *(808) 266-4646*
No-frills eatery serving
delectable salads, sandwiches,
and "plate lunches". Popular
choices include mac nut-crusted
fish, garlic *ahi,* and Kauai
lemongrass shrimp.

KAILUA: Prima $$
Italian
108 Hekili St, 96734
Tel *(808) 888-8933*
Minimally-appointed space in
a Kailua strip mall. Serves some
of the island's best gourmet
pizzas with unusual, farm-fresh
toppings. Vegetarian options
available, as also delicious
designer salads.

KAILUA: The Grove $$
New American
33 Aulike St, 96734
Tel *(808) 262-2898*   **Closed** *Mon*
Welcoming bistro serving healthy
island cuisine and American

classics. House favorites include
flat-breads, savory ribs, and fish
dishes. Good place for families.

**KAILUA: Buzz's Original
Steakhouse** $$$
Fine Dining
413 Kawailoa Rd, 96734
Tel *(808) 261-4661*
A few feet from the Kailua
Beach Park. While the chargrilled
burgers are a popular lunch
option, fine steaks are perfect
for dinner. Friendly service.

KANE'OHE: Haleiwa Joe's $$
American/Hawaiian
46-336 Haiku Rd, 96744
Tel *(808) 247-6671*
Steak-and-seafood restaurant
serving fish and beef from
Hawai'i island's Parker Ranch.
Pleasing setting overlooks a
botanical garden with colorful
foliage and lily ponds. There are
bar specials and a *pūpū* menu.

**KAPOLEI: Koa Pancake
House** $
American
91-590 Farrington Hwy, 96707
Tel *(808) 693-8855*
Dig into light, fluffy pancakes
topped with fresh bananas,
blueberries, strawberries, and
whipped cream at this eatery.
Fast and friendly service.

KO OLINA: Pizza Corner $
Pizza
92-1047 Olani St, 96707
Tel *(808) 380-4626*
This Ko Olina favorite specializes
in traditional New York-style
hand-tossed thin crust pizzas.
Toppings range from the classic
ingredients such as salami,
pepperoni, mushroom, and
black olives to the local flavors
such as *ahi poke, lomi lomi,*
and *kālua* pork. Take-out and
delivery available.

**KO OLINA:
Monkeypod Kitchen** $$
American
92-1048 Olani St, 96707
Tel *(808) 380-4086*
A funky, varied menu of fresh fish
dishes, hand-tossed pizzas, and
home-made cream pies delight
guests at this trendy restaurant
Offers a variety of craft beers.

KO OLINA: 'Ama 'Ama $$$
Hawaiian
92-1185 Ali'inui Dr, 96707
Tel *(808) 674-6200*
Considered among the best
dining options at Disney's Aulani
resort, 'Ama 'Ama offers modern
interpretations of classic
Hawaiian dishes. Soak in the
splendid views of the Pacific
Ocean from the open seating
area on the beachside.

KO OLINA: Makahiki $$$
International
92-1185 Ali'inui Dr, 96707
Tel *(808) 674-6200*
Family-friendly restaurant serving
an impressive and varied dinner
buffet. The dishes are prepared
using locally produced ingre-
dients. The house favorite
is prime rib crusted in Hawaiian
salt and fresh salad.

**PEARL CITY: Gyotaku
Japanese Restaurant** $$
Japanese
98-1226 Ka'ahumanu St, 96782
Tel *(808) 487-0091*
Bright, casual spot offering a
wide range of authentic
Japanese dishes such as sushi,
tempura, and teriyaki. Those in
a hurry can grab sushi and *pūpū*
platters to go.

**WAHIAWĀ: Maui Mike's
Fire-Roasted Chicken** $
Hawaiian
96 S Kamehameha Hwy, 96786
Tel *(808) 622-5900*
Roadside stand famous for its
namesake all-natural, fire-roasted
chicken. The free-range, slow-
cooked chicken is exceptionally
tender and perfect for picnics.
Standard sides and soft drinks
round out the menu.

**WAIMĀNALO: Sweet Home
Waimanalo** $
Vegetarian/American
41-1025 Kalanianaole Hwy, 96795
Tel *(808) 259-5737*   **Closed** *Tue*
Rustic, welcoming eatery serving
all three meals. The menu
consists of dishes that are made
using locally grown products
such as Okinawan sweet potato,
baby arugula and grape
tomatoes. Friendly staff.

Haleiwa Joe's steak-and-seafood restaurant, overlooking the botanical garden

Moloka'i and Lāna'i

KAUNAKAKAI (MOLOKA'I):
Bakery $
Bakery
79 Ala Malama St, 96748
Tel *(808) 553-5855*
Humble bakery selling snacks, beverages, and fresh, baked goods including its famous Moloka'i sweet bread. Local-style breakfasts and lunches can be enjoyed at the adjoining coffee shop's 1950s booths.

KAUNAKAKAI (MOLOKA'I):
Maka's Korner $
Eclectic
35 Mohala St, 96748
Tel *(808) 553-8058*
Diminutive corner eatery offering a low-key mix of Asian, American and Hawaiian classics as well as a healthy assortment of "plate lunches". Spartan environs and limited outdoor seating.

KAUNAKAKAI (MOLOKA'I):
Molokai Burger $
American
20 Kamehameha V Hwy, 96748
Tel *(808) 553-3533*
The first drive-through restaurant on the island dishes out fresh, home-style hamburgers, French fries, salads, and milkshakes.

KAUNAKAKAI (MOLOKA'I):
Moloka'i Drive Inn $
American
15 Kamoi St, 96748
Tel *(808) 553-5655*
Old-school, drive-up place with an ambience evocative of the 1950s. Serves kid-friendly bites: floats, shakes, chili dogs, burgers, and honey-dipped chicken, as well as fresh *akule* (mackerel), an island delicacy.

KAUNAKAKAI (MOLOKA'I):
Moloka'i Pizza Café $
Eclectic
15 Kaunakakai Pl, 96748
Tel *(808) 553-3288*
Bright, family-friendly café with a menu full of pizzas, salads, and ice creams. Daily specials include Mexican and Hawaiian dishes.

KAUNAKAKAI (MOLOKA'I):
Outpost Natural Food Store &
Juice Bar $
Vegetarian
Ala Malama St, 96748
Tel *(808) 553-3377* **Closed** *Sat*
Wholesome, nutritious burritos, salads, and sandwiches are served at this quaint country-style store. The juice bar whips up tasty, healthy smoothies.

An innovative preparation of roast chicken at The Dining Room

KAUNAKAKAI (MOLOKA'I):
Paddlers' Inn $
American
10 Mohala St, 96748
Tel *(808) 553-5256*
A wide-ranging menu encompassing a range of dishes from beer-battered *mahimahi* and burgers to *pūpū* platters and sweet potato fries.

LĀNA'I CITY (LĀNA'I):
Blue Ginger Café $
Hawaiian
409 7th St, 96763
Tel *(808) 565-6363*
One of the most renowned places on the island offering simple, home cooking. Serves hearty breakfasts, local favorites at lunch and varying specials in dinner.

LĀNA'I CITY (LĀNA'I): Café 565 $
Eclectic
408 8th St, 96763
Tel *(808) 565-6622* **Closed** *Sat & Sun*
Colorful, welcoming eatery with outdoor tables shaded by umbrellas. Favorites include pizzas, "plate lunch" specials, and filling sandwiches made with freshly-baked sub rolls.

LĀNA'I CITY (LĀNA'I): Canoes $
American
419 7th St, 96763
Tel *(808) 565-6537*
Charming, family-run restaurant offering filling breakfasts of omelets and pancakes. Lunch specials include fish and baby back ribs.

LĀNA'I CITY (LĀNA'I): Lana'i
'Ohana Poke Market $
Seafood
834 A Gay St, 96763
Tel *(808) 559-6265* **Closed** *Sat & Sun*
The beloved island classic, *poke*, is served at this tiny place in

multiple varieties, from *furikake* (dry mixed Japanese seasoning) to spicy tuna. Ideal for a picnic.

LĀNA'I CITY (LĀNA'I): Pele's
Other Garden $$
Bistro
811 Houston St, 96763
Tel *(808) 565-9628*
Popular spot that is a deli by day and bistro by night. Offers predominantly vegetarian fare, with daily soup and menu specials. Good wine list. Alfresco tables available.

DK Choice

LĀNA'I CITY (LĀNA'I): Lana'i
City Grille $$$
Fusion
828 Lāna'i Ave, 96763
Tel *(808) 565-7211*
Closed *Mon & Tue*
Celebrity chef Bev Gannon – one of the founders of the Hawai'i regional cuisine movement – had a hand in shaping this award-winning restaurant of Hotel Lana'i. The atmosphere is relaxed and the food is Pacific fusion, featuring fresh fish, prime meats, and the house signature – rotisserie chicken served with truffle mac-and-cheese and seasonal vegetables.

LĀNA'I CITY (LĀNA'I):
The Dining Room $$$
Hawaiian
1 Keomoku Hwy, 96763
Tel *(808) 565-4000*
Closed *Wed & Thu*
Set in the Four Seasons Resort Lanai, The Lodge at Koele, this restaurant features upcountry Hawaiian cuisine and opulent four-course tasting menus with optional wine pairings.

For more information on types of restaurants *see page 189*

MÅNELE (LÅNA'I): Kailani $$$
Italian
1 Mānele Bay Rd, 96763
Tel *(808) 565-2000*
Perched above Hulopo'e Bay,
Kailani enjoys an attractive
setting. The menu offers modern
Italian cuisine made from local,
organic produce. Lunch and
dinner menus feature innovative
dishes such as lobster ravioli
with vanilla butter sauce.

MÅNELE (LÅNA'I):
Nobu Lanai $$$
Japanese
1 Mānele Bay Rd, 96763
Tel *(808) 565-2000*
This cliffside hotel restaurant
overlooks a protected marine
preserve. Guests feast on the
namesake celeb chef's signature
contemporary Japanese cuisine
and new creations made with
Hawaiian ingredients.

MÅNELE (LÅNA'I):
One Forty $$$
Steakhouse/Seafood
1 Mānele Bay Rd, 96763
Tel *(808) 565-2000*
Lovely ocean-facing dining
room in the Four Seasons Resort;
offers gourmet breakfasts and
a lengthy steak-and-seafood
dinner menu. Extensive wine
list. Excellent service.

PUKO'O (MOLOKA'I): Mana'e
Goods and Grindz $
American
*Near Mile Marker 16, close to Puko'o,
96729*
Tel *(808) 558-8498*
Convenience store on the east
end of the island with a lunch
counter serving breakfasts and
lunches. The shaded picnic tables
are a good spot to enjoy basic
island and vegetarian dishes.

Maui

HA'IKŪ: Hana Hou Cafe $
Hawaiian
810 Ha'ikū Rd, 96708
Tel *(808) 575-2661*
One of the island's best places
to sample authentic Hawaiian
dishes such as *kālua* pork, *poi*,
and *laulau*. A good mix of ethnic
dishes are also featured.

HA'IKŪ:
Colleen's at the Cannery $$
American
810 Ha'ikū Rd, 96708
Tel *(808) 575-9211*
Located 2 miles off the Hāna
Highway, this casual bistro attracts
locals and visitors alike with lunch

items such as burgers and salads.
Dinner includes options such as
filet mignon and pan-seared *ahi*.

HA'IKŪ: Nuka $$
Japanese
780 Ha'ikū Rd, 96708
Tel *(808) 575-2939* **Closed** *Mon*
Izakaya-style restaurant featuring
flavorful sushi and Japanese
classics made with local, seasonal
ingredients. Casual, intimate
environs. Limited seating often
results in queues on weekends.

DK Choice

HĀLI'IMAILE: Hali'imaile
General Store $$$
Hawaiian
900 Hāli'imaile Rd, 96768
Tel *(808) 572-2666*
In the middle of a pineapple
plantation, this restaurant is
housed in a historic building that
was formerly a general store. The
island's culinary icon Bev Gannon
renovated it and continues to
be the inspiration for the inviting
menu. Her superb Hawai'i
regional cuisine, accented with
international influences, is
perfect for special occasions.

HĀNA: Hāna Ranch
Restaurant $$
American
5301 Hāna Hwy, 96713
Tel *(808) 248-8255*
Relish hearty servings of wholesome
food in a rustic setting with stunning
ocean views. Lunch includes
salads and sandwiches, and dinner
offers pasta and barbecued ribs.

HĀNA: Ka'uiki $$$
Fusion
5031 Hāna Hwy, 96713
Tel *(808) 248-8211*
A delicious combination of
traditional ingredients and

innovative cooking techniques
complemented by an enchanting
tropical setting. Seasonal vegetables and fruits are used
in the dishes.

KĀ'ANAPALI: CJ's Deli & Diner $
Deli
2580 Keka'a Dr, 96761
Tel *(808) 667-0968*
Friendly neighborhood restaurant
within the Kā'anapali Resort. The
extensive choices range from generous breakfast items to sandwiches,
"plate lunches", and pot roast.

KĀ'ANAPALI: Hula Grill $$
Hawaiian/American
2435 Ka'anapali Pkwy, 96761
Tel *(808) 667-6636*
This lovely beach house transports
guests back to the gentility of
1930s Hawai'i. Favorites include
ono (wahoo fish) and *ahi* steak,
sweet potato ravioli, and barbe-
cue ribs. The beachfront bar
serves cocktails and draft beers.

KĀ'ANAPALI: Leilani's on
the Beach $$
American
2435 Ka'anapali Pkwy, 96761
Tel *(808) 661-4495*
Beachfront island-style fish
restaurant and steakhouse. The
upstairs dining room affords
stunning ocean views, while
the downstairs cocktail *lānai*
(veranda) is a great spot for
watching the sunset. Good
choice of wines and *pūpū*.

KĀ'ANAPALI: Sangrita Grill +
Cantina $$
Mexican
2580 Keka'a Dr, 96761
Tel *(808) 662-6000*
Restaurant and tequila bar
serving delectable authentic
Mexican fare. Features one of
the island's largest collection
of tequila and mezcal.

Guests enjoying alfresco dining amid 1930s-style interiors at Hula Grill

KĀ'ANAPALI: Roy's Ka'anapali Bar & Grill $$$
Fusion
2290 Ka'anapali Pkwy, 96761
Tel (808) 669-6999
Famed for the trademark creative cuisine of celeb chef Roy Yamaguchi, this place is always buzzing with patrons. The food is served directly from an open kitchen. Award-winning wine list.

KĀ'ANAPALI: Son'z Maui at Swan Court $$$
Hawaiian
200 Nohea Kai Dr, 96761
Tel (808) 667-4506
One of the island's most romantic al fresco dining rooms where guests watch swans glide across a lush lagoon while enjoying their meals. The kitchen prepares creative Hawai'i regional cuisine with great seafood options.

KAHULUI: Da Kitchen Cafe $
Hawaiian
425 Koloa St, 96732
Tel (808) 871-7782 **Closed** Sun
Authentic Hawaiian dishes are the pride of this welcoming eatery. A good choice for feasting on island-style "plate lunches" such as *mahimahi* tempura, teriyaki chicken, and *loco moco*.

KAHULUI: Geste Shrimp Truck $
Seafood
Kahului Beach Rd, 96732
Tel (808) 298-7109 **Closed** Sun & Mon
Popular beachfront food truck offering no-frills lunch options. Fresh local shrimps are covered in a choice of tasty sauces and served with scoops of crab salad and rice.

KAHULUI: Maui Coffee Roasters $
Café
444 Hāna Hwy, 96732
Tel (808) 877-2877
Legendary java spot that serves superb coffee drinks, some made with freshly-roasted Hawaiian coffee beans. A light menu of salads and sandwiches available to go.

KAHULUI: Stillwell's Bakery & Cafe $
Bakery
1740 Ka'ahumanu Ave, 96732
Tel (808) 243-2243 **Closed** Sun
Among the best bake shops on Maui, Stillwell's churns out scrumptious bread, rolls, cakes, pies, cookies, and pastries. Savory options include home-made soups, hearty sandwiches, and salads. Pleasing, well-lit environs.

KAHULUI: Bistro Casanova $$
Mediterranean
33 Lono Ave, 96732
Tel (808) 873-3650 **Closed** Sun
Casual bistro close to the airport and Maui Arts & Cultural Center. Local ingredients such as beef and fish are used to create a variety of dishes, including pastas and tapas.

KAHULUI: Koho's Grill & Bar $$
American
275 Ka'ahumanu Ave, 96732
Tel (808) 877-5588
Family-friendly eatery with varied menu for all three meals of the day. Burgers, salads, "plate lunches", and fresh fish are popular choices. Great desserts

KAPALUA: The Beach House $
American
1 Ritz-Carlton Dr, 96761
Tel (808) 669-6200
Lunch-only spot offering tropical cocktails, salads, sandwiches, and light fare. More than 40 fully grown coconut palms form a natural canopy over the dining area. Fine views of the D. T. Fleming Beach.

KAPALUA: Pineapple Grill $$
Fusion
200 Kapalua Dr, 96761
Tel (808) 669-9600
Tropically decorated eatery overlooking the lush greens of the Kapalua Golf Club. Pacific cuisine blends local ingredients and Asian cooking. Varied wine list. Live music performances.

KAPALUA: Sansei Seafood Restaurant & Sushi Bar $$
Japanese
600 Office Rd, 96761
Tel (808) 669-6286
This wildly successful sushi spot has won rave reviews locally and abroad. Award-winning Asian rock shrimp cake, mango and

Eclectic paintings and artwork adorn the interiors of Maui Coffee Roasters

Fried Spam Musubi, a popular Hawaiian snack, served at Da kitchen Cafe

crab salad hand-roll, and Japanese calamari salad are among the signature dishes.

KAPALUA: The Plantation House Restaurant $$$
Fusion
2000 Plantation Club Dr, 96761
Tel (808) 669-6299
Perched above the blue Pacific and the Kapalua Resort area, this lovely restaurant serves all meals. The varied menus feature island cuisine with Mediterranean influences. Excellent wine list.

KĪHEI: Five Palms Restaurant $$
Eclectic
2960 S Kihei Rd, 96753
Tel (808) 879-2607
Stunning setting in the Mana Kai Hotel overlooking the beautiful white sands and sparkling waters of Keawakapu Beach. All three meals are served using fresh island ingredients. Separate sushi and *pūpū* menu.

LAHAINA: Aloha Mixed Plate $
Hawaiian
1285 Front St, 96761
Tel (808) 661-3322
Open-air oceanfront place featuring authentic Hawaiian mixed plates that offer a taste of the state's history. Classics include teriyaki beef, fried rice, and Asian chicken salad.

LAHAINA: Ululani's Hawaiian Shave Ice $
Desserts
819 Front St, 96761
Tel (808) 877-3700
Family-owned shop serving up hundreds of cups of delicious shaved ice daily to locals as well as tourists. Patrons can customize their cooling treats with a huge variety of flavors and toppings.

For more information on types of restaurants see page 189

Beachside seating with amazing ocean views at Pacific'O

LAHAINA: Cheeseburger in
Paradise $$
American
811 Front St, 96761
Tel *(808) 661-4855*
Open-air hangout offering
unparalleled views of the ocean
and nearby islands, as well as
the lively Front Street. Enormous
juicy burgers and a variety of
beers keep the crowds satiated.

LAHAINA: Cool Cat Cafe $$
American
658 Front St, 96761
Tel *(808) 667-0908*
A 1950s-style diner popular for
its award-winning burgers. The
varied menu consists of crowd
favorites such as hot dogs, sandwiches, and shakes. Patrons
can sit in the intimate booths
or the breezy outdoor patio.

LAHAINA: Kimo's $$
American
845 Front St, 96761
Tel *(808) 661-4811*
Right on the waterfront with
panoramic views of the expanse
of blue beyond the horizon.
Hawaiian fish, seafood, and prime
rib are the mainstays. Extensive
list of wines and cocktails.

LAHAINA: Lulu's Lahaina
Surf Club & Grill $$
American
1221 Honoapi'ilani Hwy, 96761
Tel *(808) 661-0808*
Fun late-night spot for casual
dining and drinks. Surf-videos
and sports play on the big flat-
screen TVs. The lengthy menu
includes pizzas, sandwiches,
and burgers.

LAHAINA: Penne Pasta Café $$
Italian
180 Dickenson St, 96761
Tel *(808) 661-6633*
Just a block from Front Street,
this place prepares Southern
Italian inspired food. An

assortment of delightful pastas,
pizzas, salads, and sandwiches
are served in casual family-friendly
environs. Kids' menu available.

LAHAINA: Star Noodle $$
Asian
286 Kupuohi St, 96761
Tel *(808) 667-5400*
Hip Asian bistro that can be
slightly hard to find. The menu
includes everything from Korean
kimchi and charbroiled miso
salmon to Vietnamese shrimp
crepes. Good selection of *sake*
(Japanese rice wine) and cocktails.

LAHAINA: Feast at Lele $$$
International
505 Front St, 96761
Tel *(808) 667-5353*
A musical tour through various
Pacific Island nations accompanies
a sit-down dinner featuring
modern interpretations of their
cuisines. The divine location
facing the ocean complements
this unique concept in dining
and entertainment.

LAHAINA:
Gerard's Restaurant $$$
French
174 Lahainaluna Rd, 96761
Tel *(808) 661-8939*
Located a block off busy Front
Street in a charming country
setting. Chef Gerard remains true
to his classic culinary roots, while
incorporating local ingredients
into his original recipes. Award-
winning wine list.

LAHAINA: Lahaina Grill $$$
American
127 Lahainaluna Rd, 96761
Tel *(808) 667-5117*
Relaxed yet elegant destination
for exquisitely prepared and
presented meals. Signature
dishes include tequila shrimp
with firecracker rice and Kona
coffee-roasted colorado rack
of lamb. Fine desserts.

LAHAINA: Longhi's $$$
Italian
888 Front St, 96761
Tel *(808) 667-2288*
One of the island's most acclaimed
dining venues that has been
serving gourmet Italian fare in
the same location for several
decades. Features fresh fish,
steaks, lobsters and much more.
Window tables offer lots of
people-watching opportunities.

LAHAINA:
Mala Ocean Tavern $$$
American
1307 Front St, 96761
Tel *(808) 667-9394*
Delectable small plates, easy
to share among groups, run the
gamut from clams in black bean
sauce to whole, wok-fried *moi*
(a type of fish). The oceanfront
setting affords wonderful
sunset views.

LAHAINA: Merriman's $$$
Hawaiian
1 Bay Club Pl, 96761
Tel *(808) 669-6400*
Owned by Peter Merriman –
one of the big names of Hawai'i
regional cuisine – this pleasantly
decorated restaurant overlooks
Kapalua Bay. The menu features
island-reared beef, fresh seafood,
and local produce.

LAHAINA: Old
Lahaina Luau $$$
Hawaiian
1251 Front St, 96761
Tel *(808) 667-1998*
Nightly show of traditional
Hawaiian music and dance
accompanies a buffet of authentic dishes including *kālua* pig,
poi, and *lomi lomi* salmon at
this restaurant on the beach.

LAHAINA: Pacific'O $$$
Fusion
505 Front St, 96761
Tel *(808) 667-4341*
Incredible seafront venue that
was once a royal Hawaiian playground. The menu features
creative modern Pacific cuisine
with a delicious Asian twist.
Uses produce from the restaurant's upcountry farm.

MĀ'ALAEA: Seascape
Ma'alaea Restaurant $
American
192 Ma'alaea Rd, 96793
Tel *(808) 270-7068*
Set in a picturesque village, this
open-air spot serves delicious
and healthy seafood. Trans fat-
free dishes on the menu cater
to health-minded guests.
Splendid ocean views.

MAKAWAO: Komoda Store and Bakery $
Bakery
3674 Baldwin Ave, 96768
Tel *(808) 572-7261*
Family-run bakery that has been a local favorite for generations. Loyal patrons arrive early in the morning for award-winning sweet treats such as cream puffs and doughnuts on sticks.

MAKAWAO: Casanova Italian Restaurant and Deli $$
Italian
1188 Makawao Ave, 96768
Tel *(808) 572-0220*
Visit this eatery in the morning to enjoy coffee, omelets, and home-baked pastries on the porch while watching people. The dinner menu features Italian specialties, including pizzas from the centerpiece wood-burning oven.

NAPILI: The Gazebo $
American
5315 Lower Honoapi'ilani Rd, 96761
Tel *(808) 669-5621*
Located right on the ocean, this eatery is a favorite breakfast option among locals. Fluffy French toast and pancakes made with everything from pineapple and banana to macadamia nuts are popular choices.

NAPILI: Sea House Restaurant $$$
Hawaiian
5900 Lower Honoapi'ilani Rd, 96761
Tel *(808) 669-1500*
This open-air beachfront restaurant affords breathtaking views of the ocean and nearby islands. The wide-ranging menu comprises Hawaiian recipes made with fresh local ingredients.

PĀ'IA: Charley's Restaurant and Saloon $
American/Eclectic
142 Hāna Hwy, 96779
Tel *(808) 579-8085*
Named after the owner's pet dog, Charley's has been a beloved local hangout for decades. The menus include everything from *huevos rancheros* (Mexican-style fried eggs) and fish sandwiches to pastas and pizzas. Pool tables and live music for entertainment.

PĀIA: Paia Fish Market $
Seafood
100 Baldwin Ave, 96779
Tel *(808) 579-8030*
One of the town's most popular eateries. Fresh fish is served in a number of ways including pasta, tacos, and salads. Fish in burgers and quesadillas are crowd favorites. Family-friendly environment.

PĀ'IA: Dazoo $$
Hawaiian
71 Baldwin Ave, 96779
Tel *(808) 579-9999*
Casual eatery serving simple but healthy fish dishes and small 'plates'. A typical dish is alii mushrooms from the Big Island sautéed with garlic and herbs. Vegetarian options available.

PĀ'IA: Flatbread Company $$
Pizza
89 Hāna Hwy, 96779
Tel *(808) 579-8989*
Flavorful, all-natural pizzas from a wood-fired clay oven is the highlight at this restaurant. The focus is on using local ingredients such as goat cheese, avocados, jalapenos, and many more.

PĀ'IA: Mama's Fish House $$$
Seafood
799 Poho Place, 96779
Tel *(808) 579-8488*
Award-winning fresh-fish dishes attract crowds to this famous oceanfront restaurant. Ethnic artwork adorns the interiors. Window tables are usually reserved in advance. Dutiful servers assist diners unfamiliar with the local fish on offer.

WAILEA: Gannon's $$$
American
100 Wailea Golf Club Dr, 96753
Tel *(808) 875-8080*
Elegant, spacious destination for chef Bev Gannon's award-winning cuisine and deluxe service. Located on a hill along

The entrance to Spago, an eminent American restaurant chain from L.A.

Wailea Golf Club's gold course, the dining rooms offer panoramic ocean views. Extensive wine and cocktail list.

WAILEA: Kō $$$
Fusion
4100 Wailea Alanui, 96753
Tel *(808) 875-4100*
Welcoming restaurant serving food inspired by the sugarcane plantation era of Hawai'i. The menu features Hawaiian dishes with Asian touches such as Korean style spicy chicken and Lumpia Filipino spring rolls.

WAILEA: Mala Wailea $$$
Hawaiian
3700 Wailea Alanui, 96753
Tel *(808) 875-9394*
Mark Ellman, one of the founders of the Hawai'i regional cuisine movement, offers innovative dishes incorporating fresh seafood and organic produce. Good dessert options and a varied wine list.

WAILEA: Morimoto Maui $$$
Japanese
3550 Wailea Alanui Dr, 96753
Tel *(808) 573-1234*
Masaharu Morimoto's Maui outpost blends island-grown ingredients with Japanese seafood to create dishes such as hand-rolled sushi and sashimi. Breezy outdoor patio.

WAILEA: Spago $$$
American
3900 Wailea Alanui, 96753
Tel *(808) 879-2999*
Celebrity chef Wolfgang Puck maintains an elegant outpost of his iconic L.A. restaurant. The menu juxtaposes Puck's legendary classics with locally inspired dishes that fuse Hawaiian and Californian cuisines.

WAILEA: Tommy Bahama's $$$
American
3750 Wailea Alanui Dr, 96753
Tel *(808) 875-9983*
Well-known store and restaurant serving large portions of fresh, island-style fish dishes, as well as salads and burgers. Offers vegetarian options as well. Choose from a range of fun, tropical drinks.

WAILUKU: Sam Sato's $
Hawaiian
1750 Wili Pa Loop, 96793
Tel *(808) 244-7124*
Drop in for island classics such as beef sticks, spam and eggs, banana pancakes, and dry mein noodles at this simple breakfast and lunch spot. Take-out available.

For more information on types of restaurants *see page 189*

WAILUKU: Tasty Crust Restaurant $
American
1770 Mill St, 96793
Tel *(808) 244-0845*
One of the island's favorite breakfast spots specializing in banana pancakes, hearty omelets, *loco moco*, and fried rice. Diner-style environs.

WAILUKU: A Saigon Cafe $$
Vietnamese
1792 Main St, 96793
Tel *(808) 243-9560*
Tucked away under a bridge without a sign, this is among the most popular Asian eateries in Central Maui. The menu features a variety of classical Vietnamese fare including a good selection of vegetarian options.

WAILUKU: A.K.'s Cafe $$
Hawaiian
1237 Lower Main St, 96793
Tel *(808) 244-8774*
Closed *Lunch, Sat & Sun*
Small café serving an assortment of delicious, local-style dishes. House favorites such as blackened *ono*, fish tacos, baked chicken, and turkey meatloaf are heart-healthy and diabetic-friendly.

WAILUKU: Asian Star $$
Asian
1764 Wili Pa Loop, 96793
Tel *(808) 244-1833*
A much sought-after lunch choice among area workers. Intensely flavored dishes include lemongrass curry with chicken and crispy tangerine beef. Casual ambience and efficient service.

WAILUKU: Tokyo Tei $$
Japanese
1063 Lower Main St, 96793
Tel *(808) 242-9630*
No-frills restaurant serving tasty Japanese dishes for more than

five decades. Teriyaki fish, salmon, pork, and exceptionally fresh sashimi are crowd favorites.

Hawai'i Island

HILO: Bears' Coffee $
Café
106 Keawe St, 96721
Tel *(808) 935-0708*
Stylish little spot, ideal for people-watching while enjoying tasty breakfasts of Belgian waffles and coffee or quick lunches of salads and sandwiches.

HILO: Cafe 100 $
Hawaiian
969 Kīlauea Ave, 96720
Tel *(808) 935-8683*   **Closed** *Sun*
A local favorite for more than 50 years. The extensive menu includes beef teriyaki, beef curry, *laulau*, *kālua* pig. The signature *loco moco* comes in more than 30 varieties. Delightful soda-fountain treats.

HILO: Ken's House of Pancakes $
American
1730 Kamehameha Ave, 96720
Tel *(808) 935-8711*
This 1950s-style, 24-hour diner is known for incredible all-day breakfasts, Hawaiian-style 'plates', and prime rib specials. A good selection of vegetarian dishes is available. Warm, friendly service.

HILO: Lucy's Taqueria $
Mexican
194 Kīlauea Ave, 96720
Tel *(808) 315-8246*   **Closed** *Tue*
Friendly eatery offering Mexican street favorites in a relaxed atmosphere Tacos, burritos, enchiladas, and tamales are the main draws. Creative margaritas such as *liliko'i* (passion fruit) and prickly pear are refreshing treats.

HILO: Nori's Saimin & Snacks $
Japanese
688 Kinoole St, 96720
Tel *(808) 935-9133*
Casual, no-frills eatery known for its delicious *saimin* noodles. Comfort favorites include teriyaki pork, hamburger steak, furikake cookies, and chocolate mochi cake.

HILO: Café Pesto $$
Eclectic
308 Kamehameha Ave, 96720
Tel *(808) 969-6640*
Friendly café in a lovely setting near Hilo Bay. The menu features regional cuisine including island fish prepared in a variety of ways, organic salads, and innovative pastas as well as pizzas.

HILO: Hilo Bay Cafe $$
American
123 Lihiwai St, 96720
Tel *(808) 935-4939*
Stylish restaurant popular with locals and tourists alike. Daily specials include a choice of vegetarian, meat, and fish options. Kids' menu available.

HILO: Miyo's $$
Fusion
564 Hinano St, 96720
Tel *(808) 935-2273*   **Closed** *Sun*
Owned and run by chef Miyo Harumi, this place incorporates Japanese and American cooking techniques with a focus on home-style cooking. Noodles, tempura and donburi (Japanese rice bowls) are made with island produce and fish. Close to the airport.

HILO: Naung Mai Thai Kitchen $$
Thai
86 Kīlauea Ave, 96720
Tel *(808) 934-7540*
Hole-in-the-wall establishment whose Thai food is hugely popular. Located near the Hilo Farmer's Market, from where the chefs gather organic ingredients to perfect delicious cooking. Serves vegetarian options as well.

HILO: Ponds Hilo $$
American
135 Kalanianaole Ave, 96720
Tel *(808) 934-7633*
Delightful eatery overlooking the scenic Reed's Pond. The classic menu includes American prime rib, lobster, and fresh fish. The friendly chef makes it a point to visit each table personally. Live music most nights.

A customer paying for an order at A Saigon Cafe, Central Maui

The in-house brewery at the famous Kona Brewing Company

HILO: Seaside Restaurant $$
Seafood
1790 Kalanianole Ave, 96720
Tel *(808) 935-8825* **Closed** *Mon*
Local institution run by the Nakagawa family for more than 70 years. The restaurant sits in the middle of ponds from where fish, caught fresh, fill the cooking pots. Reservations are recommended.

HILO: Sombat's Fresh Thai Cuisine $$
Thai
88 Kanoelehua Ave, 96720
Tel *(808) 969-9336* **Closed** *Sun*
This small restaurant grows many of the ingredients it uses in delectable, traditional fare such as green papaya salad, spring rolls, and fiery Thai curries. Offers take-out option.

KAILUA-KONA: Big Island Grill $
Hawaiian
75-5702 Kuakini Hwy, 96740
Tel *(808) 326-1153*
Offers generous portions of island favorites such as *loco moco*, chicken katsu, and beef teriyaki. Almost always overflowing with people, but it is worth the wait.

KAILUA-KONA: Da Poke Shack $
Hawaiian
76-6246 Ali'i Dr, 96740
Tel *(808) 329-7653*
Simple eatery where the namesake dish is prepared from fresh seafood, never frozen. Traditional seasonings include Hawaiian salt, *limu kohu* (seaweed), and *inamona* (roasted kukui nut). Friendly staff.

KAILUA-KONA: Ultimate Burger $
American
74-5450 Makala Blvd, 96740
Tel *(808) 329-2326*
Grass-fed, free-range local beef, ground daily and charbroiled to create some of the island's most acclaimed burgers at this restaurant. Gourmet fries are cut fresh every morning.

KAILUA-KONA: Bongo Ben's Island Cafe $$
American
75-5819 Ali'i Dr, 96740
Tel *(808) 329-9203*
Relaxed oceanfront setting offering some of the island's most acclaimed breakfast choices as well as varied lunch and dinner menus. Courteous staff and talented Hawaiian musicians ensure a welcoming vibe.

KAILUA-KONA: Kona Brewing Company $$
American
75-5629 Kuakini Hwy, 96740
Tel *(808) 334-2739*
The state's most famous brewery maintains a brewpub where fresh handcrafted local ales and lagers can be enjoyed alongside imported and specialty beers. The menu includes hand-tossed pizzas, burgers, salads, and other casual fare.

KAILUA-KONA: Krua Thai Cuisine $$
Thai
75-5705 Kuakini Hwy, 96740
Tel *(808) 327-5782*
Adventurous diners enjoy reinvented versions of traditional Thai dishes. Curries, noodles, dumplings, Thai-style chicken noodle soup, wontons, and spring rolls are popular offerings.

KAILUA-KONA: Rapanui Island Cafe $$
Asian
75-5695 Ali'i Dr, 96740
Tel *(808) 329-0511* **Closed** *Sun*
The varied menu that features a number of flavorful dishes, does justice to a variety of Asian cuisines including Malaysian and Indonesian.

KAILUA-KONA: The Fish Hopper $$
Seafood
75-5683 Ali'i Dr, 96740
Tel *(808) 326-2002*
This downtown eatery with its panoramic views of the ocean offers fresh, local seafood as well as fish shipped in from California. Tropical, colorful cocktails are served in the bar area.

KAILUA-KONA: Huggo's on the Rocks $$$
American
75-5828 Kahakai Rd, 96740
Tel *(808) 329-1493*
Family-run oceanside restaurant with fabulous views of Kona Bay. *Pūpū*, cocktails, and live entertainment attract a cheerful crowd.

KAILUA-KONA: Kona Inn Restaurant $$$
American
75-5744 Ali'i Dr, 96740
Tel *(808) 329-4455*
Set in a historic property built by the Inter-Island Steam Navigation Company in 1928. A sound choice for open-air dining with Hawaiian-themed environs and pretty ocean views. House favorites include local seafood and fine steaks.

KAILUA-KONA: 'Ulu Ocean Grill $$$
Hawaiian
72-100 Kaupulehu Dr, 96740
Tel *(808) 325-8000*
Attractive beachfront restaurant with terraced indoor and outdoor seating to make the most of magnificent ocean views. The kitchen highlights the flavors of the Pacific with dishes such as oven-roasted whole fish and tableside *ahi poke*.

KAMUELA: Village Burger $
American
67-1185 Mamalahoa Hwy, 96743
Tel *(808) 885-7319*
This casual eatery caters to burger lovers by using pasture-raised Hawaiian beef and veal in its tasty burgers. Hand-made patties are cooked to order and come with flavorful toppings.

KEAUHOU: Jackie Rey's Ohana Grill $$
American
75-5995 Kuakini Hwy, 96740
Tel *(808) 327-0209*
Lively and casual place serving well-done culinary classics from the mainland. Offerings include fresh fish, salads, tacos, chops, ribs, and steaks. Impeccable service.

For more information on types of restaurants *see page 189*

Warm interiors of the dining room at the Kilauea Lodge and Restaurant

KOHALA COAST:
CanoeHouse $$$
Hawaiian
68-1400 Mauna Lani Dr, 96743
Tel *(808) 885-6622*   **Closed** *Sun*
Impressive Pacific Rim cuisine served in the well-maintained grounds of the Mauna Lani Bay Hotel in an open-air setting. A traditional koa canoe hangs from the ceiling.

DK Choice

KOHALA COAST: Roy's
Waikoloa Bar & Grill $$$
Hawaiian
250 Waikoloa Beach Dr, 96738
Tel *(808) 886-4321*
Another one of celeb chef Roy Yamaguchi's top-notch restaurants that lures patrons from across the island. The menu features trendy Hawaiian fusion cuisine showcasing a selection of Roy's classics. The exhibition kitchen is a signature style of the chef. Well-informed servers offer pairing notes from the pricey wine list.

VOLCANO VILLAGE: Volcano
Golf and Country Club $$
American
99-1261 Pi'i Mauna Dr, 96718
Tel *(808) 967-8228*
Casual breakfast and lunch spot in the clubhouse at the Volcano Golf and Country Club. Most patrons stick to burgers, sandwiches, and local favorites such as *mahi mahi* and teriyaki chicken.

VOLCANO VILLAGE: Kilauea
Lodge and Restaurant $$$
European
19-3948 Old Volcano Rd, 96785
Tel *(808) 967-7366*
Welcoming mountain lodge with a huge and historic fireplace sets

the scene for hearty European cooking. *Hasenpfeffer* (rabbit stew) is a house specialty. Impressive Sunday brunch service and an extensive wine list.

WAIMEA: Merriman's $$$
Hawaiian
65-1227 Opelo Rd, 96743
Tel *(808) 885-6822*
Flagship restaurant owned by renowned chef Peter Merriman, one of the pioneers of original Hawai'i regional cuisine. The menu features island-reared beef, fresh seafood, and other local produce.

Kaua'i

ANAHOLA: Duane's Ono
Char-Burger $
American
4-4350 Kūhiō Hwy, 96703
Tel *(808) 822-9181*
This tiny roadside stand draws crowds for its juicy burgers and excellent fries. The Local Boy – featuring pineapple and teriyaki sauce – is a must-try. Expect a long wait at lunchtime.

KAPA'A: Eggbert's Family
Specialty Restaurant $
American
4-484 Kūhiō Hwy, 96746
Tel *(808) 822-3787*
Local favorite for more than 25 years with fluffy pancakes, eggs Benedict, and 150 styles of omelet. Serves all meals but breakfast is most popular. Welcoming atmosphere.

KAPA'A: Kountry Kitchen $
Hawaiian
1485 Kūhiō Hwy, 96746
Tel *(808) 822-3511*
The place offers hearty breakfasts and lunches of Hawaiian-accented

favorites such as fried-rice omelet, macadamia nut pancakes with coconut syrup, and *loco moco*. Great for families.

KAPA'A: Mermaids Cafe $
Fusion
1384 Kūhiō Hwy, 96746
Tel *(808) 821-2026*
Café serving healthy, delicious dishes full of island and pan-Asian flavors. Known for home-made wraps, salads, and vegan/vegetarian items. Hibiscus lemonade is a crowd favorite.

KAPA'A: Ono Family Restaurant $
American
4-1292 Kūhiō Hwy, 96746
Tel *(808) 822-1710*
Diner-style spot known for generous breakfasts. The wide variety of pancakes and Portuguese sausage are especially popular. Don't miss the shave ice.

KAPA'A: Papaya's Natural
Foods & Café $
Vegetarian
4-831 Kūhiō Hwy, 96746
Tel *(808) 823-0190*
One of the largest health food stores on the island. Also serves dishes prepared using organic products. Menu includes tofu, hummus, *tempeh* (soy product) as well as baked goods, coffee, drinks, and smoothies.

KAPA'A: Hukilau Lanai $$
American
520 Aleka Lp, 96746
Tel *(808) 822-0600*   **Closed** *Mon*
This Kauai Coast Resort restaurant serves healthy dishes in a breezy open-air dining room. The menu features items made with local produce such as Molokai sweet potato ravioli and Hamakua mushroom tart. Live music in the evening.

KAPA'A: Oasis on the Beach $$
American
4-820 Kūhiō Hwy, 96746
Tel *(808) 822-9332*
Oceanfront restaurant with great views, good food, and friendly service. Menu features fresh, locally-sourced ingredients that reflect the Hawaiian culture and international influences. Tranquil, romantic ambience.

KAPA'A: Verde $$
Fusion
4-1101 Kūhiō Hwy, 96746
Tel *(808) 821-1400*
Trendy yet casual dining/takeout spot where New Mexico meets Pacific Rim. *Sopaipillas* (deep-fried pastry), burritos, and tacos feature fresh meat, seafood and local ingredients. Kids' specials on offer.

KĪLAUEA: The Kilauea Bakery & Pau Hana Pizza $
Bakery
2484 Keneke St, 96754
Tel *(808) 828-2020*
Unassuming outlet in the Kong Lung Center serving some of the most popular baked goods and pizzas on the island. Come early before the breakfast goodies sell out. Great picnic items too.

KOKE'E: The Lodge at Kokee $
American
3600 Kokee Rd, 96796
Tel *(808) 335-6061*
Simple, welcoming eatery set within Koke'e State Park. Serves breakfast, lunch, and desserts. Portuguese bean soup is a house specialty. Try the home-made *liliko'i*, guava chiffon, and coconut pies.

LĪHUE: Hamura Saimin $
Hawaiian
2956 Kress St, 96766
Tel *(808) 245-3271*
Modest restaurant serving some of the best *saimin* on the island. Locals and tourists stop in here for signature noodles and other dishes late into the night. Fresh *liliko'i* pie is the specialty dessert.

LĪHUE: Mark's Place $
Hawaiian
1610 Haleukana St, 96766
Tel *(808) 245-2522*   **Closed** *Sat & Sun*
Popular for hearty portions of Hawaiian dishes. Offers gourmet "plate lunches", *bento*, salads, and omiyagi snacks. Quick, friendly service.

LĪHUE: Tip Top Motel & Cafe $
Café/Bakery
3173 Akahi St, 96766
Tel *(808) 245-2333*   **Closed** *Mon*
Local favorite, in business since 1916. The large dining room has 1950s-style booths. Legendary favorites include macadamia nut pancakes at breakfast and oxtail soup at lunch.

LĪHUE: Café Portofino $$
Italian
3481 Ho'olaulea Way, 96766
Tel *(808) 245-2121*
Classic old-world dishes made with flavorful imported ingredients. Breads, ice cream, and desserts are made in-house. Candlelit tables and live performances by harpist or guitarist set a romantic mood.

LĪHUE: Duke's Kauai $$
American
3610 Rice St, 96766
Tel *(808) 246-9599*
Oceanfront restaurant decorated with surfing memorabilia of famous Hawaiian surfer Duke Kahanamoku. Serves delicious food such as fresh fish, salads, and desserts. Incredible sunset views and live music.

LĪHUE: JJ's Broiler $$
American
3416 Rice St, 96766
Tel *(808) 246-4422*
Open-air dining with great ocean views. While burgers, sandwiches, and vegetarian dishes dominate the lunch menu, seafood, steaks, and pastas feature at dinner.

LĪHUE: Kauai Pasta $$
Italian
3-3142 Kūhiō Hwy, 96766
Tel *(808) 822-7447*
Modern, intimate option offering familiar favorites made with the finest ingredients. Seasonal fare ranges from simple pasta dishes to elaborate steak entrée. Good selection of wines and cocktails.

LĪHUE: The Feral Pig $$
American
3501 Rice St, 96766
Tel *(808) 246-1100*
Neighborhood hangout serving juicy burgers and other pub fare alongside a good selection of beers, including several local brews. Welcoming atmosphere.

DK Choice

LĪHUE: Gaylord's at Kilohana $$$
American
3-2087 Kaumuali'i Hwy, 96766
Tel *(808) 245-9593*
Al fresco dining destination at Kilohana, the legendary plantation estate in Kaua'i. The varied menu has pastas and fine steaks. Sunday brunch is a favorite among visitors with dishes such as smoked salmon and bagels, braised short ribs, and portuguese sausage. Impressive wine list.

PO'IPŪ: Puka Dog $
American
2360 Kiahuna Plantation Dr, 96756
Tel *(808) 742-6044*
Casual spot serving Hawaiian-accented hot dogs – typically Polish sausage in a sweet local bun, topped with a choice of mustards and tropical relishes such as *liliko'i*, mango, and coconut.

PO'IPŪ: Josselin's Tapas Bar & Grill $$
Fusion
2829 Ala Kalanikaumaka St, 96756
Tel *(808) 742-7117*
Contemporary restaurant offering unique tapas from around the world with Pacific Rim influences. Refreshing versions of Sangria such as lychee or pomegranate served table-side.

PO'IPŪ: Keoki's Paradise $$
American
2360 Kiahuna Plantation Dr, 96756
Tel *(808) 742-7534*
Enjoy island cooking, exotic drinks and live music in lush gardens on Po'ipū Beach. The menu features fish, prime steaks, and Hawaiian dishes. Tropical cocktails and more casual fare in the Bamboo Bar.

PO'IPŪ: Casa di Amici $$$
Italian
2301 Nalo Rd, 96756
Tel *(808) 742-1555*
Features Italian-Mediterranean fare served al fresco at this cozy spot tucked away in a residential neighborhood. Risottos and pastas prepared with aplomb.

PO'IPŪ: The Beach House $$$
Hawaiian
5022 Lawai Rd, 96756
Tel *(808) 742-1424*
A spectacular oceanfront setting makes this place an ideal venue for sunset drinks and dinner. The excellent menu features creative takes on island favorites made with fresh ingredients.

Lovely outdoor seating at Gaylord's at Kilohana, an iconic sugar plantation estate in Kaua'i

For more information on types of restaurants *see page 189*

SHOPPING IN HAWAI'I

Pineapples, macadamia nuts, Kona coffee, alohawear, T-shirts, tropical flowers – these are the things that top visitors' shopping lists, and they are easy to find. Traditional Hawaiian crafts, such as *kapa* cloth, pandanus baskets, and Ni'ihau shell *lei*, are harder to find and usually more costly – but beautiful, and worth the hunt.

You will find many things that look like they could be made in Hawai'i but actually come from Taiwan, Bali, China, or the Philippines. If you are determined to purchase "the real thing," check carefully. The addresses and telephone numbers of all the shops mentioned in the text are given on page 209.

A woman weaving traditional *lei* garlands, a popular Hawaiian souvenir

Shipping

For a charge, most stores and galleries will ship goods worldwide. Alternatively, you can use the **United States Postal Service** to send purchases home. Courier companies such as **DHL**, **FedEx**, and **UPS** are another option and can be contacted by phone or email. They provide insurance, delivery confirmation, and tracking, and offer a range of delivery times and costs. Some restrictions may apply to the type of item that can be sent and the destination of the package. You will be asked to fill out a form giving a short description of the goods and stating their monetary value. Keep receipts of the transaction in case any items should get lost in transit.

Where to Shop

Supermarkets, grocery shops, Long's Drugs stores, and discount shops, such as ABC Stores and K-Mart, have the best prices for things like macadamia nuts, jam, and coffee. These are the best places for cheap souvenirs, too, while museum shops are often good for Hawaiian crafts.

Anyone who likes second-hand shops should enjoy scouring shops and home sales for collectibles ("Hawaiiana"), from aloha shirts to vintage postcards, at bargain prices. The islands are big on second-hand shops and private garage sales. Check the Friday edition of the newspapers for weekend garage sales. The papers also list crafts fairs and market days.

When to Shop

You can shop 24 hours a day, seven days a week if you wish – some supermarkets and convenience stores never close.

Malls and large stores are normally open from 10am to 9pm, Monday to Saturday, and often on Sunday (but the hours are usually shorter). Small stores open from about 9am to 5 or 6pm, Monday to Saturday, and are closed on Sundays.

How to Pay

Travelers' checks in US dollars and credit cards are accepted more or less everywhere in Hawai'i *(see p236)*. However, it is a good idea to carry at least some cash for purchases at roadside stands and small, family-run stores.

Remember that sales tax of at least 4 per cent is added to every purchase made in Hawai'i, depending on the island, and that this tax will be added to the total bill by the cashier.

Fruit and Flowers

Many visitors take the fresh flavors and aromas of Hawai'i home with them. You can take coconuts, pineapples, and papayas (but no other fruit) through customs, as long as they are passed by the **US Department of Agriculture (USDA)** inspection.

It is best to buy such fruit prepackaged at airport shops or other reputable stores that specialize in "take home" fruits. There are many of these stores in Hawai'i, such as the **Maui Tropical Plantation & Country Store** near Wailuku. Someone at your hotel should know the best place on any particular island. These same places sell sterile cuttings and seeds of

Roadside stand selling tropical Hawaiian fruit on Maui's windward coast

tropical plants that have been passed by USDA. You can have your purchases delivered to the airport from which you are leaving or sent directly to your home address.

You can export all fresh flowers, subject to agricultural inspection, apart from jade vines, gardenias, and *maunaloa*. Hawai'i Island is the best place for anthuriums, while you should buy protea and exotics in Maui. You can export *lei*, but most last only a very short time; check with the florist or *lei-maker*, because some *lei* are very attractive when dried. Alternatively, you could consider buying a nonperishable *lei* made of nuts, feathers, seeds, or shells, for example (*see p33*). The best places to buy flower *lei* are the small shops in Honolulu's Chinatown, but the stands at Honolulu International Airport have a good selection, too.

If you are unsure whether or not you'll be able to take a particular item home with you, check first by telephoning the USDA.

Food and Drink

Although mangoes, guava, and *liliko'i* (passion fruit) are not permitted out of the islands, chutneys, jams, jellies, and other products made with these fruits are great buys.

World-famous Kona coffee comes from Hawai'i Island, but coffee is now grown on Maui and Kaua'i too. All coffees are available in whole-bean or ground, flavored, instant, and decaffeinated varieties.

Macadamia nuts also come in many forms, from dry-roasted and salted to honey-flavored or chocolate-covered. Adventurous gastronomes may like to try taro chips and "crack seed" – preserved and seasoned nuts, fruits, seeds, and sweets. All these products are sold at supermarkets, grocery stores, convenience stores, and specialty shops throughout the islands. **Shirokiya** (Honolulu), a Japan-based department store, also sells a great variety of unusual prepared food. Hawai'i has

two wineries. The **Tedeschi Winery** on Maui makes a couple of good red table wines, one sparkling wine, and, its most famous product, Maui Blanc – a light pineapple wine. The **Volcano Winery** on Hawai'i Island is producing some interesting wines from various tropical fruits while waiting for its grapevines to mature.

Art

Like Gauguin, many artists have followed their muse to the Pacific. Unlike Gauguin, the majority are not very good. There are literally dozens of "galleries," mostly in tourist shopping areas. Some specialize in sales of very expensive work that has no investment value – in spite of what the resident "consultants" tell you. If you need advice, someone at your hotel should be able to direct you to a reliable source; museums can often be of help, too.

There is some wonderful art to be found in Hawai'i. And much of it - in the form of lithographs, posters, and even cards – is affordable. Dietrich Varez of Volcano (on Hawai'i Island), for example, lovingly creates earth-brown linoleum block prints depicting local legends. They are glorious, easy to find, and cheap, at about $20 apiece. You will find his work in the **Volcano Art Center**. Another reputable gallery on Hawai'i Island is **Studio 7** in Hōlualoa.

The **Viewpoints Gallery** in Makawao (Maui) is a collective representing some fine local

One of the many art galleries on Front Street in Lahaina, Maui

artists. You can also rely on good quality at the **Village Gallery** and **Lahaina Arts Society** in Lahaina, **Gecko Trading** in Makawao, and **Nohea Gallery** in Honolulu.

Collectibles

Just about anything Hawaiian from the 1940s to the 1970s is now considered collectible: postcards, Matson steamship menus, even kitsch ceramic *hula* girls, and especially old aloha shirts known as "silkies."

You'll find such things in the shops on Wailuku's Market Street and in "antique" shops such as **Bailey's Antiques** and **Aloha Antiques & Collectibles** in Honolulu, and **The Only Show in Town** in Kahuku (O'ahu); **Manu Antiques** in Kamuela; **Story of Hawai'i Museum**; and the **Pā'ia Trading Company** on Maui. You may find it more fun, however, to go hunting for collectibles in second-hand stores and garage sales.

Display of blown-glass vases and other objects in a Maui gallery

Man weaving a coconut-leaf hat on a
Hawai'i Island street

Crafts

Hawai'i teems with artisans.
Hand-crafted bowls of mango,
monkeypod, or *koa* wood
make beautiful presents and
mementos. You can also buy
koa hair ornaments, chopsticks,
and key chains. Wooden objects
can be found in craft shops in
most big towns.

Hawai'i also has many expert
weavers. Coconut leaf is often
used, but *hala* (pandanus) is
better quality. Mats, bags,
and hats are all popular buys.
Ceramic bowls, vases, and plates
are also popular. **The Island's
Best** in Honolulu is a good
bet for these.

It is virtually impossible to
find any vintage Hawaiian quilts
to buy (most are treasured
family heirlooms), but new
quilts, quilt kits and other crafts
can be found at the **Maui Crafts
Guild** in Pā'ia or the **Gallery of
Great Things** on Hawai'i Island.
Hawaiian kapa (bark cloth) is
hard to find and most *kapa*
goods for sale are imported
from Samoa or Tonga.

Combing the crafts fairs
is a fun and rewarding way to
see what is available. Museum
shops are also good sources,
as are the many specialty shops,
including **Sand & Sea** on Maui
and **Ola's Hanalei** on Kaua'i.

Jewelry

Costume jewelry is made from
everything you can think of –
ceramic, paper, plastic, metals,
and more – and can be found
at crafts fairs. Fine jewelry made
of pearls, coral, jade, silver,
and gold is sold in department
stores and in the dozens of
specialty shops, such as
Precision Goldsmiths in
Wailuku and Kaua'i's **Jim Saylor
Jewelers**. "Heritage jewelry,"
Victorian gold jewelry with
names and designs inscribed
in black enamel, is popular.
It is also expensive, so be sure
to buy from a reliable dealer.

The most precious pieces
of Hawaiian jewelry available
are Ni'ihau shell *lei*. The shops
on Kaua'i are the best places
to buy them, but be sure to
do some advance research
before you make a purchase.
A simple choker may cost as
little as $25, while museum-
quality, multi-strand, waist-
length *lei* typically cost
thousands of dollars.

Books and Music

The only major mainland
bookstore still operating in
the Island is **Barnes & Noble**,
which has the best choice
of books, music, DVDs, and
more items about
Hawai'i. Museum
shops will also
have a good
selection
of Hawaiian
books for sale.
**Native Books
Na Mea Hawaii**, in
Honolulu, has a wide range
of Hawaiian-language books.

In most music stores, including
the locally based **Requests**, both
traditional and contemporary
Hawaiian music is available.

Wooden bowl from the Maui
Crafts Guild

Clothes and Fabric

The days of tourists strolling
down the street dressed in
matching polyester *mu'umu'u*
and aloha shirts seem to have
gone. Even the state's biggest
producer of alohawear, **Hilo
Hattie**, now sells attractive
cotton or cotton-blend island
fashions in its many fashion
centers. **Jagger's** (Pā'ia, Maui),
Sig Zane Designs (Hilo, Haiwai'i
Island), **Reyn Spooner** and
Macy's (a statewide department
store) stock some stunning
Hawaiian-style clothing in the
latest fashions, colors and subtle
prints. However, you might want
to think about whether you will
be able (or want) to wear your
expensive *mu'umu'u* back home.

Sarongs are popular beach-
wear among local women and
men. They are sold everywhere
and cost $10–35, depending on
the fabric and design. Most
places offer tips on how to wear
what is basically a couple of
yards of material finished on all
four sides. Hawai'i is a great place
to stock up on swimsuits, and
it can surely claim to
be the T-shirt capital
of the world.
T-shirts are sold
everywhere, embla-
zoned with every
imaginable design
and logo. In particular,
Crazy Shirts, which
has a number of stores statewide,
is considered by many to stock
the highest quality shirts with the
best designs. In Honolulu,
Butigroove sells an assortment of
trendy T-shirts as well.

Sarongs displayed outside a shop on O'ahu's North Shore

DIRECTORY

Shipping

DHL
Tel (800) 225-5345.
w dhl.com

FedEx
Tel (800) 463-3339.
w fedex.com

United States Postal Service
Tel (800) 275-8777.
w usps.gov

UPS
Tel (800) 742-5877.
w ups.com

Fruit and Flowers

Dole Plantation
64-1550 Kamehameha Highway, Wahiawā, O'ahu.
Tel (808) 621-8408.
w dole-plantation.com

Maui Tropical Plantation & Country Store
1670 Honoapi'ilani Highway, Wailuku, Maui. **Tel** (808) 244-7643.
w mauitropical plantation.com

Take Home Maui
121 Dickenson St, Lahaina, Maui.
Tel (808) 661-8067.
w takehomemaui.com

US Department of Agriculture (USDA)
Honolulu International Airport, Honolulu, O'ahu.
Tel (808) 861-8494.

Food and Drink

Shirokiya
Ala Moana Center, Honolulu, O'ahu. **Map** 3 A4. **Tel** (808) 973-9111.
w shirokiya.com

Tedeschi Winery
'Ulupalakua, Maui.
Tel (808) 878-6058.
w mauiwine.com

Volcano Winery
35 Pi'imauna Dr, Volcano, Hawai'i Island.
Tel (808) 967-7772.
w volcanowinery.com

Art

Gecko Trading Co.
3621 Baldwin Ave, Makawao, Maui.
Tel (808) 572-0249.

Lahaina Arts Society
Old Lahaina Courthouse, Lahaina, Maui.
Tel (808) 661-0111.
w lahaina-arts.com

Nohea Gallery
Ward Warehouse, 1050 Ala Moana Blvd, Honolulu, O'ahu. **Map** 2 D5.
Tel (808) 596-0074.
w noheagallery.com

Studio 7
Māmalahoa Highway, Hōlualoa, Hawai'i Island.
Tel (808) 324-1335.

Viewpoints Gallery
3620 Baldwin Ave, Makawao, Maui.
Tel (808) 572-5979.
w viewpointsmaui.com

Village Gallery
120 Dickenson St, Lahaina, Maui.
Tel (808) 661-4402.
w villagegallery maui.com

Volcano Art Center
Hawai'i Volcanoes National Park, Hawai'i Island. **Tel** (808) 967-7565.
w volcanoartcenter.org

Collectibles

Bailey's Antiques
517 Kapahulu Ave, Honolulu, O'ahu.
Tel (808) 734-7628.
w alohashirts.com

Manu Antiques
2005 S King St, Honolulu, O'ahu. **Tel** (808) 941-4901.
w manuantiques.com

The Only Show in Town
56-901 Kamehameha Highway, Kahuku, O'ahu.
Tel (808) 293-1295.

Pā'ia Trading Company
106 Hāna Highway, Pā'ia, Maui. **Tel** (808) 579-9472.

Story of Hawai'i Museum
Maalaea Shops, Maalaea, Maui. **Tel** (808) 242-6938.
w storyofhawaii museum.com

Crafts

Gallery of Great Things
Parker Square, Waimea, Hawai'i Island.
Tel (808) 885-7706.
w galleryofgreat thingshawaii.com

Maui Crafts Guild
120 Hāna Highway, Pā'ia, Maui. **Tel** (808) 579-9697.
w mauicraftsguild.com

Ola's Hanalei
5016 Kūhiō Highway, Hanalei, Kaua'i.
Tel (808) 826-6937.
w olashanalei.com

Sand & Sea
83A Hāna Highway, Pāia, Maui. **Tel** (808) 579-9377.

The Island's Best
Ala Moana Center, Honolulu, O'ahu.
Tel (808) 949-5345.

Jewelry

Jessica's Gems
Whalers Village, Kā'anapali, Maui.
Tel (808) 661-4223.

Jim Saylor Jewelers
1318 Kūhiō Highway, Kapa'a, Kaua'i. **Tel** (808) 822-3591.

Precision Goldsmiths
16 N Market St, Wailuku, Maui. **Tel** (808) 986-8282.
w precisiongold.com

Books and Music

Bailey House Museum Gift Shop
2375 A Main St, Wailuku, Maui. **Tel** (808) 244-3326.
w mauimuseum.org

Barnes & Noble
Ala Moana Center, Honolulu, O'ahu. **Map** 3 A4.
Tel (808) 949-7307.

Mission Houses Museum Gift Shop
533 King St, Honolulu 96813. **Tel** (808) 447-3910.
w museumhouses.org

Native Books Na Mea Hawaii
Ward Warehouse, 1050 Alamoana Blvd, Honolulu O'ahu.
Map 2 D5.
Tel (808) 596-8885.
w nativebooks hawaii.com

Requests
10 N Market St, Wailuku, Maui. **Tel** (808) 244-9315.
w requestshawaii.com

Clothes and Fabric

Crazy Shirts
Ala Moana Center, Honolulu, O'ahu.
Map 3 A4.
Tel (808) 973-4000. Call for the nearest branch.
w crazyshirts.com

Hilo Hattie
700 N Nimitz Highway, Honolulu, O'ahu.
Tel (808) 535-6500. Call for the nearest branch.
w hilohattie.com

Jagger's
100 Hana Highway, Pā'ia, Maui. **Tel** (808) 579-9221.

Macy's
Ala Moana Center, Honolulu, O'ahu.
Tel (808) 941-2345. Call for the nearest branch.

Butigroove
1311 Kapiolani Blvd, Honolulu, O'ahu.
Map 3 A4.
Tel (808) 589-2884.
w butigroove.com

Reyn Spooner
Ala Moana Center, Honolulu, O'ahu.
Map 3 A4. **Tel** (808) 949-5929. Call for the nearest branch.
w reynspooner.com

Sig Zane Designs
122 Kamehameha Ave, Hilo, Hawai'i Island.
Tel (808) 935-7077.
w sigzane.com

Malls and Shopping Centers

There are literally hundreds of shopping options in Hawai'i, including huge malls and shopping centers that stay open late. While shopping centers do not dominate the landscape as they do in parts of the United States, they are still a common feature of Hawai'i's main towns. Most malls have one large department store, together with smaller shops and boutiques, as well as restaurants, movie theaters, and a beauty salon or day spa. Some even have stages for performances and present a full calendar of entertainment, including *hula* shows, concerts, and amateur talent contests.

Honolulu and Waikīkī

Honolulu and Waikīkī's many shopping centers offer an outstanding selection of goods and services. The largest and most well-known is the **Ala Moana Center**, with department stores such as Macy's, Sears, Nordstrom's, and hundreds of other outlets. The **Royal Hawaiian Shopping Center** is home to designer boutiques like Cartier and Hermès. The **International Marketplace**, scheduled to open after renovations in 2016, is an open-air shopping center that offers entertainment and dining. Other popular shopping spots include the waterfront complex **Aloha Tower Marketplace**, **Kahala Mall**, **King's Village**, and **Koko Marina Center**.

The well-known Hilo Hattie logo

O'ahu

Bargain hunters can follow their instincts at **Waikele Premium Outlets**, with 50 discount outlets including Banana Republic, Guess, and Tommy Hilfiger. The **Windward Mall** has more than 80 gift, clothing, and food outlets. **Pearl Highlands Center** has stores such as Payless Shoe Source, Old Navy, Pier 1, and Sam's Club, movie theaters, and a fitness center. At **Pearlridge**, a monorail connects two shopping centers.

Moloka'i and Lāna'i

Both Moloka'i and Lāna'i each has one large town whose main street has most of its shops. On Moloka'i, shoppers can find everything from fishing gear to clothing and food on Ala Malama Street in Kaunakakai. Check out **Friendly Market Center**. Shopping on Lāna'i is centered around Dole Park, Lāna'i City. Visit **Pine Isle Market** and **Richard's Shopping Center**, an old-fashioned general store.

Maui

Maui's largest department store, Macy's, is in the island's biggest mall, **Queen Ka'ahumanu Center**. Others, such as **Whalers Village** and **The Shops at Wailea**, offer upscale shopping on the oceanfront. **Pi'ilani Shopping Village** in Kīhei has the state's largest Safeway and Hilo Hattie for souvenirs. **Lahaina Cannery Mall**, housed in a refurbished pineapple cannery, sells everything from aloha wear to fine art. **Maui Marketplace** offers The Sports Authority and Old Navy.

Entrance to the Aloha Tower Marketplace, Honolulu

Other shopping spots include **Kukui Mall** and **Nāpili Plaza**, a neighborhood-style center with a military museum.

Hawai'i Island

The main shopping districts on Hawai'i Island are in the towns of Kailua-Kona, Waimea, and Hilo. In Kailua-Kona there are several small shopping centers, including **Coconut Grove Market Place** and **Kona Coast Shopping Center**. Just outside Kailua-Kona, the **Keauhou Shopping Center** is home to one-off shops selling hand-blown glass, ceramics, mermaid ornaments, and *hula* dolls. **Waimea Center** has a supermarket, a bakery, and apparel and gift stores. The upscale **Kings' Shops** in Waikoloa are comprised of art galleries, boutiques, and designer stores. In Hilo, **Prince Kūhiō Plaza**, the island's largest mall, includes mainland brand stores, such as Sears and Macy's, and smaller outlets that carry apparel, crafts, and surf gear. WalMart, Hilo Hattie, and a food court are found in the **Waiakea Center**.

Kaua'i

The **Po'ipū Shopping Village** features an open-air garden setting and an array of services, eateries, and specialty stores selling jewelry, art, apparel, and accessories.

In Kapa'a, the open-air **Coconut Market Place** is a good spot for searching out resort wear, collectibles, and local arts and crafts. In addition to the shops and galleries at **Kaua'i Village**, look out for a heritage center and the Kaua'i Children's Discovery Museum.

Kukui Grove Center is Kaua'i's largest shopping center. Included here are well-known stores such as Macy's, Sears, K-Mart, Long's Drugs, a variety of smaller shops, and a Fun Factory. The plantation-themed **Princeville Center** has more than 35 shops and restaurants, along with a supermarket, a bank, a hardware store, a post office, and a clinic. Other popular shopping centers include **Ching Young Village Shopping Center** and **Rice Shopping Center**.

DIRECTORY

Honolulu and Waikīkī

Ala Moana Center
1450 Ala Moana Blvd,
Honolulu, O'ahu.
Map 2 F4.
Tel (808) 955-9517.
w alamoanacenter.com

Aloha Tower Marketplace
1 Aloha Tower Dr,
Honolulu, O'ahu. Map 1 A3.
Tel (808) 528-5700.
w alohatower.com

International Marketplace
2330 Kalākaua Ave,
Waikīkī, O'ahu. Map 4 E5.
Tel (808) 971-2080.
w shopinternational
marketplace.com

Kahala Mall
4211 Wai'alae Ave,
Honolulu, O'ahu.
Map 4 F5.
Tel (808) 732-7736.
w kahalamallcenter.com

King's Village
131 Ka'iulani Ave,
Waikīkī, O'ahu. Map 4 E4.
Tel (808) 944-6855.
w kings-village.com

Koko Marina Center
7192 Kalaniana'ole
Highway, Honolulu,
O'ahu. Map 4 F5.
Tel (808) 395-4737.
w kokomarinacenter.com

Royal Hawaiian Shopping Center
2201 Kalākaua Ave,
Waikīkī, O'ahu. Map 4 D4.
Tel (808) 922-0588.
w royalhawaiian
center.com

O'ahu

Pearl Highlands Center
1000 Kamehameha
Highway, Pearl
City, O'ahu.
Tel (808) 456-1000.
w pearlhighlands
center.com

Pearlridge Mall
98-1005 Moanalua Rd,
Aiea, Hawai'i Island.
Tel (808) 488-0981.
w pearlridgeonline.com

Waikele Premium Outlets
97-790 Lumiaina St,
Waipahu, O'ahu.
Tel (808) 676-5656.
w premiumoutlets.
com/waikele

Windward Mall
46-056 Kamehameha
Highway, Kane'ohe,
O'ahu. Tel (808) 235-1143.
w windwardmall.com

Moloka'i and Lāna'i

Friendly Market Center
90 Ala Malama St,
Kaunakakai, Moloka'i.
Tel (808) 553-5595.

Pine Isle Market
356 Eighth St, Lāna'i City,
Lāna'i. Tel (808) 565-6488.

Richard's Shopping Center
434 Eighth St,
Lāna'i City, Lāna'i.
Tel (808) 565-6047.

Maui

Kukui Mall
1819 South Kīhei Rd,
Kīhei, Maui.
Tel (808) 877-7073.

Lahaina Cannery Mall
1221 Honoapi'ilani
Highway, Lahaina, Maui.
Tel (808) 661-5304.
w lahainacannery
mall.com

Maui Marketplace
270 Dairy Rd,
Kahului, Maui.
Tel (808) 873-0400.

Nāpili Plaza
509 Nāpilihau St,
Nāpili, Maui.
Tel (808) 872-4318.

Pi'ilani Shopping Village
297 Pi'ikea Ave, Kīhei, Maui.
Tel (808) 874-8900.

Queen Ka'ahumanu Center
275 Ka'ahumanu Ave,
Kahului, Maui.
Tel (808) 877-4325.
w queenkaahumanu
center.com

The Shops at Wailea
3750 Wailea Alanui,
Wailea, Maui.
Tel (808) 891-6770.
w shopsatwailea.com

Whalers Village
2435 Kā'anapali Pkwy,
Kā'anapali, Maui.
Tel (808) 661-4567.
w whalersvillage.com

Hawai'i Island

Coconut Grove Market Place
75-5818 Ali'i Dr, Kailua-
Kona, Hawai'i Island.

Keauhou Shopping Center
78-6831 Ali'i Dr,
Kailua-Kona, Hawai'i.
Tel (808) 322-3000.
w keauhouvillage
shops.com

Kings' Shops
250 Waikoloa Beach Dr,
Waikoloa Beach Resort,
Hawai'i Island.
Tel (808) 866-8811.
w waikoloabeach
resort.com

Kona Coast Shopping Center
74-5588 Palani Rd,
Kailua-Kona, Hawai'i
Island.
Tel (808) 326-2262
w konashopping.com

Prince Kūhiō Plaza
111 E Puainako St,
Hilo, Hawai'i Island.
Tel (808) 959-3555.
w princekuhio
plaza.com

Waiakea Center
324 Maka'ala St, Hilo,
Hawai'i Island.
Tel (808) 961-9115.

Waimea Center
65-1158 Mamalahoa
Highway, Waimea,
Hawai'i Island.
Tel (808) 885-7727.

Kaua'i

Coconut Market Place
4-484 Kūhiō Highway,
Kapa'a, Kaua'i.
Tel (808) 822-3641.
w coconutmarket
place.com

Ching Young Village Shopping Center
5-5190 Kūhiō Highway,
Hanalei, Kaua'i.
Tel (808) 826-7222.
w chingyoung
village.com

Kaua'i Village
4-831 Kūhiō Highway,
Kapa'a, Kaua'i.
Tel (808) 822-3777.

Kukui Grove Center
3-2600 Kaumuali'i
Highway, Līhu'e, Kaua'i.
Tel (808) 245-7784.
w kukuigrove
center.com

Po'ipū Shopping Village
2360 Kiahuna Plantation
Dr, Po'ipū, Kaua'i.
Tel (808) 742-2831.

Princeville Center
5-4280 Kūhiō Highway,
Princeville, Kaua'i.
Tel (880) 826-9497.

Rice Shopping Center
4303 Rice St,
Lihu'e, Kaua'i.
Tel (800) 246-0311.

ENTERTAINMENT IN HAWAI'I

Music, song, and dance are as important to Hawaiians as the food that they eat and the air they breathe. From the musicians strumming in virtually every hotel lounge to the Merrie Monarch Festival (known as the "Olympics of *hula*"), Hawai'i is alive with the sounds of music. Besides Hawaiian rhythms, all kinds of music from country to rock, jazz, and reggae can be enjoyed, and world-class places stage both rock and classical concerts, opera, and even Broadway musicals. For information on the Hawaiian nightlife scene, from dancing the night away in Honolulu to the hotels and bars offering live music elsewhere, see pages 216–17.

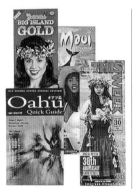

Hawaiian tourist magazines, a good source of entertainment information

Practical Information

The Friday edition of *The Honolulu Star-Advertiser* has the most complete entertainment listings; the neighboring islands' newspapers also have entertainment sections once a week. Local radio stations and posters plastered all over town are other sources, along with free local newspapers such as *Honolulu Weekly*. Your hotel should have up-to-date listings.

Ticket Outlets

It is best to buy tickets in advance for major events such as the Broadway shows that are occasionally put on in Honolulu. You can charge tickets to a major credit card for many events by telephoning **Ticketmaster**.

If you're buying tickets in person, there is usually a convenient ticket outlet near your hotel for almost any event; check with the hotel's guest services department. Music stores sell most concert tickets, for example. Local people are

not known for making plans a long way in advance, so there are usually tickets to be had at the door for smaller events.

If you want to attend the really big shows – the Merrie Monarch Festival in April or February's NFL Pro Bowl, for example – you should plan your holiday around them. Tickets for these should be purchased in advance. You should also note that hotel rooms are at a premium during particularly big events.

Hawaiian Music, Hula, and Lū'au

A great deal of the Hawaiian entertainment that is most popular with visitors – from the sounds of traditional chants and slack-key guitar (*kī hō'alu*) to traditional foods and *hula* costumes – has been "adjusted" for Western tastes. However, as a result of the cultural renaissance that has occurred in the state over the last decade, traditional Hawaiian entertainment is now accessible to anyone who wishes to experience it. Virtually every hotel offers Hawaiian music of some description on a regular, if not daily, basis, and many put on *hula* shows, too. Such performances are usually free.

The **Waikīkī Shell** in Kapi'olani Park is a magnificent outdoor spot that hosts many concerts of Hawaiian music and *hula* throughout the year.

"The Shell" was once home to the famous Kodak Hula Show, which was started by Kodak in 1939. Although the show no longer exists, the Waikīkī Shell has not lost its fame and continues to be one of O'ahu's top entertainment venues.

Small shows staged at island shopping centers are often the most authentic. They usually feature students of Hawaiian music and dance from *hālau hula* (*hula* schools) and are almost always free.

For a unique treat, enjoy the remarkable talent of the two Brothers Cazimero, whose extraordinary voices and skill on the guitar and bass combine to produce one of Honolulu's best shows. Check the listings in the newspapers or tourist magazines for details of shows.

Most of the major hotels offer *lū'au* – the traditional feasts of the islands. Prices are approximately

The impressive sight of a traditional Hawaiian feast or *lū'au* in Lahaina, Maui

Colorful pageant at the Polynesian Cultural Center on O'ahu *(see p96)*

$85–125 for adults and half that for kids. On O'ahu, try the **Paradise Cove Lū'au** in Kapolei 'Ewa, about 25 miles (40 km) from Waikīkī; tickets include the bus from town. The best place to go on Maui is, without doubt, **Old Lahaina Lū'au**, in a lovely setting overlooking the ocean.

The only waterfront *lū'au* in Kailua-Kona (Hawai'i Island) is held at **King Kamehameha's Kona Beach Hotel, The Gathering of Kings** show takes place at the **Fairmont Orchid**. On Kaua'i, be sure to make reservations in advance for the **Tahiti Nui Lū'au** in Hanalei, which takes place every Wednesday night and is perhaps Hawai'i's most "local-style" – that is, most boisterous – *lū'au*.

You can also enjoy a more authentic and inexpensive experience by checking the local newspaper for fundraisers and other *lū'au* put on by civic groups. If you get really lucky and are invited to a big Hawaiian family party, accept the invitation. You will have the experience of a lifetime.

Polynesian Shows

These shows are Hawai'i's real extravaganzas, and usually include a *lū'au*-style meal as well as exhibitions of music and dance from Pacific islands like Tahiti, Samoa, Tonga, and Fiji. All the islands have them. While they may vary in scale, Polynesian shows are broadly similar in content – never failing to deliver women wearing grass skirts.

The **Polynesian Cultural Center** in Lā'ie (O'ahu) stages several shows daily, including *"Mana!,"* an evening show featuring a cast of over 100, and the newest and most Hawaiian show, the *Ali'i Lū'au*.

The Hyatt Regency Maui offers **Drums of the Pacific**, and the *lū'au* at the **Royal Lahaina Resort** features a Polynesian show. Finally, you can also try the show at the **Hilton Waikoloa Village Resort** on Hawai'i Island.

Evening Shows

In Honolulu, mimicry features in the lively Las Vegas-style show put on by the **Society of Seven**, a group of veterans who have been appearing at Outrigger Waikīkī on the Beach for more than 30 years. **Cirque Polynesia** blends Hawaiian culture with dazzling acrobatics, including thrilling high-wire routines.

On Maui, evening shows are inspired by Hawaiian myths, legends, and lore. The **Feast at Lele** is an exquisite evening dinner show on the beach that showcases the cultures of the South Pacific. Magic is the focus at **Warren & Annabelle's**, where guests are entertained by the piano-playing ghost of the wife of a 19th-century whaler, as well as mystified by a modern magician in an interactive show. Cocktails and appetizers are available for an extra charge. **Kahuā Ranch** on Hawai'i Island draws from another part of

Hawai'i's heritage, the *paniolo* (cowboy) experience. After enjoying a hearty chuck-wagon barbecue, you can dance to live music and participate in ranch games such as roping and horseshoes.

On Kaua'i, you can enjoy an enchanted evening of musical theater, entertainment, and dining featuring a full production of the Broadway musical **South Pacific** at the Kaua'i Beach Hotel.

Concerts by big international names from Tony Bennett to Sting and legendary rock bands like the Eagles appear at major O'ahu venues such as the spectacularly restored **Hawai'i Theatre**, the **Neal Blaisdell Concert Hall**, and **Aloha Stadium**. Maui's top spot is the impressive $32- million **Maui Arts & Cultural Center**, with an outdoor amphitheater and several different auditoriums for concerts, plays, and art-house films.

The biggest stars of all are of course up in Hawai'i's night sky. Almost all the heavenly bodies in the southern hemisphere are visible from Hawai'i. Operators of star-gazing tours include **Mauna Kea Stargazing Tour** and **Haleakalā National Park**. Some hotels and charter boats also offer excursions for viewing the night sky.

The thrilling Cirque Polynesia show, a multi-million dollar spectacular

Hula at the Maui Ukulele Festival, Maui Arts & Cultural Center

Theater

For anything other than small community theater, Honolulu is the place to be. At least a couple of Broadway musicals show up each year, usually at the **Neal Blaisdell Concert Hall**. Past shows include *Les Miserables*, *Cats*, and *Phantom of the Opera*. The **Mānoa Valley Theatre** presents local productions of the cream of Broadway and off-Broadway. Hawai'i's oldest company, the **Diamond Head Theatre**, offers a mixed bag of performances each season, as does the **Kumu Kahua Theatre** – some of whose shows are written locally.

On weekends, at any time of year, it should be possible to see a performance by at least one of Maui's four community theater groups – the Maui Academy of Performing Arts, Maui Community Theatre, the Baldwin Theater Guild, and Studio Hāmākua Poko. Most often, the place is one of the two theaters inside the **Maui Arts & Cultural Center** in Kahului, although the Maui OnStage Theater uses the lovingly restored **ʻĪao Theater** in historic Wailuku.

Hawai'i Island has several community theater groups, too: Akebono Theater, Aloha Community Players, and Hilo Community Players. The lovely **Kahilu Theatre** in upcountry Waimea is a wonderful spot.

On the Garden Isle, the Kaua'i Community Players offer an almost continuous program of performances throughout the year. There is a beautiful performing arts center on the campus of **Kaua'i Community College**.

Opera, Classical Music, and Dance

The state's resident opera company, **Hawai'i Opera Theatre**, stages three or four operas from January to April each year. These are held in Honolulu's **Neal Blaisdell Concert Hall**, where Broadway productions such as *Phantom of the Opera*, *Les Miserables*, *Miss Saigon*, and *Chicago* have also been staged. You should also look out for performances by the **Hawai'i Youth Symphony Association**, made up of student musicians from all the islands.

Every year at least one of the mainland's most reputable ballet companies travels across the Pacific to perform in Hawai'i, usually at the Neal Blaisdell Concert Hall. The **Ballet Hawai'i** – the islands' oldest ballet troupe – presents the *Nutcracker Suite* every winter for the holiday crowds, plus another ballet in summer. The **Iona Contemporary Dance Theatre** perform unique works that combine dance with theater.

The **Maui Arts & Cultural Center**, which is also known as the "MACC," is Maui's premier venue for performing and visual arts. The complex includes two theaters, an outdoor amphitheater, and a gallery. Performances include classical music, rock, pop, and many other styles by an array of nationally and internationally famous artists.

The Classical Music Festival takes place every June at various Maui venues, with a series of classical concerts performed over two weekends.

Films and Film Festivals

A large and, for the most part, free film festival, the **Hawai'i International Film Festival**, takes place each November. Scores of films are shown at various theaters on O'ahu (some of which charge admission) in the first week, and on the neighboring islands the second week; even tiny communities are included.

New films normally open in Honolulu at the same time as on the mainland. In addition to the many spots that specialize in big Hollywood movies, the University of Hawai'i, community colleges, and other venues present art-house, foreign, and classic films on a regular basis. Check the Friday edition of *The Honolulu Star-Advertiser* for the latest listings. You can go to the movies on the neighboring islands, too, but the choice there is a great deal more limited. It was not that long ago that Maui got its first multiplex cinema. The **Maui Arts & Cultural Center** presents seasons of foreign and art-house films. On the island of Hawai'i, the Big Island Film Festival, devoted to independent narrative film, presents screenings, workshops, and celebrity appearances. On the neighboring islands, there are special showings of non-blockbuster films, often presented by community colleges, civic organizations, and various non-profit groups.

Sign for the top cultural place on Maui

DIRECTORY

Ticket Outlets

Ticketmaster
Tel (800) 745-3000.
W ticketmaster.com

Major Venues

Aloha Stadium
99-500 Salt Lake Blvd,
'Aiea, O'ahu. **Tel** (808)
486-9300. W aloha
stadium.hawaii.gov

Hawai'i Theatre
1130 Bethel St, Honolulu,
O'ahu. **Map** 1 A2.
Tel (808) 528-0506.
W hawaiitheatre.com

**Maui Arts &
Cultural Center**
1 Cameron Way, Kahului,
Maui. **Tel** (808) 242-7469.
W mauiarts.org

**Neal Blaisdell
Concert Hall**
777 Ward Ave, Honolulu,
O'ahu. **Map** 2 D3.
Tel (808) 591-2211.
W blaisdellcenter.com

Waikīkī Shell
2805 Monsarrat Ave,
Kapi'olani Park, Honolulu,
O'ahu. **Tel** (808) 591-2211.
W blaisdellcenter.com

Hawaiian Music, Hula, and Lū'au

**King Kamehameha's
Kona Beach Hotel**
75-5660 Palani Rd,
Kailua-Kona, Hawai'i
Island. **Tel** (808) 329-2911.
W konabeachhotel.com

**Fairmont Orchid
Hawai'i**
1 Kaniku Dr, Kohala Coast,
Hawai'i Island. **Tel** (808)
885-2000. W fairmont.
com/orchid

Old Lahaina Lū'au
1251 Front St, Lahaina,
Maui. **Tel** (808) 667-1998.
W oldlahainaluau.com

Paradise Cove Lū'au
92-1089 Ali'inui Dr,
Kapolei, O'ahu.
Tel (808) 842-5911.
W paradisecove
hawaii.com

Tahiti Nui Lū'au
5-5134 Kūhiō Highway,
Hanalei, Kaua'i.
Tel (808) 826-6277.
W thenui.com

Polynesian Shows

Drums of the Pacific
Hyatt Regency Maui, 200
Nohea Kai Dr, Kā'anapali,
Maui.
Tel (808) 667-4420.
W maui.hyatt.com

**Hilton Waikoloa
Village Resort**
425 Waikoloa Beach Dr,
Kohala Coast, Hawai'i
Island.
Tel (808) 886-1234.
W hiltonwaikoloa
village.com

**Polynesian
Cultural Center**
55-370 Kamehameha
Highway, Lā'ie, Oahu.
Tel (808) 293-3333.
W polynesia.com

Royal Lahaina Resort
2780 Keka'a Dr, Kā'anapali,
Maui.
Tel (808) 661-3611.
W royallahainaluau.com

Evening Shows

Cirque Polynesia
Hyatt Regency Maui, 200
Nohea Kai Dr, Lahaina,
Maui.
Tel (808) 667-4540.
W cirquepolynesia.com

Feast at Lele
505 Front St, Lahaina, Maui.
Tel (808) 667-5353.
W feastatlele.com

Kahuā Ranch
Waikoloa, Hawai'i Island.
Tel (808) 987-2108.
W kahuaranch.com

**Haleakalā
National Park**
PO Box 369, Makawao, Maui.
Tel (808) 572-4400.
W nps.gov/hale

**Mauna Kea
Stargazing Tour**
737 Kanoelehua Ave,
Hilo, Hawai'i Island.
Tel (808) 969-9507.
W jackshawaii.com

Society of Seven
Outrigger Waikīkī on the
Beach, 2335 Kalākaua
Ave, Waikīkī, O'ahu.
Tel (808) 922-6408.
W outrigger.com

South Pacific
4331 Kaua'i Beach Dr,
Līhu'e, Kaua'i.
Tel (808) 245-1955.
W kauaibeach
resort.com

Warren & Annabelle's
900 Front St, Lahaina,
Maui.
Tel (808) 667-6244.
W warrenand
annabelles.com

Theater

**Diamond Head
Theatre**
520 Makapu'u Ave,
Honolulu, O'ahu.
Tel (808) 733-0274.
W diamondhead
theatre.com

'Iao Theater
68 N Market St, Wailuku,
Maui. **Tel** (808) 244-8680.
W mauionstage.com

Kahilu Theatre
67-1185 Māmalahoa
Highway, Waimea, Hawai'i
Island. **Tel** (808) 885-6868.
W kahilutheatre.org

**Kaua'i Community
College Performing
Arts Center**
3-1901 Kaumuali'i Highway,
Līhu'e, Kaua'i.
Tel (808) 245-8311.
W kauai.hawaii.edu/
pac

Kumu Kahua Theatre
46 Merchant St, Honolulu,
O'ahu. **Map** 1 A3.
Tel (808) 536-4441.
W kumukahua.org

Mānoa Valley Theatre
2833 E Mānoa Rd,
Honolulu, O'ahu.
Tel (808) 988-6131.
W manoavalley
theatre.com

Opera, Classical Music, and Dance

Ballet Hawai'i
650 Iwiler Rd, Honolulu,
O'ahu.
Tel (808) 521-8600.
W ballethawaii.org

Hawai'i Opera Theatre
848 S Beretania St, Hono-
lulu, O'ahu. **Map** 2 E4.
Tel (808) 596-7858.
W hawaiiopera.org

**Hawai'i Youth
Symphony
Association**
Suite 201, 1110 University
Ave, Honolulu, O'ahu.
Map 4 D1.
Tel (808) 941-9706.
W hiyouth symphony.
org

**Iona Contemporary
Dance Theatre**
130 Ulupa St, Kailua,
O'ahu.
Tel (808) 262-0110.
W iona360.com

Films and Film Festivals

**Big Island
Film Festival**
68-1851 Lina Poepoe St,
Waikoloa, Hawai'i Island.
Tel (808) 883-0394.
W bigislandfilm
festival.com

**Hawai'i International
Film Festival**
680 Iwilei Rd, Suite 100,
Honolulu, O'ahu.
Map 1 A3.
Tel (800) 447-0577.
W hiff.org

Maui Film Festival
16 Baldwin Ave,
Pa'ia, Maui.
Tel (808) 572-3456.
W mauifilmfestival.
com

Nightlife

Traditionally, Hawai'i is an early-to-bed, early-to-rise place. Night owls may, however, find enough to keep them occupied, especially in Honolulu and Waikīkī. There is a fair bit of nightlife on Maui as well, but do not expect to find much on the other islands. Having said that, many bars and hotel lounges provide live entertainment. On any night of the week you can find almost any kind of music – rock, pop, blues, jazz, country, reggae, and, of course, Hawaiian – either performed live or spun by a DJ. Check listings in each island's local newspapers for an up-to-date guide to what is on while you are there.

Rob's Good Times Grill, a sports bar in Honolulu

Honolulu and Waikīkī

Honolulu has a flourishing club scene. **Addiction** is a swanky nightclub and beachclub, located in The Modern, a chic hotel in Honolulu. The club offers performances by leading DJ's, and a great atmosphere for drinking and dancing the night away. Dance outdoors at pier-side **Gordon Biersch**, or enjoy the casual atmosphere at the **Mai Tai Bar**. For lively parties, head to the fun Polynesian themed **Tiki's Grill & Bar**. For a lively yet affordable nightlife experience, visit on of Honolulu's many dive bars, such as **Arnold's Beach Bar & Grill**.

Waikīkī's clubs stay open late – the **Jazz Minds Art & Café**, for example, closes at 2am. **The Dragon Upstairs** has hot live jazz. For an evening of chilled-out live jazz, try **Lewers Lounge**.

Some hotels also host hip dance clubs, such as **RumFire** at the Sheraton Waikīkī Hotel (see p183), where you can dine and dance with a view.

Moloka'i and Lāna'i

Not much nightlife is to be found on either of these quiet islands. What there is takes place in the hotels. **Hotel Moloka'i** (see p184) hosts live entertainment in its oceanfront dining room, and once a week everyone and anyone brings their ukuleles and joins in a local-style jam session. It is a casual, fun, and unique island experience. On Lāna'i, you will also find a relaxed scene. Check out entertainment at the **Four Seasons Lodge at Kō'ele** or the **Four Seasons Resort at Mānele Bay**.

Maui

Most of Maui's nightspots are in Lahaina and Kīhei, where there are lots of bars and lounges offering live entertainment. **Mulligan's On the Blue** in Wailea offers a Hawaiian dinner show a few nights a week, live jazz or rock on other nights, and traditional Celtic music on weekends. In Lahaina, the **Hard Rock Café** presents a live reggae band weekly. **Cheeseburger in Paradise** and **Cool Cat Café** feature cheap eats, cold beers and live music every night.

The popular nightspots from the last century have been replaced by modern clubs such as **Ambrosia** in Kihei, where DJs spin discs for the late-night set, with state-of-the-art video, sound, and lighting technology.

Hawai'i Island

The Big Island's nightlife centres on Kailua-Kona and Hilo. However, there are great bars with DJs and dancing, and some with live bands, around the island. Again, you will find musical variety: country and western, reggae, rock, hip hop, and Hawaiian.

There is a host of bars and restaurants that feature live music and dancing at night. Among these are **Bongo Ben's**, **Don's Mai Tai Bar**, **Huggo's on the Rocks**, and **Blue Dragon**.

Just about every hotel has a lounge offering live Hawaiian music; choose from **Mountain Thunder** at Honu Bar at the Mauna Lani Bay Hotel, the open-air **Reef Lounge** at Hāpuna Beach Prince Hotel, and **Hawaii Calls** at the Waikoloa Beach Marriott (see p186).

Kaua'i

Kaua'i is not known for its nighttime scene, but live entertainment and dancing can be found in restaurants, bars, and clubs, as well as in the resort hotels. **Hanalei Gourmet** serves dinner and then has live entertainment after dark, usually modern Hawaiian or R&B. **Trees Lounge** in Kapaa offers a popular, budget-friendly happy hour, accompanied by lively tunes. **Café Portofino** in Lihue offers a varied mix of Hawaiian, classical, and DJ dance nights. There is also a sports bar, with DJs and dancing, at **Rob's Good Times Grill** in Lihu'e's Rice Shopping Center. Enjoy champagne at sunset in the relaxed environment of the ritzy **St. Regis Bar** in Princeville. It has jazz nights on Sundays.

Hawaiian dancer at a dinner show

DIRECTORY

Honolulu and Waikīkī

Addiction Nightclub
1775 Ala Moana Blvd,
Honolulu, O'ahu.
Map 3 B4.
Tel (808) 943-5800.
w themodern
honolulu.com

Arnold's Beach Bar & Grill
339 Saratoga Rd,
Honolulu, O'ahu.
Map 4 D4.
Tel (808) 924-6887.

The Dragon Upstairs
1038 Nu'uana Ave,
Honolulu, O'ahu.
Map 1 A2.
Tel (808) 526-1411.
w thedragonupstairs.com

Gordon Biersch
Aloha Tower Marketplace,
1 Aloha Tower Dr,
Honolulu, O'ahu.
Map 1 A3.
Tel (808) 599-4877.
w gordonbiersch.com

Jazz Minds Art & Café
1661 Kapi'olani Blvd,
Honolulu, O'ahu.
Map 3 A3.
Tel (808) 945-0800.
w honolulujazzclub.com

Lewers Lounge
Halekulani Hotel, 2199
Kālia Rd, Waikīkī, O'ahu.
Map 4 D5.
Tel (808) 923-2311.
w halekulani.com

Pint + Jigger
1936 South King St,
Honolulu, O'ahu.
Map 3 B2.
Tel (808) 744-9593.
w pintandjigger.com

Mai Tai Bar
1450 Ala Moana Blvd,
Honolulu, O'ahu.
Map 2 F4.
Tel (808) 947-2900.
w maitaibar.com

Tiki's Grill & Bar
2570 Kalakaua Ave,
Honolulu, O'ahu.
Map 4 E5
Tel (808) 923-8454.
w tikisgrill.com

RumFire
Sheraton Waikīkī Hotel,
2255 Kalākaua Ave,
Waikīkī, O'ahu.
Map 4 D5.
Tel (808) 922-4422.
w sheratonwaikiki.com

Moloka'i and Lāna'i

Four Seasons Lodge at Kō'ele
Keōmuku Highway,
Lāna'i City, Lāna'i.
Tel (808) 565-7300.
w lodgeatkoele.com

Four Seasons Resort at Mānele Bay
1 Mānele Bay Rd,
Mānele, Lāna'i.
Tel (808) 565-2000.
w fourseasons
manelebay.com

Hotel Moloka'i
Kamehameha V Highway,
Kaunakakai, Moloka'i.
Tel (808) 553-5347.
w hotelmolokai.com

Maui

Ambrosia Martini Lounge
1913 S Kihei Rd, Kihei,
Maui. **Tel** (808) 891-1011.
w ambrosiamaui.com

Cheeseburger in Paradise
811 Front St,
Lahaina, Maui.
Tel (808) 661-4855.
w cheeseburger
land.com

Cool Cat Café
658 Front St,
Lahaina, Maui.
Tel (808) 667-0908.
w coolcatcafe.com

Hard Rock Café
900 Front St,
Lahaina, Maui.
Tel (808) 667-7400.
w hardrock.com

Mulligan's on the Blue
Wailea Blue Golf
Course,100 Kaukahi
St, Wailea, Maui.
Tel (808) 874-1131.
w mulligansonthe
blue.com

Hawai'i Island

Blue Dragon Restaurant & Spa
61-3616 Kawaihae Rd,
Kamuela, Hawai'i.
Tel (808) 882-7771.
w bluedragon
hawaii.com

Bongo Ben's
75-5819 Ali'i Dr,
Kailua-Kona, Hawai'i.
Tel (808) 329-7366.
w bongobens.com

Don Mai Tai Bar
Royal Kona Resort,
75–7852 Ali'i Dr,
Kailua-Kona, Hawai'i.
Tel (808) 930-3286.
w royalkona.com

Hawaii Calls Lounge
Waikoloa Beach Marriott,
69–275 Waikoloa Beach
Dr, Waikoloa, Hawai'i.
Tel (808) 886-6789.
w marriott.com

Mountain Thunder
Honu Bar, Mauna
Lani Bay Hotel,
68-1400 Mauna Lani Dr,
Kohala Coast, Hawai'i.
Tel (808) 881-7911.
w maunalani.com

Huggo's on the Rocks
75-5828 Kahakai Rd,
Kailua-Kona, Hawai'i.
Tel (808) 329-1493.
w huggos.com

Reef Lounge
Hāpuna Beach Prince
Hotel, 67-100 Kaunaoa Dr,
Kohala Coast, Hawai'i.
Tel (808) 880-1111.
w princeresorts
hawaii.com

Kaua'i

Café Portofino
3610 Rice St, Lihue, Kaua'i.
Tel (808) 245-2121.

Hanalei Gourmet
5-5161 Kūhiō Highway,
Hanalei, Kaua'i.
Tel (808) 826-2524.
w hanaleigourmet.com

Rob's Good Times Grill
Rice Shopping Center,
4303 Rice St,
Līhu'e, Kaua'i.
Tel (808) 246-0311.

St. Regis Bar
St. Regis Princeville
Hotel & Resort,
5520 Ka Haku Rd,
Princeville, Kaua'i.
Tel (808) 826-9644.
w stregisprince
ville.com

Trees Lounge
440 Aleka Pl,
Kapaa, Kaua'i.
Tel (808) 823-0600.
w treeslounge
kauai.com

OUTDOOR ACTIVITIES

With its hot climate, Hawai'i is a great place for outdoor activities, many of which are focused on the ocean. All over the islands you will find people surfing, swimming, paddling, windsurfing, or fishing at all hours of the day. The abundance of coral and exotic marine life is a big attraction for divers and snorkelers, too. Whale watching is a popular activity in the winter and numerous boat tours allow visitors to get up close and personal with these awesome marine mammals. On land, there are many attractive, well-maintained hiking trails, as well as paths for horseback riding, which provide a great way to enjoy the islands' fine scenery. For more information on Hawai'i's world-leading golf courses see pages 222–3.

Snorkeler enjoying a close encounter with a trumpet fish

Snorkeling, Scuba Diving, and Snuba

Snorkeling and scuba diving are at the top of the list of Hawai'i's most popular outdoor activities. Early morning is the best time to observe the fish. Some snorkel sites are dangerous during high wave action, so check the conditions first. Darting butterfly fish, rainbow parrotfish, bright yellow tangs, and sea turtles are all common sights. For equipment rental at good prices, **Snorkel Bob's** has outlets on O'ahu, Maui, Kaua'i, and Hawai'i Island.

The leeward sides of the islands have the best dive sites, most of which are accessible only by boat. Some good dive operators are: **Aaron's Dive Shop** (O'ahu), **Bubbles Below** (Kaua'i), **Extended Horizons** (Maui), **Fair Wind Cruises** (Hawai'i Island), See pages 36–7 for more information about snorkeling and dive sites.

Another way to enjoy Hawai'i's magnificent undersea environment is snuba, a cross between scuba diving and snorkeling. This shallow water diving system allows you to go many places that snorkelers cannot reach. The approximate depth of a snuba dive is 20 ft (6 m). Snuba is not difficult to learn, there is no certification required, and few restrictions apply. Anyone over the age of eight can snub. Many snorkel cruises offer snuba for an additional charge.

Swimming

The waters off Hawai'i are cool and inviting. Maui and O'ahu have the best beaches, particularly Maui's Kā'anapali Coast and the southern and windward shores of O'ahu, where the surf is usually gentle. World-famous Waikīkī Beach is one of the best swimming spots, but locals generally prefer nearby Sans Souci. On O'ahu's windward side, both Kailua Beach and Lanikai Beach are mellow and uncrowded with lovely, clear water. Hawai'i Island's Mauna Kea Beach is also good.

If you enjoy serious wave action, look out for Hawai'i's "rough-water" swimming contests, such as the demanding summer North Shore Rough-water Swim Series on O'ahu. The ocean is dangerous. Safety tips for anyone entering the water are given on page 234.

Surfing, Body-Surfing, and Windsurfing

Athletes from around the globe flock to Hawai'i to test their mettle at some of the world's best surf breaks. With 7 miles (11 km) of excellent surf spots between Hale'iwa and Sunset Beach, O'ahu's North Shore is the surfing capital of the world, and site of the annual Triple Crown contest *(see p35)*. But there is a cornucopia of world-class surf breaks around the rest of the O'ahu coast, and also on the coasts of Maui and Kaua'i.

Waikīkī's gentle rollers are ideal for beginners. Beach boys offer surfing lessons, just like in the old days, and boards can also be rented here. Chun's Reef on O'ahu's North Shore is a good place

Surfer taking a break between rides on the Hawaiian surf

Novices being given a windsurfing lesson at Kailua Beach Park on O'ahu

for beginners. **Surf-n-Sea** rents boards here and also offers lessons.

The Lahaina Breakwall, east of Lahaina, is another popular spot for beginners. You can rent surfboards from **Honolua Surf Co.**, **Local Motion**, and other Maui surf shops. The **Nancy Emerson School of Surfing** offers lessons; **Wind-surf Kaua'i** rents boards and offers lessons on Kaua'i. Call the **Surf News Network** for general information.

You can surf all year, but the waves reach their peak from November through April, when the north shore of any island can be dangerous for experienced surfers – let alone beginners. The power of the ocean in Hawai'i is beyond description and many visitors get into trouble after paddling out into big surf. The best advice is "Never surf alone."

Body-surfing, in which riders wearing flippers lie flat on a bodyboard or boogie board (see p34), and paddleboarding are also popular. At O'ahu's Makapu'u and Sandy Beach, waves crash onto a shallow sandy shorebreak, and body-surfers shoot through the tube barely ahead of the lip of the wave. Point Panic in Honolulu is also a favorite spot. All three of these places are dangerous, but for spectators the waves are fantastic.

Beginners can get their fins wet at O'ahu's Bellows Beach and Waikīkī Beach, Maui's Wailea Beach, and Kaua'i's Shipwreck Beach. For an introduction to stand-up paddleboarding, head to O'ahu's North Shore, where **Rainbow Watersports** offers instructions and rentals. To rent bodyboards,

try **Aloha Beach Service** in Waikīkī, **Local Motion** in Lahaina, and **Progressive Expressions** on Kaua'i. Windsurfing has a big following. The sport's hub is Maui's North Shore, Ho'okipa Beach being the top spot for acrobatics. On O'ahu, Kailua Bay suits all ability levels, and Diamond Head's constant winds and breaking waves make it a windsurfer's delight. Windsurfers replace surfers at Sunset Beach when the wind blows strongly.

Lessons and equipment are available from: **Naish Hawai'i** (O'ahu), which is owned and run by world-champion windsurfer Robbie Naish; **Second Wind** or **Hi-Tech Surf Sports**, both on Maui; and **Windsurf Kaua'i** in Hanalei, on Kaua'i.

Kayaking, Canoeing, and Sailing

Kayaking is quite popular in Hawai'i. Favorite spots include O'ahu's Kailua Bay and Kaua'i's Wailua River. The kayak is also one of the preferred ways to visit Kaua'i's great Nā Pali Coast. Kayaks can be rented from **Go Bananas** or **Twogood Kayaks Hawai'i** (O'ahu), **South Pacific Kayaks** (Maui), and **Outfitters Kaua'i** (Kaua'i).

Traditional Hawaiian canoe paddling in outrigger canoes is popular, too. The October Nā Moloka'i Hoe race (see p39) is the most important contest of its kind in the world. Regattas are held on weekends in several places, but the sport is run by tightly knit clubs, making it hard

to participate. However, Waikīkī beach boys will take you out to ride the waves in an outrigger near the Moana Hotel (see p68).

Hawai'i is a major stopping-place for boats crossing the Pacific, and the state has a strong seafaring tradition of its own. Two of the world's biggest regattas, the VIC-Maui race and the Trans Pacific Race, take place in Hawai'i.

Kāne'ohe Bay on O'ahu is the best place for small boat sailing, though Waikīkī is also suitable. The **Hawai'i Yacht Club** and **Waikīkī Yacht Club** take on experienced deckhands for Honolulu's weekly Champagne Race (so named because the winners are given champagne). Races are held on Friday afternoons.

Fishing

Hawai'i is famous for its deep-sea fishing – above all on the Kona Coast, where record catches are often made of Pacific blue marlin, yellowfin tuna, and other gamefish. This area is the best for trips, but charters can be arranged on all the islands. **Sea Verse** operates in Honolulu while **Blue Hawai'i Sportfishing** is based in Kailua-Kona, Hawai'i Island. On Maui, you can arrange fishing trips with **Captain Charlie's Maui Sport Fishing Charters** and **Aerial Sportfishing Charters**. Hawai'i Fishing News is a good source of infomation.

Hawai'i's long shoreline offers lots of surf casting for smaller fish, such as snapper and giant ulua (jack). Take care if you fish; conditions in the best surf-casting places can be hazardous.

Women kayak training on the gentle waters of Waikīkī's Ala Wai Canal

Cyclist on a scenic bike ride through Waikīkī's Ala Moana Park, away from the multitudes at the beach

Cycling and Mountain Biking

Narrow shoulders and variable road quality make Hawai'i a poor place for bike riding. Mountain biking trails are limited too, but those that do exist are of good quality. Trails above Pūpūkea on O'ahu's North Shore are very popular, with ocean views and challenging riding.

South of Kula on Maui, in the Polipoli Springs Recreation Area, several miles of trails snake through ravines and forests of eucalyptus and giant ferns. An easier but extremely popular adventure is the sunrise descent down Haleakalā, a 38-mile (61-km) stretch starting in Haleakalā National Park (see pp132–3) that contains 21 switchbacks and superb views.

For quality mountain bike rentals, try **Raging Isle Sports** in Hale'iwa, O'ahu, or **Haleakalā Bike Co.**, **West Maui Cycle and Sports**, or **South Maui Bicycles** on Maui.

Hiking

An extensive network of state and national parks crisscrossed by trails makes Hawai'i great hiking territory. The terrain ranges from barren volcanic desert to lush fern rainforest with waterfalls and cool swimming holes.

There are trails to suit everyone in terms of both accessibility and difficulty. Two of the finest are Kaua'i's Kalalau Trail along the stunning, rugged Nā Pali Coast (see pp172–3) and the Kaupō Trail, which descends from Haleakalā's volcanic moonscape to the lush rainforest of the Kīpahulu Valley (see p130).

Clubs and environmental groups, including the **Sierra Club**, **Nature Conservancy**, and the **Hawai'i Nature Center**, organize hikes on a number of islands. Some of the state, national, and county parks have campsites for longer stays (see p181). Changing weather conditions can be a serious hazard when hiking; flash floods in narrow ravines are common, and hikers disappear with alarming regularity. It is dangerous to hike alone. Before you set off, leave word of your plans and your expected time of return with a friend or someone at the hotel. Pack water, a flashlight, warm clothes, and a blanket in case you become stranded.

Hiker enjoying the wild scenery of Haleakalā National Park, Maui

Whale Watching

Every winter, humpback whales migrate from the North Pacific to the warm waters around the Hawaiian islands to mate and bear their young. Although it is certainly possible to see whales from the shoreline, you will get a better look by getting out onto the water.

Almost every charter boat offers whale-watching cruises in the peak viewing season of January through April. Whale-watch cruises usually last two hours and many have a marine biologist or knowledgeable narrator on board. Try operators such as **Wild Side Specialty Tours** on O'ahu or **Paragon Charters** on Maui.

Tours may be on anything from large boats to kayaks. Boats may have a hydrophone, an under-water microphone, which allows you to listen to the haunting whale song. Humpback whales are protected by U.S. laws that prohibit approaching whales any closer than 300 ft (90 m).

A humpback whale, in Hawaiian waters from January to April

Other Activities

Hawai'i's mild climate lends itself to all warm weather activity. In-line skating and jogging are common pastimes, particularly on O'ahu. There are busy public tennis courts on the four major islands.

Two good horseback riding trails are along the Moloka'i cliffs and in Maui's Kīpahulu Valley. Horses or rides can be organized through **CJM Country Stables**, **Moloka'i Mule Ride**, and **Paniolo Riding Adventures**.

More daring activities include caving, zipping through the tree tops, or freefalling from an airplane. Contact **Skyline Eco-Adventures** or **ATV Tours** for more information.

DIRECTORY

Snorkeling, Scuba Diving, and Snuba

Aaron's Dive Shop
307 Hahani St, Kailua, O'ahu. Tel (808) 262-2333. W hawaii-scuba.com

Bubbles Below
PO Box 157, Eleele, Kaua'i. Tel (808) 332-7333. W bubblesbelow kauai.com

Extended Horizons
94 Kupuohi St, Suite A-1, Lahaina, Maui. Tel (808) 667-0611. W extended horizons.com

Fair Wind Cruises
78-7130 Kaleiopapa St, Kailua-Kona, Hawai'i Island. Tel (808) 345-0268. W fair-wind.com

Snorkel Bob's
700 Kapahulu Ave, Honolulu, O'ahu. Tel (808) 735-7944. W snorkelbob.com
Moanalani Dr, Kohala, Hawai'i Island. Tel (808) 885-9499.
3350 Lower Honoapi'ilani Rd, Lahaina, Maui. Tel (808) 667-9999.
3236 Po'ipū Rd, Kōloa, Kaua'i. Tel (808) 742-2206.

Surfing, Body-Surfing, and Windsurfing

Aloha Beach Service
2365 Kalakaua Ave, Waikīkī, O'ahu. Tel (808) 922-3111. W alohabeach services.com

Hi-Tech Surf Sports
425 Kōloa St, Kahului, Maui. Tel (808) 877-2111. W surfmaui.com

Honolua Surf Co.
845 Front St, Lahaina, Maui. Tel (808) 661-8848. W honoluasurf.com

Local Motion
Lahaina Gateway, Maui. Tel (808) 661-7873. W localmotionhawaii.com

Naish Hawai'i
155A Hāmākua Dr, Suite A, Kailua, O'ahu. Tel (808) 262-6068. W naish.com

Nancy Emerson's School of Surfing
505 Front St, Suite 224B, Lahaina, Maui. Tel (808) 244-7873. W mauisurfclinics.com

Progressive Expressions
5428 Kolōa Rd, Kōloa, Kaua'i. Tel (808) 742-6041. W progressive expressions.com

Rainbow Watersports
Hale'iwa Beach Park, Hale'iwa, O'ahu. Tel (808) 372-9304. W rainbow watersports.com

Second Wind
111 Hāna Highway, Kahului, Maui. Tel (808) 877-7467. W secondwindmaui.com

Surf News Network
Daily updates on water conditions, weather, etc. Tel (808) 593-2170. W surfnewsnetwork.com

Surf-n-Sea
62-595 Kamehameha Highway, Hale'iwa, O'ahu. Tel (808) 637-9887. W surfnsea.com

Windsurf Kaua'i
PO Box 323, Hanalei, Kaua'i. Tel (808) 828-6838. W windsurf-kauai.com

Kayaking, Canoeing, and Sailing

Go Bananas
799 Kapahulu Ave, Honolulu, O'ahu. Tel (808) 737-9514. W gobanana swatersports.com

Hawai'i Yacht Club
1739-C Ala Moana Blvd, Suite C, Honolulu, O'ahu. Tel (808) 944-9666. W hawaiiyachtclub.org

Outfitters Kaua'i
2827A Po'ipū Rd, Kōloa, Kaua'i. Tel (808) 742-9667. W outfitterskauai.com

Paragon Charters
5229 Lwr Kula Rd, Kula, Maui. Tel (808) 244-2087. W sailmaui.com

South Pacific Kayaks
95 Halekauai St, Kīhei, Maui. Tel (808) 875-4848. W southpacific kayaks.com

Twogood Kayaks Hawai'i
134B Hamakua Dr, Kailua, O'ahu. Tel (808) 262-5656. W twogoodkayaks.com

Waikīkī Yacht Club
1599 Ala Moana Blvd, Honolulu, O'ahu. Tel (808) 955-4405. W waikikiyachtclub.com

Fishing

Aerial Sportfishing Charters
Slip #9, Lahaina, Maui. Tel (808) 667-9089. W aerialsportfishing charters.com

Blue Hawai'i Sportfishing
Kailua-Kona, Hawai'i Island. Tel (808) 895-2970. W konamarlin fishing.com

Hawai'i Fishing News
6650 Hawai'i Kai Dr, Suite 201, Honolulu, O'ahu. Tel (808) 395-4499. W hawaiifishing news.com

Captain Charlie's Maui Sport Fishing Charters
Slip 27, Lahaina Harbor, Lahaina, Maui. Tel (808) 214-8510. W mauisportfishing charters.com

Sea Verse
1125 Ala Moana Blvd, Honolulu, O'ahu. Tel (808) 262-5587. W sportfishing honolulu.com

Cycling and Mountain Biking

Haleakalā Bike Co.
810 Ha'ikū Rd, Suite 120, Ha'ikū, Maui. Tel (808) 575-9575. W bikemaui.com

Raging Isle Sports
66-250 Kamehameha Highway, Building B, Hale'iwa, O'ahu. Tel (808) 637-7707.

South Maui Bicycles
1993 S. Kīhei Rd, #5, Kīhei, Maui. Tel (808) 874-0068. W southmaui bicycles.com

West Maui Cycles
1087 Limahana Place, Maui. Tel (808) 661-9005. W westmauicycles.com

Hiking

Hawai'i Nature Center
2131 Makiki Heights Dr, Honolulu, O'ahu. Tel (808) 955-0100. W hawaii naturecenter.org

Nature Conservancy
1040 Richards St, Rm 306, Honolulu, O'ahu. Tel (808) 537-4508. W nature.org

Sierra Club
111 Bishop St, Honolulu, O'ahu. Tel (808) 538-6616. W sierraclubhawaii.com

Whale Watching

Paragon Charters
5229 Lwr Kula Rd, Kula, Maui. Tel (808) 244-2087. W sailmaui.com

Wild Side Specialty Tours
Wai'anae Boat Harbor, A-11, Wai'anae, O'ahu. Tel (808) 306-7273. W sailhawaii.com

Other Activities

ATV Tours
PO Box 800, Kalaheo, Kaua'i. Tel (808) 742-2734. W kauaiatv.com

CJM Country Stables
1831 Poipu Rd, Kōloa, Kaua'i. Tel (808) 742-6096. W cjmstables.com

Moloka'i Mule Ride
Kualapu'u, Moloka'i. Tel (808) 567-6088. W muleride.com

Paniolo Riding Adventures
Kawaihae, Hawai'i Island. Tel (808) 889-5354. W panioloadventures.com

Skyline Eco-Adventures
12 Kiopa'a St, Pukalani, Maui. Tel (808) 878-8400. W zipline.com

Golf

With year-round warm, sunny weather and more than 80 challenging courses on six different islands, Hawai'i is a golfer's paradise. The courses, carved from brilliant green valleys and dramatic lava fields, are as varied as the islands. Lush fairways are bordered by tropical rainforests and sandy beaches. Distractingly scenic panoramas reveal sparkling blue sea, neighboring islands, and even breaching whales. There are championship courses across the state, created by some of the biggest names in golf – Arnold Palmer, Jack Nicklaus, and Robert Trent Jones, Sr and Jr. *Golf Magazine* lists eight in its Top 25 US Golf Resorts; no other state boasts more than two.

The challenging and scenic Turtle Bay Resort Golf Club, O'ahu

General Information

Most of Hawai'i's golf courses are open to the public. Municipal courses usually have low green fees. Resort courses are more expensive, but are generally open to all players, not only to resort guests. Private courses are for members only, but some set aside a day for non-members to play. Military courses are open to military personnel and their dependents.

Most courses have driving ranges and fully-stocked pro shops that provide equipment rental, instruction, and clinics.

Green fees usually include the use of a cart and range from less than $30 on a municipal course to in excess of $200 for a round on a plush resort course. However, many Hawai'i courses do offer discounted rates – twilight fees, junior discounts, and multiple-round discounts for those who want to play a second round on the same day or use the same course more than once in a week.

Golf packages are available at many hotels and resorts. These typically combine accommodations and golf rounds or discounted green fees with extras such as meals, instruction, video analysis, and golf logo items.

Winner celebrates at a golf championship

Major Tournaments

In January, The Mitsubishi Electric Championship, at Hawai'i Island's Four Seasons Resort Hualālai, opens the Champion's tour season. Some of the biggest names in golf including Jack Niklaus have played here. Top golfers gather again for the Hyundai Tournament of Champions on Kapalua Resort's Plantation Course, Maui where the likes of Tiger Woods, Ernie Els and Vijay Singh have played a round. January also sees the return of the long-running pro tournament, the Sony Open (*see p41*), held at the Wai'alae Country Club on O'ahu. The event has been held at Wai'alae since 1965 when it began as the Hawaiian Open. Today, it attracts more than 140 of the world's greatest golf professionals.

O'ahu

Ala Wai Golf Course is one of the busiest municipal courses in the world. Arnold Palmer's **Hawai'i Prince Golf Club** offers three challenging nine-hole layouts. Considered the toughest course in the US, **Ko'olau Golf Club** features extreme elevation changes and winding ravines. **Turtle Bay Resort Golf Club** has the George Fazio Course and the Arnold Palmer Course, where the back nine meander through a tropical forest and a wetlands bird sanctuary. The course at **Ko Olina Golf Club** has no parallel fairways.

Moloka'i and Lāna'i

Moloka'i offers the **Ironwood Hills Golf Club**, a municipal course along scenic hillsides. On little Lāna'i, **Kō'ele Golf Course** (upcountry) and **Mānele Golf Course** (seaside) are top-ranked championship resort courses. In contrast, the public **Cavendish Golf Course** has nine holes and no fees (but do leave a donation in the box).

The Kō'ele Golf Course, Lāna'i; one of Hawai'i's many superb courses

Putting at hole seven on the Blue Course at Wailea Golf Club, Maui

Maui

Maui's fabulous weather and awe-inspiring beauty provide the backdrop for some of the world's most breathtaking golf experiences. The two courses at the **Kapalua Resort** are gorgeous, with long fairways and tall evergreens running down to the sea. Opened in 1993, **Mākena Golf Course** offers some of the most spectacular views of any golf course in Hawai'i. Designed by Robert Trent Jones, Jr., it winds its way up the slopes of Haleakalā (see pp132–3), reaching an elevation of 800 ft (240 m) above sea level. At **Wailea Golf Club**, there are three courses – the Gold, the Emerald, and the Blue.

Hawai'i Island

Hawai'i Island boasts 20 world-class golf courses, many carved from black lava and overlooking beautiful seascapes. The first resort course built on the island is one of two in the state designed by legendary golf course architect Robert Trent Jones, Sr. **Mauna Kea Golf Course** has dramatic changes in elevation and incredible views of the snowcapped volcanic mountain from which it takes its name, as well as spectacular holes along the rugged coastline. **Volcano Golf and Country Club** is situated at a lofty 4,000 ft (1,220 m), along the rim of the active Kilauea volcano (see pp156–7). One of the world's most unusual golf courses, it provides visiting players with a memorable experience. The par-72 course has 18 holes and you may have to look out for wild turkeys and nene geese.

Kaua'i

Kaua'i's golf courses feature waterfalls, fern forests, and flowers on lush layouts sculpted from rainforests, canyons, and sea cliffs. At **Po'ipū Bay Golf Course**, the carts have satellite navigation systems that indicate the distance to the hole and pin placement. **Princeville Golf Club** has two courses, one with three nine-hole layouts in one.

Bunkers on Mauna Kea Golf Course, Hawai'i Island

DIRECTORY

O'ahu

Ala Wai Golf Course
404 Kapahulu Ave,
Honolulu. Map 4 F3.
Tel (808) 296-2000.

Hawai'i Prince Golf Club
91-1200 Fort Weaver Rd,
'Ewa Beach. **Tel** (808) 944-4567. 🆆 princeresorts
hawaii.com

Ko'olau Golf Club
45-550 Kionaole Rd,
Kāne'ohe. **Tel** (808)
247-7088. 🆆 koolau
golfclub.com

Ko Olina Golf Club
92-1220 Alii Nui
Dr, Kapolei.
Tel (808) 676-5300.
🆆 koolinagolf.com

Turtle Bay Resort Golf Club
57-091 Kamehameha
Highway, Kahuku.
Tel (808) 293-8574.
🆆 turtlebaygolf.com

Moloka'i and Lāna'i

Cavendish Golf Course
Keomoku Rd, Lāna'i City,
Lāna'i. 🆆 cavendishgolf
club.com

Mānele Golf Course
1233 Fraser Ave, Mānele,
Lāna'i. **Tel** (808) 565-2222.
🆆 fourseasons.com/
manelebay

Kō'ele Golf Course
Lāna'i Ave, Lāna'i City,
Lāna'i. **Tel** (808) 565-4653.
🆆 fourseasons.com/
manelebay

Ironwood Hills Golf Club
Kalae Highway, Kualapu'u,
Moloka'i. **Tel** (808) 567-6000. 🆆 molokaigolf
course.com

Maui

Kapalua Golf Club
Kapalua Resort, 300
Kapalua Dr.
Tel (808) 669-8044.
🆆 kapalua.com/golf

Mākena Golf Course
Mākena Resort, 5415
Mākena Alanui Dr.
Tel (808) 891-4000.
🆆 makenaresortmaui.
com/golf

Wailea Golf Club
100 Wailea Golf Club Dr,
Wailea Resort.
Tel (808) 875-7540.
🆆 waileagolf.com

Hawai'i Island

Mauna Kea Golf Course
62-100 Mauna Kea Beach
Dr, Kohala Coast. **Tel** (808)
822-5400. 🆆 princeresorts
hawaii.com

Volcano Golf and Country Club
Pi'i Mauna Rd, Volcano.
Tel (808) 967-7331.
🆆 volcanogolf
shop.com

Kaua'i

Po'ipū Bay Golf Course
2250 Ainako St, Kōloa.
Tel (808) 742-8711.
🆆 poipubaygolf.com

Princeville Golf Club
Princeville.
Tel (808) 826-5001.
🆆 princevillegolf.com

WEDDINGS IN HAWAI'I

Beautiful and sensual, Hawai'i is the ultimate destination for lovers. Everything you could want for the perfect romantic escape is here – balmy weather year round, magnificent sunsets, star-studded night skies, brilliant rainbows, fragrant blossoms, and magical settings. In this tropical paradise there is no end to the variety of ways in which you can get married.

Exchange your vows barefoot on a sparkling white sand beach or by a secluded waterfall. Have a traditional wedding in a tropical garden or a picturesque chapel. Sail into the sunset for a ceremony at sea, or fill a formal ballroom with family and friends. You can even declare your love under the waves or while falling through the air.

A garlanded couple exchanging rings in a traditional Hawaiian-style wedding

Wedding Details

The range of professional wedding services on offer in Hawai'i is as extensive as the choice of venues and ceremony types. Whether you want a wedding that is intimate, elegant, or unusual, wedding planners are available to assist in every way and can make recommendations to fit your personal taste and budget. The **Hawai'i Visitors and Convention Bureau** and the individual visitors' bureaux on each island have websites with sections on weddings and honeymoons. These include directories of services provided by their members. Many hotels offer wedding packages that include every-thing from a champagne toast

to a private in-room dinner prepared by a top chef, and from a fragrant flower *lei* greeting to a Hawaiian blessing. If you decide to handle the details yourself, check the *Yellow Pages* in the phone book for the island in question. Local professional associations provide useful lists of coordinators, officiants, photographers, video-graphers, musicians, and entertainers. They also list bridal gown boutiques, tuxedo rentals, hair, makeup, and nail stylists, caterers, florists, and more.

A Hawaiian Wedding

A Hawaiian blessing is just one aspect of genuine island-style nuptials. Other special features include the blowing of the conch shell to signal the start of the ceremony, soft island music, the officiant performing the ceremony in the Hawaiian language (as well as in English), and fresh flower *lei*, worn and exchanged by the bride and groom.

It is also possible to opt for a Western ceremony and the limitless stunning locations available mean you can make your vows in a memo-rable setting.

Gay and Lesbian Weddings

The State of Hawai'i does not legally recognize gay marriages and will not issue a license to same-sex couples. However, there are many gay-friendly wedding planners listed on the Internet who offer commitment ceremonies. Try www.hawaiigayweddings. org and www.alohamauigay weddings.com

Beach Weddings

Hawai'i offers countless golden beaches that make perfect wedding settings. If you get married at **Kapi'olani Park** *(see pp76–7)* on O'ahu, your wedding photos could show the world-renowned Waikīkī Beach and Diamond Head in the background. **Hāpuna Bay** *(see p144),* near Kawaihae on Hawai'i Island, has a gorgeous long stretch of white sand and sparkling turquoise water. On Kaua'i, one of the most spectacular settings is **Hanalei Bay** *(see p170),* where steep cliffs shrouded in emerald-green vegetation contrast against the dazzling white sand and deep-blue sea. Maui has mile upon mile of beautiful beaches, but

A bride and groom hand in hand on the beach at the Mākena Beach Resort, Maui *(see p186)*

Gazebo surrounded by flowers and lush greenery, an ideal garden wedding setting

it may be difficult to find one that you can have all to yourselves. The bay at **Kapalua** *(see p119),* on the west side of the island, makes a picture-perfect wedding setting. The beach here is a white sand crescent that fronts the lovely bay, with the nearby islands of Moloka'i and Lāna'i floating on the horizon.

Hawai'i's state and county beaches allow beach wedding ceremonies without a charge, but you must obtain a permit.

Garden Weddings

Foster Botanical Gardens, a serene oasis in Honolulu's Chinatown *(see p63),* is a popular wedding venue. It is well stocked with beautiful plants from tropical regions around the globe. Another popular choice is **Hawai'i Tropical Botanical Garden** *(see p151),* a short distance north of Hilo on Hawai'i Island. These gardens overlook Onomea Bay: the Twin Rocks that stand as sentinels in the bay are said to embody two legendary lovers. The **Kepaniwai Heritage Gardens** *(see p123)* on Maui are colorful and fragrant and have pavilions representing each ethnic group that has settled on the island, from the Japanese and the Chinese to the Portuguese. Gardens

that are administered by state and county parks do not charge a fee for wedding ceremonies; however, it is necessary to apply for a permit in advance.

Churches and Chapels

Each island has a picturesque historic church built in the 1800s, when Christian missionaries first arrived. Today these churches are chosen as locations for many Hawaiian weddings. Honolulu's grand **Kawaiaha'o Church** *(see p58)* once served Hawaiian royalty. On Maui, the intimate **Keawala'i Church** *(see p124)* in Mākena, built in 1832, is set on the edge of a peaceful bay and surrounded by palms gently swaying in the breeze. The oldest church on the islands, **Moku'aikaua Church** *(see p138)* on Hawai'i Island, is built of lava stone and its steeple is the highest structure in Kailua-Kona. The interdenominational **Kōloa Church** in the Po'ipū area of Kaua'i *(see p177)* also has a beautiful steeple, as well as ornate columns, high ceilings, and

Old-style steepled church, Hawai'i Island

seating for over 200 guests. Almost every hotel in Hawai'i offers wedding packages and several have lovely chapels on their own grounds.

In Honolulu and Waikīkī, there are chapels at the **Hilton Hawaiian Village Beach Resort** *(see p183),* the **Sheraton Moana Surfrider** *(see p183),* and the **Ilikai Waikiki Hotel**.

Located on a magnificent stretch of O'ahu's south shore, the lovely **Kahala O Ke Kai Chapel** is part of the gorgeous Kahala Hotel. At Turtle Bay Resort *(see p184),* on the north shore of O'ahu, the **Wedding Pavilion**, located on the tip of scenic Kuilima Point, is a dramatic glass-walled sanctuary. Here wedding parties can arrive at and depart the ceremony in the utmost style, riding in Turtle Bay Resort's own horse-drawn carriage. On Maui, the **Wailea Seaside Chapel**, part of the Grand Wailea Resort *(see p186),* is impressive and picturesque. Its exterior resembles a New England church, and inside, there are chandeliers hanging majestically from the high vaulted ceiling and glorious stained-glass windows.

On Hawai'i Island, the Sheraton Keauhou Bay Resort *(see p186)* offers a romantic white seaside wedding chapel, **Bayside Chapel**, which is secluded from the rest of the property.

The striking interior of Wailea Seaside Chapel at the Grand Wailea Resort

Tying the knot underwater, in a scuba marriage ceremony

Unusual Weddings – Land, Air, and Sea

There are many out-of-the-ordinary wedding ceremony options to be enjoyed in Hawai'i. For instance, couples can get married on the summit of one of Hawai'i's breathtaking dormant volcanoes – **Diamond Head** (see p77) on O'ahu, **Haleakalā** (see pp132–3) on Maui, or **Mauna Kea** (see p150) on Hawai'i Island. Permits are needed, but the location itself is free of charge.

Alternatively, you can let a helicopter whisk you away to your special beach or hidden waterfall. On Maui, Hawai'i Island, and Kaua'i **Blue Hawaiian Helicopters** can organize this.

Another heavenly option is saying your vows while skydiving. On O'ahu, you can arrange to do this with **Skydive Hawai'i** or **Pacific Skydiving Honolulu**.

There are a variety of possibilities for a romantic wedding at sea. You might choose to say your vows sailing into the sunset on the **Alala Catamaran** – or on a yacht provided by **Kamanu Charters** or **Shangri-La Private Sailing Charters**.

Kaua'i's legendary Fern Grotto (see p166), a natural amphitheater full of luxuriant greenery, is perfect for a secluded wedding. For the journey there, **Smith's Motor Boat Service** will provide a

private boat, on which musicians can serenade you with the romantic Hawaiian Wedding Song as you cruise up the Wailua River.

In an underwater scuba ceremony, dolphins, turtles and colorful reef fish will be your witnesses as you write the words "I do" and exchange rings. **Eve Eschner Hogan** on Maui, or **Beach Weddings Hawai'i** on Hawai'i Island can arrange to make this happen for you. On O'ahu, Maui, and Hawai'i Island, another underwater option is to charter a private submarine cruise for your ceremony with **Atlantis Submarines**.

Musician at an Hawaiian-style wedding

Legalities

Both the bride and groom must be present when the license is issued and each must provide valid picture identification (a driver's license or passport). Your birthplace, and the names of your parents will be noted on the license application. If relevant, final divorce decree information is also needed, as is written permission from a parent or legal guardian for those under 18 years of age. No waiting period, blood tests, or vaccinations are required. The license is good for 30 days and the $60 fee must be paid in cash.

The central marriage license office is located in O'ahu at the **Hawai'i State Department of Health**. An appointment to obtain the license should be scheduled directly with a license agent. For agent contact information, call the local branch of the Hawai'i State Department of Health. After the wedding, the officiant sends the license for filing as the official marriage certificate. A certified copy is mailed to the couple around 120 days later. The license agent can speed up this process by forwarding a $10 fee.

Vow Renewals

Many married couples want to do it all over again and arrange a vow renewal ceremony. These can be as creative and personal as you want them to be and there is the same endless variety of locations and ceremonies available as there is for first-timers. Since the ceremony is purely symbolic, not legal, a minister or judge is not required to perform it, nor is it necessary to obtain any form of marriage license. Outrigger Waikīkī on the Beach (see p183) and Outrigger Reef on the Beach (see p183) invite guests who are newlyweds or celebrating an anniversary to renew their vows at a complimentary ceremony on Waikīkī Beach. This nondenominational Hawaiian celebration is conducted by a practicing kahu (priest) and includes a traditional chant, hula (see pp30–31), song, and flower lei garlands.

Hawaiian dancers at a vow renewal ceremony on Waikīkī Beach

DIRECTORY

Information

Big Island Visitors Bureau
250 Keawe St, Hilo,HI 96743. Tel (808) 961-5797.
W gohawaii.com/big-island

Hawai'i Visitors and Convention Bureau
Suite 801, 2270 Kalākaua Ave, Honolulu, HI 96815.
Tel (808) 923-1811.
W gohawaii.com

Kaua'i Visitors Bureau
4334 Rice St, Līhu'e, HI 96766. Tel (808) 245-3971.
W gohawaii.com/kauai

Kaua'i Wedding Professionals Association
W kauaiwedpro.com

Maui Visitors Bureau (also Lāna'i and Moloka'i)
1727 Wili Pa Loop, Wailuku, Maui 96793.
Tel (808) 244-3530.
W gohawaii.com/maui

Maui Wedding Association
W mauiwedding association.com

O'ahu Visitors Bureau
733 Bishop St, Suite1520, Honolulu, O'ahu.
Tel (808) 524-0722.
W gohawaii.com/oahu

Beach Weddings

Hanalei Bay
Permits: Kaua'i County Beach Parks, 4444 Rice St, Līhu'e, Kaua'i, HI 96766.
Tel (808) 241-6660.

Hāpuna Bay
Permits: Hawai'i Island State Parks, P.O. Box 936, Hilo, Hawai'i Island, HI 96721.Tel (808) 974-6200.

Kapi'olani Park
Permits: 3902 Paki Ave, P.O. Box 3059, Honolulu, Oahu, HI 96815.
Tel (808) 545 4344.

Garden Weddings

Foster Botanical Gardens
Permits: Honolulu Dept of Parks and Recreation, 50 N Vineyard Blvd, Honolulu, HI 96817.
Tel (808) 522-7066.
W honolulu.gov/parks

Hawai'i Tropical Botanical Garden
Pepe'ekeo Scenic Dr, Hawai'i Island.
Tel (808) 964-5233.
W htbg.com

Kepaniwai Heritage Gardens
'Iao Valley Rd, Maui.
Tel (808) 270-7230.

Churches and Chapels

Bayside Chapel
Sheraton Keauhou Bay Resort, 78-128 Ehukai St, Kailua-Kona, Hawai'i Island.
Tel (808) 930-4900.
W sheratonkeauhou.com

Hilton Hawaiian Village Beach Resort
2005 Kālia Rd, Honolulu, O'ahu. Tel (808) 949-4321.
W hilton.com

Ilikai Waikīkī Hotel
1777 Ala Moana Blvd, Honolulu, O'ahu.
Tel (808) 949-3811.
W ilikaihotel.com

Kahala O Ke Kai Chapel
5000 Kahala Ave, Honolulu, O'ahu.
Tel (808) 739-8888.
W kahalaresort.com

Kawaiaha'o Church
957 Punchbowl St, Honolulu, O'ahu.
Tel (808) 469-3000.

Keawala'i Congregational Church
5300 Mākena Rd, Mākena, Maui.
Tel (808) 879-5557.

Kōloa Church
3269 Po'ipū Rd, Kōloa, Kaua'i.
Tel (808) 742-6622.

Moku'aikaua Church
75-5713 Ali'i Dr, Kailua-Kona, Hawai'i Island.
Tel (808) 329-0655.

Moana Surfrider
2365 Kalākaua Ave, Waikīkī, O'ahu.
Tel (808) 923-3111.
W moana-surfrider.com

Wailea Seaside Chapel
Grand Wailea Resort, 3850 Wailea Alanui, Wailea, Maui. Tel (808) 875-1234.
W grandwailea.com

Wedding Pavilion
Turtle Bay Resort, 57-091 Kamehameha Highway, Kahuku, O'ahu.
Tel (808) 293-8811.
W turtlebayresort.com

Unusual Weddings

Alala Catamaran
Ocean Sports, 69-275 Waikoloa Beach Dr, Waikoloa, Hawai'i Island.
Tel (808) 886-6666.
W hawaiiocean sports.com

Atlantis Submarines
Maui: Suite 175, 658 Front St, Lahaina. Tel (808) 667-2224. Hawai'i Island: 75-5669 Ali'i Dr, Kailua-Kona. Tel (808) 329-6626. O'ahu: 1600 Kapi'olani Blvd, Honolulu. Tel (808) 973-9811. W atlantis adventures.com

Beach Weddings Hawai'i
Kailua-Kona, Hawai'i Island. Tel (808) 328-9239.
W beachwedding shawaii.com

Blue Hawaiian Helicopters
Maui: Tel (808) 871-8844.
Hilo, Hawai'i Island:
Tel (808) 961-5600.
Waikoloa, Hawai'i Island:
Tel (808) 886-1768.
Līhu'e, Kaua'i:
Tel (808) 245-5800.
W bluehawaiian.com

Diamond Head
Diamond Head Rd, Honolulu, O'ahu.
Tel (808) 587-0300.

Eve Eschner Hogan
P.O. Box 943, Pu'unene, Maui. Tel (808) 573-7700.
W evehogan.com

Haleakalā
Haleakalā National Park, Haleakalā Crater Rd, Maui.
Tel (808) 572-4440.
W nps.gov/hale

Kamanu Charters
P.O. Box 2021, Kailua-Kona, Hawai'i Island.
Tel (808) 329-2021.
W kamanu.com

Mauna Kea
Highway 200, Hawai'i Island.
Tel (808) 933-0734.

Pacific Skydiving Honolulu
68-760 Farrington Highway, Dillingham Airfield, O'ahu.
Tel (808) 637-7472.
W pacificskydiving honolulu.com

Shangri-La Private Sailing Charters
Suite 109B, 5095 Napilihau St, Lahaina, Maui.
Tel (808) 665-0077.
W sailingmaui.com

Skydive Hawai'i
68-760 Farrington Highway, Dillingham Airfield, O'ahu.
Tel (808) 637-9700.
W skydivehawaii.com

Smith's Motor Boat Service
Wailua Marina State Park, Wailua, Kaua'i.
Tel (808) 821-6887.
W smithskauai.com

Legalities

Hawai'i State Department of Health
1250 Punchbowl St, Honolulu, O'ahu.
Tel (808) 586-4545.
Maui: Tel (808) 984-8201.
Lāna'i: Tel (808) 565-6411.
Moloka'i: Tel (808) 553-3208. Kaua'i: Tel (808) 241-3498. Hawai'i Island:
Tel (808) 974-6008.
W hawaii.gov/health

SURVIVAL GUIDE

PRACTICAL INFORMATION

Tourism is Hawai'i's most important industry. From the bright lights of Waikīkī, to the beaches of Moloka'i, the islands offer something for everyone. Paradise can be expensive – the cost of living is more expensive here than in the rest of the United States – but for those planning a money-no-object vacation, all kinds of luxuries await. Visitors on more modest budgets can also enjoy a memorable trip with a little planning ahead. With its balmy climate, Hawai'i is a great all-year destination; for lower air fares and room rates, avoid peak season (mid-December to March). Throughout the year, however, many of the islands' biggest attractions are free, while most of the rest, including national parks and museums, charge low admission prices.

Aloha Week celebration at Hilton Hawaiian Village Beach Resort *(see p183)*

When to Go

Although Hawai'i is very much an all-year-round destination, with average daytime temperatures seldom dropping below 80°F (27°C), the weather generally turns a little cooler and wetter in winter, between November and April. Since that is precisely when visitors from North America, Japan, and Europe want to escape harsher conditions back home, however, this is still the islands' busiest time for tourism. Transportation and accommodation prices rise, and with demand high, it is a good idea to make reservations as far in advance as possible.

The most important seasonal variation is that the ocean tends to be rougher in winter. Surfers come for the big winter waves, whereas families with young children, recreational swimmers, and snorkelers prefer the more placid summer. Winter is also prime whale-watching season, when the humpbacks return from Alaska.

Some visitors plan their stay in Hawai'i around special events and holidays, such as the Honolulu Marathon *(see p40)*, the Ironman Triathlon *(see p39)*, and Aloha Week *(see p39)*.

For more information about visiting Hawai'i and its events schedule, see the website, run by the **Hawai'i Visitors & Convention Bureau** (HVCB), or contact one of their many offices.

Visas and Passports

The conditions for entry into Hawai'i are the same as for the rest of the United States. All visitors are required to have a passport that is valid for at least six months after their trip and an onward or return ticket. Citizens of the UK, most European nations, New Zealand, and Australia also need to have completed an Electronic System for Travel Authorization (ESTA) application online, for which a $14 fee is charged. Canadian citizens only need to show their passport to enter the US. Citizens of all other countries need a valid passport and a tourist visa, which can be obtained from a US consulate or embassy.

No inoculations are required unless you come from, or have stopped in, an area suffering from an epidemic, particularly cholera or yellow fever.

Customs Information

Foreign visitors staying for at least 72 hours have the following duty-free allowance: 1 liter of wine or alcohol; 200 cigarettes or 50 cigars (as long as they are not Cuban), or 4.4 lb (2 kg) of smoking tobacco; and $100 worth of gifts. You are not permitted to bring foodstuffs or plants from any foreign country into Hawai'i.

Coffee of Hawai'i

All luggage is subject to an agricultural inspection on departure from the state. There are complex regulations governing which produce, foodstuffs, and flowers may be taken out of the islands – for example, the only fresh fruit you may carry with you is pineapple (also check the customs regulations of the country you are traveling to).

For full details, see the US Department of Agriculture website (www.aphis.usda.gov).

Visitor Information

At all island airports, visitor information desks provide maps and guides, and major hotels usually have a knowledgeable and helpful guest-services desk. In major tourist areas, such as Waikīkī, or Lahaina on Maui, almost all the "information centers" on the streets are, in fact, hard-sell agencies hoping to entice you on tours and activities, but the **Hawai'i Visitors & Convention Bureau** (HVCB) runs its own office on each of the four main islands.

Admission Prices

It is impossible to generalize about admission prices in Hawai'i. Many of the best things in life, of course, are free: every beach in the state offers unrestricted public access, and much of the islands' magnificent scenery can be explored on foot.

While some museums and galleries – such as Honolulu's excellent Hawaii State Art Museum *(see p61)* – offer free admission, most charge around $5–10 for adult entry. The price for the extemely popular Bishop Museum in Honolulu *(see pp72–3)*, is $20.

Commercial attractions can be more expensive still. The standard fee at the Maui Ocean Center *(see p123)* is around $26 per person, and at the Poly-nesian Cultural Center on O'ahu *(see p96)* it ranges from $50 up to $230. Both those places, and many others, offer significant discounts for online bookings, and it is always worth checking websites for discounted or free days or special events.

Opening Hours

Typical island businesses are open on weekdays from 9am to 5pm or 6pm (for banking hours, *see p236*). The biggest shopping malls, such as Honolulu's Ala Moana Center, are open 9:30am–9pm Mon–Sat, and

10am–7pm Sun. In resort areas, most shops remain open until 10pm or even later, while some supermarkets, convenience stores, and gas stations stay open 24 hours a day, seven days a week. In less touristy areas, stores tend to close between 5pm and 7pm.

Although the opening hours of attractions vary, most admit visitors daily. However, some close on major public holidays, such as Christmas and Thanksgiving.

Etiquette, Smoking, and Alcohol

Hawai'i is a friendly, casual place where hugs are common greetings. Islanders are seldom in a hurry, so prepare yourself for their leisurely pace.

Clothing is casual, too: pack sandals, sneakers, shorts, and casual evening wear. If you plan to venture above sea level – for example, in Upcountry Maui or the Big Island – you'll also need long pants and a sweater or jacket, plus sturdy walking shoes.

While it is good manners not to trespass on private land, bear in mind that no one owns a beach in Hawaii; you're always free to walk along the oceanfront.

Smoking is prohibited in all public spaces, such as shops, theaters, nightclubs, bars, restaurants, and elevators. Hotels are allowed to designate up to 20 per cent of guest rooms as smoking accommodation; how-ever, many choose not to do so.

The minimum legal age for drinking in Hawai'i is 21. It is illegal to drink in a state or national park, and to carry an open container of alcohol in your vehicle. Grocery stores, supermarkets, and convenience stores sell beer, wine, and spirits.

Accessibility to Public Restrooms

Although public restrooms are very rare in the streets and urban areas of Hawai'i, it is usually possible to walk into any hotel or shopping mall and use a restroom there. In addition, almost every beach is equipped with toilet facilities. Most beaches have running water and showers as well, though away from the main resorts and towns, a beach may have just a few portable toilets, with no water supply.

Taxes and Tipping

Hawai'i imposes a 4.712 per cent sales tax on all goods and services, and an additional hotel tax of 9.25 per cent, making a total of 13.962 per cent tax on accommodation. Rates can vary slightly between islands, so if you're visiting multiple islands check in advance that tax has been included in your room rate.

It is customary to tip good service – indeed, waiters and bar staff depend on tips for a large proportion of their income. The standard restaurant tip is 15 per cent of the check; tip taxi drivers 10–15 per cent of the fare; baggage handlers at least $1 per piece of luggage; and valet parking attendants $2.

Whale exhibit in Maui Ocean Center

Travelers with Special Needs

Hawai'i welcomes visitors with disabilities. Most hotels and restaurants, and many attractions, have wheelchair ramps, reserved parking, and specially equipped toilets.

The **Disability and Communication Access Board** website provides downloadable factsheets detailing access to beaches, parks, shopping centers and attractions, and where to rent vehicles. You can also find information about support services here, including parking permits, telecommunications, and service dogs. **Access Aloha Travel** is a Honolulu-based agency that specializes in travel plans for disabled travelers, in particular cruises, group tours and family travel.

Traveling with Children

Hawai'i is a fabulous family destination, though it is essential to remain aware of potentially dangerous ocean conditions (*see pp234–5*). Most hotels allow up to two children to share a room with their parents at no extra charge, and many also have family suites. Larger hotels often have kids' programs and babysitters. Restaurants are child-friendly, and even if there is no special menu, they will often provide youngsters with a hamburger or even a peanut butter and jelly sandwich.

Tour operators will specify if their activities impose any restrictions on children. In cars, children must sit in a safety seat (up to age four) or wear a seat belt.

Senior Citizens

Senior citizens (which in most cases means those aged 62 and over) can claim discounts at many attractions, including national parks, and at some hotels, restaurants, and shops upon presentation of their photo ID. Always ask about discounts and check publications such as the *Honolulu Star-Advertiser* and the *Maui News*, or contact the

A family *Lei*-making at Kā'anapali Beach Hotel, Maui

Department of Parks and Recreation for special events.

Members of the **American Association of Retired Persons (AARP)** receive discounts on rooms, cars, and tours. The non-profit **Road Scholar** organization offers educational trips for senior citizens that include accommodations, meals, lectures, guided tours, and activities.

Logo of the American Association of Retired Persons

Gay and Lesbian Travelers

Hawai'i shares its *aloha* with all and is equally welcoming to gays and lesbians. Gay-friendly accommodations, restaurants, bars, and beaches can be found on all the islands, and since civil unions were legalized in 2011, many local wedding planners now arrange gay marriages.

On O'ahu, Waikīkī is the hub of gay and lesbian activity. **Hula's Bar and Lei Stand** remains one of the best-known gathering places. **Pacific Ocean Holidays** organizes Hawai'i vacations for gay and lesbian travelers.

Traveling on a Budget

Although Hawai'i is an expensive place for locals and visitors alike, it's still possible to keep the costs of a visit down. The key is careful planning. Travel in low season if you can (*see p230*), and shop around for

flights. Decide which islands you want to visit, and fly out to the first and home from the last – that is, don't fly to Honolulu unless you actually want to go there, and don't pay for a pointless flight back to the island where you arrived. Do not assume you'll get the best deal by buying your inter-island flights as part of your overall ticket; it may be cheaper to buy them separately.

In terms of accommodation, if you expect to spend your days at the beach, hiking the trails, or simply exploring the islands, then stay in a more basic property a block or two back from the ocean rather than paying premium rates for a sea view. Renting an apartment or condo is usually a cheaper option, especially for families and groups. It is also possible to camp, especially on Kaua'i and Maui.

Many budget travelers choose to stay in Waikīkī, since you don't need a fancy room or a pool when the beach is so close; you can eat cheaply in local diners; and unlike on the other islands, you don't need a rental car.

Responsible Tourism

For all their beauty, the Hawaiian islands are very fragile. The land, or *'āina* ("that which feeds"), is the most important element of Hawaiian culture. Traditional Hawaiians believe that humans are stewards of the land, put here to protect and nurture it, not to exploit it. They believe that every natural

Time

Hawai'i has its own time zone, known as Hawai'i Standard Time (HST). The West Coast of the US mainland is two hours ahead of Hawai'i, and the East Coast five. Unlike the rest of the US, Hawai'i does not put its clocks forward for summer daylight saving, so some of the time differences below increase by one hour when the respective countries switch to summer time. In the northern hemisphere, this is generally from March or April to October.

City and Country	Hours + HST	City and Country	Hours + HST
Athens (Greece)	+12	Moscow (Russia)	+13
Auckland (New Zealand)	+22	New York (US)	+5
Beijing (China)	+18	Paris (France)	+11
Berlin (Germany)	+11	Perth (Australia)	+18
Chicago (US)	+4	Rome (Italy)	+11
Dublin (Ireland)	+10	Sydney (Australia)	+20
Hong Kong (China)	+18	Tokyo (Japan)	+19
London (UK)	+10	Toronto (Canada)	+5
Los Angeles (US)	+2	Vancouver (Canada)	+2
Madrid (Spain)	+11	Washington, D.C. (US)	+5

object, from a whale to a grain of sand, has life and a soul. You should therefore treat everything with great

Wildlife crossing sign cautions drivers to slow down

respect. Do not remove anything from its home – if you pick up a shell to look at it, for example, remember to put it back where you found it. Littering is both offensive and illegal.

Part of respecting the land means that locals are very careful to preserve precious resources, especially water. Most hotels and tourism developments are sited on the drier sides of the islands, where water conservation is

a major issue; follow the instructions that are posted everywhere. Some hotels are also introducing "green" door keys that turn off electrical appliances when guests are not in their rooms.

All sorts of state and federal laws aim to safeguard the islands and keep tourism responsible. Even so, it is important to be aware of the environmental consequences of your actions. Many visitors choose, for example, to eat locally sourced foods and, especially, products from the islands' many organic farms.

Conversions

US Standard to Metric
1 inch = 2.54 centimeters
1 foot = 30 centimeters
1 mile = 1.6 kilometers
1 ounce = 28 grams
1 pound = 454 grams
1 US quart = 0.947 liter
1 US gallon = 3.8 liters

Metric to US Standard
1 centimeter = 0.4 inch
1 meter = 3 feet 3 inches
1 kilometer = 0.6 mile
1 gram = 0.04 ounce
1 kilogram = 2.2 pounds
1 liter = 1.06 US quarts

DIRECTORY

Visitor Information

Hawai'i Visitors and Convention Bureau Offices
W gohawaii.com

Island Tourist Offices

Hawai'i Island
250 Keawe St, Hilo.
Tel (808) 961-5797.

Kaua'i
4334 Rice St, Lihu'e.
Tel (808) 245-3971.

Maui
1727 Wili Pa Loop, Wailuku.
Tel (808) 244-3530.

O'ahu
2270 Kalakaua Ave, Suite 801, Honolulu.
Tel (808) 923-1811.

Tourist Offices Abroad

Australia
Tel (612) 9286-8951.
W gohawaii.com/au

Germany
Tel (89) 5525 33819.
W gohawaii.com/de

New Zealand
Tel (649) 977-2234.
W gohawaii.com/nz

United Kingdom
Tel (020) 7644 6127.
W gohawaii.com/uk

Travelers with Special Needs

Access Aloha Travel
Tel (808) 545-1143.
W accessaloha travel.com

Disability and Communication Access Board
Tel (808) 586-2121.
W hawaii.gov/health/ dcab/travel

Senior Citizens

AARP
Tel (888) 687-2277.
W aarp.org

Department of Parks and Recreation
Aupuni Center, 101 Pauahi Street, Suite 6, Hilo.
Tel (808) 961-8311.
W hawaiicounty.gov/ parks-and-recreation

Road Scholar
Tel (800) 454-5768.
W roadscholar.org

Gay and Lesbian Travelers

Hula's Bar and Lei Stand
134 Kapahulu Ave, Waikīkī.
Tel (808) 923-0669.
W hulas.com

Pacific Ocean Holidays
Tel (808) 923-2400.
W gayhawaii vacations.com

Personal Security and Health

Despite its location in the tropics, Hawai'i carries remarkably few health risks (and boasts the highest life expectancy in the US). Immunizations are not usually required *(see p230)*, there are no land snakes to worry about, and there are only a few nasty creepy-crawlies. You should be aware of certain potential dangers if you go hiking or camping, but generally it is the sun and the ocean that pose the biggest threats to your health. Hawai'i does not have a serious crime problem, but take the normal precautions and use your common sense.

Police

Hawai'i is the only US state not to have a statewide police service. Instead each county – in effect, each island – runs its own police department. Your most likely contact with the police will be as a driver; each island has pretty much one main road, and local police know where speeding is most common. To report a crime, contact the nearest police station, where you can expect prompt and polite attention.

What to be Aware of

While not completely crime-free, Hawai'i is still remarkably safe, and violent crime is rare.

Use common sense. Do not hitchhike; avoid hiking alone and being in dark or remote areas at night. If in doubt, ask your hotel whether or not a particular area is safe.

Carry minimal cash when you go out, and do not take your passport unless you are required to do so. Leave your best jewelry at home, and other valuables in a safe – either in your room or at the hotel front desk. The main likelihood of theft is from a rented vehicle. Never leave any valuables in the car; thieves are skilled at dealing with door and trunk locks.

In an Emergency

In an emergency, the police, ambulance, or fire services can be reached by dialing 911. That same number will also summon help for in-shore swimming and surfing emergencies; for anything farther out at sea, call the **Coast Guard, Search and Rescue**. There is also a 24-hour **Suicide and Crisis Line**.

In the event of natural disasters, such as hurricanes or tsunamis, contact the **American Red Cross** or the **Hawai'i State Civil Defense**.

Lost and Stolen Property

Even though you have only a slim chance of retrieving stolen property, report all thefts to the police, and keep a copy of the police report for your insurance claim.

Most credit cards have toll-free numbers for reporting a loss *(see p237)*. If you need a replacement passport, contact your embassy or consulate. The Department of Business, Economic Development and Tourism website has a list of consulates in Hawai'i (www.hawaii.gov/dbedt).

Hospitals and Pharmacies

Even the smallest towns in Hawai'i have medical centers, but facilities on Moloka'i and Lāna'i are less extensive than those on the main islands. Honolulu's medical services are the state's best equipped.

Ask at your hotel if you need a doctor, dentist, or other healthcare professional. All medical care is expensive; even a simple visit to a doctor can cost over $100. Hospitals take most credit cards, but doctors and dentists usually want cash. Visitors without insurance documents may have to pay in advance. Anyone on prescription drugs should take along a supply, plus a copy of the prescription. Pharmacies are plentiful (**Long's Drugs** is present on all the islands), and supermarkets and convenience stores also sell some medicines.

Travel and Health Insurance

Travel insurance is highly recommended, mainly because of the high cost of medical treatment. Make sure the policy covers emergency medical care, accidental death, trip cancellation, and loss of baggage or documents.

Ocean Safety

The Pacific Ocean is as powerful as it is beautiful. Always pay close attention to the ocean, regardless of how experienced a swimmer you are. If you've never surfed before, don't try it without proper instruction.

A lifeguard is stationed at the most popular beaches; always ask him or her about current conditions, and heed posted warnings. Be wary of using unguarded beaches, especially

Lifeguard station on Po'ipū Beach, Kaua'i

Bright-yellow Hawaiian fire engine

if you aren't used to identifying dangerous currents. Note: many beaches can be safe in summer but pounded by dangerous surf in winter.

When you're in the water, swim facing away from the beach, to get back, swim parallel to the shore and then make your way in; if you're snorkeling, raise your head regularly. So-called rogue waves arrive suddenly and can sweep you out to sea. Should you get carried out by a rip current, don't fight it, but stay with it until it dissipates – usually 50–100 yds (45–90 m) from shore. Always check for rocks, coral, and other potential dangers below the surface. Use protective footwear such as reef slippers whenever possible. For more information check out the **Hawaii Beach Safety** website.

If you cut yourself on coral, clean the cut thoroughly with antiseptic. If you step on a sea urchin, the spine may well break off, leaving a tip embedded in your skin. This will dissolve in several days, but applying vinegar may speed up the process.

Two kinds of jellyfish are common in Hawai'i, though you're much more likely to see them washed up on shore than to encounter them while in the ocean. Box jellyfish tend to arrive on the leeward shores of the islands nine or ten days after the full moon; their stings are best treated with vinegar. The Portuguese man o' war can swarm at any time; do not apply vinegar to stings, but

irrigate them with fresh water. The website www.808jellyfish. com has more detailed advice.

Natural Hazards

Whether you're fair or dark-skinned, you must protect yourself against the harsh Hawaiian sun. Be sure to wear a hat and sunglasses, and use plenty of sunblock. Since certain sunblocks can damage coral, it makes sense to wear a T-shirt when snorkeling.

Introduce yourself to the sun slowly, and try to stay out of the sun between 11am and 2pm; even on overcast days, the ultraviolet rays penetrate the clouds. Heat can be a danger, too. Drink plenty of fluids, and avoid being out in high temperatures for long periods.

Hawaiian mosquitoes do not carry malaria but can still be a nuisance. Black widow spiders and scorpions

Warnings: currents, dangerous shore break, and big surf

are potential dangers when hiking or camping, while centipedes are also fairly common; check shoes before you put them on.

Drinking Water

Tap water is always safe to drink in Hawai'i, and bottled water is widely available. However, you should never drink from freshwater streams or pools. A bacterial disease, leptospirosis, can be contracted by drinking untreated water or exposing cuts or abrasions to fresh water.

DIRECTORY

In an Emergency

All Emergencies
Tel 911 to alert police, fire, and medical services, including to in-shore ocean incidents.

American Red Cross
Tel (808) 734-2101.
W hawaiiredcross.org

Coast Guard, Search and Rescue
Tel (800) 522-6458.

Hawai'i State Civil Defense
Tel (808) 733-4300.
W scd.hawaii.gov

Suicide and Crisis Line
Tel (808) 832-3100.
W sprc.org/states/hawaii

Ocean Safety

Hawaii Beach Safety
W oceansafety.ancl.hawaii.edu

Hospitals and Pharmacies

Hilo Medical Center
1190 Waiānuenue Ave.
Tel (808) 932-3000.
W hilomedicalcenter.org

Kona Community Hospital
79-1019 Haukapila St, Kealakekua, Kona. **Tel** (808) 322-9311.
W kch.hhsc.org

Lāna'i Community Hospital
628 7th St, Lāna'i City.
Tel (808) 565-8450.
W lch.hhsc.org

Long's Drugs
W longs.staradvertiser.com

Maui Memorial Medical Center
221 Mahalani St, Wailuku.
Tel (808) 244-9056.
W mauimemorialmedical.org

Moloka'i General Hospital
280 Homeolu Place, Kaunakakai
Tel (808) 553-5331.
W molokaigeneralhospital.org

Queen's Medical Center
1301 Punchbowl St, Honolulu.
Tel (808) 538-9011.
W queensmedicalcenter.org

Wilcox Memorial Hospital
3420 Kūhiō Highway, Līhu'e.
Tel (808) 245-1100.
W wilcoxhealth.org

Banking and Communications

Money matters in Hawai'i are the same as those in the rest of the US, so it is not necessary to take any currency other than US dollars. And since credit and debit cards are by far the most common form of currency, there's no point carrying large amounts of cash – or for that matter, travelers' checks – with you. Communications are straightforward, too, and the postal services are very good despite Hawai'i's isolation. Internet access is readily available, you can easily get online in hotels, as well as in public spaces; and for US mainland travelers, it's possible to read the same newspapers and watch the same TV shows as back home.

Banks and Bureaux de Change

The two largest local banks – First Hawaiian Bank and Bank of Hawai'i – have several branches on every island, while American Savings Bank, Central Pacific Bank, and Territorial Savings are also widely represented. If you find yourself needing to visit a bank, normal weekday opening hours are from 8:30am to 4pm; many stay open until 6pm on Fridays and also open 9am–1pm on Saturdays.

Old-style currency-exchange desks can be found at larger airports and in resort areas, and most big hotels will also change money for guests.

ATMs

Visitors to Hawai'i can expect to use their normal cards to withdraw cash from ATMs; if you are in any doubt, check with your own bank before you travel.

Many ATMs, especially those situated in convenience stores, impose surcharges, so you may have to shop around to find the best deal. In addition, it costs more to withdraw cash from ATMs using a credit card than it does with a debit card.

Credit and Debit Cards

You will be expected to use a credit or debit card for all major transactions, from hotel bills to restaurant meals and car rental. **VISA** and **MasterCard** are the most widely accepted cards, but most places also accept **American Express**, **Diners Club**, Discover, and JCB.

Overseas travelers should be aware that most credit and debit cards levy extra charges for foreign-currency transactions. It is also sensible to let your credit or debit card provider know you will be going away, so that they don't block your card if they see "unusual" charges.

Cell Phones

Check with your phone provider in advance if you are hoping to use your cell (mobile) phone in Hawai'i, and be warned that, for foreign visitors in particular, the call charges can be very high.

In addition, keep in mind that while cell-phone coverage tends to be excellent in resort and urban areas, some parts of Hawai'i are very remote indeed, isolated beyond massive volcanoes or behind towering cliffs. Hikers in particular should not depend on their cell phones for emergency use.

Hawaiian Telecom pay phone

Telephone Calls

Making telephone calls in Hawai'i is easy. The area code for the state as a whole is 808. You do not need to use the area code when making local calls (that is, within one island), but inter-island calls count as long distance, so the number must be preceded by 1-808 when dialing. Calls to other US area codes have to be preceded by 1.

Many businesses have toll-free phone numbers, which are preceded by 1-800 or 1-888. Note that these are toll-free only if dialed from within the United States.

Public phones are becoming less common. Those that do exist generally charge 75 cents to make a local call. Otherwise, conventional landline rates are at their cheapest from 11pm to 8am Monday to Thursday, and from 11pm Friday to 8am

Branch of the First Hawaiian Bank

Post-office branch in Kihei, Maui

Monday. Making a call from a hotel room always costs much more than the normal rate; for pay phones and hotel calls alike, it's worth buying a prepaid calling card at an ABC or other convenience store. Most hotels will have a pay phone in the lobby that guests can use.

The cheapest and most convenient solution may be to bring a laptop computer, so you can hook up to an online service such as Skype – though that, of course, is dependent on having a Wi-Fi connection.

Internet

Almost all hotels in Hawai'i offer Wi-Fi Internet access in guests' rooms. Many establishments impose a charge for this service, however, typically in the region of $12–20 per day. Most hotels will add any fee for Internet usage to your bill at the end of your stay, but in a few cases you may have to pay the supplier direct. Since many travelers access the Internet with their own laptops and smart phones these days, there are fewer Internet cafés on the islands than there used to be, but many hotels have a few computers available for guests' use. In addition, public libraries and independent postal services also offer Internet access for a fee.

Postal Services

Post offices are usually open from 8:30am to 4:30pm,

Monday to Friday, and on Saturday morning. Smaller post offices may have shorter hours. Mailboxes can be found on the streets of all major cities and towns. You can also purchase stamps and send mail from your hotel's front desk.

Standard US postal charges apply, and sending a letter within the US costs the same, regardless of the destination. So it costs the same to post an item within any island, from one island to another, or to anywhere on the mainland. Sending ordinary mail to the US mainland from Honolulu should not take more than four days; from the other islands, it will be more like a week. Mail to the rest of the world takes longer still.

Post box

Newspapers and Magazines

Hawai'i has a single statewide daily newspaper – the *Honolulu Star-Advertiser*. Hawai'i Island, Maui, and Kaua'i each have at least one daily paper, as well as weeklies. National newspapers, such as the *Wall Street Journal*, *USA Today*, and *The New York Times*, are easy to find in Honolulu and in stores and larger hotels throughout Hawai'i. Most newspapers also have online editions; visit www.world-newspapers.com/hawaii for a list.

Local magazines worth looking out for include *Honolulu* and *Hawai'i*, a

bimonthly general-interest publication. You can pick up all sorts of free glossy visitor guides at airports, on Waikīkī street corners, and at malls on the other islands. Many car-rental companies will provide you with a free local driving guide as part of the rental transaction.

Television and Radio

All the main US television networks – ABC, CBS, PBS, NBC, and FOX – have local affiliate stations; check listings on each island for the channel numbers. There are also a few interesting home-grown stations.

You can tune into dozens of local and state radio stations, but be prepared to lose reception as you travel around to the far side of the islands' huge volcanoes.

Reaching the Right Number

- The area code for the entire state is 808
- To make a call on the same island, just dial the number
- To call another island, dial 1, then 808, then the number
- To make international calls from Hawai'i, dial **011** followed by the country code, the city code, and then the number (Australia: 61; Canada: 1; Ireland: 353; Japan: 81; New Zealand: 64; United Kingdom: 44; United States: 1)

TRAVEL INFORMATION

Hawai'i entertains more than eight million visitors a year (roughly eight times its resident population). Almost all travelers arrive by air, though a few cruise lines include Hawai'i on their itineraries. On any given day, half of all visitors are on O'ahu, a quarter on Maui, and the rest on Hawai'i Island, Kaua'i, Moloka'i, and Lana'i, in that order. Almost all travel between the islands is by air, although there are a couple of ferry services, and a handful of luxury cruise lines available, too.

As for exploring individual islands, the only reliable way to get around is by car; public transportation is minimal, except on O'ahu.

Arriving by Air

The Hawaiian islands are the earth's most isolated archipelago, so wherever you're coming from, be prepared for a long flight. Even the shortest flight time, from Los Angeles, is about five hours; from Europe, expect up to 18 hours' traveling.

The great majority of non-stop flights from the US to Hawai'i leave from the West Coast, especially Los Angeles and San Francisco airports. You can also catch flights to Hawai'i from other cities in the US and Canada, but be aware that most involve a stop on the West Coast. While Honolulu is the busiest airport, **American Airlines, United Airlines**, and **US Airlines** all fly direct from the US mainland to Maui, Kaua'i, and Hawai'i Island.

United Airlines, American Airlines, **Air Canada**, and **Air New Zealand** are just some of the airlines that fly from Europe to Hawai'i, but you'll certainly land in the mainland US en route. All foreign travelers pass through immigration and customs where they first touch down in the US, regardless of whether that is their final destination. Admission procedures involve fingerprinting and taking a retina scan, and lines can be long – but all airlines allow enough time to catch your ongoing flight to Hawai'i.

Airports

Hawai'i's main transportation hub is **Honolulu International Airport**, 10 miles (16 km) west of Waikīkī, on O'ahu. Its two terminals handle 1,000 international, domestic, and inter-island flights daily.

Maui's major airport is **Kahului Airport**; it is always busy with long-haul and inter-island flights. Two smaller airports also receive a handful of flights. Kapalua-West Maui Airport, 6 miles (10 km) north of Lahaina, serves the Kā'anapali and Kapalua resort areas, while tiny Hāna Airport, on Maui's east coast, is mainly used by shuttle services from Kahului.

Kona International Airport, just north of Kailua-Kona on Hawai'i Island, has the state's prettiest terminal; its check-in counters and snack bars are housed in small thatched huts. It receives all the island's flights from the mainland, as well as plenty of inter-island services. **Hilo International Airport**, 3 miles (5 km) east of downtown Hilo, is also served by many inter-island flights.

Līhu'e Airport, on the edge of Kaua'i's capital, is Kaua'i's only inter-island terminal, and it also has connections with the US mainland.

On Moloka'i, little **Moloka'i Airport** – 8 miles (13 km) northwest of the main town, Kaunakakai – is served by around 20 inter-island flights per week. There's also a tiny airstrip down on the Kalaupapa Peninsula, which receives direct flights from Honolulu and Maui, as well as "topside" Moloka'i. The latter, at seven minutes, is the world's shortest scheduled air service.

Only inter-island carriers use **Lāna'i Airport**, 4 miles (6.5 km) southwest of Lāna'i City.

Hawaiian Airlines, on the runway at Honolulu International Airport

Departure building at Kona International Airport at Keāhole, Hawai'i Island

Tickets and Fares

The cheapest deals on flights to Hawai'i are generally available in off-peak months: May, June, September, and October. So-called discounted fares often come with advance purchase requirements and other restrictions, particularly involving cancellations. Check these carefully before you purchase the ticket, to avoid unpleasant surprises at the last minute. Many airlines also offer cheaper deals if you can arrive on a weekday.

Inter-Island Air Travel

It would be a real shame to come all the way to Hawai'i and see only one island. While traveling between the islands is very straightforward, with plentiful flight connections,

it can prove expensive. Many visitors, therefore, chose to fly into one island at the start of their trip and fly home from another. It's worth shopping around for inter-island flights. The best deals can often be found online and it can be worth joining the airline's frequent flier club, as this can often add extra discounts to your ticket price.

The three main airlines with inter-island flights are **Hawaiian Airlines**, **Island Air**, and **Mokulele Airlines**. Fares are usually around $100, but you may find yourself paying as much as $200 for popular flights. Note that Island Air operates smaller, turboprop planes, which might not be as comfortable as traveling in a larger plane.

Transport from Airports into Town

Approximate one-way taxi fares from various airports into town are: $25–30 from Honolulu airport to Waikīkī; $15 from Hilo airport into downtown Hilo; $30 from Kona airport to Kailua-Kona; $60 from Kahului to Kā'anapali; $10 from Moloka'i airport to Kaunakakai; $10 from Līhu'e airport into Lihu'e, and $20 north to Kapa'a. Buses and shuttle vans serve some airports and resorts – many are free for resort guests.

On O'ahu, **Roberts Hawaii Express Shuttle** runs a shuttle bus from Honolulu airport to Waikīkī for about $15 per head. **SpeediShuttle** operates similar services on the major islands.

Package Tours

Visitors have a wide range of package tours options for Hawai'i. These include air and hotel costs, car rental, inter-island travel, and often activities and meals, too. Some of the best deals are offered by the airlines themselves.

If you want to explore the natural beauty of the islands but prefer to leave the organizing to someone else, consider taking a tour with the likes of the **Sierra Club**, **Backroads**, or **The World Outdoors**.

DIRECTORY

Arriving by Air

Air Canada
W aircanada.com

Air New Zealand
W airnz.co.nz

Alaska Airlines
W alaskaair.com

American Airlines
W aa.com

British Airways
W ba.com

Continental Airlines
W continental.com

Delta
W delta.com

Qantas Airways
W qantas.com

United Airlines
W united.com

US Airways
W usair.com

Airports

Hilo International Airport
Tel (808) 961-9321.

Honolulu International Airport
Tel (808) 836-6413.

Kahului Airport
Tel (808) 872-3893.

Kona International Airport
Tel (808) 329-3423.

Lāna'i Airport
Tel (808) 565-6757.

Līhu'e Airport
Tel (808) 241-3913.

Moloka'i Airport
Tel (808) 567-6361.

Inter-Island Air Travel

Mokulele Airlines
Tel (866) 260-7070.
W mokuleleairlines.com

Hawaiian Airlines
Tel (800) 367-5320.
W hawaiianair.com

Island Air
Tel (800) 652-6541.
W islandair.com

Airport Shuttles

Roberts Hawaii Express Shuttle
Tel (808) 441-7800.
W airportwaikiki shuttle.com

SpeediShuttle
Tel (877) 242-5777.
W speedishuttle.com

Package Tours

Backroads
Tel (510) 527-1555.
W backroads.com

Sierra Club
Tel (415) 977-5522.
W sierraclub.org

The World Outdoors
Tel (303) 413-0946.
W theworldoutdoors.com

Getting Around Hawai'i

If you don't have a car in Hawai'i, your horizons will be limited. Having a vehicle provides both freedom of movement and the chance to be spontaneous. Most locals keep a swimsuit and towel in their car because they never know when the beach will look too good to resist. Anyone dependent on public transportation can reach only a few destinations beyond the confines of cities. Some of Hawai'i's most spectacular landscapes are out of bounds even to four-wheel-drive vehicles; that is when hiking can come into its own.

Green Travel

Hawaiian transportation companies show considerable commitment to minimizing their environmental impact. The largest public transit network, for example, TheBus on O'ahu, has commissioned hybrid "clean diesel" buses and recycles everything, from paint to cleaning products.

For truly green travel, you can't beat getting around by bike. There are dedicated bicycle routes all over the islands. The Kauai Path (www.kauaipath.org) is a shared cycling and walking path along the east coast of Kaua'i, while Maui also has good provisions for cyclists.

Buses and Trolleys

Only O'ahu has a completely comprehensive public transit system. It is called **TheBus**, and for $2.50 you can travel almost anywhere; simply sit on a Circle Island bus to complete a full island tour. Several routes call at the airport; in theory, bulky luggage items are forbidden, but drivers rarely concern themselves over passengers with luggage on their laps.

The more expensive **Waikīkī Trolley** loops around Honolulu and Waikīkī, charging $34 for an all-day pass, allowing you to hop on and off as desired.

On Maui, the **Maui Bus Service** runs 12 different routes. It operates seven days a week, including holidays, with a flat fare of $2. Separate routes connect Kahului with the resorts of West and South Maui; to travel between South and West Maui, you have to change buses. Only the Upcountry and Haiku routes call at Kahului Airport.

The **Kaua'i Bus** follows the main island road all the way from Hanalei in the north to Kekaha in the west, from Monday through Saturday for $2 only.

On Hawai'i Island, the **Hele-On Bus** runs various routes, connecting Kailua-Kona with Hilo via Waimea and Honoka'a; Kailua-Kona with the Kohala resorts; and Hilo with Volcanoes National Park. The fare is just $2. Schedules are built around taking employees to work rather than assisting vacationers.

Guided Tours

Many companies offer guided tours of the attractions on individual islands. The largest and most reliable of these firms are **Roberts Hawai'i** and **Polynesian Adventure Tours**. They also offer packages that include inter-island flights, accommodations, bus tours, and car rental.

Your hotel's guest-services desk should know about guided tours of specific attractions and be able to make bookings for you.

Taxis

Taxis can be found at airports and outside major hotels, but only in Honolulu is it relatively easy to hail a cab. Elsewhere, phone for a taxi. Some remote areas, such as Hāna on Maui, have no taxis.

Driving

Although Honolulu suffers with the traffic congestion of any major US city, driving in Hawai'i is generally a pleasure. Local people are seldom in a hurry, so allow plenty of time for any journey. Also, residents never use their horns, so on narrow roads check your mirrors regularly and pull over to let cars pass. If you break down, call the rental company. Always check the weather, since many roads wash out during or after heavy rain.

If you ask for directions, people will often suggest landmarks as reference points. Around Honolulu, you're likely to be told, "Go diamondhead" (southeast) or "Go ewa" (northwest), and on all the islands you'll hear the words *mauka* ("toward the mountain") and *makai* ("toward the sea"). If you find Hawaiian place names confusing, ask to be shown the way on a map.

Parking

It's fairly easy to find free parking in Hawai'i; most hotels offer it, and major hotels and many restaurants also provide valet parking. The chief exception is in Waikīkī, where hotels and garages charge $20 or more to

Waikīkī Trolley, plying the streets and sights of Honolulu

Floodlit cruise ship dominating the Honolulu waterfront

park overnight. Be sure to heed all road signs. If there's no free parking, use a parking garage; you can often get a parking ticket validated by a restaurant, shopping center, or attraction.

Car Rental

To rent a vehicle in Hawai'i, you must be over 21 (25 in some cases) and have a valid driver's license and credit card. Large rental companies such as **Alamo**, **Avis**, **Hertz**, and **National** have desks at the airports on the four main islands. They offer vehicles of all sizes, but for a four-wheel-drive vehicle you may need a specialist, like **Harper Car & Truck** on Hawai'i Island or **Lāna'i City Service** on Lāna'i. The only national chain on Moloka'i is Alamo.

It's usually easy to rent a car for a day or two from local agencies in Waikīkī, but you should book well in advance elsewhere. Fees start at about $35 a day or $150 a week.

Most visitors pay an extra $20 or so per day for Loss Damage Waiver (LDW). This protects you from Hawai'i's "no fault" policy, which holds the driver responsible for damage to the rental car, regardless of fault. Your insurance policy or credit card may cover damange costs to rental cars. Most rental firms forbid the use of unpaved roads.

Gasoline

Gas is expensive in Hawai'i, but aim to keep the tank at least half full, since in certain areas, especially on Hawai'i Island, it can be 50 miles (30 km) to the nearest filling station. Return rental cars with a full tank to avoid high gas prices charged by the agencies.

Motorcycling and Biking

Mopeds and motorcycles can be rented on all four main islands. It is not mandatory to wear a helmet, but it is a good idea to do so.

You can rent bicycles easily, especially in Waikīkī. People use them more for getting about town than for touring.

Cruises and Ferries

In the old days, *hula* dancers and *lei* greeters lined up on Honolulu's piers to welcome cruise ships filled with tourists. Almost all visitors now arrive by plane. However, **Norwegian Cruise Lines** offers regular week-long cruises around the islands, and luxury lines that call at Hawai'i include **Princess Cruises**, **Cunard**, and **Royal Caribbean International**.

The only inter-island ferry services are based in Lahaina Harbor on Maui. **Expeditions** sails multiple times daily between Maui and Lana'i, costing $30 for adults; the crossing takes about an hour and doubles as a whale-watching cruise in winter. On arrival, it's easy to get to the island's attractions.

The **Moloka'i Ferry** offers two daily sailings from Lahaina to Kaunakakai on Moloka'i for an adult fare of $72. Arrange a tour or rental car in advance, or you'll be stuck at the harbor.

DIRECTORY

Buses and Trolleys

Hele-On Bus
Tel (808) 961-8744.
W heleonbus.org

Kaua'i Bus
Tel (808) 241-6410.
W kauai.gov

Maui Bus Service
Tel (808) 871-4838.
W co.maui.hi.us/bus

TheBus
Tel (808) 848-5555.
W thebus.org

Waikīkī Trolley
Tel (808) 591-2561.
W waikikitrolley.com

Guided Tours

Polynesian Adventure Tours
W polyadhawaii tours.com

Roberts Hawai'i
W robertshawaii.com

Car Rental

Alamo
W alamo.com

Avis
W avis.com

Budget
W budget.com

Dollar
W dollar.com

Enterprise
W enterprise.com

Harper Car & Truck
Tel (808) 969-1478.
W harpershawaii.com

Hertz
W hertz.com

Lāna'i City Service
Tel (808) 565-7227.

National
W nationalcar.com

Thrifty
W thrifty.com

Cruises and Ferries

Cunard
Tel (800) 728-6273.
W cunard.com

Expeditions
Tel (800) 695-2624.
W go-lanai.com

Moloka'i Ferry
Tel (866) 307-6524.
W molokaiferry.com

Norwegian Cruise Lines
Tel (866) 234-7350.
W ncl.com

Princess Cruises
Tel (800) 774-6237.
W princess.com

Royal Caribbean International
Tel (866) 562-7625.
W royalcaribbean.com

General Index

Acknowledgments

Dorling Kindersley would like to thank the follow-ing people whose contributions and assistance have made the preparation of this book possible.

Contributors
Gerald Carr is Professor of Botany at the University of Hawai'i, Manoa and a resident of O'ahu. Bonnie Friedman runs a public relations firm on Maui, contributes regularly to Hawaiian publications, and volunteers at a Hawaiian language immersion school. Rita Goldman is a freelance writer and editor who has lived on Maui since 1978. Clemence Mclaren is a Honolulu-based writer and teacher. Melissa Miller, a native of Honolulu, is a poet, storyteller, grant writer, and nonprofit consultant. Alex Salkever is a Hawai'i-based journalist specializing in sports. Stephen Self is Professor of Geology at the University of Hawai'i, Manoa and a resident of O'ahu. Greg Ward, an established travel writer who has written extensively on the Hawaiian islands, is also the author of *Hawaii: The Rough Guide*. Paul Wood, freelance writer, editor, writing teacher, and long-term resident of Maui, is the author of *Four Wheels Five Corners: Facts of Life in Upcountry Maui.*

Revisions & Relaunch Team
Emma Anacootee, Shruti Bahl, Chris Barstow, Stephen Bere, Hilary Bird, Louise Bolton, Julie Bond, Arwen Burnett, Barbara Carr, Sherry Collins, Karen Constanti, Nicola Erdpresser, Jane Ewart, Emer FitzGerald, Fay Franklin, Anna Freiberger, Emily Green, Eric Grossman, Mohammad Hassan, Emily Hatchwell, Des Helmsley, Kim Kemp, Sumita Khatwani, Shikha Kulkarni, Maite Lantaron, Darren Longley, Nicola Malone, Linda Mather Olds, Georgina Matthews, Alison McGill, Simon Melia, Robert Mitchell, Kate Molan, Mary Ormandy, Sangita Patel, Mani Ramaswamy, Lee Redmond, Amir Reuveni, Ellen Root, Collette Sadler, Sands Publishing Solutions, Preeti Singh, Avantika Sukhia, Mary Sutherland, Rachel Symons, Conrad Van Dyk, Vinita Venugopal, Karen Villabona, Greta Walker, Greg Ward, Stewart Wild, and Tanveer Zaidi.

Special Assistance
Alana Waikiki, Sheryl Toda and Tracey Matsushima at Bishop Museum, Four Seasons Resort Maui at Wailea, Elizabeth Anderson at Haleakalā National Park, Richard Rasp at Hawai'i Volcanoes National Park, Julie Blissett at HVCB (UK), Sharon Brown at Kalaupapa National Historical Park, www.lucies farm.com, Geraldine Bell at Pu'uhonua O Hōnaunau National Historical Park, Stouffer Renaissance Wailea Beach Resort, Bill Haig and Linda Matsunaga at TheBus, the State Parks Administrator at Waimea Canyon and Koke'e State Park, and RM Towill Corporation for artwork reference.

Additional Special Photography
Philip Dowell, DK Studio/Steve Gorton, Frank Greenaway, John Heseltine, Nigel Hicks, Dave King, James McConnachie, Andrew McKinney, Neil Mersh, David Murray and Jules Selmes, Ian O'Leary, Roger Philips, Clive Streeter, Greg Ward, Andrew Whittuck, Francesca Yorke, and Jerry Young.

Photography Permissions
Dorling Kindersley would like to thank the following for their kind permission to photograph at their establishments and for their assistance with photography: Sharon Clark at the Hawai'i Film Office, George Applegate HVCB Big Island, Connie Wright at the HVCB Moloka'i, Department of Interior and the National Park Service and all other churches, museums, hotels, restaurants, shops, galleries, and other sights too numerous to thank individually.

Picture Credits
a = above; b = below/bottom; c = center; d= detail; f = far; l = left; r = right; t = top.

Works of art have been reproduced with permission of the following copyright holders: *Stage design for L'Enfant et les Sortileges 1981*, courtesy Tradhart, (c) David Hockney 1981: 75br.

The publisher would like to thank the following individuals, companies, and picture libraries for their kind permission to reproduce their photographs:

AARP: 232c; **AKG, London**: 29tc, 49tl; Museum of Mankind, London 28c; **Alamy Images**: Aurora Photos 12bl; blickwinkel 70; Steve Bly 98; Caroline Commins 130br; Hank deLespinasse 190cla; Gaertner 84-5; Douglas Peebles Photography/Douglas Peebles 10br, 131cra, 169cl; Douglas Peebles Photography/Thomas Dove 159tc; David Fleetham 26bc, 36cl; Robert Fried 226c; Blaine Harrington III 120-1; D. Hurst 191c; Imac 11tr; Andy Jackson 125br, 131cr, 225tl; Andre Jenny 164cla, 225c, 236bl; Henk Meijer 18; David L. Moore 54,138tl, 195br; National Geographic Image Collection 11cr; Ron Niebrugge 187tr; Photo Resource Hawaii/David Franzen 145tr; Photo Resource Hawaii/David Olsen 19b; Photo Resource Hawaii/David Schrichte 36br, 138bl; Photo Resource Hawaii/Franco Salmoiraghi 146tl; Photo Resource Hawaii/G. Brad Lewis 224cl; Photo Resource Hawaii/Jim Cazel 20c, 20bl, 124br; Photo Resource Hawaii/Mark Wilson 21c; Photo Resource Hawaii/Tor Johnson 20t, 222cla; Photo Resource Hawaii/Wayne Levin 21tr; Robert Harding Picture Library Ltd 148-9; Travis Rowan 37br; Stephen Frink Collection/James D. Watt 27bl; Stephen Frink Collection/Masa Ushioda 220cr; **Alexander and Baldwin Sugar Museum**, Maui: 127bl; **Allsport UK Ltd.**: Vandystadt/sylvain Cazenane 35cr; **Archive Photos**: 32tr, 48bl, 49bl; **Aston Hotels & Resorts**: 180bl.

Courtesy of **Bamboo Ridge Press**: Cover illustration From *Wild Meat And The Bully Burgers* With Kind Permission of The Artist Cora Yee 29br; **Biofotos**: Heather Angel 25cra; **Bishop Museum**, Honolulu: 46clb, 47tl, 73br, 73tl, 156bc; Charles Furneaux 139cr; Engraved By JG Woods 1878 34tr; **Bridgeman Art Library**, London: Museum Of Mankind, London 32cl, 33tl; National Library Of Australia, *Canberra Captain Cook C1820* by John Webber Engraved By Josef Selb C1820 45bl; Scottish National Portrait Gallery *Robert Louis Stevenson (1850–94)* 1892 by Count Girolamo Pieri Nerli 29cl(d); **Paul J Buklarewicz**: 30cl.

Gerald Carr: 24br, 25tc/bc; **Jean Loup Charmet**: 30tr, 44tl; **Chef Chai**: 194tl; **Chef Mavro**: 194br; **Cirque Hawaii**: 213br; **Coffees of Hawai'i**: 230br; **Bruce Coleman Collection**: Jeff Foot Productions 119br; **Corbis UK Ltd** Bettman Archive 48tr, /acme 153cla, /upi 67cla, 69b; Jon Hicks 14tl; David Muench 130tl; Amos Nachoum 27cla; Douglas Peebles 60br, 122br, 158tr, 191tl, 223tl, 226br; Roger Ressmeyer 159br; Reuters/Lucy Pemoni 21bl; Tony

Roberts 222br, 223cr; Stuart Westmorland 147br. **Culver Pictures**, Inc, New York: 45cb, 47cb, 47bl, 48clb; **Current Events**, Kailua-kona: 139c;

Da Kitchen Cafe:199tr; **Ron Dahlquist**: 24c, 35tl, 37cr, 25br, 41cra, 86clb, 87tr, 104clb, 114cla, 124tr, 125cl, 127tr, 131clb, 133br; **DoubleTree by Hilton Alana Waikiki Hotel**: 182br; **Dreamstime.com**: Darren Brode 233cl; James Crawford 94-5; Eddygaleotti 50-1; Maria Luisa Lopez Estivill 15tr; Jerryway 12tl, 14br; Scotttnz 238b; Paul Topp 228-9; Jeff Whyte 64; Alexander Yakovlev 1c.

ET Archive, London; National Maritime Museum *Death of Cook by J Cleavely 45t.

Four Seasons Resort Hualalai: 181bl; **Four Seasons Resort Lanai**: 178-9, 188br, 197tr, 201bc; **Peter French**: 23b, 24tr, 25tr, 40bl, 106tl, 139cla, 172bl, 174clb.

Getty Images: Ann Cecil 205br; Hawaiian Legacy Archive 8-9; Monica & Michael Sweet 88; **Cheryl Gilbert**: 139br; **Grand Wailea Resort Hotel & Spa**: 225br; **Ronald Grant Archive**: Paramount Pictures *Blue Hawaii* (1961) 169br; **Grapevine Productions**: 189tl.

Haleiwa Joes Haiku Gardens: 196bl; **Hawai'i Tourism Authority (HTA)**: Robert Coello 234bl; Tor Johnson 230cl, 231br; **Hawai'i Volcanoes National Park**: 159cl; Dave Boyle 158cl; Norrie Judd 158br; **Hawaiian Historical Society**: 28br, *From Voyage Autours du Monde* by Louis Choris 1822 42; **Hawaiian Telcom**: 236cr; **Eve Eschner Hogan**: 226tl; **Honolulu Academy of Arts**: Gift of Mrs. C. Montague Cooke, Jr, Charles M. Cooke III And Mrs. Heatin Wrenn in Memory of Dr. C. Montague Cooke, Jr 1951 *Nahienaena* Robert Dampier 115tc; **Hotels & Resorts of Halekulani**: 183tl, 192bl; **Georgina M. Hunter**: 237tl.

Image Quest Marine: James D. Watt 26bl, 36tr; Masa Ushioda 26crb, 27clb; **International Coffee Organisation**, London: 139cl.

Ka'anapali Beach Hotel: 185bl, 232tr; **Kapalua Resort on Maui**: 222cb; © **Kaua'i Museum**: 173tc; **Kauai Plantation Railway**: 165tl; **Kilauea Lodge**: Hawkin Biggins 204tl; **Kōke'e Natural History Museum**: David Boynton 174cla; **Kona Brewing Company**: 203tl; **Kona Coffee Cultural Festival**: 138cr.

Lahaina Town Action Commitee: 114br; **Jon Lasiuk**: 235tl; **Leonardo Media**: 180cra; **Anthony Limerick**: 114tr, 116cla, 157tc/bl, 189br, 239tl.

Maui Arts & Cultural Center: 214tl; **Maui Ocean Center**: Darren Jew 123br; **www.maui-wedding-photography**: Shasta Rose 224br; **Morimoto Waikiki**: 193tc;

Nature Photographers: Brinsley Burbidge 24clb/bl, 171c; James Hancock 173cr; Paul Sterry 173clb; **Peter Newark's American Pictures**: engraved by N Currier 1852 46tc; **NHPA**: Stephen Kraseman 25crb.

Maui Crafts Guild: Randy Miller 208c.

OSF/Photolibrary: Botanica/Bob Stefko 27crb; Pacific Stock/Dave Fleetham 26clb, 26–7, 37cla; Pacific Stock/ Jim Watt 27cra.

Pacific Stock: 44cb; Bob Abraham 31br, 38cra; Rita Ariyoshi 208br; Joe Carini 38br; Dana Edmunds 40cra; Bill Schlidge 172tr; Greg Vaughan 32bl, 33cb, 39br; **Douglas Peebles**: 9tl, 22cl, 56cla, 86ca, 99b, 127tl, 146b, 147tr, 175cr, 220bc; **Photolibrary**: David Cornwell 37tl; **Photo Resource Hawaii**: David Bjorn 34–5; David Boynton 30bl, 171tr; Randy Jay Braun 31cr; John Callahan 41clb; Monte Costa 49ca; Tami Dawson 86tr, 177br; David Franzen 61br; Nikiolas Konstantinou 140br; Jon Ogata 175tl; Franco Salmoiraghi 87bl, 135b, 161b, 144br; Joe Solem 39cra; Jamie Wellner; Lani Breheme Yamasaki 16c; Photo Tropic: David S Boynton 173br; **Photoshot/NHPA**: Pete Atkinson 27tr; Kevin Schafer 27bc; **Pictures Colour Library**: 31tr; **Planet Earth Pictures**: Pete Atkinson 93tl; John Lythgoe 25bl; **Private Collection**: 28tr, 43b, 46bc.

Rob's Good Times Grill: 216cl; **Robert Harding Picture Library**: Ron Dahlquist 110; Michael Runkel 134, 160; Masa Ushioda 2–3; **Scott Rowland**: 22bl.

Science Photo Library: Soames Summerhays 156tr; **Mike Severns Photography Inc.**: 26tr; **Sheraton Princess Kaiulani**: 183br; **The Stockmarket**: 30–1; **Surfer Publications**: Jeff Divine 35bl; Tom Servais 34bl/bc/br, 35tr; **Kevin and Cat Sweeney**: 139cb, 218cla.

Telegraph Colour Library: S. Benbow 218br.

Brett Uprichard: 33cra.

Greg Ward: 22tr, 105tc, 172cl. **Nik Wheeler**: 212br; **World Pictures**: 89b.

Front Endpaper: **Alamy Images**: Steve Bly Rtc; **Dreamstime.com**: Eddygaleotti Lbr; **Getty Images**: Monica & Michael Sweet Lc; **Robert Harding Picture Library**: Ron Dahlquist Rcr, Michael Runkel Lcl, Rbl.

Jacket: Front and Spine – **Robert Harding Picture Library**: Masa Ushioda.
All other images @ Dorling Kindersley. For further information see: www.dkimages.com

Special Editions of DK Travel Guides

DK Travel Guides can be purchased in bulk quantities at discounted prices for use in promotions or as premiums.
We are also able to offer special editions and personalized jackets, corporate imprints, and excerpts from all of our books, tailored specifically to meet your own needs.

To find out more, please contact:
in the United States **SpecialSales@dk.com**
in the UK **travelspecialsales@uk.dk.com**
in Canada DK Special Sales at **general@tourmaline.ca**
in Australia **business.development@pearson.com.au**

Glossary of Hawaiian Terms

Hawaiian began as an oral language. It was first put into written form by the missionaries who arrived in the 1820s. The teaching and speaking of Hawaiian was banned from the early 1900s, and by the time the native cultural renaissance began in 1978, the beautiful, melodious language was almost totally lost. Immersion programs are producing new generations of Hawaiian speakers. Fluent speakers are still few, and native speakers are even more rare. Still, you will hear Hawaiian words liberally sprinkled in conversation and in the islands' glorious music, and see it written on some signs.

Summary of Pronunciation

The Hawaiian language has just 12 letters: the five vowels plus h, k, l, m, n, p, and w.

unstressed vowels:

a	as in "**a**bove"	
e	as in "b**e**t"	
i		as in "c**i**ty"
o	as in "s**o**le"	
u	as in "f**u**ll"	

stressed vowels:

ā	as in "f**a**r"	
ē	as in "p**a**y"	
ī		as in "s**ee**"
ō	as in "s**o**le"	
ū	as in "m**oo**n"	

consonants:

h	as in "**h**at"	
k	as in "**k**ick"	
l		as in "**l**aw"
m	as in "**m**ow"	
n	as in "**n**ow"	
p	as in "**p**in"	
w	as in "**w**in" or "**v**ine"	

The *'okina* (glottal stop) is found at the beginning of some words beginning with vowels or between vowels. It is pronounced like the sound between the syllables in the English "uh-oh."

ali'i	ahlee-ee
liliko'i	leeleekoh-ee
'ohana	oh-hahnah

The *kahakō* (macron) is a mark found only above vowels, indicating vowels should be stressed.

kāne	**kah**-nay
kōkua	**koh**-koo-ah
pūpū	poo-**poo**

Everyday Words

'āina	**aye**-nah	land
aloha	ah-loh-ha	hello; goodbye; love
hale	ha-leh	house
haole	how-leh	foreigner; Caucasian
hula	who-la	Hawaiian dance
kāhiko	**kaa**-hee-koh	old; traditional
kama'āina	kah-mah-**aye**-nah	familiar; resident
kāne	**kah**-nay	man
kapa	kah-pah	bark cloth
keiki	kay-kee	child
kōkua	**koh**-koo-ah	help
kumu	kooh-mooh	teacher
lānai	**luh**-nigh	porch; balcony
lei	layh	garland
lua	looah	bathroom; toilet
mahalo	muh-ha-low	thank you
mu'umu'u	moo-oo-moo-oo	long billowing dress
'ohana	oh-hahnah	family
'ono	oh-noh	delicious
pau	pow	done
puka	poo-kah	hole
wahine	w(v)ah-he-nay	woman
wikiwiki	w(v)eekee-w(v)eekee	quickly

Geographical and Nature Terms

'a'ā	ah-**aah**	rough, jagged lava
kai	kaee	ocean
koholā	koh-hoh-**laah**	humpback whale
kona	koh-nah	leeward side
ko'olau	koh-oh-lowh	windward side
kukui	kuh-kooh-eeh	candlenut tree
makai	muh-kaee	toward the sea

mauka	mau-kuh	toward the mountains
mauna	mau-nah	mountain
nēnē	**nay**-nay	Hawaiian goose
pāhoehoe	**pah**-hoy-hoy	smooth lava
pali	pah-lee	cliff
pu'u	poo-oo	hill
wai	w(v)hy	fresh water

Historical Terms

ahupua'a	ah-hoo-poo-ah-ah	a division of land, from mountains to sea
ali'i	ahlee-ee	chief; royalty
heiau	hey-yow	ancient temple
kahuna	kah-hoo-nah	priest; expert
kapu	kah-poo	forbidden; taboo
kupuna	koo-poo-nah	elders; ancestors
luakini	looh-ah-kee-nee	human sacrifice temple
maka'āinana	mah-kah-**aye**-nanah	commoner
mana	mah-nah	supernatural power
mele	meh-leh	song
mo'o	moh-oh	lizard
oli	oh-leeh	chant
pili	pih-leeh	grass for thatching
pu'uhonua	pooh-ooh-hoh-nuah	place of refuge

Food Words

'ahi	ah-hee	yellowfin tuna
aku	ah-koo	skipjack; bonito
a'u	ah-oo	swordfish; marlin
haupia	how-peeah	traditional coconut pudding
imu	ee-moo	underground oven
kalo	kah-loh	taro
kālua	**kah**-looah	food baked slowly in underground oven
kiawe	key-ah-veh	wood used for grilling
laulau	lau-lau	steamed filled ti-leaf packages
liliko'i	lee-lee-koh-ee	passion fruit
limu	lee-moo	seaweed
lomi-lomi salmon	low-me low-me	raw salmon pieces with onion and tomato
lū'au	**loo**-ow	Hawaiian feast
mahimahi	muh-hee-muh-hee	dorado; dolphin fish
ono	oh-no	wahoo
opah	oh-pah	moonfish
'ōpakapaka	**oh**-pah-kah-pah-kah	blue snapper
poi	poy	pounded taro root
pūpū	poo-**poo**	appetizer
uku	oo-koo	gray snapper
ulua	oo-looah	jackfish; pompano

Pidgin

Hawai'i's unofficial conglomerate language is commonly heard on playgrounds, in shopping malls, and backyards throughout Hawai'i. Here are some words and phrases you may hear:

brah	brother, pal
broke da mout'	great food
buggah	pal or pest
fo' real	really
fo' what	why
grinds	food; also to grind
howzit?	how are you?; how is everything?
kay den	okay then
laydahs	later; goodbye
li' dat	like that
li' dis	like this
no can	cannot
no mo' nahting	nothing
shoots!	yeah!
stink eye	dirty look
talk story	chat; gossip

Honolulu Bus Routes

10 3-11-53-54-71-81-91-92-93-96-97
101-102

2

7-13-85-88

10

9-40-40A-42-43-52-62

10

1-7

7-13

7-10

2-85-88

10

10

Kalihi

7-10

7

3-11-53-54-71-81-91-
92-93-96-97-101-102

2

N. SCHOOL STREET

10

LILIHA STREET

10

2

10-19-20

10

9-40-40A-42-43-52-62

DILLINGHAM BOULEVARD

MO'OKAULA STREET

1-13

3-71

11-53-54-81-
91-92-93-96-97

101-102

4

55-56-57-57A-65-85-89

6-15

Iwilei

2-3-71

82-85-88

NIMITZ HIGHWAY

19-20

1L-11-19-20-40-40A-42-
43-52-53-54-62-71-91-
92-93-97-101-102

4

Punch

5

19-20-40-40A-42-
43-91-92-93-96

11

9

4-6-80
80A-80B

1-1L-2-3-9-11-
13-53-54-62

7

1-1L-2-3-9-1
13-40-40A-42
52-53-54-62-7

6-55-56-57-
57A-65-88-89

7

6

4-85

4-80-80A-80B-82

Sand Island

8

10

**Downtown
Honolulu**

8

5

4

15

6

1-1L-2-3-4-9-11-13-19-20-
40-40A-42-43-52-53-54-
62-81-85-96-97-101-102

7

2

3

1-1L-2-85

**SAND ISLAND
STATE PARK**

19-20-42

42

1-1L-2-85-90

6

3-9-13-40-
40A-43-52-53-62

15

17-18-4

HONOLULU CHANNEL

Kalaeola

19-20-42-55-56-57-57A

6S

Ala Moana

6

*KAKA'AKO
WATERFRONT PARK*

ALA MOANA BOULEVARD

ALA MO
RECREA

Key

— Freeway

6 Bus Route and Number

— City Express route A

— City Express route B

— Country Express route C

— Country Express route E

✈ Airport

⛴ Ferry port

▪ Main Sightseeing Areas

MĀMALA BAY

| 0 kilometers | | 1 |
| 0 miles | | 1 |

SIGHTS

1. King Kamehameha Statue
2. Kawaiaha'o Church
3. Mission Houses Museum
4. 'Iolani Palace
5. State Capitol
6. St. Andrew's Cathedral

7. Fort Street Mall
8. Aloha Tower Marketplace
9. Hawai'i Theatre
10. Hawai'i State Art Museum
11. Chinatown

1 Bishop Museum
2 O'ahu Cemetery
3 Royal Mausoleum
4 Queen Emma Summer Palace
5 National Memorial Cemetery
of the Pacific

6 Honolulu Acad
7 The Contempo
8 Lyon Arboretu
9 Kapi'olani Park
10 Pearl Harbour